THE LAND OF
BROKEN CRYSTALS

AND THE GIRL WHO KNEW TOO MUCH

JANE CELIA HATCH

Published by:
Trine Day LLC
PO Box 577
Walterville, OR 97489
1-800-556-2012
www.TrineDay.com
trineday@icloud.com

Library of Congress Control Number:

Hatch, Jane Celia.
The Land of Broken Crystal – 1st ed.
p. cm.
Epub (ISBN-13) 978-1-63424-410-7
Print (ISBN-13) 978-1-63424-409-1
1. Hatch, Jane Celia (1956 -)2. Project MKUltra. 3. Shamanism. I. Title

FIRST EDITION
10 9 8 7 6 5 4 3 2 1

Printed in the USA
Distribution to the Trade by:
Independent Publishers Group (IPG)
814 North Franklin Street
Chicago, Illinois 60610
312.337.0747
www.ipgbook.com

Contents

Foreword 1

1) My Mother and UFOs 3

2) The Wind and Atlantis 6

3) The Fairy, Sleeping in the Woods, The Raven 11

4) Indian Head River 14

5) Past Lives 25

6) The Charles River and Crystal Eyes 28

7) Jack-O-Lanterns 34

8) Hate 36

9) Crystal Blue Persuasion 44

10) The End of Religion 48

11) Popham Beach 50

12) The Light of the Silvery Moon 54

13) Watertown 63

14) Lao Tzu 71

15) Secretariat 78

16) The Ancestors and My Daughters 83

17) Solstice Celebration 89

18) Mic Mac Madness 94

19) The Four-Color Ceremony 97

20) Scott and White Buffalo Calf Woman 99

21) Full Moon and the Goddess 103

22) Helleen Kramer 110

23) Psychopathy 116

24) Queen of Spades 120

25) The Herbal Apprenticeship 124

26) Midsummer's Eve, The Curse Unfolds 128

27) Double Cursed 139

28) Academy Green 152

29) Chocolate Chip Cookies 157

30) The Witch Of Harpswell (And Even Deeper Into The Curse) 161

31) Running from Raven 170

32) Montsweag Road 175

33) Cream-Colored Sweater 182

34) Winter Wind 186

Part II

35) Layers of Death 197

36) Judge Joseph Field and Victoria Mueller 200

37) The Guardian Report 203

38) North Star 209

39) Sunset on North Street 211

40) Death and then Life 218

41) Morning Glories 224

42) Marija Giimbutas 237

43) Soul Retrieval 241

44) The First Shaman 246

45) The Consequence of Power 250

46) Gwen, The Lion and The Golden Horse 257

47) The True Face of Raven 262

48) Lesley University 267

49) Isis 284

50) Spells Unwinding 290

51) A Magdalene in A Tent 293

52) I Dream of a Fire in Bath 301

53) Healing 306

54) Very Little Strength Left 313

55) Spirit Mother and Spirit Father 316

56) Raven's Demons 319

57) My Ancestors Return to Save Us 322

58) The End 327

59) Set The Girls Free 334

60) My Mother and The Lavender Sachet 336

61) Waldoboro and The Apple Orchards 339

62) Mother Mary and 62 South Street 344

63) Escape from Maine 349

Acknowledgments 355

Foreword

A 2021 groundbreaking study conducted by Dr Richard E. Harris, PHD, of the University of Michigan, using control groups and EEG waves, conclusively revealed that the underlying neurobiology of a shamanic state of consciousness, is distinct and measurable. This study scientifically verifies that the human brain, without the usage of any psychedelics--and often just to the accompaniment of a drumbeat-- is naturally wired to experience profound worlds beyond the five senses.

CHAPTER 1

MY MOTHER AND UFOS

"What's a UFO?" I ask my mother, Polly. I'm sitting on our handmade pine kitchen table swinging my legs and feet and eating an apple I picked from the tree in the backyard of our four-bedroom farmhouse. I am seven years old. It is spring in Hanover, Massachusetts.

"Unidentified flying objects. Spaceships," my mother answers, confidently, and still staring into the mirror.

She colors her lips red in a round mirror circled in fancy gold leaves. The mirror must have come from my father's house in Bath, Maine, where he grew up. I think he lived in a big brick house next to a river called the Kennebec or something like that. It had a summer kitchen and smelled like lemons, my older sister, Sally, told me.

I can't remember ever being at that house. I just know all the pretty stuff we have came from Bath.

The lilacs and the apple tree are in full bloom outside our house. Sometimes I sit right inside the lilac bush so all I can see is purple. "Purple World," I had whispered once.

If I'm not in the lilac bush, or playing in Bunny Woods, I sit on the branches of the apple tree playing with a troll with gold eyes and long lime green hair. I love his hair. I love lime. Lime. Lime. I like to repeat certain words.

She wants the lipstick to be just right so she kisses a white Kleenex and then throws it into the fireplace where apple branches crackle in a small fire. I stare as the red kiss turns to gray ashes. She sets the pink Avon lipstick tube on the pine table and then picks up her white gloves and pulls them over her hands and fingers.

Then she looks at me.

"Janie, when you look up at the stars, you can see millions. Some of them must have life. It would be presumptuous to think otherwise," she says, confidently, and smooths down her soft white angora sweater.

I stare at my half-eaten apple which is turning brown on the inside. She hugs me. My world is my mother, apple blossoms, an Appaloosa horse named Misty (who lives way up Center Street with my friend Moira) my dog, Jonesy, trolls, plastic horses, and stars.

She steps back a bit, smiles, and hugs me. Then she smooths my hair where it had been ruffled and turns and picks up her keys.

"Oh, Polly, don't fill Janie's head with nonsense," Nanny scolds, mildly, as she repairs the hem of my white summer shorts.

Nanny sits in a rocking chair in the kitchen and is wearing a bright yellow dress, cinched at her waist with a narrow shiny yellow belt. Her short white hair is curled, and a string of pearls is looped several times around her neck. My mother often says Nanny "dresses to the nines."

"It's not nonsense, Mom. It's all over the Boston papers; the *Herald* and the *Globe*. The UFO sighting. The Hills were coming back from a vacation in Niagara Falls and they saw a flying saucer or something. Eight aliens stepped out of the UFO, they said. The Hills are the topic of our meeting tonight at the UFO club," she said, running the small black Woolworths comb through her light brown hair.

"Oh, you mean that Negro man and his wife," Nanny says with raised eyebrows, looking up now at my mother, her youngest daughter.

Nanny's only other daughter is Aunt Marie. She has black hair and wears a sparkling Spanish tiara, drinks a lot of gin (I guess), and lives in Lexington where Paul Revere rode his black horse one night yelling, "The British are coming. The British are coming."

"Yes, mom, that's what I mean. I'm all for it. I think you should marry whomever you love. What does skin color mean anyway? We're all the same underneath," my mother said, again, with confidence.

Nanny sighs, places my shorts in the basket with all the other mending, and then gets up and puts the copper kettle on the stove and turns on the heat. My mother picks up her shiny red purse from the kitchen table, clicks it open, puts in her lipstick, and then clicks it shut again.

The clicking sounds give me chills.

"Okay. Gotta go. Don't want to be late. I love you."

She kisses the top of my head.

"I love you," I say, studying her red lips. Yes, she got it perfect.

The screen door slams.

I set the apple down and run into the bathroom which is right next to the kitchen. From the window, which is low to the ground, just like the bathtub, I watch as she walks up the green grassy hill towards the dirt driveway and her car. She reaches her car and takes out her keys.

Mandy, our black cat, leans on her leg. My mother reaches down and strokes her back and Mandy arches, like a Halloween cat. Mr. Jones, our old sheepdog, bounds up to her and she crouches down and hugs him and then ruffles his gray hair. She smiles and laughs a bit when he licks her face. Then she gets into the car and backs up and drives away. Jonesy sits and watches her disappear.

I run to the back bedroom, to the window, throw open the curtain, and stare at her car until it rounds the bend towards Hansen and Indian Head River.

CHAPTER 2

THE WIND AND ATLANTIS

"I just love hanging sheets," my mother says, smiling. In bare feet, she stands on the thick spring grass and picks clothes out of a wicker basket, and clips them, patiently, one after another, onto the clothesline. Suddenly, a big white sheet snaps in the wind. I jump, because I was deep in thought about a cloud I saw yesterday that looked like a bunny.

She had come home from the UFO meeting last night. I was scared for some reason while she was gone.

"It's my favorite chore – hanging clothes. I love being out in the wind," she continues.

"After four babies, I must have hung a thousand diapers on this line,"

She seems curious. She cocks her head, raises her eyebrows, and purses her lips like she's not exactly sure how she feels about the diapers. But then she smiles, maybe decides it was okay, and hangs another shirt on the line.

"I know. I must sound like a nut. Loving hanging clothes,"

"You don't sound like a nut," I answer.

I sit on a blanket on the grass and with a real silver spoon, I eat Frosted Flakes and milk from a scratched-up blue plastic bowl. The bowl probably did not come from Bath. I'm wearing mended shorts, white sneakers, and a yellow T-shirt. My mother had braided my hair into two long blond braids and then Nanny tied green bows on the ends with ribbon from her basket.

"I had another dream about the waves last night. They were huge. I've never seen anything like them. We Atlanteans must have done something terrible," she says, quietly, then chuckles, a worried chuckle.

"I can't even imagine what that might have been," she says as she clips the end of a sheet to the line.

In another lifetime my mother lived in Atlantis. It was an island in the middle of the sea. The people who lived there healed with crystals she had said. They were special people. But Atlantis had sunk under huge waves a long time ago. What happened to all the crystals?

My mother loves rocks and crystals. And colors. She paints everything beautiful. She especially likes pink and green. She painted my room pink and white; and my sister's room, green, but not lime green; it's like sea-foam green.

Later in the afternoon, my mother and I, and Dale and Debbie (the kids in mother's playgroup) sit Indian style under the apple tree. A wolf cloud floats in the sky. Apple blossoms fall from the tree onto my head and lap.

Shivers run up and down my spine and arms. Apple blossoms remind me of something. Maybe another lifetime. but not Atlantis. It isn't Atlantis. Somewhere else.

"We are about to embark on a grand adventure," my mother says excitedly, her eyes wide.

"But we'll have to be very quiet when we get to Bunny Woods or we might scare her away," she whispers and then smiles, and looks at us, waiting for our response.

"Scare who away?" Debbie asks.

"The fairy in–," she begins.

When my brother, Jeffrey, who is thirteen or fourteen or something like that, runs out the back door holding a schoolbook and a lunch box. The screen door slams behind him.

Jeffrey's blue jeans are stiff and flat. Old Bee, our neighbor, who I'm pretty sure is a witch, ironed Jeffery's pants with spray starch yesterday. My mother pays Bee fifty cents to iron a whole basket of clothes. Mom likes everything perfect.

Once, when my sister, Sally, knew Bee was coming over to iron, she said, "Mom, what if Dick is here and Bee's here and she smells horrible? I'll be so embarrassed."

Dick is her boyfriend who puts grease in his black hair and wears a black leather jacket. He gives me the creeps.

"Now don't you go and make fun of Bee. She has feelings just like the rest of us. Any one of us could end up just like Bee and you'd be damn happy if someone helped you out," my mother said, with a kind of mock anger.

My mother hates it when Bee gets teased because Bee is old and poor and retarded. *And she is a witch.* My mother loves to help old people. Also, people who are rejected and lonely.

My best friend, Peter Gerberville (his name is German, too. Everybody's German it seems) lives in a big yellow house across from us. Peter has a goat, Sugar, an orange Volkswagen beetle car, and two Doberman Pinschers. Peter and I like to run up to Bee's door and ring the doorbell and run away – into the woods to hide – pulling Sugar on a long rope.

Anyway, Debbie and Dale just stare at Jeffrey – probably because of the black pirate patch on his left eye. My mother said Jeffrey was playing in his tree house and he fell, and a hammer fell and landed on his eye and he lost it. Now he has to wear the patch. I don't remember that either.

"Bye, Mom. Love you," Jeffrey says, picking up his bicycle which is lying on the dirt driveway. I have another brother, Robbie, who hits me on the head and only speaks Pig Latin. I think Jeffrey and Robbie are about the same age. Sally is the oldest.

"Jeff, where are all the other kids?" my mother asks, worried.

"Oh, they already left for school with Robbie," he says softly, trying to pretend he doesn't care. He swings his leg over the bike seat and begins to peddle down Center Street towards Sylvester School.

Kids don't wait for Jeffrey. I think it's because of the pirate patch.

"Well, they're gonna hear from me about that. I don't want Jeff riding his bike to school all alone," she says, sad and mad.

Last night when Mom was out at the UFO meeting, Sally, who is always telling me stories – because I am the youngest of everyone and don't know anything that is going on sometimes– said Mom belongs to a group called *The Hanover Five*. The group is my mom, her best friends, Clara, Midge, (whose daughter, Debbie, comes to our playgroup) and Barbara, and somebody else (my sister couldn't see who it was). Sally said she saw them all walking down Broadway *under a full moon*.

"They were laughing and talking really loudly. Mom was wearing about five hats," she said while sitting at a vanity in her green room, holding a metal eyelash curler tightly over one violet-colored eye. Everyone says she has *Elizabeth Taylor's eyes*.

"Go get me a Coke from the fridge. Hurry, before Dad gets home. That's all I'm going to tell you about The Hanover Five," she responds, suddenly annoyed.

The screen door slams. I'm brought back to the present.

Nanny sits rocking in a chair under the apple tree watching Mom's playgroup. On an old table beside the chair, is a silver bowl full of sugar cubes. I also see a white milk pitcher of fresh cream and a China cup with a Lipton tea bag.

"Did you take your pills this morning, Mom?"

"Yes, Polly"

"Did Bob get his lunch?"

Bob is my father. On the weekends, when he is not working in Needham, he sits on a black wooden chair in a small dark room with no windows upstairs in our house. He's working on something. He's a salesman. When he was a teenager, he drove from Bath to New York City in a brand-new Model T Ford to sell Chiclets gum to Negroes in Harlem after he graduated from Bowdoin. My father loves Negroes. He calls them "black" and corrects my mother and Nanny when they say "Negro.» I've never seen a Negro.

I can't figure out what he sells now. I don't see anything in his room. All I know is that whatever he does, he must "sit in the goddamn traffic on 128."

In the summer my father grows corn, tomatoes, beans, cucumbers, and peas in his garden. I watch him sometimes. After dinner, while my mother is washing dishes, my father sits in his chair in the living room – his light blue eyes triple-size behind his bifocal glasses– reading Science and Health with Key To The Scriptures– a dark blue book by Mary Baker Eddy who is a Christian Scientist.

We're all Christian Scientists. My mother teaches Christian Science Sunday school and I go to her class on Sundays. We don't go to doctors. Ever. Not even when I had whooping cough or my sister had scarlet fever.

"Yes, Polly, I gave Bob his lunch and gave him some tea and a muffin before he left for work," Nanny says softly, her white hair blowing in a breeze.

Nanny sips tea and leans back and stares at my mom. *She looks worried.* It's probably about what happened last night after she got home from the UFO meeting. My sister put her new black and white saddle shoes on a burner on the electric stove and the shoes caught on fire and the kitchen filled up with smoke.

"Oh. God. I've used up all my playschool money. And the doctor said Sally has to have those corrective shoes. How are we going to afford to get another pair?" my mother had said to my father, in a tired voice, while throwing the smoking shoes into the trash.

"Sally has not been the same girl since she had scarlet fever. I swear to God, Bob," she said. She says that all the time. I don't think my father listens to her. It might be true.

"*She is a completely* different person," she had added, smoke rising up from the trash veiling her face from me for a moment.

Nanny continues to stare – with her worried look – at my mom. With my father's newspaper – *The Christian Science Monitor* – she slowly fans her face and looks away towards the road.

I hear footsteps on Broadway Road. I turn and see it's Grampie who has black eyes and dark skin– like an Indian – but het's Spanish. He is a bit of a scoundrel, I heard my mother say once to Nanny, who had nodded. He's smoking his pipe and staring down at the road as he walks. I bet he was at Doc's Corner Store drinking rum with the old men at Indianhead River Bridge.

He looks up and smiles and raises his pipe and blue smoke swirls into the air. Nanny looks at him like she wants to know what he was up to and she thinks it was no good. He walks right up to her. She blushes but' she makes sure to keep a look of disapproval.

Nanny didn't like moving from her big Victorian house in Canada and coming to America and living in a small apartment in Cambridge on Ellery Street. But Grampie was something called a rumrunner and they had to leave Canada fast. I listen to a lot. That's how I learn a lot. Now, he was a diesel mechanic for the Boston Port Authority. Something like that. He fixed tugboats and ships. He had to be good at ships as he used to cross the ocean from Halifax to Boston in a boat and was always having to fix the engines while fighting off the Coast Guard, who were trying to steal Grampies rum. At least that's what my Mom and Nanny said.

To America, Nannie and Grampie brought my mother, my aunt Marie, and a little boy, who was my mother's son, Dave, from her first husband. They also brought white gloves, pearl necklaces, corn cob pipes, and a silver flask. That's all I know. Dave is my half-brother or something. He just ignores me. I think he's married and has kids anyway and lives somewhere else.

"Sadie, my love. I'll join you for tea in a moment," Grampie says, taking the pipe out of his mouth and bowing. He calls her Sadie, but her real name is Sarah Smith.

"Hi, Daddy," Mom says and kisses his brown cheek that creases into rows of crescent moons as he smiles.

My mother slides her bare feet into bright white lace-less sneakers.

"Okay," she says to me and Debbie and Dale.

We all sit up straight. The birds are suddenly quiet. Pink petals fall onto my shoulders. Nanny's rocking chair squeaks.

CHAPTER 3

THE FAIRY, SLEEPING IN THE WOODS, THE RAVEN

Mr. Jones follows me and Dale and Debbie and my mother on a path through the oak woods behind our house. He runs to keep close to a picnic basket my mother holds, maybe because of the peanut butter and Fluff on Pepperidge Farm bread sandwiches inside the basket.

My father drove a Pepperidge Farm truck in Maine when he was a teenager. He delivered white bread all over Bath, and, to his old girlfriend, Jane, from Maine, who lived way down at the end of an old winding road at a place called Popham Beach. My mother said I was named after Jane. She didn't seem so happy about it, but we still buy Pepperidge Farm bread.

Suddenly she looks around at the pine trees in the small woods.

"This is perfect," she says, happily.

She puts an old blue blanket onto the rust-colored pine needles in the middle of Bunny Woods (which is a pine forest) behind the oak woods next to our house. Mr. Jones lies beside the basket and puts his shaggy head on his paws and stares hopefully at my mother.

I kneel and hug his head tight to my chest. I'm so excited. We all sit. We are excited for the big surprise she had told us about while we were under the apple tree. Mr. Jones, who is really old, closes his eyes and goes to sleep. My mother points to the top of a small pine tree.

"I see something," I whisper, leaning into my mother, who gathers me in her warm arms – tanned from hanging clothes in the sun.

A blue cloth glitters in a single ray of sun near the top of the tree.

"Oh!" I gasp and cover my mouth. I see a pretty girl's face, then a head and blond hair and two arms and two legs. The little girl in the tree is holding a wand.

"Polly, what is it?" Dale runs over and grabs her hand. She puts her arm around his shoulders.

"It's a fairy," she says, smiling.

"Where I come from there are lots of fairies. Now everybody, close your eyes and make a wish," she adds.

A soft warm breeze swirls pine needles near my feet. The needles rustle high in the treetops. Goosebumps sprout up on my arm. Yellow and black butterflies fly in circles in my stomach. I smile and fold my hands on my lap and make a wish.

Later, near dinnertime, after Dale and Debbie have gone home, my mother and I enter the kitchen.

My brother, Robbie, who is a teenager, puts dry apple sticks, and old newspapers, twisted into bows, inside the fireplace. He lights the newspapers and they burst into yellow flames edged in blue and gold. I stare, hypnotized, at the fire, as if I'm waiting for the fire to do something other than just burn.

Nanny switches on the chandelier over the kitchen table. Mr. Jones is already under the kitchen table licking up spilled milk. Grampie, who reminds me of the old wizard Merlin, sticks a black iron spear under the logs. The flames grow. He puffs his pipe and winks at me.

My mother grabs a pillow and two of my books from the living room floor. Nanny is thumbing through the Sears catalog.

"Do you want the potatoes peeled for the chowder, Polly?" Nanny asks and puts down the catalog.

"Yes, Thanks, Mom."

We enter the kitchen again and my mother grabs graham crackers from inside a cupboard.

"Bob, I need to take a five-minute nap before dinner. I'm completely exhausted," she says, passing my father, who is making tea.

"Well, if you didn't waste half the week making that goddamn fairy, you'd probably be able to perform some of your normal chores," he says.

"Shhh!" she says, looking at me.

My father shrugs and pours milk into his tea.

"My normal chores – what in God's name do you think I was doing up until 1 am in the laundry room last night and then again at 6 am?" she asks, truly surprised.

"Washing dishes and doing laundry," she answers her own question.

He just stirs the tea.

She stares and then wipes a tear from her cheek.

"Sally, put that root beer back in the fridge right now. That's homemade and you know it's special – for parties," my father says, irritated, and ignoring my mother.

Still holding my hand, we walk out the front door. The screen door slams behind us. We cross the green lawn and then enter small woods. Mom drops the pillow on the ground and hands me the crackers and books. She kicks off her sneakers and lies down on old leaves and a little patch of grass and puts her head on the pillow. I sit cross-legged and lean against her back and pull two graham crackers from inside the wax paper and put them into my mouth.

"Heaven," my mother says, in a sleepy, happy voice.

I close my eyes and listen to birds sing and the wind rustle through the gray branches of the trees. A soft purple light sunset enters our woods through a passageway between two oak trees.

"Heaven," I repeat, and crumbs fall from my mouth.

A Raven caws. I open my eyes and look up. The Raven is circling above our heads.

"Kraa, Kraa" he says, and swoops over my head

I close *Winnie the Pooh* and stare at the Raven flying away. I drop my book and graham crackers and lean against her warm back and fall asleep, suddenly afraid of the large black Raven.

CHAPTER 4

INDIAN HEAD RIVER

I'm eight years old. It is fall.

My sister and I sit on the cold ground under the apple tree. I angrily tear grass out by the roots and throw it into the air. My fingers are stained green. Leaves, crisp and brown and curled, are scattered, like strange, misshapen, dead fairies, under the apple tree.

"Owwww!" I scream and lean away from Sally, who is trying to brush my long blond hair which is tangled all the way down to my butt.

Before my sister got dropped off here, I'd raked all the apple leaves into a big pile. I pretended to be Misty, the Appaloosa stallion that lives up the street with my friend Moira Zwicker. I'd run up and down the grassy hill, by our barn–where my mother used to park her car–snorting and prancing, and shaking my head, so my mane would fly around my face, and then run down the hill and jump into the pile of leaves.

Now, brown leaves cling to my hair and the dirty dress I'm wearing. I grab a fistful of hair and slide my clamped hand down the strands, feeling, with satisfaction, the leaves and twigs caught in the tangles.

My fat nanny, Mrs. Wright, who reads the Bible all day, and just sits in a chair farting and eating; calls me a "wild beast" when my father isn't around. Well, that's fine with me. I am a beast.

My mother is gone. Just gone. We don't talk about her. It's like she did something terrible. Maybe she shouldn't have hung sheets on the clothesline in the sun and wind. Maybe it was something to do with crystals. Again.

Everybody is gone except the old mean nanny sitting in the rocking chair my real Nanny bought from the Sears catalog. Jeffrey is gone. Sally said he drives around Cape Cod in a convertible car wearing a feathered Indian Chief bonnet and no shirt. That sounds pretty good. I don't even know what Robbie is doing. Dave, my half-brother, said he's smoking pot. But Dave says terrible things about most everyone.

The rocking chair on the porch is empty. I think Nanny died.

Sally married Dick. I hate him. I don't know why. They had two babies. I forget their names. They are both fat and one of them has red hair.

Sally lays the brush on top of my head and begins to pull it down through my mane.

"Ouch! Cut it out," I respond, angry.

She slowly lowers the brush.

"Okay," she says, quietly, and doesn't roll her eyes or stick out her tongue. That's weird.

"I was just trying to help," she adds.

She pulls a red rubber band off her wrist and gathers her brown hair into a ponytail. A large purple bruise throbs on top of a vein on her face beside her ear. She throws the brush and lies down in the leaves and stares up at the sky with her violet eyes.

She looks like a child. I think she is only like 16 or 17. Mom said she had straight A's in school and she painted pretty pictures and wrote poems. What happened? She's not in school now.

I tear at the grass, throwing it in all directions.

"Dad's lawyer made me tell the judge Mom used to take a pillow and go out into the woods to sleep. I didn't think it was bad. I tried to tell them she was just resting. It was awful. I feel terrible. Everything is my fault. They wanted me to make Mom sound crazy," she says, her voice cracking and tears filling her eyes.

"Dad said I'd get a horse of my very own if I said all those things," she chokes.

She rolls onto her side and curls up and starts to cry, her body shaking. What is she talking about?

Dick hits her face. I knew he was weird. That's why she has that bruise. Dave and my father sit in the kitchen talking about Sally and Jeffrey. It's never anything good. They don't know I'm listening.

"Sally was back in Middleborough hospital last week. I got the call. She wanted me to come and get her," my father had said, weakly, pouring hot water from the kettle into his teacup.

"She made her bed, let her lie in it," Dave had responded.

Then my father had opened the refrigerator and given Dave one of his homemade root beers. Why did Dave get a root beer and it's not even a special occasion? It's like they're a team. Why is Dave here all the time now? Whenever he is here, the way he stares at me, without smiling, I don't like it.

Dave drowned Snowball. I know he did. Right before my mother left for forever, she came into the house (when I was in the woods playing) and left me a white kitten with a note "I love you, Janie." I named her Snowball. Then she disappeared, just like my mother. Did they drown my mother, too?

Mrs. Wright is the seventh Nanny my father hired. I didn't like any of them, except maybe the lady from Germany, with the short red hair, who just lay in my sister's bed and cried. She seemed nice when she wasn't crying – which wasn't often because she missed Germany.

They all left, even the German lady. I really hated the nanny who made me ride with her to Nantasket Beach. I sat in her hot car for a long time while she was with her boyfriend in a little cottage near the beach.

The Nantasket Beach nanny got fired.

I can't stand my sister's crying.

I get up and run through my father's old, dried-up garden. The yellow corn stalks are dry and bent over at the waist – like they got shot in the back. Without looking both ways, I run across Broadway Street in my bare feet. My dog, Jonesy, is sleeping in the garden. He is depressed and old and he coughs. He doesn't follow me anymore, even if I have a peanut butter and jelly sandwich.

I run down the Gerberville's tarred driveway; past their orange Volkswagen; and their yellow barn. The old-fashioned German family my mother painted on the front of their barn, on the little door, near the eves, is slowly falling, in thin strips of paint, onto the driveway and I trample them with my feet.

I run through long green grass in their backyard. The tips of grass cut at my knees and calves. I don't even want to see if Peter wants to go to Indian Head River. I just want to keep running. I couldn't find any underwear this morning. I don't care that my father doesn't read Winnie The Pooh anymore.

I enter the pine forest behind Peter's house. No sunlight touches the floor of the cold, rust-colored pine forest.

It smells of wet sticks and stones and pine needles. I'm weaving quickly around the tall pine trees and I'm breathing heavily by the time I reach the river and the soft green mossy banks. The cold rushing water is dark amber in the middle where it is deepest, and golden amber on the edges near the banks, where it is shallow and foamy.

"Hello, River," I say.

The river has been here for forever, I think. It never leaves.

I touch the wet rocks on the bank of the river, and chills run up and down my arms. I can feel something; or hear something; a voice; or maybe it is a feeling…

My tangled hair, still dotted with dry apple leaves, lifts off my sweating neck and forehead in a sudden wind.

"Thank you, wind," I say.

With hands on my hips, I stare down river and through the lowest tree branches. A raft is hidden somewhere. My brothers made some pine rafts but Peter hides them because he thinks Robbie and Jeffrey might come back and steal them. They aren't coming back. No one is coming back.

"One thinks he's frigging Indian and the others a pothead," my half brother, Dave, said to my father last night – about Robbie and Jeffrey.

Who would ever want to come back now? My father and Dave and Mrs. Wright are all mean. I don't believe anything they say. They just make me mad. I don't believe Mary Baker Eddy either. I don't believe in Christian Science anymore.

I spot a raft and run along the wet mossy bank and then jump onto the raft, which is tied, with an old dog leash, to one of the pine trees that bends so far over the river that its roots are exposed. I untie the raft and push off from the riverbank with a long pine pole Peter had left leaning against a tree. The fast current quickly pulls the raft into the center of the river. I stand with the pine pole in my left hand and my hair blowing in the wind as we head towards Doc's Corner Store and the small waterfall.

"We are about to embark on a great adventure" I hear my mother's voice in my mind. It is more like remembering a dream. Maybe my mother was only a dream.

I smell smoke. I'm pretty sure that, around the next bend, Mrs. Cogers, the school bus driver, who lives on Broadway, is burning old leaves. As I round the curve, I see flames rise from her huge pile of fall leaves.

After my mother disappeared Mrs. Coger's, who is pretty old – like, maybe, 35– and Jeffrey, who was only 15, had an affair. My father and Jeffrey were arguing about it one night. I was sitting on the stairs in the dark in my pajamas holding my stuffed dog. My father started slapping Jeffrey in the face.

"My eye. My eye. That's my bad eye," Jeffrey cried out, holding his hand over his fake eye. I started to cry and buried my face in my dog.

The next day my father was so mad he drove Jeffrey to New Hampshire and tried to give him away to anyone who would take him, but no one would take him and so he brought him back and that's when Jeffrey went to the Cape and became an Indian.

The sky is blue and white puffy clouds float along above my head. Birds sing from the trees. Fall is my favorite. The leaves on the maple, oak, and aspen trees are yellow and orange and red. I feel sad for Jeffrey.

I sit on the raft and place the pole across my lap. "I'm Queen of the River!" I say to the world, to somebody. I don't know who. I know something or someone must be listening.

I drag my fingers in the water and create ripples of brilliant colors from the leaves overhead reflected in the water. The river winds through a grove of old oak trees whose leaves have turned orange, red, and yellow. I know they're oaks because the leaves are huge, and acorns are scattered all over the forest floor.

I breathe in deeply and take my hand from the river and wipe the sweat from my forehead. I exhale. Cool water streams down over my eyelids and nose and lips and chin and neck.

I stare down into the river. As I drift, I feel I'm carried away to another world.

The raft stops abruptly in a tangle of branches and logs. I gasp and jump. Then I sit motionless, the pole across my lap, and stare into the water. I see a woman with long black hair in a tan dress with fringes in the oak trees, reflected in the water.

She might be an Indian. Maybe it's my mother. Maybe it's my mother in her past life. She told me she was an Indian once. The woman crouches, picks up a handful of acorns from the forest floor, looks up at me and smiles, and offers the acorns.

I gasp again, straighten my back, tuck my hair behind my ears, and look away from the image in the water and into the oak woods. I shield my eyes from the glare of the sun, but I can't see the woman. Maybe it isn't an Indian, but my mother and she has come to get me. Is she hiding from Mrs. Wright and my stepbrother, Dave, and my father? She would be hiding, right? She knew she would find me here on the river!

There is only darkness deep in the woods. I give up and lie down on the raft and stare up at the clouds. I lay the pole over my chest and let my hair drag in the river water as the raft passes through and out of the oak grove.

The raft bounces against the soft long grass on the banks of the river all the rest of the way to Doc's Corner store, where Grampie used to ride Sally's big brown horse, Colonel, to buy rum. I pull the raft onto the sandy shore and then walk up the steep bank to the road. I pass Doc Cook's store

– he just has alcohol and cigarettes – and then head up the hill to Jeff's Corner Market to buy candy.

At Jeff's, I buy fireballs and Tootsie Rolls and then slowly walk up Broadway towards my house. Halfway, I wander into the woods near Bunny Morse's house and fall asleep on the pine needles with pink goo drooling from my mouth. I wake up, remembering my mother is gone. It's hard to move or think. It's like I'm floating around outside myself. Eventually, because there is no place else to go, I head back to the house.

Sally was gone. I stand on the porch in the cool air of twilight.

"Just swept and it's not dinner time," Mrs. Wright hisses through the closed screen door, one eyebrow raised high and the other squinted. She has a tight grip on my mother's broom.

Rolls of fat push against the faded pink roses on her thin housecoat. Sweat leaks from the fat on her neck. Tendrils of thin white hair float around her face like snakes waiting to strike. She slams the door.

I shudder and gasp and tears threaten my eyes.

I turn away and just stand on the porch. What to do next is a mystery. A dry brown leaf blows by my feet.

"Peter!" Peter's mom shouts from somewhere.

I walk to the end of the porch and stare across Broadway Street. Peter's tall, redheaded mother hollers from the open front doorway of his house.

"Brian, Billy," she continues, holding one of their Doberman Pinchers by its silver choke chain. Peter and Brian run across the lawn towards the front door of their house. She wraps her arms around their shoulders. I look away quickly. It feels like the world is about to go dark.

A light is turned on in the Spinzola's kitchen. I look over at Bee's little house. Bee Webb died. The weeds are growing up around her house. The rock slab steps are hardly visible under the weeds.

I step off the gray-painted porch where Nanny used to sit in her rocking chair drinking Lipton tea and walk around to the back of the house to the rock wall beside my father's old garden. Nothing much grows there anymore. Just a bunch of weeds.

Did Nanny die? I can't remember. Where is she?

The sun slowly sinks behind the trees in South Hanover where Indian Head River flows dark amber under Broadway. The street is quiet. The neighborhood children have vanished. No barking from the packs of dogs that roam our neighborhood. Even the dogs have gone home.

Gold and red and orange rays of the setting sun warm the old gray rocks on the wall, transforming them into huge jewels. I sit on a ruby glowing red. "I am Queen of the Jewels," I think to myself and sit on the ruby which is part of my kingdom of trees and flowers. Maybe I'm from Atlantis, too.

Later, with an open palm, I stroll between rows of old yellow corn stalks in my father's garden. I brush the stalks with my hand. They rattle.

I climb to the top of the apple tree and stare up at the sky and the stars and the moon. The Universe. My mother said it would be presumptuous to believe we were the only living beings in the universe. I believed her. She also used to tell me that the world was my oyster. I'm not sure what that means.

I walk by the barn and think of my old bunny, Fluffy. I found him dead with one cold pink eye staring up at the small window under the peaked roof of the barn.

Down at the bottom of the hill from the barn, in the sand box, I sit Indian-style and sift cold sand through my fingers. Inside, in the kitchen, the light of the chandelier illuminates Mrs. Wright's head. She pulls a pan out of the oven, dumps a can of something into it, stirs it with a wooden spoon, and shoves it back in.

I rest my head in my hands and stare at the sand. I look up at the tree house where Jeffrey fell, and the hammer knocked out his eye.

"How come you have to wear that black patch on your eye?" I had asked him recently; while we sat on the grass, waiting for someone to pick him up. I'm not sure why he was here at the house.

"The doctor wants me to wear it until I can get another eye. A good one," he answered, and then took a cigarette out of his shirt pocket and lit it.

"How did they fix your eye?"

He picked at the green grass.

"At the hospital, they covered both my eyes with a white bandage."

How could you see?"

"I couldn't. I couldn't see at all for a couple of weeks. I heard people's voices. I heard Mom's voice. And Nanny and Gramps and Aunt Maria and Uncle Dick," he continued, sounding a little happier with each person.

"Mom came every day to see me," he said, excited.

"I knew it was her because she always walked her fingers from my knee all the way to my chin. Like this!" he said and walked his two fingers down to his knee. He didn't smile or laugh. He looked confused.

"I think she did it because it made me laugh."

He laughs, just a little.

"Did Dad do that, too?"

"I don't think so"

"Are you an Indian?" I had asked him, finally, after he had finished his cigarette and then snuffed it out in the grass. "Sally said you were dressing up like an Indian Chief. She said you were wearing feathers on your head."

"Yes," he answered and then, exhaling smoke with the words, "I am an Indian. My name is Two Crows."

And then someone came and picked him up and he was gone.

The headlights from my father's car, as he pulls into the driveway, shine down the hill onto the grass near the sandbox. It's almost pitch-black outside.

Mrs. Wright opens the door.

"Janie. Get in here right now and get cleaned up," she hisses.

A half-hour later we are all seated at the pine table in the kitchen under the chandelier. Jonesy is under the table asleep, as usual.

"Now Mr. Hatch, we both know evil is a creation of the human mind and only that which is from love and truth is real," Mrs. Wright says, in a singsong voice, to my father.

She never talks nicely like that when my father is not here.

She is quoting Mary Baker Eddy's book, *Science and Health and Key to the Scriptures*. It's one of the books my mother used to read to us at Sunday School at the Christian Science Church.

Mrs. Wright serves my father green beans, mushroom soup, and onion ring casserole from a wooden spoon. A huge clump of the casserole is heaped on my father's plate. Almost as a regrettable afterthought, she adds food to my plate.

"We all know it was a terrible thing that she did, but we must know the truth. Know the truth. Understand the truth. Know that Love is the only true reality in the universe," she says, her eyebrows raised and her face pink.

She is a Christian Scientist, too. It's probably why my father hired her. They use the words "she" and "her" all the time, but I know they are talking about my mother.

She has a clean red apron tied around her waist. On top of her big head is a white bun the size of a quarter. She put on red lipstick after the apron, I'm guessing. Most of the time she is wearing her old bathrobe and sleeping on the Sears upholstered rocking chair. The teakettle whistles on the stove. My father pushes back his bench and starts to get up.

"No. No. Mr. Hatch, you sit down. You've worked hard all day. I'll get it," She says, starting to rise, awkwardly. She must weigh a ton.

"I can take care of it, Mrs. Wright. Thank you though. Please stay seated," he responds, rising easily. He takes a few steps to the stove and lifts the small shiny kettle and pours steaming water into his teacup. He dips his used Lipton tea bag (from breakfast) into the hot water.

"Why do you use all those old tea bags?" I ask, not really caring.

"Don't want to waste anything, Janie. I grew up in the Depression," he explains.

"My father lost the shoe business that had been in the family for three generations. But Hatches paid all their debts before they closed the store. No IOUs for us. It's important to be thrifty – to conserve as much as possible. You never know when hard times might come again," he adds.

"We must be strong and stand steadfast along with Mary Baker Eddy," Mrs. Wright says, trying to draw his attention back to her and away from me.

"I'm not sure about Mary Baker Eddy anymore," I say, not really eating, just playing with my food.

"Mary Baker Eddy was a very notable woman, Janie, way ahead of her time. She ushered in a great spiritual revolution in this country. She founded the Christian Science Church in Boston. I have a great deal of respect for that woman," he says and takes a sip of tea.

My father likes respectable people. Mrs. Wright's neck and face are bright red. She puts down her fork and clears her large wobbling throat.

My father, who is amused by her antics, says loudly and with a grin,

"And thank you, Mrs. Wright, for your extremely encouraging words. You are a faithful Scientist, I believe, and a great influence for Janie."

I'm confused. Mrs. Wright lies. When my father got home tonight, she told him she had made me Welsh rarebit for lunch. I wasn't even home for lunch. I was eating fireballs at Jeff's corner store.

"Thank you, Mr. Hatch. I do my best," she says, demurely, her cheeks flushing.

I eat a few spoons of green bean casserole and a biscuit with butter and then, after a slow game of cribbage with my father, lay awake on my bed in the upstairs corner of the house. I pick at the little balls on my white cotton quilt my mother had said was a "popcorn" quilt.

"Popcorn," I say. I like that word.

It's windy and dark. I pull the covers up to my chin but still shiver. I hug my one stuffed animal, a dog named Brownie. Down the hall, past my father's small dark office, and across from Jeffrey and Robbie's old bedroom, the wind wails through the eves in the attic. I'm afraid to go into the attic these days. One day when I was playing in the sandbox, for some reason, a woman waved at me from the attic window. A grown-up woman. She was a ghost.

In the moonlight, on my nightstand, sits a small ceramic statue: it is a little girl with white wings and a gold halo around her head. "January Angel" is written in gold letters on the trim of her white gown. My mother gave me the January Angel because my birthday is January 12th. An April Angel had stood on Sally's nightstand but now the nightstand and the angel are gone.

The puffy green quilt and her bed and vanity and bureau are still in Sally's room. I had drawn circles in the dust on the glass vanity on my way through her room tonight. Gone are the red lipstick kisses on the tissues in the silver trash can under her huge mahogany bureau from Maine.

I grab the angel and hold her and my dog tight with both hands up against my chest. I lie perfectly still on my side staring at the pink cameos on the wallpaper and listening to the wind howling through the attic.

Is Dick beating up Sally tonight?

Jeffrey told me once, when Sally and Dick were at the house before they got married, Dick had Sally on the floor in the living room and was beating her "to death with his fists." Jeffrey said he got a baseball bat and he was going to kill Dick, but he called the police instead.

"They wouldn't do anything," Jeffrey said about the police.

I swing my legs out from under the bedspread and step out onto the cool, white-painted wood floor and then open the top drawer of my bureau and pick up the purple rhinestones brooch I stole from Mrs. Pettigrew, a lady who used to be our nanny.

I slip my feet into white sneakers and pull a red sweater over my head and then tiptoe down the silent, steep, dark stairs, gripping the rail with sweaty hands.

If the ghost woman appears, I'll just run fast to get away. I'm not sure if she is friendly or mean. The stairs creak.

At the bottom, I open the front door and step out under the old white wooden arbor which is draped with brown vines and faded roses, and withered leaves. Roses were my mother's favorite.

One night, a long time ago, when I was seven, after my mother left, she came back and went into my bedroom and wrapped me in my popcorn bedspread and then carried me out of the house at night under this rose arbor. My father grabbed me from her, and I saw stars and the moon while he was running through the yard with me back into the house.

My mother was crying, and she said, "Please. Bob. Please."

I had smelled her lilac perfume and touched a strand of her brown shiny hair.

I step out onto the damp grass. I walk quietly past my father's bedroom windows and his old garden and the withered corn and then sit cross-legged on the grass. The cold ground sends a chill up and down my legs and arms.

I pull the broach out of the pocket and hold it up to the moon and rock it back and forth. Will my mother see the rays of starlight reflected into the sky? I hope she can send a message back. It is a secret language and safe from my father and Mrs. Wright and Dave.

"It's safe now Mummy. You can talk to me here. Everyone is asleep. They won't hear you."

I wait in the grass, staring up at the stars. There is no message in the sky. I wait and wait. I slowly walk back to the house and up the stairs and fall into my bed with my sneakers still on. I hear a voice.

"I am here, in the stars. I was with you in the beginning. I am with you now. And in the end, I will be with you then, too."

I dream of waves bigger than my house rising over my father's cornfield and Indian Head River and all of Hanover. And then there is nothing but darkness.

CHAPTER 5

PAST LIVES

Early the next morning, I jump out of bed, pull on dungarees and a T-shirt and run outside and around to the backyard and pick two red apples from the tree. Apples in hand, I pass my father's new blue Impala car and head down Center Street.

I run all the way (taking bites of the apple) to Moira Zwicker's house. The whole family is at church, probably because it's Sunday morning.

Misty, the small Appaloosa stallion, is grazing in the center of a green field next to their barn. He raises his silver head, looks at me, and snickers. I smile and walk over to him and offer one of my apples. He gently takes it from my hand, and after a few bites, it's gone.

I run up their driveway and into the barn. From a rusty iron hook, I pick up an old black bridle. The reins are worn to white along the edges. A big black bull, with a gold ring through his nose, stands squarely, staring angrily, through the gaps in his pen.

With the bridle in hand, I quickly depart the dark musty barn for the green field where Misty is tied with a long rope to a stake set in the middle. Misty stares and whips his long black tail at flies on his muscular front legs.

"Hi," I murmur and stroke his silver neck and forehead under his forelock. I wrap my arms around his neck and lay my head on his warm silky mane.

I slip the reins over his head and unbuckle his halter and let it slide to the ground.

I nudge the silver bit into Misty's mouth. He bobs his head and prances. I jump, trying to avoid his hooves stomping on my bare foot. I step onto a field rock and hold the reins and pat his gray muzzle, and he whinnies.

Combing his black forelock with my fingers and I turn in circles on the rock, leading him around and around, and then, when he is close to the rock, I grab his mane and the reins with both hands and throw my right leg over his back and press my thighs with all my strength on his silky back.

He rears and paws at the sky. I clench muscles from my toes to my neck, trying to stay mounted. He lands with a thump and begins to circle with his hind legs and then rears up again at the morning sky, which is light blue veined with streaks of red and orange at the horizon.

His black mane, shining in the thin streams of morning sunlight, reminds me of the Indian woman on the banks of the Indian Head River. I thought she was my mother.

I hold him at a fast trot down the driveway and then onto Center Street. The hollow clip clop of Misty's hooves is the only sound on this Sunday morning as we head towards the entrance to Bunny Woods.

Where is everyone? Sometimes I feel I'm alone on the planet.

The entrance to Bunny Woods is a few yards ahead. Misty's back muscles begin to quiver. His neck and body contract into a coiled mass of muscle. Midway around the curve into Bunny Woods, he leaps forward with his front legs and his muscular hindquarters propel us faster forward than I expected.

I press my legs into his sides, drop the reins, and gather fistfuls of mane with my hands to try and stay mounted on what feels like a flat sheet of running silver silk.

I look down for an instant – his unshod black hooves are a blur and seem not to touch the slippery rust-colored pine needles on the old logging trail. His hooves must touch the ground because the sharp sweet smell of crushed pine needles fills my nostrils.

The young pine trees on each side are vertical beings that form a tunnel – a passageway. The wind whips my hair into my eyes, and they sting. Tears are ripped from my eyes by the force of the wind. I am bent low over his neck and his mane, and my hair are entangled, black and blond.

Later, we reach the end of the logging trail and the forest. Misty slows to a rolling canter and then, abruptly, a bouncy trot. As we enter the thickest part of Bunny Wood, we walk.

I hold out my arms like I'm a human cross. Misty snorts his approval and navigates his lean body forward into the woods where there is no trail, only trees and a carpet of rust-colored needles. His steps are quiet and soft, as though he were tiptoeing.

A small pine tree draws my attention. It is the tree with the fairy. The tree where my mother said a fairy lived.

A black claw scrapes at the sides of the hollow inside my stomach. I lean forward and cradle my stomach with my arm.

"Hello, Janie. Hello," the trees say in unison, just like a bunch of little children.

"Hello sisters. Hello brothers. Hello. Hello. How are you?" I say, in my mind, but know they hear.

"Don't fall off the horse, Janie. Don't fall off the horse, Janie," they say, in unison.

They really don't want me to fall.

The young pine trees in Bunny Woods act differently than the old Pine and oaks and Maples along Indian Head River. The old ones speak slowly, and clearly, with deep voices and only one at a time.

We reach the top of a hill and Misty stops; he snorts and bobs his head, rattling the chain on the bridle. Earth loosened by his pawing, crumbles and tumbles down the hundred-foot-high sandy cliff below into the sand pits.

I sit tall and straight and fold my arms across my chest. I am an Indian Chief looking over the yellow grass plains beyond and my people – the women and children and young warriors and old men with gray braids.

I sense an enemy. Maybe they are in the woods behind me. Someone like Dave or Dick. I turn quickly. Fear runs down my arms and legs and into my fingers and toes.

I lean forward over Misty's neck and press my heels into his strong black side. He runs down the side of the cliff, sending more clumps of dirt and rocks into the pit ahead of us. My heart thumps hard against my chest – I only have a few minutes to save my people.

Misty paws at the sand and I wait for a clue; a raven flying west or east; a rabbit running into a hole, or the wind changing direction.

Two crows caw loudly and turn and fly east towards Indian Head River. I lean forward and guide Misty toward the east; he gallops across the open sand pit, dangerously close to large holes where dirt has been dug up and carried away by the machines. The flick of Misty's mane in my eyes causes tears to stream down my face and every muscle in my body is strained to burning in the effort to stay free.

"Hey. Hey. Hey," I yell.

I want the enemy to follow. I'll save the lives of The People. Misty shakes his head and gallops faster and faster, passing the thousands of brown Buffalo who thunder in the endless yellow plains under a clear brilliant blue sky. My red face has black and yellow paint marks across my forehead and cheeks and my long black braids are blown straight back with the force of the wind.

CHAPTER 6

THE CHARLES RIVER AND CRYSTAL EYES

I'm gonna tell you a story.
I'm gonna tell you about my town.
I'm gonna tell you a big bad story, baby.
Aww, it's all about my town.
Yeah, down by the river
Down by the banks of the river Charles,
That's where you'll find me
Along with lovers, muggers
and thieves.
– *Dirty River* by Ed Cobb and The Standells – 1966

I'm thirteen years old and riding a chunky black Morgan horse, Venus, along an old dirt track road beside the Charles River in Needham, Massachusetts, where we moved in 1967 when I was ten. A horn blast on Route 128 – the highway on a bridge above my head and Venus rears.

"Damn," I say, angry and a bit afraid.

I slide back on the saddle and the reins tear from my hands. I grab at the front of the English saddle and pull forward. Venus lands with a thump on her front feet and I'm jerked forward. My small butt hits the center of the hard saddle.

"Ouch!" I exclaim because I don't have much padding back there.

I push my long hair off my sweaty forehead. It must be 5 pm – rush hour. The cars on Route 128, above my head, are at a dead stop. Lawyers and doctors who work in Boston but live in Needham, are probably sitting in their cars swearing at the other drivers and chain smoking. Wives in ranch houses in Needham are cooking steak, mashed or baked potatoes, and canned corn or lima beans.

I never learned to cook, except for apple pie and butterscotch brownies – which my mother taught me to make. I used to sell the brownies to our neighbors in Hanover so I had money to buy candy. None of my nannies, and now a stepmother, Marion, ever let me into the kitchen.

I look to my left at The Charles River. It's kind of gross. . Slime-drenched weeds, an orange chemical oil floating near the edge, a boot, a trash bag, and a dead fish, float in the water. I don't love that dirty water.

I clench my thighs into the English saddle and lean forward a bit, nudging Venus into a canter and away from the river, towards Dedham Town Forest. When we are far enough from the river that I can no longer smell it, I pull back on the reins and Venus slows to a wobbly trot and then a walk, her hooves and legs brushing aside big piles of dry brown leaves as if we are a boat cutting through waves. Orange and red leaves drift down from the huge old oak trees and land on my head and on Venus. It feels like a blessing.

"No more god damn 128 traffic for me," my father said last night, happily cracking open his favorite newspaper – *The Christian Science Monitor* – and easing into his leather chair.

At 5 PM every night, after work, he watches TV and eats Cheez Whiz swirled onto Triscuits, and drinks a whiskey" highball" with a cherry. His new wife delivers it to him on a fake silver platter. No more real silver. Where did it all go? No more real cheese. Where did all the real cheese go?

His business, Hatch Associates, is here in Needham, at Needham Industrial "Park." That's the reason we moved – so he wouldn't have to drive on Route 128. He also kept saying Needham had the "best schools in the state."

I didn't want to move. I hate it on Dunster Road, where we live, and I hate my science teacher at Pollard Junior High who keeps dropping pieces of paper so he can bend over and look up my mini skirt. I mostly hate my stepmother.

Before we left Hanover, when he told me his business was in a "park," I imagined green grass, trees, and a waterfall or a pond. Maybe it wouldn't be so bad to leave the river and the woods and trees and fields of Hanover…

I cried when we drove up in his new powder blue Chevy Impala to the concrete and tar park that is Needham Industrial Park.

When my mother dropped the custody battle in 1967, my father married Marion Frohog, a divorced Baptist. I guess she was a bookkeeper or something in Brockton, an ugly factory town near Hanover. They sent me off to camp in Vermont, and without telling me, packed up everything in Hanover, and moved to Needham.

It's like Hanover disappeared, just like my mother did.

I remember one of the last conversations in Hanover between my father and my stepbrother, Dave, and my old nanny, Mrs. Wright (before Marion was on the scene).

"She's dropping the case?" Mrs. Wright hissed and lurched forward from the cushiony Sears living room chair that sagged in the middle. The chair had clumped and bumped with the weight of her exertions. I was in the bathtub dribbling lukewarm water onto my scarred dirty knees and watching it stream off in tiny streams without taking away any of the dirt.

"Yeah, what a nutcase," my stepbrother, Dave, muttered.

He was talking about his mother. What is wrong with him?

"Polly told her lawyer she's dropping her custody case. She doesn't want Janie put in front of a judge," my father responds, dully. He set down his silver spoon etched on the handle with a fancy "R" for Robert.

"Well, I really had no intentions of putting Janie through all that by myself," my father concluded.

My stomach had tightened.

Yes, you were. You were going to make me tell a judge I was scared of my mother because she had tried to take me out of the house in the middle of the night. You said I was going to get a horse of my very own. Just like you told Sally.

I didn't get a horse of my very own. I got a rented horse. My father rented Venus from a horse stable in Sherborn–a town about ten miles away–where Dave lives with his wife Sue, and their children David and Greg and Laura and Jennifer.

Maybe it was because I never had to testify against my mother that I never got a horse of my very own. I don't think Sally ever got a horse of her very own either, even though they did force her to testify.

Rage runs through me and I lean forward and press my knee in hard. I want to run away from it all. Whatever it is, it is getting closer to me.

"Goddess on the mountaintop, burning like a silver flame. The summit of beauty and love. And Venus was her name. Her weapons were her crystal eyes, making every man mad." I sing the lyrics from one of my favorite songs, Venus, by Shocking Blue.

Crystal eyes and a silver flame and Goddess on a mountaintop. The words slip off my tongue so easily.

When we first got to Needham, I tried to leave it as much as possible. I rode my black bicycle ten miles to the rural town of Dover where I met David and Greg; sons of Dave; who were my age – and who had ridden their bikes from Sherborn. We bought candy at the Dover Country Store, rode in circles around the town green, broke into abandoned houses, and threw rocks into the streams.

None of us seemed very happy. Dave screams at Greg and David and his sweet wife, Sue. I've heard him when I visited their house in Sherborn. I've heard him scream until he makes Greg cry.

Venus shakes her head and yanks on the reins, trying to eat from a clump of grass aside the trail. I stop and drop the reins on her neck and let her munch on the grass.

I copy Twiggy the skinny model from London. Today at school I wore a tangerine turtleneck, a green and orange polka dot mini skirt, white go-go boots, and white fishnet stockings. I also put on black eyeliner and white frosted lipstick.

I pull a tube of lipstick from the pocket of my skin-tight riding pants and cover my lips with more frosted lipstick. I catch a whiff of the green Eau de London perfume I had splashed on my wrists this morning.

In the stall, where I keep Venus, I had taken off my Twiggy clothes, stuffed them into a Woolworth's bag, and then pulled on my tan riding pants, a white stretchy turtleneck, and tall black leather-riding boots.

The English saddle creaks as I lean forward to push away a fly from Venus' ear with my riding crop. I don't need another temper tantrum, which a bee or bug might provoke. I urge her forward along the trail. I sit up straight and begin to trot and then look down at my lower body to ensure my knees, shoulders, and hips are aligned.

"If I held a drop line at your shoulder, the line should cut precisely down through your hip and ankle," my riding teacher at the Dover Riding Academy says every Tuesday and Thursday afternoon, as her students, including myself, trot our horses in circles in the dirt riding-ring under the Sugar Maple trees.

I gather up the double reins, slide my pinky fingers in between them and close my hands into two tight fists – holding them low and close to my pelvis – and continue riding towards the Dedham Town Forest.

Judy, my best friend, who usually rides with me on her own horse, had to go home after school to do chores. I don't think I've ever had a chore in my life. My stepmother won't let me touch anything in the kitchen and my father just can't be bothered trying to hold my attention for something unpleasant to which I might rebel. He just doesn't have the time I guess.

Yesterday, while Judy and I were smoking Kool cigarettes in the girl's bathroom at Pollard, our popovers burned in Mrs. Marr's bright white ovens. When Mrs. Marr– our home economics teacher– told us to scrub the burned pans, Judy called her "cyclops eyes" and laughed.

I felt bad for Mrs. Marr. After all, *she was cross-eyed.*

A brownish-yellow haze hovers, like a semi-translucent monster, over the dirty river. Maybe it even has eyes and is watching me. It creeps me out.

I press my knees into Venus's wide black chunky sides and urge her into a canter. Brown leaves crunch under Venus's hooves and the wind blows my hair. It is October, my favorite time of year. It feels different, like neither here nor there, a misty portal, between summer and winter, an opening in a world where a Goddess on a mountaintop might live.

The trail curves close to the river again. Dead fish float in the weeds near the bank, their vacant eyes forever staring upwards into the haze. Venus shakes her head and stomps her hooves.

Please don't buck or rear.

"If you fall into the Charles River you gotta get a tetanus shot, it's so polluted," Judy had said a few days ago while we were riding along the Charles.

Then the edges of her mouth had begun to curve up and she had that *look.* I *knew* that look. It always appeared before *an event.* A bad event. Like a kid at Pollard Junior High School getting hit on the head with her math book. It always made me wince. Sure enough, she had reached over and hit Venus's rump with her crop and Venus lunged forward, towards the river, throwing me back on the saddle.

"Judy, why the hell did you do that?" I had stated, with only about half the anger I felt. I didn't dare get mad. I hardly dare to speak anymore, never mind get angry or show strong emotions. It was all being buried inside of me somewhere.

"I'm sorry. I didn't know she'd bolt," she offered.

I stared at her face. She wasn't sorry. She wanted Venus to bolt. The only time she was usually mean to me was when cute guys were around; like Chris Jensen or Rob Claus or Jimmy Kerner.

I put my feet back into the stirrups and press my legs against his sides and urge Venus into a canter. The play of sunlight onto the path through the oak trees is peaceful, *even mesmerizing.*

The hoofbeats are steady and predictable. Over dead leaves and acorns, she canters, and I feel relieved to be moving away from the dead river. Indians made flour from these acorns, I think.

I can see them pounding the acorns. I feel like I can feel the Indians. They've left their shadow; like the faded outlines of a drawing after you erase with an Etch-A-Sketch. Just like in Hanover, I could feel the Natives in the woods, even when I couldn't see them.

I'm low on Venus's back trying to avoid being hit by tree branches. Venus trips on a pile of small gray rocks but quickly recovers. Her stocky neck is shiny with a thin layer of sweat.

I suddenly remember shiny black silk cloth – the witch's cape – my mother made me one Halloween. I can't think about Halloween anymore. Don't think. Don't remember. It's almost like I don't exist.

Eau de London perfume, Maybelline frosted lipstick, moss, and withering oak leaves, intermingle in my nose. A chain-link fence, at least ten feet high, suddenly appears ahead of us. I pull back on the reins and Venus's hooves slide on the slippery, doe-colored oak leaves.

Angry, I rein Venus around. She throws her spirit into the run home *towards hay and grain and water.*

We reach the river, I hang onto her neck and loosen the reins, so she has her head. Venus wants to find her feed bucket, but I am trying to find the Goddess. We gallop along the Charles River; the wind whips my hair. My hard velvet riding hat is strained by the cord around my neck; the colored leaves are a blur as is the dirty river. I do not think a Goddess would live on this dirty river.

But the wind is here. Is this the same wind and sun my mother loved? Should I not love the wind?

CHAPTER 7

JACK-O-LANTERNS

Twenty minutes later, I walk Venus slowly up and down the dirt driveway at Whitte's house on South Street where I board Venus. When she is cool, I lead Venus into the dusty old barn and crosstie her in the stall and pick up a metal comb and slowly pull it through her long silky black tail, removing sticks and grass and other debris caught on our fast ride back to the barn. The repetitive motion of combing is soothing.

If I focus on combing, I don't have to think about home on Dunster Road.

The wind whistles through the tall Maple trees. Two orange jack-o-lanterns are perched on a wide gray slate step in front of the main door. A fluorescent orange VW van, decorated with psychedelic lime green and pink flower power stickers, is parked sideways on the driveway as if it just flew in helter-skelter through a magical portal, onto the driveway. Even the color lime hurts. I look away quickly and shove the comb back on the shelf of spider webs.

The Whitte's barn reminds me of the barn in Hanover. It has a calm, watchful silence and a sweet smell of hay and grain. The occasional solid thud of Venus's hoof on the dusty floorboards is comforting.

Ten minutes later, Mrs. Whitte, opens the front door and walks outside with a box of matches. She homeschools some of her children (I don't know how many. I just hear them laughing and talking) and she allowed her son, Tony, to ride in his pony cart, pulled by his Shetland pony, King, all the way to the Montreal World Fair.

She lights a candle inside the Jack-o-lantern. Did my mother light Jack O lanterns? *A black silk witches cape.* The water bucket is half empty, so I refill with the hose and then wrap my arms around Venus's neck and give her one last hug.

"Good girl."

I grab the bag of Twiggy clothes and exit the barn and then turn and shove the wrought iron lever on the barn door, sidewise and then up. The solid clunk of iron against wood signifies the door is soundly locked. Venus is safe. Maybe.

I step towards my bike and then stop.

Is it possible to stay here and sleep in the horse stall, like Tony? Panic seeps into my heart at the thought of going "home."

Maybe the Whittes could adopt me.

I pick my black three-speed English Raleigh bicycle off the ground and pedal past the VW with the flower power stickers and out onto South Street and the beginning of the three-mile ride north and uphill, all the way to Dunster Road.

It is almost dark when I lean my bike against the garage wall attached to a small white Cape Cod house my father bought in March of 1967. A new powder blue Dodge Charger is parked on our steep driveway, which is lined, in the spring, with blue Hydrangea bushes.

Blue is my father's favorite color. Five or six Spruce pines, planted in a crowded single file, form almost a solid wall of privacy from our neighbor going uphill towards the water tower at the top of the road. My heart pounding, I enter the small screened-in breezeway and then turn the dented brass doorknob on the door that leads into the kitchen.

Chapter 8

Hate

The worn gold-plated doorknob hits the edge of the mustard-colored Formica counter in the kitchen as I open the side door. The white wooden shutters on the door rattle (a dreaded sound). My stomach tightens; my heartbeat accelerates, and my mind goes blank.

Marion, my stepmother, wearing thin and frayed plastic slippers, and a formless polyester housecoat, rounds the corner into the kitchen from the den. I hear Walter Cronkite on the black and white TV in the den. He drones on emotionlessly, about the soldiers in Vietnam.

"You're late," she growls and throws a dish into the sink and it crashes with another one. I jump. My heartbeat accelerates. Is she trying to break dishes? I'm confused.

I untie my sweater from my waist and drop it on the kitchen counter.

"God … damn … it. When are ya gonna learn to put things away?" she hisses.

She takes one long threatening step from the sink to the counter and grabs the sweater which is right in front of me on the counter. I step back. What is she going to do? She races to the cellar door and opens it and throws my sweater down the stairs. A soft muffle and the tap of the zipper signal the sweater has hit the floor at the bottom of the cellar stairs.

"Where it needs to be," she mumbles, enraged.

"Dinners on the table in five minutes" she adds, in the same menacing tone.

I turn towards the den and the TV. Walter Cronkite. Black men rioting. The usual. I don't know what to do, but I move, just to do something. My insides are tied in knots. My mind is blank. My heart is racing in fear.

I walk through the dark hallway from the kitchen into the den where my father sits. A large black and white photo of Bobby Orr hangs on the wall above Marion's chair in the den. Kool cigarettes, a silver lighter, an ashtray (full of crooked dirty cigarette buts), fingernail polish, and a metal nail file, clutter her side table. Stale cigarette smoke hangs in the air in the small, dark, wood-paneled den.

"God damn girl doesn't…" I can hear Marion saying in the kitchen, even over the gunshots and rioting on TV.

In plaid pants and a white shirt dribbled with red shrimp cocktail sauce, my father sits on a leather recliner and stares at the TV. He takes the last sip of his highball.

"Hello Janie. How are you?" my father says, not looking up. He seems small, but treacherous in the dark, smoky den.

"Fine," I mumble.

"Ready to have some of Marion's delicious casserole?" he asks and almost looks at me.

I'd rather die – I want to say – but don't. My mind is still blank, my body heavy with adrenaline and fear.

What is the point of telling the truth to him anymore?

"Dad, Marion is so mean. She screams and calls me a "whore" and a "bitch." Don't you hear her? I mean we live in the same house. I hardly dare breathe. I just want to die. There is no reason for me to live," I said to him one night a few weeks ago, tears streaming down my cheeks.

I believed, with all my heart, if he just knew; really understood, what was happening; he would save me. He would stop it. He could stop it. He had all the power. I had finally gotten up the courage to speak. He just came home from a YMCA board meeting and Marion was out grocery shopping.

"Marion is a good cook, and she keeps the house up and she's very good with the bookkeeping," he responded, cracking the *Christian Science* newspaper, so it opened wider, while he sat down on his Lazy-Boy leather chair in the living room.

"What?" I whispered, disbelieving I'd heard him correctly. If he knew my feelings, he would help, wouldn't he? I felt, at that moment, part of my spirit drain out of my body. It felt like cold blood, down my legs, through my feet, and into the avocado living room rug.

He didn't even look at me.

"I asked you if you liked her and you said you did and so I married her. You needed a mother. If you recall, you hated Mrs. Wright," he added.

"Dad," I said, fresh tears pouring down my cheeks, "I was just a little girl. Marion let me take bubble baths at her apartment in Brockton,"

"There's not much to do about it now," he had said, still reading the *Monitor*.

That had been the end of it all. With no siblings (to speak of, since we had all been alienated from each other and no one wanted to visit Needham, since Marion made everyone (except Dave) feel as if they were unwanted) and no mother (I had heard she was coming back from California) and no relatives and now no Indian River or Misty, or Bunny Woods, my father was all I had left.

Now, he was gone.

Is it possible to be completely alone on a planet filled with people?

"Well let's eat. We don't want all Marion's hard work to go to waste," he says, monotone, resigned. He delivers Meals on Wheels to old people. All the neighbors love him.

At the dinner table, Marion stands on her Woolworth slippers and pours boiling water from a tea kettle into his coffee mug, into which the obligatory teaspoon of Sanka coffee and a white artificial sweetener has already been deposited (by Marion, before my father got to the table). I feel like she is slowly poisoning him.

My father doesn't even like her, never mind love her. Hot steam burns her wrist –

"God damn it," she hisses and jumps up and runs to the kitchen sink, tearing a towel off the mustard yellow Formica counter on her way. My heart races and another release of adrenaline floods my body. I can't understand why we are all living like this – like there is no way out. Isn't life supposed to be about love, like Mary Baker Eddy always says?

"God damn it," she continues, her outrage building.

No one cares about her "pain." My father is just waiting for dinner to be over so he can escape to a Yacht Club meeting; or to an aerobics class at the YMCA; or to deliver some meals on wheels, leaving me alone to absorb Marion's fury.

"That's enough Marion," he says, weakly. It's a pathetic and useless nod to my difficult circumstances.

I sit next to the window. It's my seat. Cold air seeps into my back and, shivering, I stare at mashed potatoes and some kind of Betty Crocker hamburger casserole, and a small pile of canned corn on my blue plastic plate. I don't recognize anything. What happened to everything we had in Hanover?

A green plastic ivy plant shoved into a chipped turquoise Fiesta Ware pitcher is the centerpiece. No more real flowers. I force myself to eat a bite of potato. I feel like I'm eating hate. I drink milk through a constricted throat.

Later, after dinner, after my father has gone to his aerobics class at the" Y," I walk into the large living room carpeted with a wall-to-wall avocado green carpet. The walls are painted mental hospital mint green. *She doesn't like me to go in here.*

Only John and Steve (her adult children) and special company are allowed in the living room. Begrudgingly she allows my father, but she won't let him make a fire in the fireplace because they "stink" and they're "dirty."

The green velvet Victorian armchair from my grandparent's house in Bath, Maine, and a print of the Hatch Coat of Arms are the only two recognizable objects in the living room. Nothing else made it here from Hanover.

A crushed orange velvet armchair, a red leather chair with wooden arms, two green and white striped cushioned armchairs, my father's brown leather recliner and Marion's floral on white cushioned armchair, are oddly positioned and there are large spaces – several feet in some cases – between all the chairs.

One thing is clear. No chair exists for me.

Marion's and my father's chair's face the television (which is hidden in a cabinet) and are about twenty ten feet away from the TV. All the other chairs face away from the television and towards the back yard. So, if I were to sit down, I would be facing them, while they are staring past me at the television set and we would all be about ten feet apart.

There is no couch. My friend, Judy, and I call it the "funeral parlor." All the room needed was a casket with a body to make it complete. It certainly feels as if there is a decaying corpse somewhere in this house. Maybe it is just Marion's heart, slowly rotting.

If I must go in there, I stand around like an unwanted dog, and leave as quickly as possible. It is a room designed to eject.

Oh, there is the old clock from Hanover with gold Roman numerals on the fireplace mantel. Tick Tock. Tick Tock. For me, it counts the seconds of the slow hours in the funeral parlor at Dunster Road.

The Hatch Coat of Arms *had been hung in a remote corner.* She must have needed *something* to fill in the corner. I walk over, across the seemingly miles of avocado rug, to touch the red shield in the center of the Coat. Will she see me touching it?

The lions on the Hatch Coat of Arms remind me of the lion in the Wizard of Oz. The lions walk onto the shield through an invisible doorway. A knight's silver chest armor rests on the shield. Gold and red leaves and winding green vines border the image. What does it all mean?

Safer With Hope Than With Arms and *Hatch* are the words inscribed, in black calligraphy, below the knight's armor and the lions. I trace the perimeter of the knight's shield with my finger.

"You don't need to be in there, do you?" Marion warns. I jump and turn my head quickly towards the kitchen.

She stands and glares from the doorway between the kitchen and the living room. Her glasses are steamy from doing dishes in scalding hot water; her hands are in yellow rubber gloves.

My heart thumps hard against my chest. She stomps into the living room. Oh God, what is she going to do?

She rushes past me like she is running from a fire or holding a hatchet she wants to slaughter with. She slams the doors on the wooden cabinet that hide the television. Adrenaline surges through my body again; my legs are weak and shaky.

"God damn it, doesn't anybody around here close doors?" She hisses as she walks back towards the kitchen, crouched forward, like a lizard, with yellow curled hands, large round misty eyes, and worn and frayed hooves.

I want to pull her hair out by the roots and then throw her through the plate glass window in the living room that looks out on our perfect green lawn with the blue hydrangeas. Imagining her blood streaming down shards of broken glass provides me with a moment of emotional relief.

Later that night, in the darkness, I shiver in my bed under a thin brown cotton blanket – it actually has holes in it – and a paper-thin flower-power orange and pink polyester bedspread. It's about sixty degrees. The automatic heat monitor (encased in a locked hard plastic cover) in the living room lowers the house temperature at night and it can't be adjusted – just like everything else in this house.

When they moved to Needham from Hanover, Marion put the extra blankets (except the dual control electric blanket Marion and my father use) in an old wooden trunk with frayed leather straps. She keeps it locked and at the foot of my bed. I'd told my father I was freezing at night and he'd mentioned it to Marion. Ironically, warmth rested in the old trunk so close to my bed, yet, that too, was locked.

"The blankets in the trunk are for John and Steve when they visit," she uttered, forcefully, with a threatening darkness.

Defeated, he'd gone back to reading the Monitor – the newspaper created by Mary Baker Eddy – the founder of the Christian Science religion, who had taught me Love was the only true reality on the planet.

A three-drawer plastic bureau (stuffed with unfamiliar clothing), a hatbox, and a couple of strange leather suitcases have suddenly appeared in my room. Is she turning my room into storage? Does my father know?

Am I moving out? Is someone moving in? Is my father going to make me go live with another family like he tried to do with my brother, Jeffrey?

My father *had* liked me for a while.

I roll over and over in my bed. I am terrified he is going to bring me to New Hampshire, like he did Jeffrey. Although almost anything would be better than this life, even an orphanage. At least I would be warm.

The horror with Marion began after she had married my father and the first Christmas we lived in Needham. I had made a red and green construction paper chain and hung it, as a Christmas decoration, in the kitchen. That night she ripped it down while I stood watching, helplessly. She said something about the chain being "a filthy mess." I could not speak. I felt a part of me leave my body.

The phone rings in the upstairs hallway outside my bedroom and Marion's heavy, hard footsteps soon follow on the avocado carpeting on the stairs. My heartbeat accelerates in fear.

"Hello," she says, out of breath, and irritated. I pray it's not one of my friends.

Then her tone changes completely.

"Oh, hello dear," she says, gaily.

It is either John or Steve, one of her sons.

"No. Not at all, dear. I don't mind, Steve dear. It's not that late," she says brightly.

"Oh, I'm okay. Three down and one to go. That's how I see it. (pause). Oh, but this one. She's a real beaut. She's had detention three times this week already" she adds.

She is talking about me. *The three down* are my three siblings. They are trying to get rid of me. I knew it. I cover my mouth to stifle a gasp and then quickly wipe tears which have sprung in my eyes. Doesn't my father hear her? She's right outside their bedroom.

When the house is completely dark, the moon is high in the night sky, and she is finally asleep, I creep down the stairs to the kitchen, not daring to turn on a light. It's so cold, but I'm so hungry.

I open the refrigerator.

"DO NOT EAT' signs (for me) are taped onto the little plastic yogurt tubs of strawberry yogurt and on a new, unopened package of Kraft cheddar cheese. Nothing else looks appealing – especially the meatloaf leftovers in an old plastic Tupperware container.

I open a kitchen cabinet door and search, in the dark, for the Planter's peanut jar. It's harder for her to monitor the peanuts. I pour a pile in my hand and then throw them into my mouth and hungrily chew and quickly swallow. I'm afraid to be caught eating. I cannot eat at dinner the atmosphere is so threatening

In the dim light of the moon that filters through a window into the kitchen, a slim black book leaning on a red Betty Crocker cookbook pulls my attention. I slide it out and open the book and read the first page in the thin stream of moonlight.

Favorite Recipes Tested and Proved by The Ladies Auxiliary of the Epiphany Lutheran Church, 1931, Elmhurst, Illinois.

Marion was from Illinois. I quickly flip the pages. This is Marion's recipe book. There are recipes for salt pork fruitcake, tutti frutti cake, chag po, and veal rosettes. It's the kind of stuff she cooks for Steve and John.

Marion was a Lutheran? She goes to the Baptist church in Needham. My God. Religious? Does she think she is spiritual? What do people think it means to be spiritual?

My father still attends the Christian Science Church.

I flip to the next page and a "poem."

We may live without POETRY,
MUSIC AND ART;
We may live without CONSCIENCE,
May live without HEART
We may live without FRIENDS,
May live without books;
But a civilized man cannot
Live without COOKS.

I shut the book and shove it back next to the Betty Crocker cookbook. I throw a handful of peanuts into my mouth and then pour a cup of milk and wash them down with it. I hesitate. I stand in the dark holding an empty glass. I'm afraid to leave the cup in the sink, but even more afraid to wash it. Either action, in the morning, would provoke Marion to slam cupboards and stream venomous condemnations – either for leaving the cup or washing it inadequately and leaving it "filthy."

Maybe I should go outside and throw the cup into the small cluster of trees at the back of our yard. No, too many doors and locks to jangle and squeak or slam in the wind.

I don't know how to eat or drink here. I set the glass in the kitchen sink and hope the punishment will not be too severe.

I creep up the stairs and into my room and the cold bed. I fall asleep shivering and dream someone is at my window. They speak, or more like they growl, like an evil spirit.

"Janie, come out. Come out and play" it says, menacingly.

I wake up from the nightmare. I'm shivering.

It is still dark, and my heart is racing. I want to run, to someone; to somewhere, but quickly remember there is nowhere to run. I would not dream of knocking on their door.

Eventually sleep arrives to take me from one nightmare to another. I sink into a stream of terrifying images and feelings of despair, hopelessness, and eternal aloneness.

CHAPTER 9

CRYSTAL BLUE PERSUASION

I wear an orange sweater and a flower-power mini skirt (I made it in Mrs. Marr's home economics class), white fishnet stockings, and white go-go boots, and lean against the plain gray wall at my father's office. I'd just had detention at Pollard Junior High and then walked to my father's office on Great Plain Avenue in Needham

I reluctantly scan his new office.

He had moved from The Needham Industrial "Park" to downtown Needham. Three employees, two men wearing gray suits and black ties, and a secretary, Helen, are all sitting at their gray desks, lined up against the opposite white wall. My father's desk is at the front of all of them, near the big windows and the front door.

"Sure, Mike, we'll get those conductors shipped out right away. You won't be sorry. On the double," my father says, very loudly, over the phone, to someone who is probably either in California or Japan.

Everyone he talks to is either in Japan or California: at Raytheon or Honeywell: and they all make microchips or semiconductors or something like that. What is a microchip?

Holding the phone receiver, he slowly leans back in his office chair until the phone cord is stretched into a straight line and he is looking directly up at the white ceiling.

I glance at a letter on his desk. A black and white drawing of a chicken stepping out of a broken eggshell is the symbol for "Hatch Associates" and it is on all his stationery. It's sad. The baby chicken is all by itself.

"Very funny. You know it's the guys at Harvard making us dumb guys rich. They're the ones who made the microchip. Or was it MIT? OK. Yeah. We'll talk to you then. Goodbye Mike. Good talking with you," he says, even more loudly.

What does he do? I never see anything for sale; just men talking on phones. He lurches forward and his swivel chair squeaks. I flinch and my heartbeat accelerates. Sudden movements scare me lately. He hangs up the phone.

"So, Janie, you probably want some money, right?" he says, a moment later, still smiling about his phone conversation.

"Yeah, Judy and I are going for pizza," I mumble. I know he doesn't really care about my reply. It's all about him.

"Well ... let's ... see ... what ... I ... can... do," he continues, standing up.

My heart slows while he fishes in the back pocket of his plaid pants trying to get his faded brown leather wallet. Almost everything my father owns is old. He never wants to waste anything. It's Yankee thriftiness. He eats every part of the lobster. He saves glass jars and paper clips and junk mail and brown paper bags and old and stained clothes.

I ask him for money all the time. Maybe if I keep asking him, he'll understand there is something important I need.

"Hey Helen, you got a few bucks for this young girl here? Think I'm broke," he says, with a smile.

They laugh. *It would be nice to be like them. To be able to laugh and joke around.*

He's making a lot of money these days, that's why it's a joke. I guess. I'm not sure why they are laughing. I'm completely removed from my father's world where people seem happy and relaxed.

Helen smiles, shakes her head at his *crazy* joke, and keeps typing. Helen is the ex-wife of someone my father knew at Bowdoin College where he went to college.

One of his employees, a man with a black briefcase on his desk, suddenly rolls towards me on his chair which is on a clear sheet of plastic. I gasp silently and stare at the man. His sudden movement had surprised me.

"Your father is a highly respected businessman, Janie. He has a reputation as being one of the most honest men in the business." the man says.

My father, honest? Really? What does that mean? To whom is he honest? I just stare without responding.

"Well, thank you, Jim. That's awfully nice of you," my father says quietly. I look down at my transistor radio. I play with the dial. The man slides his chair back to his desk.

"Here you go Janie," my father says and walks over and gives me a five-dollar bill. I take the bill. Anxiety. Fear. Anger. It all rises. My palms sweat. I want to get out of his office.

"Thanks," I respond stiffly and stuff the money in my rawhide, fringed purse, and then push open the door.

"See you at dinner" he adds, but he is already turning towards Helen. He probably has a funny story.

"Did I ever tell you…" I hear him say as I exit.

Later that night, after another one of Marion's hate-filled dinners, I grab my radio and exit the house, and walk, in my red Dr. Scholl sandals, down the perfect, black-tarred sidewalk which is lined, on both sides of the street, with lush, green, manicured lawns; and blue hydrangeas and yellow forsythia bushes. The houses are mostly two-story Colonial and Cape Cod-style.

My father's house is located at the highest point in Needham, so, except for the water tower, everything is downhill. At the bottom of Dunster, I cross Lindbergh Street and run through the backyard of a white colonial house with black shutters, and into a small patch of woods.

I reach a special flat rock hidden from all the streets and houses and surrounded by tall oak and Maple trees. I sit on the rock and look around and imagine I'm back in Hanover in the woods near Indian Head River where the bridge crosses over to Hansen. It feels peaceful.

I take matches and a crushed cigarette out of my pants pocket and light the Kool cigarette stolen from Marion. I take a drag and then exhale and watch the smoke rise into the sky.

Kim used to meet me here. We both smoke Kool cigarettes. She lives on Brookline Street. This year maybe I'm too wild for Kim. She comes from a nice Italian family. I'm kind of a mystery. Everyone else has a mother.

"Crystal Blue Persuasion, It's a new vibration," I sing along with my favorite song.

"Every green field and every town, they'll be peace and good. Brotherhood. Crystal Blue Persuasion," I continue.

Really? Will that really happen? Peace and good? I start to walk towards the Mitchell School field, the baseball diamond, and the swing sets.

"I been tryin' to get to you girl for a long time, cause constantly, you been on my mind. But, babe, I was wrong. Took too long," I sing. I start to dance, a little.

"You wanted love and affection, now you won't look in my direction, The Expressway to your heart…the expressway." I sing a little louder and dance now, in circles.

Later, I walk across the empty baseball field and then hang out on the swing sets near Mitchell School. When the sun has set, I reluctantly head towards "home." I drag my fingertips across all the blue Hydrangeas and the yellow forsythias bushes on Dunster Road as I slowly move towards the house.

Later, at "home" I sit on my bed – on the thin polyester bedspread with large orange and yellow flowers – and try to write a paper for my social studies class about what the people eat in China.

"GOD DAMN THAT GIRL." Marion screams and slams a cupboard in the kitchen. My body shakes and adrenaline seeps out from my stomach and into my body.

I drop my notebook and pen on the bedspread and wrap my arms around my legs, put my head on my knees, trying to brace for the next SLAM and DAMN.

Where is my father? Oh, he's doing Meals-On-Wheels. The old people. He doesn't hear.

Something happens. It's awful. It's strange. The orange and black flowers on my wallpaper look like they are melting. My body shrinks until I'm the size of a dot. My heart races and my hands break out into a sweat. I'm dying or going insane. I am big and small at the same time. Hot and cold. Still as the surface of a quiet pond on a windless day and terrified of a monster deep inside the pond, underneath me.

"Father-Mother-God. Adorable. Thy kingdom…present…earth… heaven (I could feel my heart beating faster) Feed the famished…love is love…for God is infinite power and all and all and all," my father says in a low, deadly serious tone.

He is suddenly sitting on my bed reading from Mary Baker Eddy's *Science and Health with Key To The Scriptures*. Did I tell him I was dying?

None of it made sense. My heart banged against my chest. I'm going to have a heart attack. Droplets of sweat pour off my forehead and my temples.

Thank God my father stopped speaking. I couldn't understand what he was saying or why he was saying it. *I thought he thought I was dying.* There was something wrong with my hearing. Sounds are too loud and then too soft. My whole-body shakes can't stop anything. It goes on and on and on, like a train off the tracks headed over a cliff, but you never really get to the cliff –

CHAPTER 10

THE END OF RELIGION

"It was an anxiety attack," he told me last night and that was it.

Today, on Sunday morning, in his new Dodge Charger, we drive to the Christian Science Church on Great Plain Avenue in Needham. He goes upstairs to church and I go down into the basement to Sunday school. He talks to everyone we meet, but I'm silent, not even smiling. I'm still shaking inside.

"You mean the chair I'm sitting on and this table is not real," I ask my Sunday school teacher, in a confrontational tone, after we had settled in for the lesson and she had said that everything material is unreal and "temporal."

The white walls, the plain wooden tables and chairs, and the floor of the Christian Science Church Sunday School are unadorned, plants or art or rugs. Christ is not bleeding to death anywhere, No Virgin Mary's. *Especially no Virgin Mary's.*

We are a no-frills religion, unlike the Catholics and all their "hoopla and shenanigans," as my father called the Catholic services. He hates holy smoke and holy water and holy crackers; and statues of saints and virgins and dying Christs. He calls the Pope a "goddamn idiot."

I agree with him about the Pope.

"Liar" I'd said under my breath watching a televised Catholic sermon just recently. I'd also watched the Pope on television as he was in a car being driven down a crowded street in Rome. Massive amounts of people bowed and threw flowers on the street that preceded his vehicle.

"Idiots," I said out loud and scribbled out a poem, "A Rose is a Rose is a Rose." The poem criticized the people for not believing they were equal to the Pope, and the Pope, for lying and deceiving. For weeks my father raved about my poem and showed it to anyone he could get to sit down and read it or he read it out loud to them. That was unusual.

"That's right dear. They are just a manifestation of the human mind. Love and God are the only truth," my Sunday school teacher says in her sweet, monotone tone.

Oh really. Well, you should spend a night at my house.

"I have to leave," I mumble, picking my coat up from the back of the *chair that didn't really exist.*

I departed under a big red EXIT sign I'd been staring at for several weeks.

CHAPTER 11

POPHAM BEACH

It's July, six months after the first anxiety attack. I'm sixteen years old and my father, Marion, and I have just arrived for our annual two-week summer vacation at Popham Beach in Maine. I have already thrown my suitcase into the screened porch of our brown, with red shuttered two-bedroom rented cabin and run down the gray, weather-beaten wooden steps to the beach.

I kick off my Dr. Scholl sandals, unbutton, and pull down my faded bell-bottom jeans embroidered with flowers and a rainbow.

Free at last. Free at last.

In a white fringed bikini, I stand and stare at the ocean.

The wide dark blue choppy Atlantic Ocean stares back at me. Gray herring gulls stand motionless on floating driftwood. Blue waves infused with silver mica, sparkle in the sun. The waves crash rhythmically onto the pure white sand.

I hold my hand to shield my eyes from the sun and stare to the right to Fox Island. Yup, she's still there. It's my first stop.

I jog along the shore, leaping over long brown rubbery strips of seaweed as wide as boards. My sterling silver peace sign earrings bounce against my cheeks. Multi-colored sea pebbles, white clamshells, sand dollars, and bits and pieces of green sea glass, softened on the edges, line the shore and glisten wet from the most recent wave.

I try not to step on any sand dollars. Etched on each fragile dollar is a five-petal flower that I do not want to harm.

Halfway to Morse River, at Popham Beach State Park, I see three tanned lifeguards perched, like lions, on chairs on top of the white stands. Two of the lifeguard's stare at me strangely. They used to ignore me.

Maybe the white bikini was a bad choice, especially the fringe. I lean down and pick up a long piece of driftwood and pretend to be interested in drawing a line in the wet sand, staying on the far side of my line away from the lifeguards.

A little blond girl is playing with a blue plastic pail and shovel.

She finishes digging a hole in the sand, only to have it immediately filled in by an incoming wave.

"Mommy!," she screams.

Her mother, who had been reading a book, drops her book, runs over to the little girl, and cradles her in her arms.

Pain edges in on the few moments of freedom I had felt. I start to run. Ahead in the water, a teenage boy paddles a surfboard straight into a large incoming wave. There are several large ones behind that one. I continue at a slow jog, passing Fox Island; a huge rock rising from the ocean on which flowers and a bit of grass grows.

I stop and flip over a crab with my stick and see it is only a shell; the rest of it is gone and probably already digested by a seagull.

I bear right and inland and now I'm completely alone.

The ocean has given way now to the fifty-foot-wide Morse's River. The sparkling clear river originates at Spirit Pond and then empties into the Atlantic at Fox Island. Archeologists found a Viking Rune at Spirit Pond not too long ago.

I run on the sandy banks along the river which are steep and soft. In most places, the sand gives way under pressure from even a light footstep, and you can easily fall into the river. I'm not afraid.

I stop and stare down into the river.

The water is infused with silver mica. Shells, mostly white, tumble and cartwheel towards the sea in the river current. The current can easily sweep you out to sea. Seagulls screech in the sky. I look up at the gulls and then to my right and the light green dune grass as it sways in the warm breeze as it has since I was a child.

Driftwood bleached white has been deposited incongruously every which way on the river beach like old, twisted bones dropped from the sky from another planet, whose beings have skulls like tangled tree trunks. I wonder, fleetingly, if the earth is a cemetery for these aliens.

I continue walking towards the swimming hole at the end of the river. I suddenly remember an old black and white photograph of my mother, pregnant with me, my father (still handsome and wearing his bifocals), and my three siblings, Robbie, Jeffrey, and Sally, sitting on the sand on Morse's Beach – which is right up ahead.

I run the last few feet and then plop down on the sand. I am in the photo too. And they are all beside me, here. We are all together. What would it be like, to have a family; or someone, at least one person, who cared about me? What would that be like? I stare down into the river; deep, cold, and pure. This is the swimming place. Not a soul in sight. A hawk with a fish flies over my head in the blue sky.

I get up quickly and get ready to do "the dive." You had to do "the dive" at Morse River. I had watched my father do "the dive" for ten years every summer.

"You're next Janie," he'd say after he did the dive into the frigid water and then had ascended out like a Sea God covered in sparkling sand and salty water.

He'd wipe his shoulders and chest with the towel then throw it around his neck and stare at the river, his arms crossed on his chest. It was just the two of us.

Now I'm alone.

I take a deep breath and dive into Morse's River.

I kick hard with my long legs and pull forward at the deepening water with strong breaststrokes as I inch closer to the bottom of the river. I fight not to be swept towards the ocean in the current. The tips of my toes and fingertips tingle as my body temperature descends.

Pressure builds on my temples. My lungs hurt. I'm aware I'm moving with the current towards the ocean, but I'm detached. My blond hair floats around my head gently touching my lips and eyes and mouth.

I touch my hair like, I've never seen or felt it before. Pure white clam shells float along beside me, on their own journeys. Do they have a destination, or they are just floating through life, aimlessly, like me?

I swipe the bottom of the river sand with my hand, raising a small cloud of silt. Satisfied I've touched the bottom of the river, I push off hard from the ground with both feet and look up towards the sunlight. A few moments later, I burst through the surface of the water and gulp for air.

Fox Island – surrounded by seagulls and crashing waves. I've drifted too far. The ocean and the riptide are only moments away. I'm only remotely concerned. I've been swimming in dangerous waters my whole life.

I struggle against the current. I swim towards the bank of the river. I get to the bank and latch on, but it collapses under my weight and the sand falls into the river. I try again and again, but the soft riverbank keeps collapsing.

The bank, maybe because it's closer to the ocean and the hard sand of the beach, suddenly does not crumble; I'm able to latch on and climb onto land. Breathing hard, I lie on the sand beside the river.

I close my eyes and rest my head on my folded arms, on the hard sand bank, breathing heavily into a small space between my arms and the beach. Tiny flecks of mica and sand jump and swirl with every inhale and exhale.

Motionless and covered in sand and sparkling silver mica, I might have looked, from a seagull's perspective, like an alien that had crashed to earth.

CHAPTER 12

THE LIGHT OF THE SILVERY MOON

There are so many things
That will not die, nor seek a shadowed past where they belong.
White sand that blazed beneath a summer sky,
The lyrics of a slight, enchanted song.

The quiet tread of dusk,
the purpled light turned softly down that day might sink to sleep.
And lips that framed against the gathered night,
The promises they would never keep.

There for a while the song was sweet and low,
And there was wine to quench an ancient thirst.

There for a while we managed not to know
That all dreams fade, and those we hold close go first.

And so, the wind blows chill across the sky
And ghosts come out to watch a summer die.
By Pauline Hatch (my mother)

*T*hat *night there is a storm.*
I shiver in my sleeping bag as the cold ocean wind sweeps through the screened-in porch where I sleep. My shell chime, which I had made from purple clam shells that had natural holes near the neck, clatters, and the strings whip until it is a tangled mess that ceases to move.

Lightning flashes in the black starless sky. Waves pound against the shore. It is high tide; the waves seem very near to the back steps that lead to my porch.

I get up and stare out at the black ocean. The Sequin Lighthouse casts a forlorn stream of light across the ocean, almost to my cottage. It is a lonely, long, forbidding light.

The next day the waves are still high. The sea is gray and choppy and forbidding. I sit on the wet sand on the beach and stare at the morose gray waves pounding the shore. I am compelled towards them like they are calling.

The undertow today is dangerous. I want the frigid waves to numb the pain in my body. I throw off my clothes and run, in my bathing suit, un-thinking, towards the ocean.

My father and his brother Dan watch from the ledge above the beach near Ocean View Restaurant. They wear yellow rain slickers and L. L. Bean boots and are drinking coffee from paper cups, like a half a dozen other storm-watchers.

I dive headfirst into a huge gray blue wave littered with driftwood and seaweed. Immediately, in the churning gray ocean, I try to decide what is up and what is down. Driftwood; even logs; a few dead fish, and seaweed clutter the ocean, making it hard to see or to understand my position in the ocean.

It is always lighter towards the sky. I look up and see seagulls and then move my body into a space about a foot below the surface where I'll be somewhat protected from the crashing waves and the undertow.

It is quiet and peaceful. It might only take one wrong move, a dive downwards, towards the undertow. Freedom forever from Marion; from the anxiety attacks; the terror; the sense of hopelessness; the feeling that I don't really exist–that I am out there somewhere. Waves were crashing on the shore. Any minute and I might be sent spinning out to sea like the boy from Canada.

The Canadian boy had drowned at this very spot two years ago. Jessie the cook – who worked at Ocean View Restaurant – with the greased-back black hair and white T-shirt – had run out of the restaurant and dove straight off the rocks into the huge waves to try to save the boy. I had swum beside the boy that day, but knew the waters better than him, and dove down deep to avoid the crush of the waves and slid onto shore on my stomach.

Now, from within my watery world, I see my father running down the steps to the beach. He looks worried; an unusual expression for him; as his life seems to be an ongoing party; golf on the weekends, Tanqueray and tonics at five, board meeting at the YMCA; trips to Europe with Marion; Power Squadron meetings; and fishing trips with Dave on his new speed boat named after his mother, Clara.

It was always Dave, hardly ever one of his biological children, who tagged along with our father. We had been lost to him. We, as a family, had been broken, not as much by the divorce, but by slander. My father was easily influenced by stronger personalities than himself, and Dave, with his bravado, and snake oil salesman personality, had turned him against all of us children and our mother.

Dave had not had his own father as a child, so I think he wanted ours all to himself. He never wanted our family united. A united family would have put us, all the Hatches, together. He would have been on the outside again, looking in–not because we were a mean lot of people– but because he was nothing like any of us. Not a streak of creativity, spirituality, or compassion in him–that I could see. My father, never being the cool guy– mostly an intellectual nerd with bifocals as a child–and then as a teen, a slight, non-muscular, but funny and smart kid–but who never got invited into the sports clubs or fraternities at Bowdoin–now he thought he was finally one of the cool guys.

He was just weak.

It was almost like someone, or something had sent Dave and Marion into our lives to destroy us. Is that possible? Could it have anything to do with the microchip? How could so many things go wrong?

Why go back? I have lost everything I love, including my dog Jonesy who died of a lung disease. I had tried to keep him alive with a blue coat I made, but Marion had called the coat "filthy" and it was taken away and he had been put to sleep one night when I was having a sleepover with a girl I hardly knew in Needham.

Suddenly, there are rays of sunlight streaming into the ocean above my head. Thousands of tiny particles of silver mica sparkle and swirl in the water. I am a mermaid inside a snow globe of glitter and white shells. Crystal water. Maybe it was the crystals from Atlantis. I suddenly remembered the apple tree in Hanover and Misty and Indian Head River. I reach out to touch the sparkling mica at my fingertips.

I swirl it with my hand in circles in the incoming sunlight.

I turn and watch for the swell of the next incoming wave that is indistinct from the rest of the water except to an experienced eye. I have been swimming in turbulent waters my whole life. I can feel it as much as I see it. When the wave is right above me, I shoot forward towards the shore.

The same force that moves the waves and the tides and the moon, maybe, propels me away from death. It is the same force that changes the leaves from red to gold to green, and the flowers burst to life; I do not know why but cannot stop myself from choosing life.

My lungs near bursting, I kick hard to become part of the swell as it builds to its crest. I ride the cresting and then breaking wave until its very end; until it dissolves into nothingness.

My father, who is standing on the shoreline, still looking worried, holds his hand out. Embarrassed by his attention, I take his hand anyway and slowly stand up with his support. Vertical streaks of blood are intermingled with seaweed and black and white and gray pebbles on my stomach. Broken shells had torn my skin.

My eyes meet my father's briefly. I see something. He looks vulnerable. He's not making a joke or telling a story. I also see something else that can't be named.

"Are you okay, dear?"

"Yes, I'm all right," I say.

"Dear?" Did he just use that word?

"Hey, great dive," he says, getting back to his old self. In a way, it's a relief.

With one of the ragged towels from Needham, I wipe the blood from my bare stomach. Pebbles have embedded themselves in the long bloody scratches. My bikini is torn and filled with sand.

My father walks back up to the ledge to meet Dan and I lean down and cup sea water in my hands and then pour it over my wounds. I wince as pebbles and pieces of seaweed and shells are tugged from the wound.

My blood is a thin stream amongst the sand, shells, pebbles, and driftwood, as it is all carried out into the ocean with the receding tide. I stare at the stream of blood and somehow know that my life will be a sacrifice.

On the next sunny day after the storm, my father and I made our annual visit to Jane Stevens. Jane had been one of my father's high school girlfriends. Or at least they dated. Her quaint white cottage was perched precariously (I thought) on the edge of Fort Baldwin Hill and overlooking Atkins Bay, Fort Popham, The Kennebec River, and the Atlantic Ocean. I had to admit, the view was spectacular. Her home was neatly enclosed inside a white picket fence draped with wild roses. I always felt welcome here. It was a rare feeling and I dared not trust it.

Behind her house, hidden at the top of the hill, in the thick deciduous leafy green trees, and thorny bushes, were the mossy decaying ruins of

Fort Baldwin. It was a fort manned during the American Revolution and built on the highest point at Popham with a view of all incoming and outgoing ships and boats.. canoes..whatever. It had military armaments, underground prisons, an outlook tower, and near her house, her long-time theory that her house sat on the first European settlement in America.

Jane had told us, on a visit prior, that George Popham– an English nobleman who brought colonists to Popham in 1607– had died the first winter after his arrival believing, erroneously, that his name would be forever associated with creating the first English settlement in the New World.

Jane was excited about a small shard of English China she found in her yard. It had been carbon-tested, proving, along with other archeological findings at a dig site, just a few yards up the road, that Popham Beach was the location of the first English settlement in America.

"They hated the cold, and they made enemies of the Indians. They built a boat, The Virginian, and sailed back to England shortly after Popham died. But he was the first, He was the first," Jane said, emphatically.

"I always knew it, "she added, her face glowing with satisfaction.

She had white hair and pink cheeks, and she wore a sailor's hat. When she looked at me, her smiles were deep and generous. I was shocked at her warmth.

"More blueberry cake Janie?" she stopped suddenly, trying to include me.

"Oh, no, thank you," I managed to respond, smiling and trying to act normal, like pleasantries were a part of my everyday life. While my father had made an art of escaping our house to avoid Marion's wrath, I was primarily stuck. I was quite literally shaken to my bones most of the time.

I mused on Jane's words as I ate her homemade blueberry cake. I might be sitting on top of George Popham's bones. It wasn't just any bones, but the bones of maybe the first white man to ever have stepped foot on North American soil. If not the first white man, then the first "English nobleman.»

She had been an investigative reporter for the Times Record newspaper in Brunswick. She'd also written a popular book called "One Man's World" about her father's life as a ship Captain.

Suddenly, as the adults talk and laugh and reminisce, in my mind, I'm seeing a carnival game. The kind where you throw a ball and hit the top half of a pin, which is a monkey head or something, then it spins around to reveal the bottom half of the pin which is something entirely different like a horse head or a person or another image.

I felt someone or something– a portal opening in time– had pitched a ball and I had spun up to the top and George Popham was on the bottom – and upside down looking up – at me. I was on top. What did it mean?

The next day, we visited my namesake, Jane Donnell; the lady my father delivered Pepperidge Farm bread to when he was a teenager–she was always the last stop on his route.

A long wooden walkway grayed by the sun to a perfect stone color leads neatly from the beach at Popham through the long green dune grass to Jane's three-story red Victorian cottage.

The thigh-high grass, whipping in the wind, stings my bare, tanned legs. Brown as a bear from long days in the sun–swimming, boating, fishing– at Popham and his skin rugged from exposure–, my father did not seem to mind the lashing sea grass. . He was preoccupied and obviously excited to see his old girlfriend. Maybe they have always been just friends, I'm not sure.

"Bob darhhhhhling how deeelightful to see you (pause) And Janie how are you dear? " Jane says warmly in her husky Katherine Hepburn voice, from the top stair of the forest green wooden wrap-around porch, as we neared the cottage. Her reddish-blond hair is windswept in the front and loosely gathered in a bun in the back.

When we reached the top step, the adults kiss, and hug.

"Would you like a highball, Bob? And Janie, dear, would you like some lemonade?'

"Glad you asked. Sure would. I've been waiting all summer for one," my father jokes, smiling.

"Yes, please," I answer, quietly, and follow them onto the porch.

Jane brought out our drinks and the three of us sit on the old green wicker chairs on the porch. Jane and my father sip their drinks and watch the waves breaking on the shoreline on the beach in the near distance.

"Bob, dear have you tried the fish chowder up at Spinneys this summer. It's heavenly," Jane asks.

"Well, as a matter of fact, I haven't. So, how about you and me- Saturday night- at Spinneys? Is it a date?" my father responds, deadpan.

She smiles knowingly. My father laughs and slaps his bare brown knee as if it is the most amusing thing anyone had ever said.

I could only think of one word "Why?" Why were we stuck with Marion if you knew women like the two Janes?

Oh, yes, I remember. Marion was good at bookkeeping.

I simply stare.

Straight ahead on a bank against the sea grass, white granite rocks are wedged with huge chunks of silver mica sparkle in the sun. It's almost blinding to stare at them. It's beautiful. I think of Atlantis again and the crystals. Had they shattered into millions of pieces and been reformed into the mica of Maine?

I listen to the soft thud of tennis balls on the red clay tennis court behind the house and the ker-chink of little ice cubes being dropped into frosted beach glasses in the summer kitchen.

It's like a fairy tale. Both of the Janes make me wonder, how we got stuck with the troll Marion. She is probably down on her hands and knees, grumbling, and scrubbing sand off the bathroom floor at the cottage, with a Red Sox game, on her small black and white TV, blaring in the background.

The next night a bonfire at the beach spews sparks thirty feet into the night sky, illuminating the faces of a couple of dozen or so children and adults. It is the last big bash of the summer.

We eat steamed clams and lobster drenched in butter off of paper plates. I toss my plate into the fire. It sizzles before turning to ash. Tanqueray and tonics– the preferred drink of Yankee WASPS– had quenched a deep thirst in my father, Betsy, the two Janes, and Uncle Dan. They talk loudly and laugh uproariously at everything that one of them says.

The ice in the red and white Igloo cooler plunked in the sand was almost all melted. The lid was open more than shut, I had noticed. An empty Emerald green Tanqueray gin bottle lay abandoned near the Igloo. I thought it was beautiful. The bottle. I simply stared at it squinting my eyes, thinking maybe I could make it move or transform.

I stood separate from most everyone with a pretty teenage girl with a French accent-who was about my age- and a couple of tanned lifeguards. We were secretly passing around a bottle of Blackberry Brandy. Through blurred eyes, I move my gaze from the green Tanqueray bottle to the blazing fire. I step back from the fire and into the shadows and closer to the dark ocean, and my friends follow. The tide was incoming, and the waves were crashing in a steady cadence. I held the brandy bottle up to the moon and took a long slug.

"I can't believe we actually think it's fun to boil a lobster alive, " I muse, slurring my words slightly, holding the bottle loosely in my hand, by my side. I simply didn't care anymore who saw it.

"Let's get out of here," I add.

"That zounds gewd to me," Chloe murmurs.

"I'm game," said one of the lifeguards. He picks up a rope that had a white buoy attached to it and his backpack.

"Let's go to Fox Island," said the other lifeguard, who had brown eyes and dark wavy brown hair and a body as compact as one of the Maine tugboats that chugged up and down the Kennebec River,

I set out with my three brand new friends under the universe of stars.

Chloe and I wear shorts and halter tops. The boys had on orange jackets with LIFEGUARD emblazoned in big black capital letters on the back.

We had been on Fox Island for at least an hour–finished off the brandy and started our own little fire and we were talking and laughing–I had a LIFEGUARD jacket draped around my tanned shoulder– when someone said, "Oh fuck,"

The rest of us continue to stare into the fire. We are surrounded by crashing cold deep sea and an endless black sky of stars. It was the same ocean, the same location where Dale Hatch had fallen into the crashing waves and never been saved.

The next thing I knew one of the LIFEGUARDS was carrying me across rushing water that looked about three or four feet deep. I drag my hand through the moon-dappled ocean. So beautiful. The Canadian girl held onto the buoy tied to the rope being dragged by the other lifeguard.

My head is against his chest, and I feel the pounding of his heart. I take my hand out of the water and clench my hands around the back of his neck and try to shift my weight to make it easier for him. When I adjusted myself upwards, I look straight into his eyes. They seem to be reflecting the starlight beaming down into the ocean. I wonder how many aliens are looking down at us from above. I remember my mother saying there were millions of them. Did they like me, these aliens?

"I don't wanna go back to the lobster bake," I murmur softly into his ear.

"I'm not taking you back" he utters in a strained but sober voice. "But I am going to make sure you get back to shore alive,." He hoists me higher on his chest.

I am so close to his wet lips I could easily kiss him. I do not remember anything else until I was being gently placed on dry sand and covered in a blanket.

The next thing I recall is a flashlight in my eyes and my father's angry voice. It was still dark, but the sun was a thin strip of light on the horizon.

"What the hell is going on here?" he says, angrily.

I slowly sit up and then peel a small lobster claw off of my cheek. It dawned on me that I had passed out in the sand in a pile of lobster carcasses from the lobster bake.

"Gross," was all I could think of to say.

I looked across at Fox Island. I also suddenly realized we had almost been trapped out there at high tide, but someone had had enough sense to get us all back before the sandbar had been completely covered by a rip tide. I smile, remembering a beating heart against soft skin. Dark eyes reflecting starlight; the warm feeling I had from the brandy. They were feelings of happiness, I guess. It was unfamiliar. .

I was ignoring my father and looking around for the LIFEGUARD. I dimly recall someone had been lying next to me on the sand.

"Get the hell back to the cottage,"

I was still staring in the direction of Fox Island.

My father's voice got dimmer and dimmer until I no longer heard him and then he was gone. Only an empty space existed where he once stood. He was now lost to me, as a father, as someone who was supposed to have protected me, for forever.

I grab an L.L. Bean blanket left on the beach, pull it over my shoulders, and lay back down. I wonder vaguely if one of the waves might take me out to sea- to Seguin. Am I too close to the shoreline? I think of mermaids, and underwater dragons, and dolphins, and starfish and all kinds of Beings who I might me in the water world.

The salt, the ocean, the mud, the wind, the waves, had cleansed, me maybe, of a thousand angry words shot at me by Marion. Maybe the earth was healing me again–like she had done in Hanover.

I remember a song my mother used to sing to me at night … or someone. It was vague.

"The owl and the pussycat went to sea, in a beautiful pea green boat … They took some honey and plenty of money…. And hand and hand on the edge of the sand, they danced by the light of the moon …the moon"

Then, wrapped in the blanket, listening to the pounding of the surf, I fell into a deep sleep, warmed with memories of being carried in strong arms over dark waters.

CHAPTER 13

WATERTOWN

I'm homeless somewhere near Boston. Maybe I'm in Brookline or Newton. Or Watertown. The sky is gray and thick wet snowflakes fall from silver clouds. A sliver of a moon peeks out between clouds.

I had been kicked out of the house in Needham. I had become "a problem." My anger. My "rebelliousness." Maybe, mostly, my drinking. Brandy and the LIFEGUARD and the warm skin and beating heart had imprinted on my brain. I had been trying to get back there in my mind since our vacation had ended six months ago. I was desperate to find an escape from my anxiety and depression, and so, instead of peanuts, I was stealing liquor from the kitchen cabinets.

They had tried sending me to a Freudian psychologist in the posh town of Dover. Mr. Smell sat in a big black leather chair and smoked a corn cob pipe and asked me questions about my sex life. I knew there was something wrong. I didn't just guess. I knew. I did not trust him or his pills. He wanted to give me valium.

I had seen the devastating effects of prescription medicines–especially sedatives – on Dave's sons' – David and Greg – who Dave, – yes, the same guy, my half-brother – had committed to a mental institution for some reason I will never totally understand. It seems one day we were riding our bikes along the streams in the woods of Dover, the next they had been put away. I was shocked.

David had somehow made it out of the asylum, Greg – with the sweet smile, the beautiful green eyes with thick black eyelashes – the shy Greg – one of the few boys or men, who treated me with respect, had never made it out.

It seems anyone who was nice to me paid a price or they just disappeared. Why?

When I had visited them at the drab scary institution, afterward, I had also said to myself "They will never get me. They'll never put me away."

So I never took the valium. The pills were like nails in a coffin or bars on a window, I thought.

Drops of cold melted snow stream down my face, probably washing the black Clinique mascara from my eyelashes onto my cheeks and chin.

With the back of my hand, I wipe the black mascara water off of my cheek. The red garnet ring framed in gold leaves on my right-hand catches my eye. It had been a birthday present from my old boyfriend Billy Jergin.

I close my eyes and remember.

It was snowing then, too, the night of my birthday a year ago in January. Billy and I had stood outside in the dark beside a telephone pole at the corner of Dunster and Lindbergh Ave. in Needham. He had reached into the pocket of his black leather jacket and handed me a small gray fuzzy ring box.

I looked up at him, questioning him with my eyes- as if I didn't know what was in the box. I was just stalling for time. It was difficult for me to know how to act in these circumstances – when I was supposed to be kind or intimate– or anything other than afraid or angry.

"Happy Birthday," he said, a slight smile on his lips.

In the silence, the snow gathered on his blond hair.

"You know…I was thinking that you look like someone in the Irish Republican Army," I said slowly, stalling.

I pointed to his army boots and then I touch the collar of his black leather jacket.

"A real rebel" I had said, in response to his gift. Lame

I had been thinking about my favorite book at the time, Trinity, by Leon Uris who wrote about the Irish fighting back against the English occupation of their homeland.

He gently lifted my chin until I was looking straight into his eyes. He looked amused and kind and infinitely patient.

"Go ahead, open the box, Janie," Billy said. He let go of my chin.

"And my God, Sean, your grandfather is a leprechaun," I added, smiling, thinking of his grandfather, an elegant man even at 95, who wore a long black cashmere coat, still had a thick Irish brogue, and still drove a taxi in Boston.

I thought I had found my escape by trying to amuse him.

"Janie, come on. I worked a month of Friday nights at Filene's to buy that present," he said, only partially joking.

I opened the box and gasped. It was really the most beautiful ring. It had a red garnet stone set inside petals of gold.

"I love you," I heard him saying, above the howl of the wind.

It made my stomach hurt thinking about Billy. It was over a year ago. It was all over – again- maybe for the tenth time. I forced myself to think about something else.

Snowflakes melted rapidly after they hit my fringed rawhide jacket. The jacket was wet. I shivered. I must have been walking for two hours. I didn't have a hat or gloves or a scarf. I wore tan-colored leather Frye boots my mother had bought me in a small shoe store in Harvard Square.

It was soon after she had arrived back. About three years ago. We had walked downhill from Harvard University through a maze of cobblestone sidewalks, deep into the Square. I hardly knew her. In fact, I couldn't remember the first time I saw her again. I really couldn't.

I do remember the shoe store had creaky wooden floors. Bright sunlight had streamed in through the long windows. Frye boots in cardboard boxes were stacked high – from the dusty wide pine board floor – almost to the ceiling (in some stacks). It smelled like leather and wax and clean cardboard. The salesgirl was busy with the crowd of boot buyers. Frye boots are the rage in Cambridge.

It had been just my mother and me on that beautiful blue October day – when the leaves on the maple trees around Harvard University had turned to brilliant shades of scarlet and orange and yellow.

As a child, I had begged God to bring her home. I dreamed about her. I imagined what she might be doing, where she was. I carried her bright red purse into the woods like it was her.

But now, she was back, and I did not know her. Hardly a memory remained. She seemed very nice but unrelated to my mother; the mother I dreamed about every day of my life until I did not dream anymore.

Now, she was like a Good Fairy whose magic wand streamed Clinique make-up, Dean sweaters, Calvin Klein jeans, Frye Boots, ice cream cones, pizza, Chinese food, gold necklaces, and almost anything else I wanted.

"The sky's the limit," as she would always say, giving me a big smile, chin up, as we sped along Massachusetts Avenue in Boston in her bumble bee-yellow Honda Prelude convertible.

But the trinkets from my mother did not hold my attention for very long and it was all very weird. All the money came from my stepfather, Hal, who was an alcoholic. He beat her and he had molested me. I've kind of blocked it all but that's why I can't go back there. It's why I'm homeless.

I had tried living with them in Watertown after I got kicked out of Needham. It lasted two months.

One day, while I was with her in Watertown, I had watched her one morning from my yellow-painted bedroom– filled with Chinese and frog figurines in addition to a Mayan calendar–window. She had a small lawn, but she had managed to grow roses, daffodils, and, in the spring, pansies.

She stood on her small patch of green lawn hanging white sheets on a revolving clothesline. I squinted my eyes until all I could see was my mother. She wore all white; even her sneakers were blindingly white. She bleached clothes with Clorox so often and with such intensity, they glowed in the sunlight.

Maybe she thought if her clothes were white enough it would distract from the ugly dirt of Hal. While I stared at her that day, she put a clothespin in her mouth and the wind lifted the sheets. I thought of my old dog Jonesy. I smiled and felt unnaturally good, as if someone had prayed for me. I couldn't quite find the words to identify the feeling. It was something to do with the wind.

I had given her the book *The Last Temptation of Christ*, but I doubt it was read. A stack of *People* magazine and *National Inquirers* dominated her nightstand beside her waterbed. How weird. A waterbed.

But despite Hal, there was life at my mother's house – some kind of life – my mother hanging out my clothes to dry on the little turnaround clothesline; my mother smiling and making homemade meatloaf bakes in the oven; roses growing up the white fencing in front of the front porch; The keys to her car left on the kitchen table; clean clothes on my bed; the overhead light in the small porch still on at night –no matter how late I got home. The violence was better than the neglect in Needham.

But, In the end, it was too terrifying. The last night I'd spent there Hal had chased her with a butcher knife. What had happened to my mother? Why was she with this monster?

So here I was on the streets. The snow fell harder. No stray dog or other homeless person hovered under a doorway or walked in the darkness. My feet are freezing. The tips of my toes are frozen. Frye boots had no liners. The thick sole is good for walking over dry cobblestone in Harvard Square in the fall, but the whole boot, at least my boots, were generally bad for snowy, wet New England weather. Maybe they just weren't any good if you were homeless.

Suddenly, a dark four-door sedan pulled out of a road up ahead and took a right, towards me. Its headlights swept the wide road and the unblemished blanket of snow. The cold had numbed my brain. I stared at the oncoming lights thinking about how hard it was snowing. The car was slowing down. Then it stopped.

I started to run. I had no idea where to go. I remembered a winding brick path that lead up to the apartment buildings. Was there a doorman? I headed off the road and into the woods, following the winding brick path. I didn't look back until I was deeply hidden in the trees. When I did look, the car seemed to have disappeared. I relaxed a little and sat down on a concrete bench located between a couple of concrete gargoyle lawn ornaments.

I stared at the small pools of water that gathered in the gargoyle's paws and wings. I remembered the Hatch Coat of Arms, the lion's tails that wound around gold filigree. "Safer it Hopes then With Arms" What did that mean? I had never been safe.

I twisted the gold ring and thought about Billy again.

"Janie, here's five bucks for some lunch at McDonald's. And get some gas, it's getting low," Billy had said when we were still together, before I had broken up with him – the last time.

I had been sitting in the driver's seat of his 1966 white Corvette convertible with red leather bucket seats. The car idled at the bottom of the long driveway that leads up to Needham High School. The black top was down on the Vette. Billy was leaning on the windowsill. He took a few cigarettes out of the Marlboro pack and handed them to me. His black leather jacket creaked with almost every movement.

"Thanks," I put two cigarettes on the passenger seat and one in my mouth.

I pushed in the round lighter.

"Pick me up after school, OK," he added.

Now he had both hands on the car sill. He was still wearing the black onyx ring I had given him, even though the silver band had broken. He had tried to repair it with masking tape.

"Yeah. Ok. Billy. Where?"

"Right here. See ya after school"

He smiled and turned away. I smiled after he had turned around.

"K. Thanks," I said quietly.

I lit my cigarette with red coils and watched him walk up the hill towards Needham High School, which was made of bricks and set on top of the hill like a castle. Al and Steve, two of the guys in his rock band, who were also wearing black leather jackets, soon joined Billy, who was their drummer.

Billy always went to school. Everybody I hung out with went to school. Steve turned and waved at me, then Billy did, and he gave me a kind of salute.

My anxiety attacks were so bad I couldn't even sit through a class without feeling terrified the walls were melting and I was shrinking. Billy gave me the Vette whenever I needed to get away. What a freak I am.

I took one drag of my cigarette and then set it in the ashtray.

I pushed one of his eight-track tapes into the rectangular slot above the radio.

Disturbing sounds filled the car. It hurt my body. I pulled it out and read the artist label.

"Black Sabbath.... God help me," I said out loud, with the cigarette between my lips and threw the eight-track onto the seat with the cigarettes. All the music sucks these days.

Not since Crystal Blue Persuasion and Michael Jackson and Motown had I really cared about music. It had changed. It made my stomach hurt.

I pushed in the clutch and pressed down on the accelerator. But as I let up on the clutch, the car lunged forward- the engine roared, and the tires shrieked- and the back of the car shimmied. I had only moved a few feet forward. My heart was racing.

I lifted the cigarette from the ashtray, put it in my mouth, and just let the car idle in neutral. How could I not roar off school grounds in a Corvette? If the bald principal came out and started asking questions like "Why aren't you in school, Miss Hatch?" I wouldn't be able to answer. It's all so complicated.

The beast of an engine that lived under the white fiberglass hood of the Vette could not easily be tamed, at least for me, a new driver.

"It's easy, Janie, just slowly, slowly, let up on the clutch" Billy had said to me, patiently, with a cigarette in his mouth, and smoke swirling around his face, numerous times. He always remained calm. I couldn't understand how he could be so nice, and, on some level, it made me not trust him.

I took a puff on my cigarette and blew the smoke out the window. It wasn't that much fun being without my friends even if I did have the Vette and some money and a few cigarettes.

"If I were the king of the world, I'd tell you what I'd do, I'd throw away the cars and bars and the wars and make sweet love to you," I sang.

I had screeched out of the parking lot leaving behind two long black snake curves on the gray asphalt. And that was that for Needham High School.

I don't know where to go. I'm hungry and my right leg is starting to hurt like it always did when I was cold. It had been slammed up against the door of the Fiat (Billy's car before he bought the Vette) when we had crashed into the side rails on Cape Cod during the blizzard and now it always hurt when I was wet or cold.

I knew my mother loved me.

I laughed out loud at the irony of everything. The gargoyle, surprisingly, did not laugh with me. Why are there gargoyles all over the place?

I gasp. Up ahead, to the right, under a telephone pole, was a parked car. It was a white Vette. It can't be. It is. Billy. What is he doing? I start to run – my heart pounding. His blond hair and leather jacket were unmistakable. He got out of the car and took a drag on a cigarette.

"Billy" I yelled and ran in his direction.

He threw his cigarette on the street and snuffed it out with the heel of his boot.

"Billy" I yelled one more time. Why wasn't he answering me?

He swiped his bangs to the side, crossed his arms over his chest, leaned back against the car, and finally looked in my direction.

I came closer to him until we were only a few feet apart and stopped.

"What are you doing out here? It's so late. I mean. How did you know?" I stammered.

"I have my ways," he said, taunting.

It was a bit awkward. How many times had we broken up? I'd lost track.

"I think you've got about a million angels watching over you," he said. He looked away and then straight at me.

"I'm not always gonna be here ya know. You've made it pretty clear you want to be left alone. That is what you want isn't it?"

It seemed ridiculous. I simply couldn't answer. It was way too complicated. Just like when the school principal had come out to the parking lot and said, "Why aren't you in first period, Miss Hatch?" Then, I had just taken off in the Vette without replying. I couldn't just run away from Billy now. It would be dangerous. Or could I?

"Where do you want to go," he asked, finally, a bit frustrated.

"Well, I can't go to Needham. I was thrown out. They've locked up the house and gone to Europe," I answered.

"Jesus," he responded, shaking his head in frustration. It dismayed him and his family and many other people in Needham, who were aware of the abuse at my house. No one could understand it.

"Billy, you know I can't go back to Watertown. You know what happened with Hal," I said, quietly. He looked away. He didn't want to talk about the sexual abuse.

The vette's engine purred loudly. Snowflakes fell on his blond hair. He shoved his hands into the front pockets of his jeans and then stared at me. He wore the ring I had given him.

He grabbed my arm. His look was stern. He was always looking out for me, it seemed. I guess. I didn't know. When I ran away when I was fourteen and my father put out an All Police Bulletin. Billy had put together a search party and scoured most of Needham. They found me asleep in a tree outside Pistol Pete's house.

I shook myself loose from his grip.

"Janie, what the hell are you doing?"

I could hear him yelling my name as I headed into the darkness.

"Janie ... Janie." he persisted.

I wish he would stop. It hurt. It hurt so bad. Just like the song I had heard a hundred times playing on the old fashion record player in the cafeteria at Pollard Junior High School where I had first met him.

I remember our first dance at Pollard. I wore a yellow and lime-colored mini dress with an empire top. I had put on O'De London perfume and white "frosted" lipstick in the girl's bathroom before the dance. My father wouldn't let me wear make-up, so I snuck it at school.

Whatever happened to the dancing shoes I had worn? What happened to my Mary Jane's and my sterling silver charm bracelet imprinted with Aztec Gods and my pearl necklace and the post cards with the paintings of little animals, sent to me from my mother when she was still in California, that I had saved in an old shoebox? Probably thrown away or stuffed into garbage bags and thrown in the attic or the back of the basement.

Nothing about me mattered.

Tears fell in streams from my eyes and the buildings and trees and streets where I ran were a watery blur.

CHAPTER 14

LAO TZU

A disco ball slowly revolves above the wooden dance floor sending colored streams of light into the furthest corners of the dark windowless bar. I'm living in Maine – near the University of Maine at Orono – and working as a waitress at a bar known for knife fights, drugs, and drunken after-hour parties. I'm eighteen-years-old.

I couldn't have sunk much lower.

I sit at the long bar with an amaretto brandy in a snifter glass, staring at the ball, mesmerized by the Light. It's only five PM. I haven't even clocked in yet.

I had run from Massachusetts to Maine. I was trying to find the LIFE-GUARD, instead, I found an x-con, named Peter, and his girlfriend, Terri who was only sixteen. She was running away too, and so we went with him, and rented a house in the snow, under an icy blue sky. A river ran by us down at the bottom of the hill.

I kind of knew Peter. He had worked at Ocean View Restaurant at Popham. He often opened the restaurant at night, after hours, and we – myself, Peter, Terri, my cousin, Steve, and a few other teenagers–would raid the fridge. He made us anything we wanted. Clam rolls, lobster rolls, french fries. Bottles of blackberry brandy were also often thrown into the late-night seaside parties.

I didn't know if he was dangerous, but I didn't care, really. As it turned out he was another protector, at least for me – not Terri.

It's early on a Friday night at the bar, the students and Indians have not arrived yet, but football players from the University of Maine, who are our bouncers, stand outside in the cold Maine night, near the open front door of the Outside Inn Bar. The belligerent UMaine fraternity guys, when drunk, often antagonize the Indians and we never knew when a fight might break out.

The Inn has a blank-faced front and is in a nearly empty plaza, on a lonely dark stretch of road, about halfway between Indian Island and The University of Maine.

I hear male voices and look up as six young Indian males with long black hair enter the bar and slowly walk across the dance floor towards a table in the recesses of the Inn. The disco ball light flickers on their dark hair; streaking it with red and green and blue. They're beautiful.

"How ya doin, Janie?" asks Peter, my roommate, and the bartender, who looks like Charles Manson.

I look away from the Indians. Peter has his own glass of creamy-looking liquid set on the bar. It's a coffee brandy and cream. We both drink all night while we work and often until early morning – not leaving until four or five a.m. sometimes.

He takes a sip of his drink, his eyes on me still. Peter has long dark wavy hair pulled back into a ponytail. He wears a bandana around his head, lots of hippie beads and he's about thirty years old, I think. A dumbbell or something hangs from his belt. It's a weapon.

"Did you have some dinner," he asks. I think he feels responsible. He'd known me as a child at Popham. He knew my father. He knew my relatives. It's nice to have someone care about me, even if he is an x-con that looks like Charles Manson.

"I'm OK. I. Yes, Jess made me a cheeseburger," I answered.

Jessie, who had been the cook at Ocean View Restaurant at Popham is here with us too–the guy with the slicked back black hair–who wore white T-shirts that accented his muscular body–who was married to Roseann, who claimed to be a country western singer.

Jessie had dove head first into the hurricane waters to try and save the Canadian boy at Popham. I'll never forget that.

The short (like Jessie) blond, blue-eyed Roseann mostly sang country songs while she flipped hamburgers. She often lamented publicly that her marriage to Jessie had cost her a potentially lucrative singing career in Nashville. I felt embarrassed for Jessie when she did this.

Jessie was kind and respectful to me although his highest aspiration for me was that I become a Playboy bunny with a black belt in karate. I couldn't imagine what he was talking about. So much for going to Wellesley or Smith College in Northampton, which had often been suggested by my father, before he threw me out of the house. So much for following in the aristocratic footsteps of my namesake, Jane Donnell.

"You need to get the black belt though," Jessie had said more than once. I honestly had no idea what he was talking about, but he was nice, so I usually just smiled and laughed.

"I'll get 'em," Peter says, about the six Indians.

He's giving me an opportunity to settle in and finish off my first drink. I had just arrived for work. I'm wearing a rawhide fringed vest, bell bottoms, and Eskimo boots (which I was told to please not wear again by Peter, who had laughed at first) and my hair is braided. I have leather earrings and jewelry. I decided it was white men who were the problem. After all, I had been molested, raped, slandered, drugged, and abandoned by white men. It had to be them, right?

Peter walks out onto the floor, with his purposeful, cocky, in-control walk. He takes their order and comes back to the bar.

"Six whiskeys, straight up," he said, lining up six gleaming glasses on the bar.

The Indians had sat at a round table in a dark corner of the bar about ten feet from the dance floor. I stared over at them through the darkened interior, watching their cigarette smoke turn blue, purple, and red, under the disco light. We had a mutual enemy I thought.

I watch Peter pour the dark amber liquid into the glasses.

Before work, I had sat on Terri and Peter's bed, upstairs in our two-bedroom house, reading Lao Tzu, the Chinese philosopher. Terri sat cross-legged on the bed smoking pot. Terri, named after St. Theresa of the Roses, had become my best and only friend.

"A journey of a thousand miles begins with a single step," I read out loud.

She had brought the book home from her new school.

I looked up to see her response.

She smiles and raises her eyebrows like she thinks the passage is interesting, but she is holding the pot in her lungs and can't talk or exhale. Waiting for her to exhale, I look around their room. It's neat and clean, like the rest of the house. She attends an alternative high school in Orono called Skitticut or Skit-a-something. I can't remember. It's an Indian name. When she's not in school she's at home cleaning, smoking pot, drawing, or doing her homework.

We have many long talks when we are alone – when Peter is at work – and while we are staring out at the snow-covered forests and the Stillwater River in the distance.

"You should write, Jane. You're always saying smart things like Lao Tzu," she said, in spurts, as she exhaled.

Through the pot smoke, I stare at her almond-shaped dark brown eyes and long brown hair. With one hand she held the joint up and away from the bed and the new Indian blanket that covers it, and with the other, she picked up a spiral notebook from a pile of about ten on the floor beside the bed.

"Here, take one. Peter got me a bunch," she said.

I take the notebook downstairs to my bedroom and write about how terrified I had been of my stepfather and how he had molested me and abused my mother. I wrote about how a man, not a blood relative, had raped me when I was only seven. It was all coming back to me. It was just too much. I wrote about Dave staring at my breast my whole life. I had written it all out and then thrown the twenty pages of writing on the floor, and just stared at it. It did feel better to have it outside of me, rather than inside. It was the beginning of me writing out my life.

Peter picked me up to go to work at 4:30 PM.

By one in the morning, I'm drunk on shots of Wild Turkey. Alcohol is no longer enough so I've also taken speed and smoked a joint with one of the Indians. The Outside Inn is packed and loud and filled with suffocating smoke. Peter and I hang out at the bar, just waiting to close the place.

A drunk jock, at a round table with a few of his buddies, stands up.

"Hey, too fuckin bad Chief Sockalexis couldn't hold his liquor. He mighta made something outta you fucking Penobscots," the jock yells out at the Indian men.

There is no response from the Indians, they are staring at the floor or into their drinks. Their faces are grim.

"Deerfoot of the Diamond my ass," the jock continues, slurring his words and holding out a hand to keep himself from falling. His friend laughs loudly and a couple of them slap him on the back.

"Damn shit right," a friend announces.

A tall lean Indian, with long black hair, stands up slowly.

Even in my inebriated state, my senses are aroused.

Louis Sockalexis was the pride of Indian Island. He was recruited by Notre Dame. The story goes that he only played for the majors for two years, when he got drunk at a party, fell out a window, and broke his ankle. Things were all downhill from there for him.

A jock motions for me to come over to his table.

"Hey Zweetie, over here," he slurs.

Peter looks at me and shakes his head. Negative.

"Closin' time. Bars closed," Peter says loudly enough for the jock to hear. Steam from a sink full of hot soapy water partially veils Peters's face but I see he is gazing over the crowd with a furrowed brow and a growing concern at the level of tension which is palatable.

"No, fuckin way," the jock says."Itz zonly 'bout nine o'clock."

I walk slowly out onto the floor to get what looks like about fifty dirty beer glasses on tables pushed together by a crowd of university girls who had departed an hour ago. No tip, I realize as I get closer. College girls are cheap.

A jock leans way over in my direction and then hooks me around my waist with his left arm.

"Where you goin' sweetheart?" he says, grinning, like a lizard.

"Let go," I say, softly.

I try to uncurl his fingers from my waist, but his grip tightens. His crooked fingers on my side hurt as he pulls me backwards towards him and his crowd. Fraternity assholes. The local newspaper had reported a rape at one of the Fraternity houses last month. I look up for Peter. I can't see him through the smoke.

An Indian guy is coming toward us, his jaw set with grim with determination. Determined to kill the jock, I hope.

"Peter!!" I scream, finally, because I really don't know what the Indian or this jerk holding me are going to do.

I fall backwards and try to grab at the table but miss. It falls over. I see three Indians headed towards us. They're all under the disco ball; flashes of blue and green light on long black hair. It's kind of mesmerizing, but, Jesus, one of them has a knife in his hand. Something gleams silver in the light. Where the hell are the bouncers? And Peter, where is he?

Glasses from my tray shatter and my money floats into the air and onto the filthy floor. There is broken glass, shining like crystals, I thought, in the blue green red disco light, all around me.

"Peter!" I scream again and see his face, finally, behind the bar. He must have been in the kitchen. He leaps over the bar, like it's the horse in a high school gym. Then his face is above me and he yanks on the guy's arm that is still around me somehow.

"Get your fucking hands off her, Skip," Peter says menacingly. In my drunken daze I wonder why he was in prison, and for the first time, I hope it was for murder.

The guy cinches me tighter. Peter kicks him hard in the groin, once, then twice. He screams and his arm wilts away and he holds it close to his body.

Two bouncers are talking to the Indians. By their gestures I guess they want to see what one of the Indians has in his hand. Red police lights flash through the front door onto the dance floor. Police sirens coming up Stillwater Avenue. Peter must have pressed the emergency button.

"Get the hell out of here and don't come back. You're banned from the Inn for six months." Peter screams at the jock who is slowly standing up.

Then Peter pushes him hard, toward the door. He keeps pushing him – hard – right in the middle of his chest – with his open palms – five , six , seven, times. Boy, he is pissed. The jock looks like he's going to vomit as he is backed up. I stare. I feel kind of happy. I can't believe someone has stood up for me–stopped a man from abusing me. Finally.

The Indians disperse back to their tables. Two cops with large flash-lights enter the Inn. No matter what went down, the Indians would be blamed.

I get off the floor and run, not in a straight line, towards the bar. I duck under the bar ledge and sit down on the thick rubber mat which is gucked with sweet sticky liquor and beer spills. It smells like vomit.

My heart races and my hands shake. I grab a bottle of amber liquid from a row of top shelf and a glass and pour myself another shot of Wild Turkey. I like the name "Wild Turkey." I love the name, really. I drink the shot fast and then put my head down and wrap my arms around my knees.

I wake up on my bed in Orono hours later still wearing my clothes. I also have on my fringed leather jacket and seal skin boots. Someone had thrown a blanket over me. I am groggy and disoriented.

The angle of the moon tells me it's about four in the morning. My German Shepard, Brandy, wags her tail at every movement I make. "She's alive. She's alive," I know what she's thinking. Guilt punches me hard in my heart, or that space below my neck where I used to have a heart. My body shudders.

"Hi girl," I manage to say and reach out and pat her soft brown head, hoping to God I fed her.

An empty Wild Turkey bottle and a couple of empty beer bottles are beside my bed. An ashtray filled with old buts is on the windowsill. Clothes are strewn on my bed and floor. I pick up a Bic lighter and, with an unsteady hand, light the three wicks on a sand candle beside my bed on a small table. I wonder if it is made of crushed sand dollars.

I pick up my Lao Tzu book. With one hand, I pat my dog and with the other, hold up the red book and turn the pages trying to find something. Anything. Anything that might make me want to live.

The next thing I remember is opening my eyes and looking at Brandy standing in a downward dog position beside the bed and barking. The candle busted into pieces on the floor. There is intense heat near the top of my head. I wonder if it is a side effect of the alcohol. Then something burning and I crawl out of the bed towards Brandy, and then spin around and gasp at the flames consuming my blue bedroom wall.

I start screaming for Terry and Peter to get out of the house. "It's on fire. It's on fire" I yell.

CHAPTER 15

SECRETARIAT

I mostly just laid on my bed staring out the window. Sober. Late night visits to an oversized white plastic jug of commercial-grade peanut butter, aside of which was a toaster and endless loaves of cheap sliced white bread – in the small kitchen were one of my only interactions with the world.

I smoked in the courtyard. I barely got dressed to do it. I threw a ski coat over my Lanz nightgown and pulled on my L.L. boots.

It was cold in western Massachusetts in February at the Sorority house I lived in at the University of Massachusetts in Amherst. Snow was piled four feet high against the outside concrete walls of the Sorority, and my breath, on the exhale, was almost as white as the snow.

Day after day; I was sober and staring out the window of my room at the leafless gray branches and the sky; blue to gray; white; slate; pussy willow; thin clear blue; black with stars and moon. Never bright, mostly darkening from thin white to gray to black. Naked and black and nothingness.

Sinking deeper and deeper; inside and out; half asleep, asleep, awake and staring out the window, until there was a silent nothingness; free of pain. In a vision I saw a woman journeying on a canoe through a jungle river of snakes and reptiles and piranhas, but separate and protected.

Then I arrived at an inner space where there was something like Holiness or Light; separate and untouched by my pain; still me.

Billy had showed up at the bar in Old Town one day. I was shocked.

"Let's get you out of here," he had said.

It didn't take much. I had thrown my clothes in a bag, put a leash on my dog, and with Brandy, – my one true love at the time– and jumped into the white van Billy had driven from Amherst, MA to Old Town. The house had not burned to the ground, but my walls were black, and I had only survived because of my dog, barking. Terri had left already. I guess Peter was abusing her, I don't really know. My cousin Steve had rescued Tarri. They are together now. Everything was falling part.

Soon after I arrived in Amherst, Brandy was killed. I was devastated.

It had been eight months since Brandy died. I wanted to die, again. It seemed everything I loved was always taken. Just when I almost felt it was safe to love.

I took a deep breath – and still standing in front of the bowls of sugar and pitchers of cream – the answer to my question became clear in an image of myself dumping my fringed leather jacket and bear claw necklace into a dumpster behind the sorority. Good riddance. I didn't want anything to do with love or feelings.

Bracing myself, I pick up the sugar bowl and, unsmiling, and chin up, I walk across the dining hall and back to my seat at the head of the table. Marsha stood inside the kitchen with her hands on her hips staring at me with her usual blank, dull expression. She's an idiot.

The next morning, I and fifteen other pre-vet majors, and our professor, Dr. Border, board an American Airlines plane to Louisville Kentucky to study farm animal husbandry and to visit some of the Thoroughbred horse farms. Meeting Secretariat, the horse who had won The Triple Crown, was on our agenda.

On the plane, sitting next to Professor Border, who fussed nervously with his wire rim glasses, I wondered how I had gotten into college, especially in a major that required extensive knowledge of science and math.

I had missed almost the entire four years of high school and already many of my college classes. The signs and symbols and words on the huge overhead projectors in physics and biology and chemistry and algebra were meaningless. Overwhelmed wasn't a strong enough word to describe my status as a pre-vet major.

Horses seemed to be important. Horses came to mind when they made me declare a major. I chuckled out loud and Mr. Border looked at me quizzically.

"Oh, it's nothing. Just thinking about horses and stuff," I said, quickly. He resumes looking out the window at the Atlantic Ocean, as if he were searching for someone or something.

And then, two days later, I stood in a green field of Kentucky grass, looking at Secretariat, the magnificent golden-brown stallion who had won the Triple Crown in 1973. He had also run, some would say, the greatest race of all time, at the Belmont stakes, and won by 31 lengths.

On the other end of the spectrum here I stood, terrified; suffering from PTSD, depression, alcohol addiction, extreme loneliness, abandonment, low self-esteem, and multiple traumas, but as I watched Secretariat, I inhaled and a breath of life returned.

"Don't get too close," warned Secretariat's bodyguard, a tall, muscular man who wore a silk scarf and who had once been a Miami Dolphin's football player.

I step back a half a foot from the fence, as Secretariat runs towards me, but I'm transfixed. He rears and rears again and sounds like thunder on the ground. He stomps and runs wildly up and down in the seemingly endless pasture of green and then back along the perfect white fence where we all stand.

His massive golden brown body seems sculpted into the likeness of some kind of Roman Pagan God. I feel from him an intolerance for oppression or suppression. He was now, unridden, and he had a fierce wildness; an aloof power; an incomparable strength and he had total freedom in his thousands of acres of the green grass.

His presence touched my soul. It reminded me of something within me that was also powerful.

I watch him rear, paw at the sky, and neigh, and shake his head; warning us off. I step forward – I must touch him; his face; like I had Misty a hundred times.

"Don't," warns the Miami Dolphin.

I put my hand down, but Secretariat is right in front of me, behind the fence, staring. I feel his spirit and strength and power. Maybe I also heard him say,

"Don't give up. Don't ever give up. You can win. Win."

Tears threaten my eyes. I do not want to feel *hope*. I do not want to feel *anything*. I said goodbye and thank you in my mind to Secretariat and I turned and walked away – from everyone. I followed the perfect white fences towards the forever green fields of Kentucky.

I graduated with my class, with a degree in journalism, but just barely. I was one of the many thousands of nobodies in black graduation hats at the University of Massachusetts. I was embarrassed I had not attended a noteworthy school like Smith or Wellesley.

I *had* loved taking ballet at Smith College (participating in classes at other colleges in the UMass area was part of the UMass five college program); I loved riding beautiful Morgan horses at the UMass Equestrian center (I was with the horses at the center so much the Chi Omega "sisters" called me "Calamity Jane.") A few of my journalism professors were helpful; and swimming in unison, in the college pool; being I was a Naiad, had helped quell my anxiety and depression; but basically, I felt like a failure and was still completely alone.

I did not have one friend at UMass. I was strange. Unusual, I guess.

My father wouldn't attend my graduation because he said, "it wasn't real." It was true, I guess. I still needed to do an internship and needed more credits but was scheduled to graduate with this group and to take the extra credits the following summer.

I looked out at the crowd of thousands of people who had come to support the graduating class. It was a sea of browns, grays, and taupe suits and dresses. Color was considered garish by most New Englanders. I hoped to see someone from my family. But there was nobody. I'm not sure anyone in my family even knew I was at college. I had no family and no friends.

Then I saw a person dressed in yellow – yellow pants and a yellow top. And I looked closer and realized it was my mother. She was alone in an ocean of gray and brown, like a daffodil in a huge patch of brown earth. I stared at her, disbelieving. I actually had someone in the audience for me?

No one had even acknowledged it; no cards, or phone calls, or anything. I tried to wave. I waved.. I think she saw me, and she waved back, smiling, happy, as if she did not have a care in the world, as if her life had been easy, as if she was not also all alone in the world.

I look down at the grass. I have traveled so very far away from my heart. I had run from the earth and my love of animals and the spirits of the earth. What a snob I had become; in attempts to be part of the winning team; to run from all the mistakes I had made in Old Town, Maine.

I had been trying to escape the horrors of the world, which I realized, at that moment, I had placed the wrong person – my mother.

(I wanted to interject here, looking back as an older woman, with a broader understanding of what happened to me back then. I want to take the story out of the first person for a moment. I wrote this *book from*, the point of view as a child, of seven, then eight; and then as a teenager, and young adult, primarily because I thought it was important for people to see the effect of "matricide" – -the killing off of the mother – from the perspective of a child and teenager. The drawback of the viewpoint of the child, is the reader, like the *child, does* not yet see the larger picture. So before we go on, I wanted to say as a mature woman and a fully trained shaman, that I was, at this point in the book, suffering from multiple soul losses and MK Ultra trauma based mind control.

The MK Ultra had been imposed on me using repetitive trauma, in the form of continual loss and betrayal. sexual abuse, drugs and abandonment, MK Ultra, a Nazi based program of torture, had been imported into America in the 1950's and it is used, in part, to traumatize Americans to the pont where they (the Deep State) could impose a New World Order. Please see any work by survivor and writer Cathy O'brien, to fully understand MK Ultra. Shamans, historically, are often the first to be killed off during a regime takeover because they can see it coming. they cannot be mind controlled. The MK Ultra was delivered to me potentially through a microchip as well as Satanic curses. And while, at this point where the new chapter begins, I have survived – mostly because I have had so much protection on the spirit level – and I am about to enter into the happiest time of my life – what they had in store for me in the near future was unfathomable. They brought out the big guns. I include this brief synopsis so that the reader, unlike the child, and the teenager, and even the young adult, understands what is happening in the larger context)

CHAPTER 16

THE ANCESTORS AND MY DAUGHTERS

Five years later my life has changed for the better. I had found my heart. I had married, and given birth to two beautiful daughters, Arianna and Gwen. I was divorced but happy for the first time in my life.

I lived with my daughters in a beautiful four-bedroom antique Victorian house at 62 South Street in Bath, Maine. It was located at the bottom of a steep hill and only one block from the banks of Kennebec River where my paternal grandparents once owned a brick mansion.

In the winter here, the sun seems to set around three PM.

I sit cross-legged on an old double-wrought iron bed wearing an ankle-length flowered rayon Renys dress pulled down over my knees. I wear thick wool L.L. Bean socks. Filaments of dust spiral around in the last few rays of light streaming through the bedroom window.

This beautiful, three-story, old house is dusty. An ancient oil burner, almost as big as a Volkswagen, sits in the cellar on a foundation of granite rocks, throwing dust up into the air and grinding on and on, night and day.

I try to keep the two wood stoves fired up to reduce the oil bill. A gleaming blue enamel wood stove sits on top of a brick base in the center of the power blue and white kitchen.

A minister owned the house for twenty years before John, my ex-husband and I, bought it, shortly after we had been shown the property. I had fallen in love, not only with my husband but with the Victorian. It was like something from an English fairy tale.

The house was also only a block from Bath Iron Works, a private company which contracts with the US Navy to build Arleigh Burke Destroyers – massive war ships – often armed with nuclear warheads which are considered the "deadliest" ships in the American fleet.

Ironic, I had thought, for me to have chosen a magical fairy tale house right next to a factory spitting out war machines. Opposites. Contrasts. It was the story of my life; I was beginning to think.

Despite its proximity to war machinery, I loved the wide-open rooms, the bright blue kitchen, the gleaming pumpkin pine floors, the ten foot high ceilings, the chandeliers, the huge front parlor with floor to ceiling windows, a winding staircase to the upstairs, and, on the second floor, four bedrooms, two of which were perfect for little girls. It also had an attic with a small diamond-shaped window which looked out over the Kennebec River and Bath Iron Works.

But now it is just my two little girls,

Gwen and Arianna and I, living in the house. John, I think, is still living on his boat, which is docked at Popham Beach, my childhood romping grounds where I had once picked blueberries, swam at Morse's River, watched the Destroyers – launched at Bath Iron Works – glide down the Kennebec to the Atlantic Ocean.

Popham Beach, like so many other situations in my life, was a study in contrasts. The beautiful ocean, the beaches, the peaceful and serene Crystal Lake, the blueberry patches, the sweetgrass, sparkling silver mica wedged into the many granite rocks, contrasted dramatically with the military forts, Fort Baldwin and Fort Popham, which both had been armed and did include prison cells.

I had just woken up from a nap and was dreaming of lions. I listen to the house. I don't want to miss anything that reminds me of how much I love it here. The tic toc of the clock that Jim, John's brother, gave us for a wedding present is ever-present in the entryway at the bottom of the long staircase. Even the thump and click of the furnace gives me comfort. It feels like the heartbeat. The flicker of flames in the woodstove. The creak of old wood floors.

It is quiet in my daughter's rooms just down the hall. They are still asleep.

I should get up and light a fire in the kitchen wood stove downstairs. But it is hard for me to let go of moments that are peaceful. I have had so few in my life. I pull up the handmade quilt I bought at a yard sale. It is getting chilly. The shadows lengthen through the window in my bedroom. It gets cold and dark fast in Maine.

An oil bill on my nightstand catches on the quilt and falls to the floor. I reluctantly pick it up and lay it back on the pile of other bills. Shit. It's ruined the peace.

I grab an electric bill, pick up a pen and write $200 on the back of the bill. It's my income per week as a reporter for the Kennebec Journal. On a good week. I make $60 per story so I don't always make the $200.

I sigh heavily. How the hell was I going to survive? Something will certainly happen to help me through all this. I refuse to put the girls in daycare, so I can't work full-time. It is sad to hear the babies in the factory daycare next door. Babies. My God, it seemed unnatural for a woman with babies to have to work full-time at the factory, in my opinion.

I take the girls with me while I'm working as a reporter and photographer. Last week I did a review on a new art exhibit at the Chocolate Church –a midtown renovated church painted a dark chocolate bar brown – and they played on the shiny wooden floors and stared at paintings and asked me lots of questions and we had tea and cake with the director Patricia Conn.

The girls also followed along when I covered the opening of a new bookstore, The Treehouse. The same day we had gone to Crystal Works, a new store where a little Irish guy, John, sold crystals and sage and books by Shirley McClain, who had written Out On A Limb. Everywhere we went the girls had fun playing and talking with the people I interviewed – we always stopped for treats and snacks either at the Bath Deli or at the Truffles.

So far, I had successfully refused to work at the local shipyard, Bath Iron Works, where they made Navy war ships armed with nuclear warheads.

"Everybody's got ta' to go work," my former brother-in-law, Eddie, said to me, accusingly. He worked at Bath Iron Works. I wondered how long it would be before he had black lung disease.

"You're no different, are ya'?" he laughed, but I could see the venom in his eyes. As usual, people were uncomfortable around me; outright hated me for reasons I didn't understand.

I stand up and walk over to a window. A middle-aged man wearing a yellow hard hat and carrying a tin lunch box is trekking hard up the street in work boots. He is an early release from the yard. At exactly 3:30, a half an hour from now, a siren will blast and almost instantaneously South Street will be bumper to bumper with cars – people fleeing from work – anxious to be home to open the first bottle of beer and dig into fish chowder or other heavy meat dish.

I walk away from the window.

"I love you," John, my husband had said, before he walked out of the bedroom and down the stairs and out the door six months ago, never to return. The screen door on the porch banged once and then twice, again, in the wind.

The tinny sound of the Fiat engine starting up in his little brown sports car came next. Then the distinct low rumble of the car as it went up the hill, stopped, and turned left on Washington Street towards Popham Beach.

I had wondered, as he drove away, if the new amethyst crystal ball he had installed at the top of the five-speed gear shift, replacing the regular hard plastic one, was somehow related to his leaving me, like he was going through a spiritual evolution. He was a former football player and now a merchant marine and didn't naturally interact with crystals.

Now, alone, on my bed, I listen for a click of a Lego from Arianna's room or Gwen talking to her stuffed animals. The house is still silent. They are still asleep. It made sense. I'd only slept a half an hour.

But I had to see them.

I pad down the long hallway in my stocking feet to Gwen's room. I had painted her room a bright yellow. The floors are wide-board pumpkin pine golden-orange; the same beautiful color as the rest of the floors in the house.

The sun streamed into her room. The sun on the yellow walls made them glow. I stepped quickly over to her crib with a feeling of urgency. A thin film of sweat was on her forehead and her cheeks were flushed a bright pink. She sleeps deeply. I quickly loosen the soft cotton blanket I wrapped her in, papoose-style, an hour ago when she went down for a nap.

She might still be too hot. I gently tug at the blanket, rolling her a bit back and forth, until it's free. I place it over her loosely. The air can flow more freely.

I open her window and a cool breeze enters the room. I grab a clean white sock out of her drawer and wipe her forehead. I kneel and stroke her soft hair with my hand. The golden blond curls still astound me. I feel she had arrived, not through me, but out of the pages of a fairy tale.

Long black eye lashes rest like little waves on creamy white flawless skin. The bright pink in her cheeks is softening to a pastel and I relax.

I gently twirl one of her curls. I think of the old gold locket with the gold curl. Exactly like Gwen's curl but it is my hair. My mother had saved one gold curl of mine for thirty years. She had given me the locket and the curl recently.

"I cut that curl off your head the day you won the beauty contest. You had a head full of blond curls. You were only a year old and I entered you in the contest and you won first prize," my mother said recently, during one of her recent visits from Watertown. Then she handed me the golden lock she had saved for many decades. I was astonished and speechless.

I continue to stroke Gwen's hair. I cannot imagine being separated from children. What had it been like for her? Up until now I only thought what it had been like for me as a child and lonely teenager.

I imagine my mother during her last day in Hanover. She is rummaging through dresser drawers where she keeps her perfumed white gloves, a few odd pieces of jewelry, and her bobby pins. She is trying to find what meant the most to her. What one thing represented her love for her children? She must have scooped up the locket and a black and white photograph. In the photo, I was fat and wore a white taffeta dress, and had a huge smile. I was startled by my smile. I couldn't imagine being so happy. But then, I realize, I had my mother.

I blank out the image of my mother desperately going through her drawer, looking for one blond curl.

Gwen's fingers are curled next to her mouth, and I touch her hand, marveling. I still cannot believe a being so perfect lives with me. I feel like the nursemaid who will be usurped at any moment when the real parents arrive back from wherever they have gone.

I pad my way to Arianna's room. A robin's egg blue wall-to-wall carpet covers the floor and lace curtains flutter in the wind. A sweet floral print wallpaper of small pink and blue flowers on a white background makes the room cozy. Stuffed animals of every type and variety sit and lie and are positioned on her bed and in corners and on her bureau. Dozens of books cover the floor, are stuffed into a white metal bookshelf and are on the nightstand and bed.

The branches on the huge maple tree in our neighbor's backyard tap against her window. It is a peaceful room of flowers and wild animals and books.

Arianna, my first born, has slung her arm over the furry brown Gap bear my mother bought. She is comfortable in the cool shade of the room. Her cheeks are flushed a light pink. The birth of this child resurrected me from the land of the dead; where I had been for most of my life since my mother left and I had repeatedly failed at living at college.

Arianna is still sound asleep and so I amble back to my bedroom and put my head on my pillow. Tears. I feel so alone. Just when I thought I had a real family. John's mother and his brothers and sisters are gone. My own family rarely talks to me. I guess I do miss him. John. I close my eyes to stop the tears. Then the world fades as I fall into a deep sleep.

I am in a tunnel whirling around, like I am being pulled away. Then I fall gently and land in a field of yellow grass. Long grass. I look around with a sense of wonder. It is so beautiful. And clean. The sky is blue, bluer than I have ever seen a sky. Somehow, I know this is the Great Plains of America before the coming of the white man.

I look down. I am bareback on a Painted Pony. A single Eagle feather is tied to the bridle at the head of the Pony. It drifts in a slight breeze.

I touch my hair. Long black braids.

Up ahead, over a ridge of a bank, are three Native American men, also on horseback. One looks like a chief. He wears a full headdress. They are riding through the grass towards me, but I am not afraid. I am joyful. Finally, my tribe has come.

Then they are in front of me. I see the horse's breath. I feel their energy. The elder is strong, wise, and brave. Tears stream down my face.

"We are your ancestors," the chief says.

"You are to be a bridge between the two worlds. The white and the red. Mother Earth is bleeding. She is hurt. She is crying out. You must help to heal her. You must be strong. There are hard times ahead. You will teach people how to honor Mother Earth and the feminine. You will teach them to honor women," he said.

"I want to come home. I'm tired," I said in my mind.

"There will be a time you may return to us. That day will come. But it is not now," he said patiently.

"I have been all alone. All of my life," I answered out loud.

"We will give you strength. In your darkness hours, know we are here. We will be waiting for you. Go in peace and strength,"

He smiled slightly and nodded. They reined their horses around and headed back towards the ridge.

I leaned down on my Appaloosa stallion and let the tears from the pain of three decades on earth stream down the black silky mane. I cried from the bottom of my gut. I cried for all that was lost for me and for my mother. For never having my father stand up for me. For being alone all my life. I cried for the earth and it seemed like it was all one and the same.

CHAPTER 17

SOLSTICE CELEBRATION

It was Christmas time and it was still just the girls and I at home but we were happy and John and I cooperated together in a shared custody situation.

I was working part-time as a reporter for *The Kennebec Journal* in Augusta. I often took the girls with me when I had simple and/or uncomplicated assignments.

Today, we were on Front Street in Bath. It was cold and snowing lightly, but the sky was not dark. It was a light gray and the street was festive with old-fashion Christmas decorations.

The local Bath townspeople, in rehearsal for Edie Doughty's Medieval Solstice Celebration, began to appear in costumes on the snowy sidewalks of Front Street. The girls smiled as a jester in a green velvet hat hung with jingle bells walked up to us and bowed and smiled and then went on his way. A Queen in her crown and red velvet dress and gold slippers tromped up Front Street toward the rehearsal hall. The King in his starry robe, also passed us, winking at the girls.

Fresh evergreen boughs tied with red ribbons hung from lanterns and people carried gifts wrapped in green and silver foil. Edie Doughty, the owner of 88 String Guitar and the producer of The Solstice Celebration and the overall grand dame of Bath theatre, ran down the street, snow in her blond hair, with a white wig in her hand, chasing after an actor.

She wanted everything perfect.

I had snapped photographs of the king and queen and then slung my camera over my shoulder and grabbed Arianna and Gwen's small hands and walked forward towards the smell of fresh baked bread and pastries.

The strong wind up from the Kennebec River blew my hair into my face. I didn't mind. It made me feel even more alive. I made sure the girls' snow jackets were zipped up snug. I re-tied Arianna's string knot under her chin and tucked Gwen's blond curls deeper under her hood.

My hair just kept blowing in the cold wind. I never wore a hat. I loved the feeling of the wind in my hair.

I wondered if the scene on Front Street that day was at all like Christmas when my great-great grandparents were here in front of Hatch's shoe store a hundred years ago

The girls, and I held hands, and walked along the snow-covered sidewalk until we entered the Bath Deli. I ordered three hot chocolates. I got coloring books for the girls and myself, the local newspaper, the Times Record. The girls colored in reindeer and Santa Claus and Christmas trees with green and red and gold.

I was filled with a golden glow of joy and contentment. I loved watching everything they did. I love their laughs, their giggles; the way Gwen always acts like a clown or a performer. Her beautiful blue eyes, pink cheeks and golden curls were almost too much for me. I could not believe she was my daughter. Nothing or no one so beautiful and loving had ever been in my life.

I was happy for the first time in my life. The girls were my life. Almost nothing they did was uninteresting to me. I was in awe of motherhood. It was everything I had ever dreamed of and more. I loved cooking with them. I loved reading to them. Their favorite books were *Grandfather Twilight* and *The Velveteen Rabbit*. I loved washing their adorable clothes and helping them get dressed. We baked bread and cookies and made flour playdough. We planted flowers. We walked along the ocean, in the local parks, and along the tree-lined streets of Bath.

My ex-mother-in-law, Pat, who perceived child raising as something done with a robotic sameness, and without creativity, perceived my mothering style as ridiculous. She would have rolled her eyes if she did not always try to at least appear supportive of me. Ultimately, I think, behind my back she and her son, Eddie, a BIW shipyard worker, who was definitely headed towards lung disease, gossiped incessantly about me. At least that's what I found out later in life.

I missed them on every other weekend when they were with their father, but my own life was expanding intellectually, spiritually and emotionally. I had many friends (my friends, for the most part, – at this time – were intellectuals, back-the-earthers (in some cases) and also often spiritual and creative My friend Taffy Field had just written and published a book *Short Skirts*) I had one or two boyfriends and I was beginning to expand my spiritual consciousness taking classes in crystals, reiki, sound healing, drumming and whatever else showed up on my radar that appealed to me. I could always easily fill in the gaps when they were gone.

The girls were like ancestors, I had not seen for centuries, who were suddenly in my midst, daily. Every day was a celebration because we were able to be together in physical forms. Every day was healing for me. I had finally found a world which was safe. My stepmother, my stepfather, my half-brother, even my father, were fading into the background and becoming irrelevant.

My perception of motherhood may sound saccharin, but if you had lived a life of total darkness for over two decades, every moment you are not in that darkness, seems like a miracle. If you have only known darkness, then the moments of light become all that much brighter and profound.

I also loved my work – writing and reporting for the Kennebec Journal. I felt I was contributing to the knowledge and enjoyment of my community as well as uncovering important, unexplored issues. I had light-hearted interviews with writers, artists, and entrepreneurs – like the interview with Edie Doughty today about the Solstice celebration – but I also did hard news stories which were difficult and controversial.

I had taken an assignment for *The Kennebec Journal* covering sexual harassment at Bath Iron Works. It was not necessarily appreciated in the way I imagined.

It was an unspoken rule, I, at the time, was oblivious of, which was you *don't mess with Bath Iron Works (BIW) the biggest employer in Maine.* Local people didn't like anyone threatening their income, even if women were being systematically emotionally destroyed in the process. Eventually, sexual harassment laws were enacted because of the coverage and the exposure of the issue by the women at Bath Iron Works.

Bath Iron Works employee Jane Smith described to me, when I interviewed her, how a naked effigy of her was hung from the work crane at BIW. Officials waited a week to order it be taken down.

Linda Noble, the first female electrical engineer at BIW, found used condoms on her desk top most mornings: her chair was constantly dismantled; she was chased off the road one night in a snowstorm; every night, almost, there were hang-up calls. The verbal abuse and alienation by her co-workers and managers was worse.

After my story of sexual harassment at Bath Iron Works was printed in the Kennebec Journal, Linda Noble and I continued to meet at my house and/or at coffee shops. She developed trust in me and agreed to tell her life story. There was a universal truth I searched for in between the lines of Linda's own life. Something about the status of woman in general. Something about the earth. Something about the Goddess and the Divine Feminine. It wasn't about feminism everyone was talking about. It was something else.

My mind saw dramatic images. My outlet was a screenplay. I took a screenplay writing workshop in Rockport and then, under the chandelier in my rose dining room, late at night, when the girls were in bed, I wrote the screenplay.

I also learned grinding paint off of the ships at BIW created a toxic chemical everyone called black beauty. This chemical concoction spewed into the air and landed mostly in South Bath, where I lived. Cases of lung disease and lung ailments were epidemic. BIW dumped hydrocarbons, chlorides, sulfates, PCB's into the land and water at Tarbox Hill. It seemed everyone up there was sick and I wrote about it and my stories were continually published in *The Kennebec Journal* in Augusta.

The local newspaper, the Times Record, avoided controversial issues involving Bath Iron Works.

I had also written about anti-nuclear activist and Catholic Priest Phil Berrigan and the Plowshares Seven, when Berrigan and five other activists broke into Bath Iron Works and poured goat blood down the side of the The USS Sullivan, an Aegis destroyer. The plowshares said their purpose was "turn swords into plowshares." The Camden Shakespearean group paraded down Washington Street dressed as corpses during a ship launching and I covered their political position in detail.

I was reporting for anti-nuclear protestors Chuck Hagan, Catholic Priest Ray Shadis and former Maine State representative Maria Holt who all wanted to (and ultimately succeeded) in shutting down Maine Yankee Nuclear Plant in Wiscasset.

I thought I was on a roll, defending woman and the earth and being a full-time mother to my beloved daughters.

The girls and I finished our hot chocolate, and we zipped up and re-tied all the clothing and hats and we walked along Front Street again, this time admiring the white and purple Christmas lights as the sky was turning dark and it highlighted the electric lights.

At home, we ate corn chowder and chowder crackers and cider and then, I read them Grandfather Twilight, and tucked them into their beds, under the glowing fluorescent stars and duck mobiles. A wind-up music box, with a twirling ballerina, played *Silent Night*.

I look out the window at the starry Maine night. Maine nights are so black they are almost blue. Then I drop the white curtain and it falls straight, blocking the stars. I turn away from the window and tuck clean folded clothes into Gwen's dresser.

(Looking back, little did I know then, at that moment – while the girls were sleeping peacefully, and I was busily putting away clean little white ankle socks – that we were inside a kind of all-seeing crystal ball being watched by powers far greater and much more evil than The Wicked Witch of the West. I believe, even way back then, our fate had already been sealed.)

CHAPTER 18

MIC MAC MADNESS

Will Peter find his way here tonight from the Mic Mac reservation in Canada? It is already so late. About 11 pm. Peter, with the long black shining hair hanging down to his waist, had called and said he would be entering into a sweat lodge ceremony at the reservation but then later would climb into a black car, a sedan; the reservation transportation; and drive south to Maine.

They would drop him off here at my house.

"The spirit of my grandfather speaks," Peter said two weeks ago, while he wove strips of cedar bark. He sat cross-legged on the gravel parking lot outside Chuck Hagen's Native Arts Indian store on Route 1 in Wiscasset.

Five chairs of Peter's were for sale on the porch of Native Arts.

I had been hanging around the store waiting for Chuck. I was about to interview him about his recent protest against the Maine Nuclear Power Plant. He waved at me through the glass window from the back of his Indian store while he was showing a customer a Kachina doll. Chuck was an apprentice to the powerful Mexican shaman Tlakaelel. I had lost count of how many times Chuck had done the Sun Dance or how many times I interviewed him

"Is Tlakaelel here yet?" I asked him after he was out on the porch, his hands stuck in his front pocket and smiling sheepishly. He looked up. His dark brown eyes always got to me.

I could feel Peter's eyes on my back.

"Yeah. He's getting ready. You can come in. He'll talk to you."

Leaving Peter behind, Chuck and I entered his store. I was immediately on sensory overload. Crystals, sage, drums, sweet grass, turquoise jewelry. It all felt familiar and like home. We descended the stairs and into a rather large room where Talakaleal, a short husky, middle aged man with eyes like a panther, and his assistant, were preparing for his lecture. Chairs were set up in front of the room where Talakael and the other elders would speak. Copal burned in a dish in front of the chairs.

Talakael shared his truth in lecture halls all over the world and at Harvard and MIT and other universities in the states. A powerful, compact energy swirled around him and I realized I was slightly afraid of him. I interviewed him about his feelings about Mother Earth. He spoke only Mexican, but his wife translated in English.

"We are in a solar system which is moving. Mother Earth is alive. She moves, she breathes, she has her own energy and movements. And the human beings, we are interconnected – our brains, our minds – with all other human beings," she translated.

"The totality of our mind is the mind of Mother Earth. We are connected with the animals, with the plants and with all the beings that exist. But we have forgotten this. And now the few people who can move these forces because they know them – because they feel them – we call these people witches or medicine men or shamans. But anyone can do this. We all have the same capacity for comprehension" she had said.

I wrote as quickly as possible. It was a half hour interview, and I took some photographs and then thanked him and turned to go.

"Miss," I heard his wife say, " Talakael would like to speak to you alone."

I was surprised, but I went and sat on the native rug with the elder and his wife, and this is what he said, as translated through his wife.

"In another lifetime you were a healer. In Europe. Many people were condemned. They were called witches. Good witches. Healers. The Inquisition. Very bad time. Lots of people were killed. It was the same in Mexico. Everywhere. All over the world the people were killed. You still have these qualities of healing. You are still this person."

"They will not be able to hurt you in this lifetime. Not physically. But be aware. Be prepared"

It was ominous and I departed Chucks store feeling like I had received much more than a news story. I had been given an insight into my past lives. I had also made a "date" with Peter, the Mic Mac who wove willow into chairs.

I heard a car stop, a door open, then loud Native American men, then a door slam. I suddenly felt afraid. I didn't know why. I ran down the stairs and into my front parlor. My heart was racing. I opened the door.

"Hi Peter," I said.

He just looks at me. Brown face. Long black hair. One hundred percent Mic Mac. He strode into my house. It was strange, how people could enter differently, just based on their culture.

"How are you?" he said, without looking at me.

We sat on my rug and he lit a rope of sweet grass. We talked about the weather, about how horrible it was to work at BIW, and that his old girl-friend had thrown a hatchet into his front door.

"Where are your children?"

"They're asleep," I answered, nervously.

I got up and showed him a photograph of Arianna and Gwen.

"Oh. One is blond and blue-eyed. They are the worst"

I almost hit him across the face. I was furious.

"I'll make some tea," I said, getting up. I was stalling for time, trying to figure out how to get rid of him. Dr. Clarissa Pinkham Estes, who wrote the book Women Who Run With the Wolves, suggested that at moments like these, women should behave like wolves, and bare teeth, growl, snap, and possibly even bite – to ward off dangers to ourselves and our children.

Instead, as a socialized woman, I was trying to make him more com-fortable. I didn't feel I had the right to tell him to leave.

I put on my leather jacket and went upstairs instead. I just wanted to look at my daughters. I went into each of their rooms. Touched their warm faces, curled their hair behind their ears. My heart raced.

Why did I invite Peter, an Indian from a reservation in Canada, who I really did not know at all, into my house?

Maybe because I had developed a racism towards white men, and now thought red men were OK. It was all in my head. Why had an ex-girlfriend thrown a hatchet at his door? I didn't want him to follow me, so I ran back down the stairs.

I stood at the bottom of the stars, in the room I loved – with the em-erald green wallpaper with cream-colored hydrangeas and saw the front door flung wide open.

Smoke from sweet grass hung thick in the house, but as I stepped into the living room, I realized Peter was gone. Apparently, he had departed into the night – alone. He would be walking the streets. It was so strange. It was as if he had been chased out of the house.

I walk over to the front door and stare out into the dark night. Maybe my only true Indian ancestors were in Spirit. Maybe it was men, not just white men, who were the problem. My concepts of who was evil were changing.

CHAPTER 19

THE FOUR COLOR CEREMONY

Two weeks later my friend Linda, a young Cherokee Hispanic girl, struggled to erect the old canvas tent while I enter the woods in search of dry kindling for a campfire. Arianna, Gwen, Linda and I drove four hours to Wampanoag Reservation in Freedom, Massachusetts for Talakael's Four Color Ceremony.

It would be the first in the world. He would honor the four races. And he had personally invited me after my private session with him.

"Find some good hot dog sticks," I said to Arianna and Gwen, who were already running ahead of me into the darker woods. Arianna stopped to twirl around a tree.

I looked back over my shoulder. Lots of young white people were hanging around in the clearing setting up camps alongside ours.

Later that night we sat around the campfire cooking hotdogs and breathing in the cool night air. Through the blue tips of the fire, near the ceremonial ground I saw Wildcat, Chuck, Talakael, Slow Turtle, Drifting Duck, and Medicine Story. I knew them all. I wondered, briefly, why they were all men. *It was men in front of the church itinerary all over again.*

Medicine Story, a Wampanoag Indian, was told by his grandfather that his people came out of the ocean to live on an island. Thousands of years later when the island was about to sink under the water, his people departed in canoes and ships, landing at different spots along the east coast, all the way from Florida to Nova Scotia. These people were called Bringers of the Light.

I opened a package of hot dogs, stuck two of them on sticks, leaned them up against the rocks and then just stared into the fire and listened to the laughter of the children. I looked up. Arianna and Gwen had already found friends. I smiled and watched them lovingly. When they were happy, I was happy.

Later, the bonfire, the plumed feather bonnets on the shirtless Mexican dancers; the incessant, loud drumming; the painted faces, became surreal as I watched from behind the crowd. The word "Aztec" filtered into my consciousness, and I recalled, for some reason, the Mayan calendar my mother had on her wall in her apartment in Watertown.

The next day Linda and I entered a sweat lodge with ten other women and Talakael's wife. At first, the female children ran in and out of the lodge. Then they stopped. It grew too hot.

"Silent night. Holy night. All is calm," Arianna sang. I could hear her right outside the lodge.

It was her favorite goodnight song. I fended off the rising anxiety that accompanied the closing of the front flap of the lodge. Nuggets of white copal hissed after they were thrown by Talakael's wife onto the pile of hot stones in the center of the lodge. Red sparks flew into the air.

The lodge closed in on me. Nothing, I thought, could be more confining. Restricting. Suffocating. God, I'd only been in three minutes and felt I was going to die.

Sweat rolls down my dirty face. My lungs will burst. Fear. Fear of being alone with my stepfather. Fear of my stepmother's voice, like a hatchet in my heart. Tiny spears. Spear. Arrows. Chunks of black inside of me. The darkness.

"Close your eyes," It was Talakaelel's wife's somber voice.

"Notice there is no difference in the lodge. It is not with your eyes that you can see the truth," she said.

Her dark, round face, and brown eyes were hardly visible through the smoke, even though she was sitting across from me and seemed to be looking into my eyes.

And then I fell asleep or fainted.

"Janie,"

It was Linda, tugging at my sweaty arm. I exited the lodge with her help feeling like I had left a piece of me behind. A weight of some sort. I felt lighter. The cool wind on my skin was so tangible.

Chapter 20

Scott and White Buffalo Calf Woman

Snowflakes, from the brief walk from his car to the Guthrie theatre, melted on the black velvet collar of his evening jacket. Once seated in an upper row, in front of the railing, looking down onto the theatre, we leaned into each other so that every inch of our bodies could touch wherever it was possible.

We held hands so tightly it felt our hands might meld into one. My heart counted the hours we had left together.

I gently brushed the wetness on his velvet collar with my fingertips and stared at his profile, the hard Danish jaw, the dark, thick hair. I reluctantly turned and stared down at the performance of Charles Dickens' *A Christmas Carol* from the top row of the dark, round womb of the Guthrie Theatre in Minneapolis.

But it was all about him. I was breathing in his essence, so I could remember. Scott.

Later that night I lie naked under crisp pure white cotton sheets on the bed of our large old English-style room at the Victorian bed and breakfast on a lake in St. Paul. A fire still flickered in the fireplace at three in the morning. And wind from the lake rushed through the chimney and it shook and the flames shot higher.

I realized Scott was not beside me and I looked up. He stood beside the fireplace. He must have gotten up to feed it more logs. I sat up on my elbows and stared at him. I did not want to fall back asleep. I wanted to memorize him.

He leaned against the fireplace mantel with one long muscular outstretched arm. A baseball player's arm. Long and lean and muscular. His strong fingers gripped the mantle with more force than necessary. The fire illuminated his face. He held a thick white towel closed at his waist with his other hand.

He stared into the fire. Against the far wall, away from the fireplace, l stare at a long flickering shadow exaggerating his bowed stance. He was feeling the pain already. I knew it. I hadn't even left. It made me wild. His pain.

I tore off the sheet and huge white down comforter and, with bare feet, walked quickly over the thick oriental rug and through his dark shadow. I touched him gently on his well-muscled back with my open palm. I didn't want him to be alone. The touch brought tears to my eyes. The wind howled across the endless deep and dark lake. The chimney shook slightly, and the flames rose with the rushes of cold lake air. The hairs on my stomach and upper arms bristled slightly with the chill. The snow caressed the windows in loud rhythmic waves with each gust of wind. I shiver.

The lake is deep and dark and frozen. He turns slowly. His face was in the shadows, but I knew it well. Strong wide jaw. Hazel eyes. Dark thick hair. Broad Danish brow. I couldn't look into his eyes even though he stared at me. I closed my eyes and touched his cleft chin with two fingers and then gently raised my hand so that my fingers were on his lips.

Do not speak. Do not speak. I cannot stand to hear his voice. I would fall into despair. I felt the wetness on the tips of my fingers on his lips. His tears. Then his arms were around me and the towel dropped softly onto the rug.

I have to stop thinking of Scott, or remember our last night together–my first love after the divorce from John.

I swing my feet off my bed, pulling the old torn quilt half onto the floor of my bedroom in Bath and run into the center of the room. As if I could run from the pain. As if I could actually run from memories of Scott. The action was foolish. I knew that. The book *Black Elk Speaks* by John Neihardt falls from its hiding place in a rumple in the quilt and thumps onto the floor. I don't care. I am tired of male Indians. I wasn't reading it anyway. It's been there for a week. I'm glad it fell. I was re-reading *White Buffalo Calf Woman Speaks* when… I made the mistake… of thinking about Scott.

Brooke Medicine Eagle, a Lakota medicine woman from Montana, had just published her first book, *White Buffalo Woman Comes Singing.* Brooke explained in her book why, in order to follow her true spiritual path, she broke away from her own tribal authorities and traditions; mostly positions and philosophies held by men. A medicine man, a person of high degree, who guarded the ancient medicine pipe of White Buffalo Calf Woman, the spiritual leader of the Lakota, had made sexual advances toward her.

I flop down on my bed and pick up another book, *The Gift of The Sacred Pipe*. I open to the first page.

> Early one morning, very many winters ago, two Lakota were out hunting with their bows and arrows. As they were standing on a hill looking for game, they saw in the distance something coming towards them in a very strange and wonderful manner. When this mysterious thing came nearer, they saw it was a very beautiful woman, dressed in white buckskin, bearing a bundle on her back.
>
> Now this woman was so good to look at that one of the Lakota had bad intentions and told his friend of his desire. But this good man said he must not have such thoughts, for surely this is a wakan, or holy, woman.

This was White Buffalo Calf Woman. What happened next was the young scout who looked upon her with evil intent was turned into a pile of snakes. The first experience on earth for White Buffalo Calf Woman is to evaporate a male who was disrespectful to the feminine? *Why was the importance of respect for the feminine her very first teaching to humanity?* Did the male Lakota understand this message? Did they care?

> "Look at this bowl," said White Buffalo Woman. Its stone represents the buffalo, but also the flesh and blood of the red man. The man buffalo represents the universe and the four directions, because he stands on the four legs, for the ages of man. The buffalo was put in the west by Wakan Tanka at the making of the world, to hold back the waters. Every year he loses one hair, and in every one of the four ages he loses a leg. The Sacred Hoop will end when all the hair and legs of the great buffalo are gone, and the water comes back to cover the world."

I smell meatloaf cooking. I sigh, drop yet another book on my bed and, in my stocking feet, run down the stairs and through the parlor, to the kitchen. Maybe food will help. Something.

Dressed in yellow polyester pants and matching shirt, my mother stands beside the stove, holding, with a lobster potholder, a pan of cooked meatloaf. She smiles brightly and I slump into a chair and rest my head on my hands, like a kid. She serves me meatloaf, baked potatoes, and peas, already slathered in butter and seasoned with salt and pepper. It is Friday night. The girls are with John. He picked them up from nursery school.

Tonight, I will find out more about my mother's dreams. Maybe there will be some answers to my questions.

I am thirty-three and it has been almost three decades since she first told me about Atlantis. I had started out my life trying to find my mother and then finding her, I realized I was really looking for the Goddess, but now it seemed I was trying to find the root of evil.

CHAPTER 21

FULL MOON AND THE GODDESS

It was a beautiful crystal-clear Maine night, and the moon was full. Halloween was in three days. Arianna, Gwen, and my friend Michelle and I were on my front porch at 62 South Street in Bath. The girls sat happily talking and laughing in the wicker loveseat. They were also eating chocolate cupcakes with white frosting. On top of the cupcakes, I'd created pumpkins with orange and green icing.

Michelle sat on the steps smoking a cigarette. I was rocking in the wicker rocker.

The girls and Michelle and I had just returned from Witch Hill Spring in West Bath. We had brought my blue Carnival glass chalices and filled them with freshly drawn water from the spring. We had blessed each other and the four directions and Mother Earth and Father Sky with the water. It was a ceremony we had in Suzannah Budapest's new book *The Witch's Bible*. We were experimenting with the concepts. But it didn't feel like a new idea. It felt old and familiar.

We did the same with sea salt and with sage smoke.

I had found Michelle's name and phone number on an index card on a bulletin board at Morse High School. She was a great babysitter, and we quickly became friends. I was a mother for her too, especially when she was kicked out of her house by her father, who is a welder at Bath Iron Works. She sleeps on the couch occasionally. I understood couch-surfing from when I was a teenager with two abusive stepparents.

"Hey, we forgot to give the girls a Goddess Blessing," Michelle said.

"Girls, do you want a blessing?" she continued.

"Yes," they both said in unison, casually – they were used to this stuff – their mouths filled with cupcake. Words like Goddess and crystals and medicine wheel and blessing and smudging and SamHain and Winter Solstice were familiar and routine.

"What do you think, Jane?" Michelle asked.

"Of course. It is almost Halloween," I replied.

She set her cigarette on the brick beside her cupcake. The tip burned bright orange in the darkening twilight. She dipped her fingers in the chalice of Witch Spring Hill water.

She walked over to Arianna and dribbled it on her forehead. Arianna hunched her shoulders. Michelle laughed. Arianna licked the drops along with the white icing on her lips.

It was meant to be fun. A Halloween thing.

"The Goddess blesses you with strength and power. May you always be strong and brave and true to the Goddess and The Great Mother…" Michelle began.

The brilliant moon came out from behind a wide cumulus cloud. Sky riders raced across the starry sky. The wind blew dry leaves down South Street. The small Maple tree branches tapped against the porch screen.

She went to Gwen who was drinking cider.

"Hi Michelle" she said into the glass.

Her words were muffled and funny-sounding like she wanted them to be. I could see her smiling.

"And to you Gwen. The Goddess bestows upon you magic and strength and the ability to see through the dark veils of ignorance. Know, in your heart, even in the darkest times, you are always protected by the Great Mother."

The squeak of my rocking chair was the only sound.

"Be at Peace," Michelle said, her voice fading…

She sat down on the step. We ate our cupcakes as the moonlight shone onto the green leaves of my rose bushes and green lawn, making them appear they had been brushed with silver. We felt Her Presence. It was a powerful night, and in hindsight, a powerful blessing. For a couple of hours, we all talked and laughed and shared stories and the girls played happily.

Later that night, in the parlor, from the long windows, the girls and I watched my mother turn into our driveway in her yellow sports car. It isn't the same if we miss her arrival. It would be like seeing Santa standing in your kitchen, rather than sliding down the chimney or landing on the roof in his sleigh pulled by reindeer.

I pick up Gwen and hold her close. She holds a Teddy Bear. Arianna places her palms on the window and stares smiling out at her grandmother. I see Arianna's reflection. Long thick ash blond hair. Almond-shaped hazel eyes. Full lips and a strong jaw. Tall for her age and slender. She wears a white sweater with pearl buttons. I place my hand on her head, still believing she might not be real and want to feel her substance under my hand.

The first two years of Arianna's life John was out to sea. He was a merchant marine. When she was born, she and I lived alone in an old ramshackle of a house in Popham on Route 209. The heater was often broken and the wind blew in through holes in the walls. I was afraid to light a fire in the woodstove. The chimney was falling.

It was free. No rent.

I had fun bathing her in the big white ceramic sink in the kitchen with the cracked window that looked out on the steep hill of crystal and mica, but I was afraid at night. I held her against my side in the big cold bed and listened to the waves crash and the wind in the trees and the foghorn out at Sequin Island.

The wiring was so old I thought the place might catch on fire in an electrical storm. I was always cold, but I kept her swaddled in layers of blankets and close to my side all night long. She was born in February, in the height of the stormy weather in Maine, and I was alone with her in an almost deserted roadway into Popham.

We moved a couple of times. John kept trying to keep us somewhere cheap or free, but I got upset and looked for a house. I found this one and fell in love. He bought it. I was shocked. Maybe he got tired of me complaining.

I made her food by hand in a grinder. My mother bought a sturdy old wooden high chair and painted it bright blue. She painted a watermelon on the tray and other bright-colored fruit down the legs and on the back. I bought all her clothes 100% cotton from The Gap.

If I went somewhere, she was in the car seat in the back seat of the Peugeot or in a Snugli on my stomach. Or in her new baby carriage. That was my favorite. I walked most everywhere in Bath in all four seasons.

As we walked, I talked to her about the colors of the leaves in the fall and the flowers in the spring, and in the winter, about the snow that fell on her lips. I read books while we snuggled under layers of quilts or in a rocking chair beside the woodstove with the snow brushing up against the window.

She took her first steps on the gleaming pumpkin pine floors in the parlor. She wore a long-sleeve pink cotton shirt and Gap jeans with suspenders and tiny work boots with orange shoelaces.

John's mother, Pat, stood behind Arianna holding her hands up.

"Now go see Mommy. See if you can make it. Go on."

Pat was excited. This amazed me considering she had seven children and at least ten grandchildren. They were a large Catholic family.

I was on the other side of the room holding my arms out for Arianna. Arianna wasn't sure what we wanted, but she knew it was important. Pat let her go and she started moving, like Frankenstein, her arms out and up like she was ready to catch a large incoming ball. She teetered back and forth and then leaned forward and willed herself across the room. She fell into my arms and I hugged her. Pat clapped her hands.

"Good girl, Arianna!"

"You are so smart," I said.

I held her in my arms in the stream of sunlight.

"Oh My God. Pat. Wait till we tell John."

"Oh. He'll be so excited," she said, beaming.

Gwen puts her tiny hand to her mouth. I am brought back to the present and my mother stepping out of her car. Gwen's eyes widen. I follow the direction of her stare. In the front passenger seat of my mother's Prelude are several shiny white Reny's bags. Grocery bags from Shaw's fill the back seat. There's probably enough food for all of us for two weeks.

I hold their hands when we walk to the driveway to meet her.

"Jane. Arianna. Gwen. How are you?" my mother asks, breathlessly. She has emphysema.

She is all in pink. Pink shirt, pants, and sneakers. Gold necklaces and a gold bracelet. Eva Gabor short blond wig. Big zirconium diamond on her right hand. Short white cotton socks. A shiny white plastic purse. Pink Mary Kay lipstick. She is a fairy. Without wings.

She embraces us all. I smell strong perfume. Gwen jumps up and down and knocks off my mother's glasses. My mother laughs and picks them up from the driveway. She could care less about material possessions. At least that's what she says.

"Nana. What's in the bags?" Arianna asks, excitedly.

Arianna's hands are clasped in front of her mouth like a chipmunk with a nut. Her eyes plead. She learned this stance from my mother. My mother imitates Arianna.

"Oh, we'll see won't we," she says.

I look into her purse for a pink Mary Kay make-up bag. Something for me. Maybe. Night cream? I see People and Star Magazines and a half-eaten Snickers bar and her pills and wallet.

"How are you? Come on in. The girls have been so excited."

"Well, let me just grab a couple of bags here,"

She sticks her key into the lock on the trunk and it springs open. L.L. Bean and The Gap.Two bags of clothes.

"I stopped in Freeport on the way up. I just wanted an ice cream, but I got sidetracked and went into a couple of the stores. They were having the best sales. And everything is so beautiful. I couldn't resist. I just got the girls a couple of things," she says.

She made us a big pot of macaroni and cheese for dinner and ice cream cones for dessert. Playdough, slinkies, fart pillows, birthday party horns, crayons, coloring books were spread out on the living room floor following dinner.

After a very long fun night, and the girls are finally tucked into bed and my mother is resting in her own room, I lie in my bed with a new face cream sinking into my face and wearing a new white cotton nightgown from Laura Ashley. I smooth the crisp cotton gown down on my flat stomach and wish Scott could see me in it.

I open a People magazine that features a story called "Life Without Di." It was about Prince Charles turning 40 and worrying about bad omens in his dreams.

Then Barbara Bush, in all her blue blood, white-haired glory. *The First Lady*. Something about Barbara bringing back a simple, old-fashion Yankee style to the White House. I threw that one on the floor. Nothing simple about that woman.

I settled on Princess Diana. I love Diana.. I understood her. She and I experienced similar childhoods. We lost our real mothers when we were seven years old and were raised by a series of nannies and then … ta … da! An evil stepmother. Just like in all the other fairy tales.

I fall asleep and dream of Diana on an island in a lake surrounded by black swans. It did not feel good. What did it mean?

The next morning Arianna and Gwen went to nursery school in new Calvin Klein white button-down shirts, white cotton cardigans, pink and blue plaid pleated skirts, white cotton anklets, and expensive brown leather penny loafers from L. L. Beans.

On Thursday night, after dinner, my mother and I sat with our tea in the living room near the warmth of the woodstove watching the girls color in their new Disney coloring books. I always like the second night of my mother's visits. It's calmer.

Michelle and two of my best friends, Liela and Nyree Thomas, stop by. My mother always draws a crowd.

Nyree is from England and is the children's librarian at the Patten Free Library in Bath. We both love children's books. I've known Leila since I was seventeen. She is an actress and singer and works part-time at the local bookstore.

I met Leila on the beach at Popham when we were both teenagers in bikinis. Her family now owns a huge chunk of the summer cottage rentals at Popham.

Leila and I share a love of books and philosophy. Our ancestors go way back in Bath history. It bonds us in some way. I love it when she arrives at my door with some new book hidden under her purple wool coat. She doesn't have any children. Books are her babies. She protects them from the snow and wind.

"Jane," she will say very seriously, after she has knocked and I have opened the door, "Do you have time for tea?'

I know we will have an exciting conversation. Her concerns are the environment and equal rights for women and girls. We also talk about men. She is interested in my spiritual journey and asks thoughtful questions. We can talk for hours.

Towards the end of the night on Thursday my mother gave a beautiful white cardigan sweater to Nyree and a wool coat to Michelle. We drank tea and coffee and ate cake from Kristina's bakery. Leila showed us a new Tarot deck they were carrying at the bookstore.

Now it is Friday night. My mother sits at the table eating a Snickers bar and leafing through a *Star* magazine while I eat my meatloaf. Wow, she certainly is addicted to sugar. I think she ate half a Shaw's cake by herself this afternoon.

"Gwen looked just like a little cherub today. Those gold ringlets. Those dear little girls. I've never seen anything so precious in my life. I just adore them," she says.

Her pants, shirt and sneakers are yellow today. I wear a flowing ankle length cotton dress in earth tones of green and brown and maroon. I feel like a brown wood troll next to my mother who, with her blond wig, is as bright as a lemon drop from head to toe.

"Mom, do you remember when you told me you had dreams of Atlantis?" I say, setting down my glass of soy milk.

"Of course I do," she says and firmly places her *Star* magazine flat down on the table. She is a fire sign. Aries. She does everything with gusto.

"I remember very distinctly. I've dreamed of Atlantis my whole life. I remember when the water came. We were overwhelmed. I think I must have drowned. I only remember the waves and I was terrified and then it was darkness," she said.

"I wonder what it was like on Atlantis. Why did it sink?" I ask.

"Well, I'm not sure of all that… It's kind of hazy but I've always been interested in Egypt. I did paint the picture of Isis. I wanted to be an archeologist," she answers, matter-of-factly.

I raise my eyebrows in surprise.

"You're kidding?"

"No, I am certainly not. I thought it would be exciting to go out on digs," she continued.

I ponder all of this. I'm a Capricorn. I go slowly and think much more deeply than my Aries mother.

"Do you believe there is a relationship between Egypt and Atlantis? "I ask.

"There could be," she says.

"I wonder if there was a culture a long time ago that honored women more than they do now," I ponder.

"Well, I sure as hell hope so."

I laugh.

"Maybe it was some place in the stars"

She sighs.

"Like Pleiades"

"Yes, like Pleiades"

CHAPTER 22

HELLEEN KRAMER

"She seems a bit odd," Helen says in her crisp upper-class English accent.

A couple of weeks after my mother's most recent visit, my friend Helen and I sit at a small round table at Tridles, Helen and Matthew's tea and pastry shop, located on the corner of Front and Water Streets in Bath.

We sip hot tea brewed from loose leaves and Emileen and Jonathon, Helen's two young children, play amongst the antiques. I'm a little sad that John isn't with us today. It used to be fun, the four of us adults and the four children, Arianna, Gwen, Emileen, and Jonathon. The kids would play and run around the store and us adults would be having a good old chat over tea and scones.

Helen and Emily have long straight red hair. Jonathon and Matthew, Helen's husband, are blond. The primary visually uniting feature amongst them is that they all wear clothes from Goodwill. Helen loves Goodwill so much she works there part-time as a salesclerk. They don't really need the money. Matthew's mother, who lives in an ashram in India, sends them all they need as far as I can tell. Of course, they also work extremely hard running the tea shop and selling antiques

"She has narcolepsy," Helen continues, her red eyebrows raised, her eyes wide.

"She can just fall asleep anytime I guess," she continues, and then sips tea.

An alarm goes off inside me. It is muffled, like it's under a pile of pillows. Helen and Matthew had lunched recently with John and his new girlfriend, Helleen Kramer, at the Bath Delicatessen.

They were giving me an update. This is the first time I heard anything about this girlfriend. I just knew John was dating someone new that he had met at an Alcoholics Anonymous recovery group.

"What? What do you mean? She falls asleep?" I ask, not believing I'd heard her correctly.

"Narcolepsy. It's an illness. She could fall asleep anytime. Even driving," Helen says, nonplussed.

I suddenly feel like I am at an underwater tea party. Helen is talking in gurgles and she is moving slowly. I'm trying to access something in my brain. What is it?

"I still can't believe you and John broke up," Matthew chimes in from behind the glass pastry shelf heavily stocked with freshly made scones, muffins, biscuits, and rolls.

His handsome face is covered in a fine film of white flour as if someone had sifted it over him. A big blob of white dough rests in front of him on a wide wooden board. Matthew smiles and his perfect white wet teeth gleam inside his floured face. He ignores the flour blob and smiles expectantly at me. He loves town gossip – even more than Helen.

What went wrong for John and I?

I have a flashback.

I'm twenty-four-years-old and in Pensacola, Florida. I'm wearing a pink dress and sitting in John's brown convertible Fiat which is parked at Cumberland Farms. A dark pink azalea is tucked behind my left ear. It is several shades darker than my dress. I had picked it from a bush beside our front steps on my way out the door – as if it would help. As if it made me larger and brighter than I really felt when he was on the phone with his mother.

John stood on the asphalt parking lot outside the car, arguing with his mother on the pay phone. We didn't have a phone yet at our new apartment, so we went to the gas station to make calls. He'd been on the phone for half an hour. I rolled my bare feet over the sides of two beer bottles on the floor of the car in front of my seat. The cool glass felt good on my soles.

"No, Mom. I can't come back to Maine next week. I'm gonna' be in New Orleans(pause) I gotta' work. I dunno'. I think she's got a job at a restaurant. We're going up there now. (pause) No, I'm not drinking. (long pause) No, I don't want to talk to Father Murphy," he says angrily.

His voice is strained.

I roll my eyes and angrily kick the dripping brown beer bottles and set my feet back on the floor of the car. White sand from the car floor, mixed with beer, sticks to my toes. I wiggle my toes and watch the glittery white sand fall to the wet car floor.

I sigh heavily and then throw the wilting flower out the window. Half the petals were gone anyway. It all seemed so hopeless. The night would be ruined. Just like a half dozen other nights. He turned his back to me. His voice became muffled and angry.

John is Catholic. His mother believes we are living in sin because we aren't married. He thinks he might go to hell. Having grown up a Christian Scientist, I had no concept of hell except that which we create with our minds. The notion of a real hell seemed absurd, almost comical, like a place in a Saturday morning cartoon. Maybe that was one reason he loved me. I was kind of the opposite of a Catholic if there was such a thing. A living antithesis of Catholicism.

We had moved to Florida when he got the job on the oil rig off the coast of New Orleans. When he asked me to go, I immediately quit my job as a receptionist for Bath Iron Works president Bill Haggett, sold my newly painted red Pontiac Le Mans, and abandoned my messy third floor apartment in an old Victorian house in Brunswick near Bowdoin College.

I happily jumped into his new Fiat (earned from one trip to Alaska as a third mate on a merchant marine ship) and we headed south on the Maine interstate with only my one suitcase and his duffle bag in the small trunk.

Every two weeks, when he got off the oil rig, he raced, "about 90 or 100 miles per hour" (he told me) on the long hot highway with the top down on the Fiat – his shoulder-length reddish blond curly hair blowing in the wind – to Pensacola, where we had rented an apartment in a brick duplex. The three-bedroom apartment was across the street from an ocean bay with a long wooden walkway where I sat at night under the stars in my pink dress when John was gone. A Blue Angel pilot lived next door to us and, on quiet nights, we sipped beer and talked about flying in formation in the sky.

When John was home, we danced and drank and ate dinner out at The French Quarter restaurants with all the Top Gun-type officers (and their girlfriends) from the Pensacola Navy Base and training center. We shopped for pans and dishes at the local hardware store, made love in one of the three bedrooms, and swam and sunbathed on the sand holding hands.

On one hot sunny day, after more than our usual amount of beer, we ran naked along the shoreline of a white sandy beach at noon. We had parked the car in an empty parking lot in between two huge white sand dunes.

We were alone – no other people on the beach. John held, from its plastic rim, three cans of beer left from a six-pack. They bounced off his leg. I was about ten feet behind him watching the blue waves wash over the cans and his tanned body, making them both shine in the sun.

We were laughing so hard. Was it the waves, the way they were almost pushing us over and we didn't quite care if we got pulled under in all the foam and sand and warm turquoise water? It was so different from the steel gray and dark, blue-collar shades of the cold Maine ocean that was so often threatening and whose churning waters along the Kennebec, near Fort Popham, could suck you under and out to sea in a half a second if you weren't careful.

Maybe we also knew that day on the beach, we had it all. Beauty. Youth. Money. Love. Passion. Freedom. When we walked into a barroom in the French Quarter in Pensacola, all eyes turned to us like we were a prince and princess. That's the way it had always been for us.

We were the youngest in two large families. His mother doted on him in an unnatural way, like he was her husband. He was the replacement for the real husband, John's father, who had died from a brain hemorrhage before John was born. She held onto John with fear and guilt until she couldn't hold on anymore until he had fallen in love: with me.

I was his first attempt at freedom. He had decided to fight against her control. Fighting had meant leaving Maine. Maybe that's why we had been smiling into the brilliant blue waves and laughing so hard.

How could we go wrong? We had it all.

But it had gone wrong. Toward the end, before we left Florida, and went back to Maine, our relationship was challenged. I was immature and wanted to be taken care of like a little girl. He felt lost and directionless. He depended more and more on his mother to direct him.

We went back to Maine and even though we were partially separated – trying to figure things out – I had gotten pregnant, and we married. It did not last long. He was a recovering alcoholic and I think he felt lost trying to be the head of the household. I was still recovering from my own child-hood. We were in love, but we were lost. He left one day and just went and lived on his sailboat. I think it could have been temporary – the separation – if other forces had not moved in to make it permanent.

"Jonathon!" Matthew's voice brings me back to the present.

Matthew chases Jonathon down the front steps and grabs him just in time to keep him from crawling off the curb and under the front wheels of a passing police car.

"She mentioned you," Helen grunts as she bends down to pick up a Beatrix Potter book from the floor.

"Who mentioned me?" I say, my stomach trying to turn itself upright again after watching Jonathon almost crawl off the curb. I was awakening from a daze of jumbled thoughts of the past with John.

"Helleen."

"Who?"

"Helleen. Oh God. I can't remember her last name. John's new girlfriend," Helen says through a thick wall of long red hair that swings forward each time she bends down to pick up another book.

"It's a Jewish name. Isn't that it Matthew?"

"I … think … so," Matthew says, his voice strained from carrying Jonathon who is kicking. He flashes me a big smile. I know he loves the mayhem and the mystery of relationships..

"She's a strange one. That's all I know. And thin. She's quite ill, wouldn't you say, Matthew?" Helen adds.

"Oh yes. She's not quite right. I think John said she was bulimic," he quips, meaningfully.

"What do you mean she mentioned me? I've never met her in my life. This is the first I even knew she existed."

"Oh, it was something silly."

Helen crouches down in her three-quarter length polyester blend pants. I smell Goodwill. She yanks her pants up with her fingertips, freeing her knees so she can kneel on the old Indian carpet. She tucks her hair behind her ears and patiently piles children's books into her arms. The juxtaposition of their Goodwill clothing to their fine antiques and oriental rugs and exotic and expensive furnishings of their home and store, always made me shake my head a bit. They were eccentric but had been close friends of John and I for over a year before we divorced.

"Something about Arianna's sweater. (pause) Oh, I know. She said Arianna told her you didn't have enough money to buy a sweater she wanted at Reny's. Helleen got her a new one. The one she wanted," Helen says, somewhat absent mindedly.

She slowly stands up holding onto the side of the pastry shelf and sets the books on the table with the daffodils and reaches out for Jonathon. She automatically knows when to relieve Matthew of a child.

"What?" I ask.

Helen shrugs.

I try to imagine a sweater I had not been able to buy at Reny's. What sweater? I feel confused,

"What do you think of this?" Matthew asks Helen.

He holds up an old wooden crucifix. Religious items were not usually Matthew's thing. I stare at the crucifix.

Large splats of rain streak the floor-to-ceiling windows of the bakery. Raindrops on the roof are loud, like muffled gunshots. A cold air sweeps in under the wide gap below the closed front door and I shiver and rub my arms. It thunders. Goosebumps rise on my forearms and thighs.

I stand up and walk to the window just in time to see lightning strike over the steel gray Kennebec River. I stare at the repeated strikes of lightning.

The small, warm, steamy English bake shop; the laughter of children; the carefree chatter of adults; fades away. My life, and the short years of happiness, are now over I intuitively knew. It would never be the same.

CHAPTER 23

PSYCHOPATHY

"Are you okay, Jane?"

My roommate, Martha, walks up behind me. She speaks with her mouth full of noodles. I stare out the small, beveled glass window in the middle of the front door of our house on South Street.

"I'm worried about the girls," I answer, my voice heavy.

"Why?" She looks alarmed, even with her cheeks puffed out with noodles.

"I'm not sure. I'm just nervous. I think it's something to do with John's new girlfriend."

"Jane, you're such a great Mom. I'm sure you can handle anything that comes up."

"Thanks."

"Well, I mean it. You're an amazing mom," she chirps, holding her next spoonful of noodles inches from her mouth. I look at her and smile and laugh and relax just a little.

An hour later, the girls are still not home and I am, as a diversion from the growing sense of panic, scrubbing burnt milk off the bottom of the heavy iron soup pan. Martha had gone upstairs to sleep. I can't stop thinking about Arianna and Gwen. That's not unusual, except my thoughts are clouded with fear and trepidation. I've never felt this way about any of John's girlfriends.

I poured the unburned chowder into another saucepan and put it on the stovetop on low. It would be perfect for the girls when they get home. I stick my finger in the soup. Good, it's not too hot or too cold. I open a cupboard door. The bag of round white Chowder House Crackers is still about half full. Arianna loves them. Good. I don't have to run out to the grocery store.

I hear voices at the door. The girls! I drop everything and quickly wash and dry my hands. It sounds like they are pushing against the door at the same time. It's strange, like they are trying to break the door down to get in. I head towards the front door.

"Oh, we'll do it again soon. That's for sure"

A woman speaks loudly. The hair on the back of my neck stands up.

The front door bursts open and Gwen runs into the front foyer and stops suddenly and looks around, almost frantically. She grips two white plastic Reny's bags, one in each hand. The palms of her right hand and the inside of those fingers are red. My heartbeat accelerates. What's wrong with her hands?

"Mommy!" she yells not yet seeing me in the hallway. I enter the foyer and our eyes meet and I smile and her body relaxes.

"Hi. Gwen!" I say, excited.

"Mommy!"

The wild look in her eyes evaporates. She drops the bags and runs past me towards the kitchen. A half empty bag of red licorice falls out of the bag onto the floor. That's good. My heart slows. It looked like blood on her hands.

"What are you cooking Mommy?" she calls back.

"Corn chowder," I answer, happy I have made her favorite dinner.

"Mhhhhh" she utters to herself.

I continue towards the front door in search of Arianna. Arianna enters the house and turns quickly right into the living room and flops down on the couch. Chocolate or something brown, is smeared around her mouth and her hands and even, it looks like, on her hair and coat.

"Hi Mom," she says, languidly, not looking at me, or smiling, but staring straight ahead at the woodstove. Her light pink coat hangs off her right shoulder. My stomach inflates with apprehension.

"Hi honey," I stammer. My heart is racing again. I swallow my excitement. It is as if a wall has been erected between us. Why?

A tall thin woman steps through the threshold of the house. She passes like a shadow into the small entryway and then into the light of the larger front foyer, my favorite room in the house because of the morning light and the forest green wallpaper with the cream hydrangeas.

I flash on Christmas day in this room two years ago. John and Arianna and Gwen and John's mother and my sister Sally, and her son, Tommy, and my mother, were all here. A Cabbage Patch doll's head appears out of gold cellophane wrap and Gwen, still in her little white nightgown, cries out delight, her eyes disbelieving her good fortune.

Blue string lights twinkle on a large Scotch pine tree cut by John in the woods in Woolwich near Eddie's house. The grandmother's Christmas cookies are passed around and everything is funny and amazing, as I remember it. Even the Bath Iron Works crane, a Christmas tree with blinking lights perched on its head, had seemed, through the foyer window, as if it were smiling down on us. A benevolent and festive dragon for the day. I knew the next day it would be carrying large hunks of Navy frigate ships, like they were torn pieces of the stale dead carcasses of other weaker reptiles. I had finally found a family. I was so happy on that day.

"Hi. I'm Helleen," the woman said.

I'm brought rapidly back to the present. Three chunky blue veins raised from her skin run the length of her unnaturally long thin white arms. I shudder and revulsion forces me to close my eyes. I open them. It's not so much her appearance, but the feeling I have about her. I feel sick and slightly dizzy.

I force myself to look at her; after all, we are the only ones standing in the foyer. On her right arm the blue veins are thicker, tighter, raised higher because of the tug caused by a large black plastic bag that she is carrying which is half full and lumpy.

My stomach lurches and I quickly look over at Arianna, who is staring blankly at the woodstove. What is wrong with Arianna? She is usually so happy and excited.

I look back at this person. Her face is pale and hollowed under large wide cheekbones. Bushy shoulder length light hair parted on the side, frames a larger than normal head.

Crooked thin long lips, glossed; rise at both ends.

I suddenly feel like I'm under water again, like I did when I was with Helen the other day at Trifles.

"We got lots of candy" Arianna says quietly and throws wrappers on the floor.

The lips on Helleen's face rise on each end. I assume it is a smile, although no light emanates from her face. Her face is very clean. There are no chocolate stains on her lips or face or teeth or clothes. Her clothes are perfect, as if she had changed into them only moments ago.

"Yeah. Sorry about that. The girls went a little crazy in the candy department at Reny's," she says, and then looks down at the floor and then at Arianna, then at me, as if she is scrutinizing both Arianna and me and the floor.

How did they go crazy? If one of my friends had made the same statement, my heart would not be beating so rapidly. We would have laughed and imagined what it would be like to be kids again.

"Where's John?" I ask.

"Oh, he's working. We're saving for a house now. He'll be working a lot. I told him I'd take care of the girls for the day. I hope that's okay with you."

She holds her hair tightly away from her eyes with her free hand and she leans her head forward, jutting her large forehead with the vein in my direction. She is waiting for an answer.

"Oh…um… I guess it's okay," is all I can manage to say, but my stomach is burning. I feel disoriented.

Why did I just say that's okay?

The wall clock chimes twice. It's too early for the sun to set but it feels dark and cold inside my favorite room.

Gwen skips into the foyer. She grabs my hand and swings one of her chubby white legs. Color has returned to her cheeks; I am happy to see. Love fills my heart and I want to pick her up and swing her around, but I don't.

"Helleen fell asleep," Gwen says nonchalantly.

The blood drains from my face into my feet. I recall the conversation with Helen at Trifles.

"I feel sick," Arianna says to the ceiling. She is slumped so far down on the couch her butt is in the air and she is about to fall onto the floor.

"I think Arianna ate an entire bag of malted milk balls." Helleen says and chuckles and now the lips are smiling broadly. It's a long smile with lots of gleaming white teeth.

My heart is beating rapidly.

"What? What happened?"

How could I have forgotten for an instance what Gwen had just said?

"I just need to get my prescription refilled. It was a little lame. Yeah. I've got this sleeping problem."

She smiles and snorts self-effacingly.

She wears designer clothes in shades of Safari taupe and expensive penny loafers and bright white socks. A simple gold around her neck and an expensive watch on her right wrist. No chocolate anywhere.

I imagine Arianna and Gwen, loaded up on sugar, in the back of a moving van, with the driver slumped over the wheel asleep.

I erase the image.

"Oh, these are for you," she says and drops the lumpy black plastic bag on the floor.

"The girls said you needed some clothes."

I stare at the garbage bag and listen to the tic-tock of the clock, a wedding present from Jim, John's brother, who had been killed in a freak car accident at night on black ice. He had been a friend, the only person in John's family who seemed to have truly cared about me..

Chapter 24

Queen of Spades

"I have a buyer for you," my realtor, Andrea, says.

She looks official in her below the knee plaid skirt and black business jacket and holding an L.L. Bean canvas bag and wearing L.L. bean boots. It makes me nervous.

"A buyer?" I respond quietly, looking, suddenly, into her eyes, as if I am trying to wake up from a dream. We stand in the front foyer of my house, almost in the same positions as Helleen Kramer and I had stood two weeks earlier.

I cannot concentrate on my discussion with Andrea. My mind is stuck in the confusing, stressful series of conversations I had had with John after my first meeting with Helleen.

What is Andrea talking about anyway? A buyer? My mind travels back to the most recent conversation two nights ago with John.

"Jane, I think you're a little paranoid," John said, darkly, with a severity that was surprising. It was during a phone conversation we had two nights ago. I could feel his tension and anger in his voice.

"What?" I asked slowly. Was he really talking to me? Was there someone else in the room with him?

"What? What are you talking about? I don't think so, John. Gwen said Helleen fell asleep. Helleen didn't deny it. In fact, she laughed apologetically and then said she had let her prescription run out."

Silence.

"John, you even told Matthew and Helen, she had a sleeping disorder," I said, more emphatically, like I was trying to break down a wall – or break a spell – or I was trying to help him understand something that should be simple.

More silence. Why were we arguing? What was there to argue about? It seemed simple. Just make sure Helleen takes her medicine when she is with the girls. I wasn't blaming her for anything.

"What the hell am I being paranoid about? Aren't you worried about the girls?" I asked, finally, rage creeping into my voice. What was he doing? Why wasn't he talking?

More silence.

"I'm not surprised you are being so defensive," he said, finally, dully.

The statement was weird.

Maybe he was talking to someone else who had just come into the room.

"Helleen said she felt like you didn't like her, that you didn't really approve of her spending time with Arianna and Gwen," he continued, robotically.

"What?" I retorted.

But in my mind, I quickly tried to reconstruct the series of events and discussions, which transpired that day. I always doubt myself. I knew I had been cordial and kind. It was just my way. Especially with women. Especially to women who I feel have been abused. I had ended up feeling like she had been the victim of some kind of horrible abuse because she was emaciated. John's accusation did not make any sense whatsoever.

"You know Jane, you're just going to have to get used to Helleen. We plan to move in together in the condos in West Bath."

Was his final statement before I hung up, exasperated. Wasn't he at all concerned his daughters could be killed if she fell asleep while driving? What had happened to him? Was I overreacting? Life suddenly seemed out of control, confusing and depressing. John and I had always gotten along. What was happening?

"Yes, and the young couple just loved this room. It's probably the wallpaper you put up. You did a great job," Andrea was saying.

She has a cute short hairdo and freckles and an accent – maybe she is from Boston too.

"So when do you think you could move out?"

I suddenly realized I did not put the house on the market to sell it. I was just doing what I was supposed to do to make it look like I was in control of the situation. The situation being that my house was in foreclosure. The girls loved this house. It was our home. It was the only home, other than Hanover (which I could hardly remember anymore) that had ever been a home to me.

"Oh … yes … okay … I'll think about it," I murmured to Andrea.

She looked a little surprised. I stood to make a lot of money if I sold the house.

Late that night, long after Andrea had departed (confused about my non-committal attitude) and after the girls were asleep and Martha had gone out with her friends, I crouch before the open door of the wood-stove and stoke the fire with a wrought iron prong. It is extremely cold out. *It is February.*

I put the small copper kettle on the stove and turn on the burner. I grab a bag of Red Rose tea. It was the tea Nanny used to drink when she sat on her rocking chair on the porch in Hanover.

I go to the kitchen table and clear off the surface. I remove the cribbage board I made for Arianna out of a piece of firewood. It was a Christmas present. I stare for a second at the board. In yellow and red and green I had painted Mayan or Indian symbols on the top of the board.

I grab a pack of blue Ace playing cards from the junk drawer under the built-in cutting board and hold them in my hands. On the kitchen table, my tea is steaming in a mug. I listen to the crackle of the fire and the wind rattling the icy branches on the tree outside the kitchen. The reflection of the golden flames dance on the glowing pumpkin pine floor.

The room feels more alive tonight. Maybe my Native American ancestors are present. I feel a rush of pain knowing I may only see this beloved kitchen a few more times.

What did I want to know about my life? Where should we go? What about that woman, Helleen? Was I wrong to feel so awful when I was around her

I lay the cards in an arrangement previously discussed with the woman, a stranger, who I had talked to over the phone. A fortune teller.

"Four horseshoe shapes. Eight cards in each horseshoe," she had said, solemnly.

"She's amazing, Jane," Leila had said about the fortuneteller.

"This woman was so right on about everything to do with Steven and I. You've got to try and connect with her," she expounded excitedly, while I quickly scribbled down the woman's phone number on the back of an electric bill, a week ago.

When I was done placing the cards on the table, I recorded their placement on a lined piece of notebook paper I tore from a Rachel Perry notebook.

The ice-laden fingers of the tree branches tap wildly against the narrow rectangular window above the radiator in the kitchen. The tree grew in my neighbor's yard but the branches reached my windows, the houses were built so close. A stoneware plate on the windowsill seemed immune to the wind and stood still in its precarious position.

"LOVE. LOVE. LOVE" I said out loud.

I was reading the words imprinted in black in capital letters all around the perimeter of the plate. Half of the LOVES were upside down from my perspective.

The plate had been a gift from my father, who had recently been diagnosed with prostate cancer. He had discovered a spiritual practice based on the teachings of Joel Goldsmith and was trying to be loving to everyone, including me. At mountain top retreats with Goldsmith my father learned how you can heal yourself of cancer.

"I drove up to Bowdoin College recently. I had made an appointment with the president. Wow. Wow. Wow. Can you believe it Janie? I told him I forgave the college for not letting me into a fraternity," my father told me.

Then he had laughed, the same way he did when he told me his father had taught him to swim in the dangerous current of the Kennebec River.

My father had made a list of everyone he held resentment towards and apparently was making amends. The stoneware "LOVE" plate had arrived in the mail in the midst of his healing work. I had sat on the couch in the living room, the bubble wrap all around me, simply feeling the words LOVE with my fingertips, like Helen Keller. I felt nothing.

Later, after both the fire and the wind had died down, I sealed the playing card information inside a stamped envelope and then slipped it into the mail slot on my front door.

That night I dreamed I was bitten by a water moccasin snake.

CHAPTER 25

THE HERBAL APPRENTICESHIP

It is March in Maine. Mud season. It's pouring outside. The car I am sitting in, stops.

"What are we doing?" I inquire, anxiously, from the back seat.

I wipe a clear space on the fogged-up window. I can't see any buildings, just a field and woods in the distance and puddles on the driveway and an old, rusted car. A wooden sign with letters long ago faded, creaks at its hinges in the cold wind. The paint is buckling and falling off in strips. A wet chicken walks by the car.

I think of the sign in the *Wizard of Oz*, "I'd turn back if I were you" and roll my eyes.

Tess, blond and blue-eyed and smiling, is in the passenger seat beside Gail who is driving the old Toyota wagon. She takes what I hope is one last toke on a short joint and snuffs it with the tips of her pretty white fingers. Doesn't it hurt? I shift uncomfortably in my seat and kick an old Snickers wrapper on the floor.

I notice several more candy wrappers on the floor.

"Whattsmatta Janie," Gail asks, glancing in the rearview mirror. She treats me differently from the other women. I'm not sure why. There is a hidden cackle in her question.

"Nothing. I'm fine," I chirp.

I straighten the bottom of my lacy white shirt, which is creeping up on my stomach.

It's a lie. I suddenly don't know why I am in this car in the middle of Timbuktu with three stoned women. Well, maybe two stoned women. Anita, who is beside me in the back seat, is probably sober. And it's not actually Timbuktu, but Mattawamkeag. Or something like that. We have all signed up for an herbal apprenticeship with a woman – I have never met but who lives somewhere out here. We've been driving inland and north from Bath for two hours.

We are sitting in a puddle in her driveway

Anita tucks her long brown hair behind her ears and reaches into a slightly battered white canvas L.L. Bean bag. Everyone in Maine has these bags. Except for me. She pulls out a half-eaten sandwich. She smiles and takes another bite of a ham and cheese on white

I am not stoned. I hate pot and alcohol. They both remind me of my insane family. My Aunt Marie, who looks very Spanish and used to wear a diamond tiara on top of her black hair, is now dying of liver toxicity from too many shot glasses of straight vodka. My stepfather Hal was an abusive alcoholic. My sister is a prescription drug addict. I think one of my brothers is a pothead.

I am painfully sober. All the time. As soon as I knew I was pregnant with Arianna, I stopped smoking cigarettes and drinking alcohol. Completely. It wasn't even an issue. I was actually more comfortable without my spirit and body being artificially stimulated. Plus, I scared myself straight after the brief six month episode in Maine at the Outside Inn, when I was 18, and had abused alcohol and drugs to try and suppress the pain of so many memories of abuse. Had I remembered everything? Was there more that was hidden?

The car engine dies.

"Damn," Gail says in a way that means something is damn funny.

I want to be back home with Arianna and Gwen baking chocolate chip cookies and moving my Victorian couch to the other side of the parlor and sipping on Earl Grey English Breakfast tea and staring at my beautiful green wallpaper. More and more I want to be with my daughters. I am fearful that our world is changing.

"What is it?" I ask, truly afraid.

"Oh nothing. The car won't start," she says, and giggles, as she turns the key for about the tenth time. The grating sound is getting to me.

"Jesus," I mutter.

"Oh … here we go," she says. The low murmur of the engine indicates success and we begin to creep along the driveway again.

"I think this is it," Gail says, suddenly, with a cottonmouth.

I sit bolt upright.

What is it?

I roll down the window because I can't see through all the pot smoke and fogged up windows. I inwardly recoil. I observe broken down rusted cars up to their hubcaps in mud and weeds and grass and an old white porcelain bathtub in a field.

This is her driveway.

I am worried about the cost of the apprenticeship. John had stopped paying child support ever since he moved in with Helleen at the West Bath Condominiums.

The Kennebec Journal had discontinued their coastal edition. My last story as a reporter for them was about a ghost in a house in Bowdoinham. They closed the coastal edition, my edition, without explanation. I vaguely wondered if the shutdown of *The Kennebec Journal* and the consequential loss of my job, had anything to do with me reporting the truth about Bath Iron Works and Maine Nuclear Power Station. My conversation with the editor of the Journal was short and somewhat curt. He had no explanation except to say it was "no longer profitable."

The Shelter Institute had built its own dormitories. Receiving rent from two-week borders, like Scott (who I could still not think about without tearing up) and his father was now non-existent for most of the people in Bath who had once derived a substantial income from Shelter students.

Where would I get the money to pay for the nine-month apprentice? I didn't know. I only knew I was supposed to be here because of the dream.

"Oh Jesus," Gail says, in a stoned, isn't this riot kind of way, and the car tips left and then stops. I forget about my money problems. She is silent, and then cackles, like a baby who just saw a ball bounce up into the air, but wasn't sure at first if it was funny.

"The dogs are blocking us now," she says, amused.

Irritated, I stare at the back of her little head, waiting for her next comment. Gail is very short with fine black flyaway hair. She wears glasses but they don't always seem to help. We are back in a watery ditch.

Three skinny, growling German Shepherds, teeth bared, approach the car on my side, bringing me quickly back to the present. I roll up the window and listen to the growls and stare at the seam between the door and the floor. I'm waiting for the water to seep in, the puddles are so high.

I breathe. I'm supposed to be here today, aren't I? I did have a dream last night. *The dream.*

While we sit in the rut, I think about the dream. I force myself to remember it so I can convince myself I am supposed to be here in the pouring rain stuck in a mud puddle with three stoned women I barely know, in a town I had never heard of until recently

In the dream, I floated above a long wooden table draped in a white tablecloth. In the center of the table white candles burned in black iron holders. The room was dimly lit with candles but a pink haze hung like a fog over a bouquet of roses. Silverware and napkins and bowls of hot steaming soup, for eight people, were set, with individual place settings, on the table. I hovered in my ghost-like state.

I noticed the soup brew sparkled like it was magical. I moved down the table becoming aware of people who were entering the room – two men and five women. I recognized Gail the woman and maybe Tess. As I suddenly found myself floating above a table setting unoccupied, I heard a voice.

"This is your place at this table. You are meant to drink this magical soup," a voice in the dream said.

When I awoke this morning, I immediately remembered the dream and panicked. It was clear! I was supposed to be at the apprenticeship, right? Gail was in my dream. I had been so happy; I had not felt the joy I felt in the dream – ever, in my life, that I could remember; like I had come home to my tribe. It had to be a good omen.

"Oh My God," I had said out loud to the long streams of morning sunlight warming the pumpkin pine floors in my large bedroom. It must be past nine.

I swung my feet out of my double bed with the blue painted wrought iron headboard. I pulled on my leather-bottom Acorn slippers and ran out of the bedroom and down the hallway to the bathroom (past Arianna and Gwen's empty bedrooms). They were with John. The knowledge hit me fresh in the mornings when they were gone. These days the knowledge was like a cold ghost stepping into my body. I shuddered.

John was evasive about Helleen's falling asleep at the steering wheel problems. He was evasive about everything to do with her. Before Helleen, even though I missed the girls when they were with their father, I knew they were safe. And we would talk often. We had been co-parenting and everybody was relatively happy and relaxed.

All that was gone.

Arianna came home last week and said she didn't like our car anymore. She liked Helleen's car better, a brand-new white van.

It was just so strange, for a little girl, who normally had her head in the clouds, reading books, dancing, playing with her dolls, talking to trees and flowers, to suddenly care about cars. Gwen had seemed confused when she came home – in a daze like she'd been watching a strange, disturbing movie all weekend, she did not know how to process or accept.

Something was terribly wrong.

CHAPTER 26

MIDSUMMER'S EVE, THE CURSE UNFOLDS

By mid-summer the herbal apprenticeship experience had begun to define who I was on a spiritual level. I roamed the woods and fields behind Hyde school in Bath, with Arianna and Gwen, looking for wildflowers like Hyssop and St. John's Wort. I picked Horsetail, which I knew gave you strong hair and gums and fingernails. It grew hidden in the field and marshes near the Kennebec River. Horsetail was estimated to be 50 million years old.

On my way to a Dawnlanders sweat lodge in western Maine one night I stopped in a field of purple clover. I harvested a basketful of clover and presented it to the Native American lodge keeper and his wife. They looked at me like I was a mystery.

I dried bundles of St. John's Wort, horsetail, lemon balm, and wild nettles and hung them in the darker corners of the kitchen and from the crystal chandelier in the dining room. Big old pickle jars from Burgess Market were filled to the brim with echinacea and hundred-proof vodka. I had carefully placed the jars into the dark recesses of my kitchen cupboards.

"For about six weeks and away from the sun. The sun drains power from the medicine," Gail had said.

"A Great Goddess culture once existed," Gail, our teacher, had explained at the rose ceremony.

"For thousands of years, humanity honored a female deity. The Goddess. She was revered in pottery and paintings and jewelry, in most cultures," she said, sitting beside baskets of rose petals.

"The patriarch, as it exists right now, did not always exist. In fact, it has been around for a few thousand years only. Before that, a Goddess was honored the same as God is now. Women were the priestesses, the shamans, the astrologers, and spiritual leaders. The earth and women were respected as a natural extension of the Goddess herself," said the other Gail, who was in her Owlish mood, and taking notes, after the wild dancing at the ceremony.

With all these thoughts in my mind, and halfway through the apprenticeship, which met every other week, I sit at the kitchen table with Arianna and Gwen. A large blue glass pitcher (made of Carnival Glass), which has grapes and flowers embedded on it, is filled with cold lemonade. Slices of real lemons float with the ice on the surface.

A thick-stemmed chalice made of the same carnival glass and filled with lemonade is on the table in front of Arianna and Gwen. A white candle burns in a Goddess candle holder on the oven and Brook Medicine Eagles' flower song plays on the recorder on the kitchen counter near the stove.

"Flower song oh flower song…"

The table is covered with Echinacea roots, flowers, stems, and leaves. I chop the roots, already cleaned and dried, with a sharp cutting knife on the top of a butcher block.

Arianna has woven purple flowers into a ring and placed the flower crown on her head. She holds her Velveteen Rabbit tighter against her chest than usual. My mother had given her the stuffed toy and the book by the same name. It was the story of a stuffed animal rabbit who became real after he had been loved.

Gwen, flushed pink with excitement, has made two perfect rows of flowers and is counting them, over and over again, with her little fingers.

"1, 2, 3, 4, 5, 6…"

Arianna is silent and staring at her book, but not really reading, I noticed.

"Arianna, are you okay?" I ask, and my heartbeat accelerates a bit.

Fear, like an uninvited guest, leaps into my chest. She had not been herself at all lately. Almost since the day she came home gripping chocolate balls in her hand and the girls had been out with Helleen Kramer for the first time.

"Yeah," she said grumpily. A shadow flickered across her face like the lie itself was a being that had a shadow. My stomach clenched.

On Monday, two days ago, the day the girls came back from spending the weekend with their father, John had called me on the phone and said Arianna did not want to come home. He said she was upset because I wouldn't take her to the doctor when she had a cough last week.

"What?" I was shocked.

I didn't know why I was shocked. Bizarreness dominated all my conversations with John these days. We argued all the time now and spoke less and less in the old, familiar friendly tones we had shared even after our separation. Everything had changed.

"She goes to see Dr. Kitfield. She was there last week," I said, but it seemed the truth was starting to become irrelevant to him. There was something else more important. I couldn't quite figure it out yet.

"You know, the doctor who delivered her and who we have been taking her to for seven years," I said, in a futile effort, as I knew these facts would not be entered into his thinking.

"Well, she said you wouldn't take her anymore." He continued as if I had not even spoken.

It was getting scary. I hardly knew him anymore. He had changed almost completely and overnight. He sounded robotic. I also knew, from experience now, that it would be impossible to prove to him the truth by asking him to call the doctor. It was like he wasn't interested in the truth.

Futility had suddenly drained like a slippery mud into my feet and into the ground underneath me and I was seized with fury but I tried to maintain my calm.

"I'll just come and get her," I had said, and hung up the phone before I had to hear his zombie-like, infuriating reply.

Heart racing, I had driven the five miles to the new condominium at the reservoir in West Bath where John now lived with Helleen.

My heart softened and I relaxed a bit when I saw Gwen outside playing in the front yard with her overnight bag on the walkway. Thank God, I had said to myself. She had quickly dropped the toy and ran up to my car.

She had the same bewildered look I saw the first time she was with Helleen and it had dissolved until I stopped and got up and picked her up. Then her eyes had softened and her whole body had melted into mine like she was a ray come back to the sun. I felt she had been out of her body and was dropping back into it for some reason. Gwen seemed safe. I put her seat belt on and she immediately picked up her stuffed duck and started talking.

I had turned back towards the house in time to see a curtain pulled back from the upstairs living room window. But I saw no one. John opened the front door and stood at the threshold with Arianna who was scowling. My heart thumped against my chest. With the fear of a gladiator entering a coliseum of lions, I moved forward – making myself break down some wall I felt. My God. This was my daughter. What was I feeling?

"Arianna. Come on honey. It's time to go home," I said as pleasantly as possible when I reached the front door. I could hardly hear my words, my heart was thumping so hard. She looked at me through her bangs which had fallen into her face. She looked dirty and unkept and had unfamiliar clothes on. Where were the nice new clothes she had worn to her father's? I shook my head in confusion.

"What's wrong?" I asked.

She was silent. The curtain moved again and Helleen came into plain view for me, but not for Arianna or John. There was something wrong here. A mother knows her young daughter completely and this was not the tap-dancing, flower picking, dress-up in the wedding gown and golden slippers, I love my Mommy, little girl. She looked and acted like a rag doll.

"She doesn't want to go," John said, lamely.

I gently took Arianna's hand and walked back down the sidewalk towards the car with her in tow. John stood with his hand on his chin shaking his head, like I was an unreasonable person he would have to figure out how to deal with at a later date. This would not be the end. In fact, I felt I had played with some kind of dynamite, but next time it would explode in my face.

I thought I might have a heart attack. Why? The danger here was profound, but I wasn't sure why. Helleen turned away from the window and disappeared into the interior of the house. The danger was as clear as if a rattlesnake, or something worse, was in the grass, about to poison my daughter with its fangs. I pulled her more quickly.

I wanted to attack or kill something or somebody, but I remained calm on the drive home. I watched Arianna through the rearview mirror and she seemed drugged. I wanted to get her home and on safe turf and hopefully, fed and relaxed, before I asked her any more questions.

On Wednesday night, after school, I went into Arianna's room with the beautiful blue carpet and pretty flower wallpaper. She sat on her bed reading. Books were stuffed sideways and lengthwise into a white metal bookcase. It had been a shelf for flowers but I took it inside in the winter for all her books. Stuffed animals, Barbie dolls, more books, Legos, and plastic horses were happily scattered about on the carpet and bed.

"Arianna, honey, I just wanted to check in with you and see how you are doing," A lace curtain blew

No comment.

"How are you feeling?"

"Fine," she answered without looking up from the book.

"Oh, good."

I paused and picked up off the blue rug a pair of her jeans and a blouse and folded and put them on a pile on her bed.

"Well, I was just wondering why you didn't want to come home from Daddy's house on Monday when I went to pick you up?"

"I dunno," she mumbled and tossed her long thick hair, still staring at her book.

But then I asked the question I'd feared.

"Did you tell your father you didn't want to come home with me on Monday because I wouldn't take you to the doctor anymore?

My palms broke out into a sweat. My heart raced. Why was I so afraid?

"Yes!" she yelled and threw down her book and got up and sat on the rug and picked up a Barbie Doll.

My heart plunged. She had lied. I was not afraid for myself. I was afraid for her. This was totally out of character.

"But honey you know you go to see Dr. Kitfield, a lot."

"Helleen told me if I went to her doctor, he'd give me candy. She said I could go to her doctor if I stayed and didn't come back here," she continued, almost in a whisper.

It seemed like all the fresh wholesome air had been sucked out of the house, leaving a deadly kind of vacancy you feel in a hospital operating room waiting to be cut open.

The only sound is the rhythmic flop of wet clothes in the dryer and the inevitable click and tap of the buttons on Gwen's white sweater inside the dryer. I envision my mother sewing the buttons on the sweater the first day of school last September. It had been such an amazing day. I think about it all the time.

I try to stay calm. Her answer was the one I had most feared. She had been manipulated.

"Well, I think it's important for you to keep going to see Dr. Kitfield and Sarah. They've known you for a long time. Since you were a baby. They love you."

"Well, I want some real candy. Not that carob candy from the Grainery!"

I couldn't think clearly anymore.

"We'll go to Reny's and get some real candy. Don't worry!"

I was furious. As soon as the girls were outside in the yard on the swing set, I picked up the phone and dialed John's number. I told him the whole conversation.

There is a moment of silence. I can hear him breathing like he is trying to remember what he is supposed to say or trying to formulate a strategy.

"Well, Jane, like I said before, you are going to have to accept Helleen in my life. She warned me you might try to make her look bad. So here it is. Helleen would never do that."

"John, are you in the same universe as me? This is your daughter. She's lying about her mother. Do you have any idea how dangerous that is for her?" I say.

"Helleen made an appointment for Arianna to go see her doctor," he said, calmly and without emotion or concern for Arianna.

I stammered. I felt I was going into some kind of shock – everything was slipping away. It wasn't about what doctor she went to, but he wasn't getting it. Something much more malevolent was at play here.

"What? What are you talking about?" I ask.

"Helleen said there's a scrape on Arianna's knee that looks infected, and she didn't think you would take Arianna to the doctor."

He had thrown me a curve ball. His voice was louder now, more self-assured. I struggle to maintain my composure.

It was becoming like a game, with the rules being made up as we went along. The problem is the girls' lives were center stage in a game with arbitrary rules. I focus on Arianna's knee. Her knee. What was happening? I can barely think.

"She scraped her knee two weeks ago playing beside the quarry, by herself; where the hell was Helleen? Gwen said they were all alone. She scraped her knee and nobody bothered to put a band-aid on it. I took care of it when she got home. It's fine. It's scaled over," I responded. I was shaking.

"Well, that's not what Helleen said," he said, smugly.

"Did you look, John? Arianna's your daughter, not Helleen's. Did you look at her knee?" I shot back.

I might as well have been speaking to the wall next to the phone.

"Jane. You're jealous and you're paranoid. Helleen would never leave Arianna or Gwen alone beside the quarry. It's fifty feet deep and dangerous!," he yelled.

I hung up the phone, shaking. The girls were in mortal and spiritual danger. I knew it with every fiber of my being.

Gwen ran in from the yard to be with her toys in the foyer. All her stuffed animals are lined up on the Oriental rug like the front-row audience of her theatre performance. I walk and smile at her as she places a daisy in front of every animal.

I walk into the foyer and kneel down beside her and straighten the collar on her little white shirt, and tuck her hair behind her ears. She smells like fresh air and her eyes are bright and happy and excited. My heart is beating so hard that I fear I will have a heart attack. My hands begin to perspire.

"I love you," I say, trying to stay calm.

"I love you, too Mommy," she says and hands me a daisy.

I gather her into my arms.

"I love you," I whisper into her ear.

I want her to completely understand what my love feels like. In her body, not just in her mind and heart. I want her to know it in her bones. Deep in her bones. I knew she must remember this love. She must. I realize her life depends on it.

The next day I go visit Arianna's first-grade teacher. It is lunchtime and the kids are all out at recess.

"I'm really worried about Arianna. Her Dad is in a new relationship and I…don't know…how to say this, but there's something wrong… It's confusing, but Arianna is kind of in the middle and she's depressed. I think. If you could… just keep… an eye on her, make sure she's okay," I stumble on my Words. I can feel something is wrong. Already. It's a shift, almost imperceptible, but real. I already know before she speaks, that her attitude about me has changed.

"Well, that's funny," she said.

"What?"

"Is her name Helleen?"

Yes," I said, feeling the slow, creeping terror associated with her name.

"She was here early on Tuesday. She said she was worried about both you and Arianna. She said she felt you were lonely and having financial problems and that this was having a negative effect on Arianna," she continued matter-of-factly, as if she was ready to move along to the next bothersome parent or she needed to correct some papers before the children returned from recess.

"Lonely? I'm far from lonely… I… and yes, I'm struggling a bit…but the girls don't even … "

"Well, it's hard for us teachers to know exactly what's going on with mixed families," she interrupts.

"At any rate, she wants to come in once a week to help out. We're always happy to accommodate a volunteer," she says, cheerily.

What is that smell? Like earthly?" she said, sniffing, and not altogether pleased.

It's a perfume … something I made … from roses … it's natural."

She raises her eyebrows. In interest or alarm, I wasn't sure.

"Well, nice of you to come in, Jane!"

I was being dismissed.

I left feeling I had accomplished nothing or worse. How could I have made it worse? I was just trying to help. Maybe the teacher thought I was desperate and lonely or lying. Everything is so confusing.

I see Arianna on the playground and feel a rush of love and pride. She is so beautiful, and I bet she had made up the cute game they all are playing with chalk on the pavement. Oh, yes, she is so creative, it must have been her idea. They are jumping in and out of circles drawn in chalk. Her hair is still in the French braid but a few strands in the front, and on both sides, fall prettily and frame her face. I smile and stand for a moment beside the metal fencing, my hand resting on the bar.

Her pink My Little Pony lunchbox leans up against the sunny brick wall of the school and I hope, with a brief moment of alarm, she already ate her tuna fish sandwich with lettuce. Did she eat her apple? I always pack an apple. Most of the time the apples go to school and come home again, along with the girls. I smile. I am sure she ate the Reese's peanut butter cup. I bought a whole bag from Reny's. Did she read the note? "Hope you like your candy, but don't forget the apple. Have a great day. I love you. Mom."

A kid who just got tagged screams and Arianna turns in my direction. My heart leaps and I smile and wave excitedly. She looks at me, right at me, I know she sees me and I get excited. I wave again, with my arm extended higher and my wave more exuberant. She does not smile or wave and just turns and goes back to playing.

I feel a knife-like stab into my chest. Into my heart. Maybe she didn't really see me. No. She looked right at me. I forced myself to start walking. We lived two blocks from the school. I would just have to keep walking. I was in shock. A mother knows her child. A thousand times since she was a baby she had held out her arms in joyful greeting. A hundred times a day in seven years. My blood had turned to ice. My legs were shaking.

I stepped onto my front walkway just as the postman did. He handed me a pile of letters, mostly bills. A disconnection notice from the electric company. A letter from the bank where I had my house mortgage. Something from my father. Probably an article he had torn out of the Christian Science Monitor. Something about the starving children in Africa.

Tears were streaming down my cheeks. Through my tears, I noticed one envelope which was handwritten. Somehow the address had a meaning to me deep in the recesses of my mind. I tried to hide my face from the postman with the letters. Once inside, I threw them all onto the couch.

I put on the kettle. I opened a brown paper grocery store bag and grabbed some motherwort herbs and then opened another bag of lemon balm and pushed both the herbs into a stainless-steel tea ball. My hand was shaking. Motherwort. It would help the pain in my heart and calm me.

With a cup of steaming hot tea in my hand, I picked up the phone and called Brenda, the local psychic, who had also been a friend of mine and John's.

"I need help, Brenda. I feel like my children are in danger. It's partially John. He is not the same person we both knew. He's changed. It's something about Helleen. I've never been so revolted by anyone in my life. It's something about her Brenda. I'm terrified. I feel paralyzed. Could you see me today? I asked, my voice wavering.

"Come in at one," she answered matter of factly.

"I have some information to share with you," she added.

Later that day, after I had drank three cups of motherwort and deeply pondered the abstracts of my life. Specifically, and most recently, the joy of learning about healing herbs and being reunited with Mother Earth and with my own mother, and then, the flip side, my daughters in danger.

Brenda ushered me through her healing area which smelled of patchouli, and we parted a crystal beaded doorway and passed pictures and statues of Jesus Christ and Mary and other saints and angels. A Crucifix, an amethyst, and a water fountain shared a small table covered in lace.

"Sit!" she said, when we were in front of her large round kitchen table. I think there were about eight people in her family now and she needed the table space. She had married and settled down since the days she had been uprooted and homeless and I had allowed her to live at my house for a few weeks with her three children.

I sat. She served me coffee, cookies, and homemade brownies. I explained to her what was going on in my life, while trying to catch the cookie crumbles as they fell off of my chin.

"She's got him right by the balls." Brenda shot back, without hesitation.

She wore a black satin dress, purple amethyst on her neck, and yellow citrine earrings. A large crucifix hung on a wooden beaded strand from her neck.

"I've known Helleen was a nut since John brought her to meet me," she continued. "He's still trying to convince me how great she is. I know better. I feel so sorry for those girls, Arianna and Gwen, having to spend time with her.

This last sentence gave me a sinking feeling.

"How is she doing this to him? I mean, he was fairly sane, at one point… anyway," I inquire.

She slowly leans forward, her face somewhat blurred behind the steam of her tea; her necklace is chunky and long, and it clatters as it hits the table and half of it folds up as if to sleep. She stares intently at me through the steam. Even her cross-eye seems focused.

"Sex," she whispers. I blush

"How do you know?" I whisper back, horrified.

She leans back in her chair as confident and cool as a cat.

"I still see him, you know. He's still my client. I know things in this town. I don't usually share this kind of information, but in this case, it's an emergency. I can feel what is happening to Arianna. I can read it in your energy field. They are in danger," she added.

"She's turned him into a pile of jelly. He's lost his will. I mean that in the most serious way" she said.

I was too shocked to reply, although any explanation at this point was better than nothing.

The transition to the healing room wasn't easy at first. I lay on the table while she held her hands above my body, my mind kept going over the shocking and revealing details of our conversation.

Could it be John was under some kind of sick mind control? I was desperate for answers, and at the time, this didn't seem too unrealistic. He used to be under the control of his mother, a stern Irish Catholic woman. Maybe it was more comfortable for him to be controlled.

"Jesus Christ. Father. God. I pray you heal your daughter," she whispers, her eyes closed, her arms outstretched and her soft palms above my body. A brown incense stick glowed red on the end and swirls of smoke floated upwards from the tip. An angel painted on the ceiling above my head smiles down on me.

"Our Father who art in heaven, hallowed be thy name. Thy kingdom come, thy will be done, on earth as it is in heaven. I fall asleep and then wake up about a half hour later feeling a weight has been lifted. The two large rose quartz crystals are beside an angel and the waterfall.

The family is gathering for dinner. Brenda was the type of person who would have let me sleep there all night. A small angel clock, chimes. It's 2:30. I grab my coat and purse, wave to her through the crystal curtains, and run out the door. Brenda, standing in the center of the kitchen holding a platter of spaghetti, surrounded by her husband and her children, stays in my mind until I get home. It must be nice to have a family.

I'm back at home going through my mail.

The first envelope has the return address of the bank in Brunswick that held the mortgage on my house. I open it slowly. It is a copy of a letter sent to my father, Robert B. Hatch, 40 Dunster Rd., Needham, Mass. outlining an agreement. It appears my father had paid some back taxes or something. Taxes? My mind got fuzzy around numbers, especially if there were a lot. It seemed the house would avoid foreclosure but it would be taken back by the bank in thirty days.

What? What had my father done? Saved the bank a discomfort, but the girls and I were to leave in 30 days. I couldn't understand what he had done. How could someone spend so much money? It looked like about $10,000 or more – to have their daughter and granddaughters removed from a house.

I barely reacted to the next letter which was a disconnection notice from Central Maine Power. The power was to be shut off tomorrow – Friday.

I threw the disconnect notice. It landed undramatically on the couch beside me.

The final envelope had a handwritten address label. It was from a woman in Bowdoinham. I did not recognize the name, but at least it was from a woman.

I tore open the envelope, ravaged it really, and let it fall to the floor of a house that no longer really belonged to me.

"Dear Jane" it started out in neat cursive words. I trusted her handwriting and my heart warmed a fraction of a millimeter.

I read on. I slowly understood it was the result of a reading this psychic woman had done from the playing card formation I had sent to her in the mail a couple of weeks ago. The two horseshoe shapes. I had almost forgotten.

She told me of impending financial problems, a turn of events, like the "wheel of fortune" – except reversed – a bad turn of events.

"There is a woman in your immediate environment who is an enemy. Something like your mortal enemy. She is from another lifetime, followed you here. She will try anything to destroy you and your children. She has no morals. She is jealous of you but she will not reveal this to anyone. She acts innocent, but it is a veil. It will begin slowly as town gossip but quickly accelerate. You are in grave danger."

The letter slipped from my hand to the floor.

Chapter 27

Double Cursed

I stand on the porch of my house and smile and wave goodbye to the girls as they speed away in the new white van – with John driving, thankfully. But I know this is short-term. Helleen will be behind the wheel as soon as she chooses. I feel we are on the precipice of a cliff.

I have been inside John and Helleen's new condo, and there is an ominous presence. Something that turns my stomach. Whenever I stand at its threshold I feel I'm staring into a cursed cave that eats butterflies and buttercups and little girl dresses and Velveteen bunnies; anything of the Light gets chomped.

But it is never full. It is always hungry. It is insatiable. John has already been consumed for whatever nourishment he provided and then regurgitated into a pitiful shadow of his former self.

It is pathetic. It is Helleen. I am sure of that now. I am terrified now when the girls leave for the weekend with their father and stepmother, but for their sake, I pretend otherwise.

I turn to go into the house but stop and stare for a moment at the dent a bullet made in my front door, a week or so after I wrote the story about sexual harassment at Bath Iron Works. I'm still confused. Who shot at my door and why? What is happening to our lives?

I run up the winding stairs and into my bathroom, which is small and pretty and papered in colonial blue with floral wreaths repeating. I empty a glass jar of dried lavender flowers and rose buds into the surging hot water in the bath. I dried the flowers myself on a screen in the downstairs hallways where it is dark and airy.

I had learned to make herbal tinctures, cough medicines, salves, dried flowers, lip ointments, and much more in the apprenticeship; and almost all my beauty products were homemade.

Who cares? It all seems insignificant now. Nothing matters but the girls.

I shut off my brain. I do not want to think. Especially about Arianna and Gwen and where they are going tonight. Just for one night. I want to escape the constant fear. I slip naked into the tub and soak in the nourishing flower scents and the healing hotness. I focus on roses.

Finally, I shave my legs, wash and condition my hair, and try not to count how many baths I might have left in this house.

Thirty minutes later I try not to look at the girl's rooms as I pass, dripping, wrapped in a cotton towel.

The emptiness in their rooms is terrifying.

Dripping water on my bedroom floor, I pat my body dry and then slather on my arms and legs a comfrey and cocoa butter concoction made by Gail. It comes in a little round tin. I rub two layers into my thighs and calves and ankles and feet. My feet and lower legs are always dry and cracked like alligator skin. A physical characteristic of Capricorns. Something about having hooves instead of feet. For lots of mountain climbing.

I slip on jean shorts and a white cotton T-shirt and ceremoniously lay a triple strand of amethyst around my neck. From my pine floor, I grab a rose mohair sweater bought at Walfield Thistle antique store on Old Bath Road. I had found, in a dusty corner there, a box of twelve mohair sweaters in every color in the rainbow. They were strewn about my bedroom floor. A few were on my bed, like rootless flowers.

Painting my toenails pink is defiant. Like even in hell there is pink. I imagine a conquered but defiant Cleopatra lining her eyes with kohl before she put the poisonous snake to her breast.

Where was I going? I wasn't sure, but felt compelled, like Dracula's bride.

Was there a Goddess who instructed us to make ourselves beautiful before an execution? I wonder about Joan of Arc. Did she do anything to her body in the hours before she was burned to death at the stake? I knew very little about her. Can't even pick up a book about her anywhere in my house. I knew we were both born in January and the same people she had defended, betrayed her.

My stomach contracts. I erase the image of her burning on the stake and focus on pink, letting it seep into my heart, eventually easing the pain.

I tie the ribbons on the gold sandals my mother gave me.

Half an hour later I stop at a gas station, ignoring the leering attendant. I have no time for men. The girls were the center of my life now. I fill up the car with gas bought with my last twenty-dollar bill.

With the windows wide open I drive north on the Maine interstate highway past tall dark evergreen trees, which get taller and darker the further north I drive. My blond hair blows across my eyes but I can still see the sun setting in gold and orange and red streaks to the west beyond the trees.

I play with the amethysts at my throat. A gift from Raven. One of the many. He also gave me a malachite necklace set in silver, a ring carved from a moose antler, purple Native American glass beaded earrings, and several rose quartz stones.

In June he laid an old sterling silver flask at my feet where I sat cross-legged on the dirt in front of a campfire in West Athens at Gail's house. I smiled. It was as if I was some kind of goddess or saint. He had not spoken, just simply nodded at the flask, and backed away into the darkness of the night beyond the light of the fire.

I picked up the flask and brushed off some of the dirt around the neck and looked up at him with a questioning smile.

He also wrote about how he had traveled from Montana to Maine in an old school bus. He stopped at various locations where they were clear-cutting forests.

He gave me his poncho that same night of the silver flask. It was a cheap Mexican polyester blend.

"I slept in a snowbank in a snowstorm in Montana. It… kept… me… from… freezing," he stuttered.

I stood in his poncho that night staring as the rain on his bare muscular shoulders slowly traveled down onto his clavicle and then to his chest and to the center of his flat hard stomach. He did not bathe often. He said too much water and soap could wash away power. Many of the raindrops beaded on his soft oily skin and he shimmered in the thin coat of water. Finally, some of the raindrops broke free, reached the edge of his jeans, and sank into the faded blue cotton.

I had wiped my eyes to get a better view of the black panther tattoo wet and shiny on his lower right arm and then turned away. I was both repulsed and intrigued by the panther. I could feel his eyes on my back.

That was two weeks ago.

The round white moon rose in the clear sky. There were hardly any cars going either north or south once I passed Augusta, the capital of Maine, and the home base of *The Kennebec Journal* where I worked for a year. I was a journalist and covered coastal Maine from Bath to Damariscotta. One of the best jobs of my life. One of the only jobs, I remind myself. I had never been a nine to fiver.

But I didn't want to think about jobs or anything associated with Bath. Just wanted to feel the cool night air on my skin and relax into the widening expanse of land between myself and Bath and the tall pine trees and the night sky and long winding mostly empty highway. A deer ran into a field between the forests along the highway. It reminded me of one of the opening scenes in the screenplay I was writing. I was obsessed with the screenplay. It had to be written.

Hawks, or maybe an eagle or two, darted and swooped in the darkening sky. Mostly hawks. No moose tonight.

I wanted to get to Raven while the moon was still high and the sky cloudless. It would be almost impossible for me to navigate through western Maine in complete darkness.

I'd never driven to Raven's odd dwelling, which was an old school bus painted brown and parked in a field in Solon. I'd walked to Raven's bus from Gail's house one-day last month – midsummer's day. He told me he wanted to show me something and we had just disappeared from our herbal class in the middle of the day. I wonder now what had compelled me to leave without notifying my friends or thinking hardly at all about my decision. Like I was under a spell.

We walked barefoot through the grassy back trails and woods and fields of West Athens and Athens and then Solon. It was an eight-mile hike and an African drum was strapped to his bare back for the entire trip. He looked like Tarzan. Shirtless, I could not help but notice he was slender and muscular, and tanned. Every muscle on his body was toned and fit and prepared to respond. His body was all he had, it seemed.

He kept a long shiny knife strapped into his belt buckle. Holding up my ankle-length white skirt to keep up with him, I felt I was in an old movie playing myself, Jane. It was a dream world. I was Cathy and Raven was Heathcliff. I was Jane and Raven was Tarzan. In some way, I thought I was living my childhood dream. I was Cathy running through the Moors of England with her love.

I did not know yet, what a curse felt like. I did not know that curses and spells are often woven from our own fantasy and dreams.

We jumped over clear, fast-running streams, and ran through a grove of willow trees and several small hills radiating with the mid-summer colors of purple and yellow. There were apple trees. I could not contain my joy around apple trees. I stopped to pick up apples from the ground and, smiling, I ran to catch up with Raven. I presented him with the apples and his expression indicated he shared my feelings. We munched on the apples, and he grabbed my hand and we walked hand and hand through the open fields and orchards laughing and smiling and eating our apples.

We passed two or three hippie houses. A naked fifty-something man stood beside his mailbox puffing on a joint. He smiled and waved and then let his arm drop languidly, and looked away, as if, in his mind, he was on to other more important matters already. Important in this part of the world anyway. Tending to the pot gardens, playing with the latest batch of newborn kittens, making herbal tea, taking a sun shower, smoking a joint, or waiting for the wife or husband to return home from being with their other wife or husband. I had learned a lot about West Athens during my apprenticeship.

Gail's husband, was a tall, big man with a wide smile, a large stomach, and a red beard, who often had a black iron shovel resting on his shoulder, was shared with another Athens woman. Jack dug holes and repaired fences, and patiently did whatever else Gail asked of him when he was around.

I never understood exactly how many children this man had fathered with Gail, but three happy redheaded kids lived with Gail. They were like wildflowers. I watched them run barefoot in their ragamuffin clothes through the fields as if they were in search of their old homes. Why else would they constantly stop and just stare at the ground?

The only vehicle Raven and I saw in Solon that day was a beaten-up postal truck which sped erratically along the dirt road, often coming close to the sides. It was as if the driver couldn't wait to get out of Athens and its numberless houses and falling down mailboxes. I could hardly blame him.

The big brown bus, Raven's home, looked like an alien spacecraft that had run out of gas and fell to earth into an unsuspecting and otherwise normal neighborhood. The bus had not moved in many months judging by the tall grass and weeds and dandelions around the sunken wheels.

I had stepped in tentatively. An old thin mattress and a sleeping bag and a yellow-stained pillow had been dropped on the floor on the right just inside the bus. Raven picked up a piece of paper from the mattress and handed it to me.

It was a simple pencil drawing of three intertwined circles. I didn't get it. He seemed like a ten-year-old boy showing me his stick figure drawing.

" A circle within a circle within a circle," Raven said.

"This is it, Raven. This is what you brought me to see?" I said with as little sarcasm and as much interest as I could muster.

I felt like Jane in the Tarzan movie where he drags her miles into the jungle forest to show her a dirty monkey skull. I ignored the drawing while I pulled burrs off my shirt and picked up my foot and rested it on my knee and, with my hand, brushed off the grass and twigs from my sole.

He stood waiting patiently. I look back at him. He smiles but a dark shadow crosses his eyes and it is unnerving..

I held the lined paper closer to my face wondering if it had come from the same planet as the bus or if he'd bought a notebook from CVS. I simply could not imagine Raven in a store. He was so uncivilized.

"Well, what does it mean Raven?"

"It's about the Goddess and you and me."

Was this whole day a well-designed pickup? Deep down, no doubt, I was scared of men. My stepfather still haunted my dreams. I had nightmares about my brother-in-law Dick McIlvene, my sister's abusive ex-husband. I was alone on the bottom bunk bed at night in a little house in Easton and his shadow loomed in the threshold of the door. I would wake up terrified.

I realized I was completely alone with Raven. There were stories about him. Not all of them were good. He had been accused of theft. His strength was local legend.

None of us really knew where he had come from exactly, only that he had lived most of his life in Montana and Washington and then, later, in North Carolina. He landed in Solon, Maine, in the winter and lived inside the bus encased in half a foot of ice, like an igloo, for most of the winter. The people who left baskets of food outside his front door that winter told their neighbors he must be alive because they saw smoke coming from the small pipe that led to his woodstove in the bus.

There were also footprints. And drumming.

He mumbled and stared into the fire while he talked. It was hard to understand his words. He rolled his own cigarettes and smoked. Smoke often obscured his face. We –the apprentices, myself, Gail, Tess, Anita, and myself – heard half sentences. maybe he had even made everything up. Nothing was clear.

There was something about Raven that was either superhuman or less than human. I was not sure which. I watched him maybe more than anyone. Especially when he thought I was asleep in my sleeping bag and he was alone and smoking and staring into the campfire. He kept the fire lit. I never saw him sleep.

"Right after I met you…. I fasted for eight days… and on the last day of the fast, I ran and ran… for fourteen miles. When I got home I dreamed of these circles," he continued, trying to describe the three circles on the dirty piece of paper I had let drop onto a table – or something – maybe it was a stump of a tree covered in dark rocks and crystals.

Three circles were not much reward for so great a sacrifice, I thought. But these were the most words he had ever spoken in one breath. It must mean a lot to him. Maybe it wasn't just a pick-up line. I stared at the circles. I was dizzy, angry, scared, confused, and hopeful.

And then on that day, I had become aware of Raven's closeness to me; of his heat and sweat and the grass and the oat straw tops stuck to his body. I realized that I too was covered in grass and straw. It seemed we were both mirrors of the heat and the sun and the summer flowers and the golden wheat right outside the bus. I was feeling light-headed around Raven, as usual. I was not myself, but isn't that what I wanted? I wanted to escape my world which was becoming increasingly scary.

I turned my back on him to look around at the bus.

Natural rose quartz stones covered the wide dashboard. I wondered if he drove with rocks on the dash. A few feathers and plain gray and brown and green rocks were interspersed with the quartz. I picked up a small pink stone. I felt strong pulsations on my palm where it rested. I wondered what was up with the color pink. It seemed to be a theme for the day.

"Pink dunes in Utah. Just south of Devil's kitchen," he said. "That's where I got them."

I looked towards the back of the bus. Rocks and crystals, of all shapes and sizes and colors, sat, like a large mysterious unblinking family, on makeshift wooden and metal shelves and on the floor and bed and even on the woodstove. A moose antler hung from a broken wooden rack. A dozen or so small clear bottles of glass beads decorated a log stump. Purple. Pink. Red. Green. Blue. They reminded me of the antique braided rug in my living room. Or my mohair sweaters.

A curved, thin needle, wax thread, a spool, and two pairs of long, beaded Indian earrings, unfinished, also rested on the log, inside the life rings of the stump. There was a silent but rhythmic thumping in the bus, a singular heartbeat that joined the crystals and the rocks in some kind of powerful earth harmony.

"What do you eat?" I asked, feeling defensive. There was no refrigerator or oven or any food that I could see. I wanted to talk about something normal.

"Rabbit. Pine needle tea. Pine spaghetti," he said, picking up a lime green stone, about the size of a softball, which was veined in thin black lines.

Carvings; triangles and deep kiva grooves; revealed the carved interior of the odd lime green rock. It looked alien and maybe had arrived with the bus from outer space. His answers did nothing to ease my fears and return us to a sense of normalcy. Oh, well, when in Rome.

"What's pine spaghetti?" I asked, almost sarcastically. I was both stressed and mesmerized.

"It's from inside the pine bark. You peel it off the tree," he answered and looked away quickly.

I realized he might be embarrassed and suddenly felt guilty. I could be impertinent and thoughtless. Especially with men. I had an ax to grind.

He handed me the green rock.

"What kind of rock is this?"

"Magical," he answered quickly and looked away. I stood holding this strange green rock, not knowing what to say but thinking "Yes, of course."

I focus on the image of Raven and the rock as I drive faster toward Solon. A strange green light on the horizon ahead captures my attention.

Mary Summer Rain, in her many books about her relationship with her Native American teacher No Eyes, spoke of a green light which would appear as a warning the earth would soon rotate on its axis provoking massive earthquakes and tsunamis all over the world.

I recall, with the wind still blowing in my face, and the sky rapidly darkening, the dreams I had as a child of huge waves covering the earth. And my mother telling me she had drowned in the ancient sunken city of Atlantis when it had been overcome by ocean waves.

Maybe the green lights are the landing lights of a spaceship that would take the girls and me away to another planet. I know in my heart aliens would have more compassion than some of my fellow human beings.

I smile, imagining the three of us flying across the night sky. Gwen's little face pressed up against the window, her eyes wide with amazement. Arianna would be free to sit on my lap and hug me and love me and I her, like we had done all of her life until now.

Is my imagination a weakness or a strength? If it makes me think and feel – even for a minute – that I am okay, that the girls are okay, isn't it okay? Or am I delusional? Who am I really that I can journey away from reality into my imagination and find peace and even joy in those moments?

The closer I get to the light the brighter it is and the more expansive. On top of the horizontal green, with most of the sky sideways, as if a giant artist had brushed it in a state of great joy and hope, are vertical strokes of red and orange and pink and yellow.

Is it the exhaust of a departing spaceship? The aftermath of the Fourth of July? No. Too late for that. Then I remember the Aurora Borealis. The Northern Lights.

"Oh My God," I say in hushed awe, my hand over my mouth. I am dramatic like my mother.

They are named after the Greek Goddess of Dawn.

A stirring of hope remains within me for the next hour as I continue on the highway and then exit into the complete darkness of Solon and Athens. I slowly make my way along winding back country roads, enveloped, except for the narrow snake of the road itself, in deciduous trees; tangled, wild, and black against the fading Northern lights and the moonlit sky.

The Northern Lights are as much a part of me as the dark shadows on the old country road and the ominous complexities of my life. They are all a part of my creation. I understand we are co-creators in this universe. But why, dear God, would I create someone like Helleen Kramer? She was much more dangerous than John. He was a helpless puppet under her spell.

A half hour later, I leave the back road and enter a dirt driveway and then into a field in Solon. Miraculously, in my headlights, in a field, is the bus. Could a bus sleep? Would I be disturbing something it did at night, like dreaming or hunting? God, I can't turn back now without written directions. What was I doing here?

Women understand, maybe more than men, that there are certain events, like giving birth, that can't be turned back. Accepting my fate with this kind of certainty, I take a deep breath; turn the keys and the engine dies.

Why was I always on these adventures? I had anxiety in normal life, never mind putting myself into strange circumstances. I sigh again, more heavily.

It was my mother and her ancestors, the Spanish, especially the girl with the flowing black hair, who had dared to leave her Spanish village and elope and sail the seas with the love of her life, the Scottish Sea Captain who was my great-great-great grandfather. It was her fault. It was in my blood. I had to explore unknown territories. Or is it something else? What had motivated me to drive alone at night to visit a strange man who many believed was a criminal?

I step out of the car. I think it is grass. I can't see. I scratch an itch on my calf. A bug or the tips of the grass?

Crickets chirp and a small raven or a crow (who could tell, everything is black, it could be a vulture or a vampire) disturbed from its perch, maybe, by my headlights, makes a hurried departure; its wings pushing air. Why was he flying away? Didn't they ever see headlights up here?

Is Raven even here? Where would he go? What am I doing here? Don't I know what is normal?

Scott, a missionary in India, is probably wearing a long black robe and preaching. Was he the old fashion fire and brimstone kind of preacher? Traitor. My eyes fill with tears.

I still love him deeply.

As mad as I am at his choice to become a missionary, I wish he were here tonight. He could hold up a crucifix at the front door of Raven's bus. For a few wild seconds, I seriously consider Christianity, in the traditional sense, and then give it up, knowing I love the earth. Why would I even consider for a second they considered opposing forces? They certainly are not.

Well, I am a Christian anyway. I love Christ. I grew up a Christian Scientist. He was a great man whose teachings had been insanely perverted by the Christian male hierarchy. I thought the Pope was a nut. A cult leader.

My intuitive feelings about Christ had been acknowledged and deepened when I recently read The Gnostic Gospels by Elaine Pagel. Unable to put the book down I read it through the night, excited that Christ's true teachings were being revealed to the world. The secret gospels of Christ were buried deep in the Egyptian desert and were unearthed by an Arab peasant, Pagel had explained. Carbon dating had proven their authenticity.

I felt in my heart they were Christ's true teachings. He spoke of a deep love for the divine feminine he called Sophia. He had wanted his wife Mary Magdalene to carry on his teachings after his death. He believed that humans and God were indivisible. The Divine existed in all of us.

No wonder his gospels had to be hidden. The priests would have lost control of the masses of people doomed to find God only through the Christian hierarchy of men; and women, and their powerful connection to the earth, would have been honored and respected.

As I waded through the thigh-high grass, I thought about the other normal men in my life.

My heart races, and my palms break into a sweat, but it is better than the dread I felt in Bath tonight.

I walk closer to the bus, the long-wet grass lapping and tickling my legs.

A dirty kerosene lantern hangs from a pine tree branch. From its subdued light an elongated, troubled shadow crosses the door of the bus. I hear Native American drums. Does he have a tape player? Sage smoke drifts in the air. I step closer. Through a grimy bus window, I see three small white candles are lit and perched inside of a piece of gnarled wood, like three swans on a rowboat on a dark lake.

Three priestesses in white and Avalon and the apple orchards and the lake where Lady Morgaine threw Raven's sword Excalibur. What made me think of Avalon, the legendary home of the ancient Goddess culture?

I knock. The door opens immediately, squeaking. He must have been watching. The stairs are dark and dirty and the rubber is torn and hanging from one of the steps. Not much like the entryway at my house, with the forest green wallpaper with the cream-colored hydrangeas, wrought iron lamps, the Victorian couch, and the antique wool braided rug.

He stands, staring down.

"Hi, Raven. It's me. It's Jane. I didn't have anything to do tonight. Thought I'd come for a visit," I pile the words on top of each other. I suddenly don't know what drew me here. Why am I here?

He is silent. He holds a thread and needle in one hand and a half-completed earring in the other. Purple. A purple beaded earring.

"I would have called if you had a phone (pause). Guess I could have sent smoke signals."

Oh, that's great Jane. Start out with a solid dose of Hatch sarcasm, which is always a thinly veiled insult.

"No. I'm sorry. I shouldn't have said that. Sorry. I …Can I come in?" I ask, meekly.

I am all alone and defenseless and have insulted him.

He moves aside. Why isn't he speaking?

My inner monkey urges me to make things really bizarre by mentioning Tarzan. "No," I think, reprimanding myself silently.

I walk up the stairs and stand in front of him. He is half naked, as usual, except for pants. Old, torn jeans. He never wears a shirt. Barefoot.

I look at my feet and my pink-painted toenails. I'm reminded of cotton candy. My toenails and gold slippers seem suddenly garish and cheap beside the dark stones on the floor

I imagine the stone family trying to be polite but whispering amongst them, "Look at that carnival pink nail polish. Nothing earthy about her!"

I try to shuffle at least one of my feet under an old newspaper, but before I do Raven comments.

"Your toes look pretty," Raven says, setting down the needle and thread and earring.

I find his comment endearing and suddenly think maybe he has lived other lives when he wasn't just a Tarzan guy; a lifetime he was a gentleman; distinguished; refined. I think of England. I see a beautiful old mansion in the city. We are together. Not as a couple, but as something else. Could we have lived another life together, the way I did with Scott and Donny? How did he fit into the complex web of my soul's purpose?

I hear a loud crack. I turn my head quickly in the direction of the sound.

"It's the fire," he says quietly," I just added more wood. To make it hot, for you." He was talking in a whisper.

"You're always cold," he adds, like he knows me better than I know myself.

"Thank you."

I am not sure what he means or if I should thank him. He did bring me hot stones to sleep with the night we had all camped in the field next to the ceremonial grounds. I am cold a lot.

He sets down the needle and thread and the earrings. He must want his hands free.

I think of the deer that he killed with his knife. Jesus Christ. It was another story told around the campfire. Raven had hidden himself in a tree on a mountain in Washington. He was hungry. He spent a lot of his time watching animals, so he knew their habits. He waited silently for four hours in the tree and then jumped onto the back of an unlucky buck as it passed under the tree. He slit its throat with his knife. At least that's what he told us.

I put my hand to my throat

I feel the life seeping from the deer and I breathe deeply to remind myself I live. I am not the deer. Or am I?

"I'm sorry I just showed up here ... I'm sorry. I just. There's a lot going on in my life. I wanted to get away."

His face is mostly in the shadows, except for the left side of him, which is illuminated by the candles and the flicker of the flame from the small wood stove. Strong jaw, wide forehead, large head, dark hair, just like Scott. I realize they are both Danish.

He stands, smiling, a thumb hooked on his belt loop. I remember the rain soaking into the rim of his jeans.

"Well, I knew you were coming," he says.

"You did?"

"Yes. There were signs."

I don't know what to do or say. I'm frightened, but still glad. I am grateful for the distraction he provides. I look at the rose quartz and pick one up and hold it to my heart.

I lean against the long steel pole still holding the pink stone. Judgments about myself and Raven begin to evaporate. My heart is beating in unison with the pulse of the stone. The fire seems merry now. My breathing is steady. My daughter's faces appear in my mind. My whole body is heavy now.

"Can I sit?"

"Yes."

He pulls out another stump from somewhere and I sit. I tell him my story of what is happening. He smiles and nods when it is most helpful. Finally, the tears fall.

His strong hand grips my wrist. It is like the hand of a tree, if a tree could reach out to me. Solid. Gnarled. Dark. Ashes or burnt wood. He pulls me towards him. He gathers me into his arms and I lean my forehead on his chest where there were raindrops. My tears roll down his chest.

His arms fold around me like the dark wings of a Raven. Am I being enclosed, shut off, or enveloped into love? I'm not sure. It is another world inside the black shiny wings of Raven. But this was my goal – to leave behind, at least for a night, a life that was becoming unbearable.

The drumming is loud; the rocks vibrate with the beat of the Indian drums. A collective heartbeat. I enter a world of brilliant blue skies, and herds of roaming buffalo; my ancestors are alive and well. I see a chief. A feathered bonnet... He looks familiar... He looks like Raven...

In his arms I become who I was or what I am but I have somehow forgotten. Clean, clear swift-moving rivers. The fish are not dying. Wild paint ponies run free in pale yellow fields. Is this what is inside of me? He takes me away to a world so far away, yet right inside of me. Deep inside.

There is more. In him, I feel a rage. Deep. Betrayal. Who betrayed him? Oh God, what path have I chosen? It did not matter, for this night I am again riding a Painted Pony across The Plains and my long black braids are whipping in the wind and I am free.

CHAPTER 28

ACADEMY GREEN

"What did Daddy say, Mommy?" Gwen asks, her eyes hopeful, almost excited, but also, something else, fearful.

It's two months later and I have lost my house, and we are living (Gwen and I) in a low-income housing division beside Hyde School. John is planning on going out to sea for three months and wants the girls to be with Helleen. Arianna will no longer come home at all. I've asked John if Gwen can, at least, be with me. I'm only barely holding myself together, as I'm in constant anguish for the loss of my first-born daughter. Night and day are a nightmare. John will do nothing to help Arianna. he considers it a victory that Arianna has been alienated from me. He wants to be with the winners. But Gwen is so excited that she and I will be together full time. I've asked John if he will agree that Gwen needs to be with me.

Her perfect face is pale.

I want to take her and run as far away as possible. Where would I go? I have no family or money. I see my friends less and less. I feel isolated from the community these days. Helleen has planted seeds of suspicion.

If Arianna had died or been kidnapped, the town would have gathered around me with praise and support and love and money and tuna fish casseroles. Instead, people assume I am a bad mother or a drug addict or both.

People talk in whispers now at Burgess Market. If I dare to go into Arianna's school or call the new doctors, officials are skeptical and unresponsive to me. The receptionist at the dentist office had held her hand over the phone.

"It's her. The mother," she said. They said they could not reveal any dental information about Arianna.

Sometimes I knew exactly what Helleen told people, other times I could only imagine. If I defended myself, if I was upset; if I got angry, a certain cynical knowingness flickered in people's eyes and they would withdraw further from me. It was as if, by asking the question, I had confirmed the negative information.

"He's going to talk to Helleen," I lied.

I could not tell her that within a matter of five seconds he had rejected her truth. But what do I say? What do I withhold? What will break her? What will give her hope?

Her face pales even more. I am horrified. I have made it worse. I want to scream. I want to murder them both. John and Helleen. But then they will have won and Arianna and Gwen will be completely alone and I will be in jail for the rest of my life. In any court system, but especially in Bath. When I was a reporter, I was told disturbing stories from the women, mostly poor women, who passed through the judicial system in Bath whose words and testimonies were ignored or twisted against them.

It is a misogynist system at best. I suspected worse. Much worse. There were stories about how they garnered power. My fate would be horrifying.

I gently gather her hands in mine and smile. Her curled fingers are cold. Her fingertips are the tips of icicles on my palms. She is motionless and stares at our hands, tears falling onto her knuckles and then dripping off and disappearing.

"Oh," she says, weakly.

God give me strength. To truly stand with her. There are no words now. I kiss her cheek and put my arms around her and hold her close. I feel there is not much time left for her to understand love.

The next weekend she came home on Sunday from a visit with her father. She looked far worse, even (if it was possible) than when she had left on Friday. She departed with dark circles under her eyes and an outbreak of shingles on her neck and upper chest. She was also wetting the bed.

Her father and Helleen dropped her off with her overnight bag and made a hasty departure from the Academy Green Parking lot. I was looking out Gwen's window when I saw them and Arianna's head through the back window of the van. It was her. I knew her hair. The shape of her head. To see her, but to never talk to her or hold her hand or just be her mother in all the thousands of ways mothers are mother; the visible and invisible; to know if she slept well or didn't; to take her shopping like other mothers and daughters; to see her school work; to meet a new friend; to tie her sneakers; to read a book; mostly just to be. To be together. Each breathI breathed was shattered glass in my lungs. Living was almost unbearable. I thought about her a thousand times a day.

I ran down the stairs to meet Gwen.

Before I even open the door, she enters wearing her puffy pink ski parka. She was looking down, her hair covering her eyes. She looked worse than when she left on Friday. If that was possible.

She departed with dark circles under her eyes and an outbreak of shingles on her neck and upper chest. She had wet the bed four out of five nights. I told her she did not have to go back to her father's. She said she had to go back. She had to see Arianna. She mumbled something about "Dad will be mad" if she didn't. I advised her not to go until we could figure everything out.

My concern increased her anxiety. I observed her expressions of doubt and fear and confusion when I suggested this. She was getting confused in some very deep way. I sensed she was unsure of the world in general. I sensed her pulling away from me. Somewhere inside of her I was suddenly one more person trying to control her actions. She was going inside of herself. This was terrifying...

I had to let her go...back to her Dad's. At least it made her feel in control. Of something. Her physical body.

But she was home now. Thank God. I followed her gaze down her arm to a few sheets of lined paper she held stiffly in her right hand.

"Hi. Honey,"

Like someone who is drowning is happy for those she loves whose heads are still above the water line. I was grateful she was home. Each time she departed I thought she might not return. I knew the pressure she was under not to come back to me. On Sunday afternoons Helleen invited her to parties or to go shopping in Freeport or rent special movies or get ice cream cones. The list was endless and mind-boggling. Gwen, for one so young, bravely declined. This infuriated Helleen.

She would tell her she was grounded for the next visit or would be left behind on a trip to Disney World or not receiving any new clothes when she and Arianna went shopping next weekend. If she was mad, and Gwen was there during a weekday, she had Gwen walk two miles to school alone with her trombone and heavy backpack in the rain.

Helleen contained within her psyche a mind-boggling array of both threats and rewards. If there was a witness, she delivered her lines within a context of being helpful.

For instance, if a friend like Mathew or Helen or Janie Crowley or a relative, like John's mother, was at their home at the time Gwen was scheduled to leave to come home to me, she would invite Gwen to stay, adding, with a sincere and humble smile, I had "difficulties" these days. She inferred Gwen would have clean clothes or get to bed on time or get her homework done if she stayed with Helleen.

If an opportunity to discredit me arose unexpectedly she could create a dialogue with her as a victim within seconds.

She committed crimes against children without remorse or guilt. Lies spilled from her mouth as if within her she had an endless reserve and she would never be discovered. The lies were told without consciousness. No trace of guilt.

I often learned what Helleen said from Gwen, who would let it slip, during dinner or while walking, or when we paused during reading books. She never wanted to implicate anyone, even Helleen. She just repeated things she was told or had overheard. Helleen talked about me in front of her and over the phone to friends and family. To anyone who would listen. Gwen wondered why Helleen would say those things as she knew they were not true. To me, John robotically repeated Helleen's accusations.

Matthew and Helen repeated to me what was being said around town; so did other people includinng Janie, Jessie, Victoria, Nyree, Leila, Helen, Matthew; teachers at school, librarians, book store owners, receptionists, the local dance teacher. Helleen knew my paths. She knew my trails. She infiltrated in seemingly innocent ways; she always wanted to "help" by dropping seeds of doubt in people's minds about me.

Many people fell for her lies. Some people were confused. Only a few had the strength and courage and insight to completely reject her. Those people often paid a high price. They would soon discover rumors circulating about them. Helleen would find inroads to their friends or jobs or other family or social circumstances and begin to discredit them.

I saw a pattern in the people who were most likely to fall under her spell. It was those who considered themselves the most intelligent, the most educated and sophisticated.

The poorest of the poor were not as easily fooled. They also had nothing to lose. They were becoming my allies.

It was astonishing what was happening in the town.

My stepmother and stepfather, compared to Helleen, now seemed like simple fools in a scary old fairy tale. Hardly malevolent. Neither of them intelligent or calculating.

Nothing in my entire life prepared me for this level of insanity and evil. Helleen is intelligent. She is also educated; a Bowdoin college graduate with a MSW degree in social work. It made her dangerous. She is also a certified mental health therapist. She can spin therapeutic verbiage that sounds logical and helpful. Who would suspect her?

She did not make mistakes.

It took me two years of watching and observing to totally grasp the truth; to understand the gravity of our situation. I learned she perceived herself as saintly and self-sacrificing and wanted the rest of the world to adhere to this image. Her self-promotion was powerful.

The lie is so big, it is almost invisible. Unless you see it every day on your child's face. I cannot walk away. My mother, unable to bear the pain of losing me, went to California with Hal to try and escape. But it did no good.

Every little girl she saw was me. Every child on bicycle was me. Every little girl on a swing was me. She tried to kill herself. I Knew from her experience there was no escape. I would have to bear witness to this unfolding horror. I could not run away. Again, in my life, there was nowhere to run.

CHAPTER 29

CHOCOLATE CHIP COOKIES

The phone rings and I pick up the phone in the kitchen and the whole house darkens. My stomach turns acid. But that's the way it is now. All the time. When I answer the phone.

Ever since Gwen's letter, it's gotten worse. I could feel it. It felt like a predator was watching me from atop a high tree hidden in dark, lush, foliage. It was watching with curiosity and a growing hostility because all former attempts to kill me had failed and now he or she was analyzing how to make a more efficient strike.

It had found I could not be manipulated or threatened. Nothing in the world would make me believe Gwen had lied. It was Helleen, of course. I was feeling a change in her energy. I should be hopeful. John was leaving in two weeks.

Arianna would have to return. Gwen would be freed from her task of visiting her sister and her father – feeling responsible for both of them. Gwen would be free from the confusion, the lies, the betrayal, the extreme loss, her nightmares.

She would begin to heal. Arianna's nightmare would end and her childhood restored. My nightmare, which began when I opened my eyes each day, would end.

Arianna could be freed from her enslavement. Helleen understood this. She somehow knew that I was the one who could free the girls. No one else. Certainly not John who had become enslaved himself. Certainly, none of our friends or John's family had come to rescue Arianna and Gwen.

It seemed the entire community had been silenced, restrained, cursed by this woman – either by overt or covert threat – or simple confusion. If all else failed she would fill people with conflicting information until they simply retired into the simplicity of their own lives,believing, suddenly, it was all none of their business.

I sensed a shift in the level of her malevolence. Helleen was assimilating new information about me. I could not be manipulated. She no longer bothered to call and convince me that Gwen was lying. Even John was at a loss for words, which only meant one thing. She was no longer telling him what to say. The onslaught of verbal sewerage had retreated to its origins – the deranged mind that lay beneath her enormous skull. She was thinking.

Through the airwaves that linked all living beings, I felt her brain flipping through an inexhaustible supply of cataloged recipes for causing despair and grief. These were always executed in her perfect demeanor of humility, sacrifice, intelligence, and slight confusion – as if she would rather be changing her babies diapers or shopping "at the market" as she called the grocery store, than talking about me. She was more perfect than perfect in her disguise.

There was a reason I was beyond her threats and manipulations. It was simple. It was inconceivable to me that Gwen lied. I could see her soul as clearly as her face or the rainbow that crossed over Academy Green that day I met the angel. To doubt Gwen, even for a millisecond, was beyond my comprehension. It would be to doubt the existence of the universe. They were both plain to see. My body registered the completeness of her truth as did my mind and spirit.

It felt as plain as a blade of grass. Who wouldn't feel the same about their daughter? Who wouldn't do exactly as I did? Aren't we all the same like that? We see the truth and speak it? What else is there to live for? What else but love and truth gave life meaning and purpose?

But still I felt the shift in Helleen's game – almost imperceptible, but distinct, like a change in the direction of the wind.

I picked up the receiver. The bell on Gwen's bike ding-a-linged in the parking lot where she was riding and she laughed. Raven dropped the wrench against another. It must be a heavy one to clunk, not clink, on impact.

"Hello," I said, nervously. My throat went dry. My heart thumped hard against my chest. My hands were sweating. What horrid rumor would I hear about myself that Helleen had told? I sometimes thought I would hear that Arianna was dead and no one knew who killed her, but Helleen would be leading the funeral ceremony. My terror knew no bounds these days. Five times a day. Seven days a week. My body went through this torture when I went to answer the phone.

I had no choice. I had to answer. But How long could my heart last? It could only go so long under the constant adrenaline. I had to answer. If Gwen was gone it could be her. She needed me to come get her. She was scared. If Gwen was here, it could be the one time Arianna calls me to tell me she wants to come home. I had to keep putting my hand into the fire hoping one day her hand would be there to meet mine.

"Jane. Yeah. It's John," I hear.

Now my heart is beating in terror. This could be horrible. He hasn't called in a while.

His voice is empty, callous, unfeeling.

I lean against the kitchen wall and close my eyes and brace myself for incoming pain. What horrors will flow? Dear God, now I know why my mother fled to California when she gave up the custody battle and lost me. The torture my father inflicted on her must have been unbearable. What cruel men my mother and I have known. It is strange they are both from Bath and the coveted and spoiled sons of overly adoring mothers. I did not know what that meant. I only knew I could not run away from Arianna and Gwen. I knew the agony that would follow for them. I also knew it did not help my mother. She tried to commit suicide in California.

"What?" I respond, quietly. It's hard to speak.

"Yeah, ah... I'm leaving next week for California. I'm shipping out," he says.

There's something wrong. This should be good news for Arianna and Gwen and I; my stomach has shrunk to the size of a piece of acid rock.

"Well, I know. I'm expecting Arianna back..." I say, but feel I am on the Titanic and we have just hit the iceberg and no one knows but me.

"Yeah. Well, I don't think so, Jane," he says, icily.

"What? What do you mean?" I respond, acting as if hell and death were descending.

"Helleen thinks we shouldn't interrupt her schedule." He responds. His rage is contained but I can feel it threw the wires.

"Helleen thinks... what do you mean, Helleen thinks..." I ask, my heart beats wildly and hard against my chest. Terror.

"Yeah... she thinks..." he begins, more confident, now that he has gotten the evil words out of his mouth.

"What Helleen thinks doesn't matter, John. You're their father for God sake... I am their mother. You and me, John. It's our decision. If you love Arianna and Gwen... if there is anything left in you that is human and compassionate ...and you care at all about the emotional health of your two beautiful daughters you have to wake up. Please."

Silence. I feel – no. I know I have reached him. Somewhere inside I've touched him.

1....2.....3.....4.....5....6....

The seconds pass. It's taking too long. I am furious, but I soften my voice.

"John?" I beg.

8....9....10....

It's too late. I've lost him. It's over. I can feel it. He almost reached his heart, and then it was over.

"No...no...Jane. That's not true. Helleen is an expert in these matters. She's a licensed therapist for God's sakes. She knows what's best for the girls," he says, with a callousness that is both stunning and horrifying.

"And you're fucking paranoid. Everyone knows that, Jane. You think Helleen's out to get you and you think there's an evil triangle out there" he continues, with vengeance, with a growing sense of victory and, sadly, tragically, while destroying what remained of the mental health of his daughters.

It was not enough for him to tell me his wife wants to keep both of my daughters away from me permanently. He wants me to think I am insane. He had to pour salt on a weeping wound. He had to try to totally crush me even if it meant destroying our daughters, too. Why? Why? What had I ever done to him? I'd loved him and our daughters and never said a mean thing to him. I'd cared about his family – been a loving mother. I even just let him walk away from me without any kind of fight. Just gave him back his freedom.

I hang up the phone...

I slip to the floor and bury my head in my arms.

CHAPTER 30

THE WITCH OF HARPSWELL
(AND EVEN DEEPER INTO THE CURSE)

Purple glass earrings glitter in a single beam of moonlight filtering through the soft night clouds. It is all part of the spell that I still believe is my dream.

I sit crossed-legged in long beach grass holding the earrings in my open hand. The meadow, by day a yellowish green in the sunlight, by starlight, softened to a milky dark blue. I am bordered by clusters of healthy pine trees, damp from the ocean air; their needles glistening in the moonlight. A comforting energy seems to both rest and move silently through the woods.

Beyond the trees, both to my left and right, and straight ahead, past Bailey Island, is the cold Atlantic Ocean.

This is Harpswell, Maine. A small fishing village seven miles from Brunswick and a solid fourteen from Bath.

I hold the earring between my thumb and forefinger and stroke the beads with the pad of my thumb. I shudder in response to their perfect smoothness and brilliance in the moonlight.

I suddenly remember the night, when I was a little girl, when I sat on the wet grass beside my father's corn garden in Hanover and held a rhinestone broach up to the moon, hoping my mother would see its light reflected and know I was trying to communicate.

No one would let me talk to her or see her and I thought we could have a secret code in the stars. It was the same night I dreamt about the waves covering Hanover.

I am still waiting for my mother to come home, even though she visits me now in her yellow Honda Prelude. It's not the same mother. It's not the little girl's dream.

Recently, I dreamed of waves rising over Bath.

Waves as tall as mountains.

Down the hill is the teepee, where Raven and I now sleep. Inside, Raven made the purple Indian earrings by the light of the campfire with a thin, curved metal needle and wax thread. I had watched him, silently, from deeper inside the teepee; hypnotized by his rhythmic motions, the hot fire that crackled between us, and the howling of the ocean wind around the teepee. The wind disturbed me, as if it was trying to communicate something ominous.

How was that possible?

I had escaped Bath – at least. I close my eyes, feel the damp, cool wind on my cheeks. The air is pure. So different from Bath.

Something nasty is growing in Bath. Whatever beauty – physically, emotionally, spiritually – I had once experienced there, is gone. It saddens me. I am desperate to find home, to find relief from the agonizing pain of my daughter's being away from me and being abused by their stepmother.

I rise swiftly to my feet from my Indian posture (I am limber from doing yoga every morning, so do this in one smooth movement) and stroll through the grass to the top of the mound and look to the ocean, brilliant, breathtaking, and black, with thousands of diamonds where the moonbeams touch the waves, as far as I can see.

Bath is beyond these waves. Closer by sea than by land. I blink back tears.

English ancestors, the Hatch's, had lived in Bath since the 1800's. I think they came from Plymouth, Massachusetts and before that, Devonshire, England. I knew my father went back to Bath, England once to visit some Hatch's there. Maybe they were ancestors of those who had fled England during the short reign of the infamous English Queen, Bloody Mary, who was burning Protestants who would not revert to Catholicism.

One thing I was sure of. My father hated the Catholic religion, and the hierarchical structure, including, and maybe mostly, the Pope. And for no reason I could fathom.

The people I knew who disliked or hated Catholicism were Catholics. Like my old boyfriend Billy from Needham. He got hit by nuns with rulers at Catholic school. Or my ex-husband, John. He grappled with images of burning in a fiery hell for having slept with me before we were married.

The only living Hatch relative from Maine was Uncle Dan, my father's younger brother. I think he was afraid of me. He had never invited me to his cottage on the ocean in Popham, even when I was a young mother, living alone with my baby (Arianna) in an old house on Route 209; a half a mile from him and his new wife, Ann. I chuckle. He had divorced Betty, who, sometime in the sixties, took acid one day and ran out of the house, happy and naked. It must have been quite the scene in their conservative town of Bedford.

Adventuresome women did not fare well with the Hatch men.

I was beginning to realize I wore the scarlet letter, daughter of infidel and had all the uningratiating qualities (to the reserved Hatches) attached to an infidel.

Suddenly, as I continue to gaze out over the diamond-strewn ocean, and brush the tips of the wild grass with my fingers, I feel an unusual closeness to my father, even though I was now further exiled from his life

My father is a heretic, as am I, I realize, almost laughing out loud at the irony.

Mary Baker Eddy, founder of Christian Science, would have been hung from the highest tower in Catholic England. Yet, my father had fully embraced the teaching of one of America's leading female "spiritualists."

I would never forget, as a young girl, visiting, with my father, the French New Orleans-inspired Captain's houses on Washington Street in Bath, the homes of my father's childhood friends. I was a wide-eyed little girl enchanted with chandeliers, oriental rugs, ballrooms, thick silk curtains set to the sides of the long floor to ceiling windows … and something else I could not name back then, which I now know as elegance and grace. I was his little princess.

I had been in a state of speechlessness at the ornate colorful beauty of the homes; so different from the flat, unadorned white ranch houses of suburban Needham.

Bath felt like home. I spent my life, until I was 24, waiting to come back.

When did it become dangerous? It was not just Helleen. Something fundamental had changed in Bath. Had she ushered in this change when she arrived? She couldn't be that powerful. Maybe there was an alignment between the negative forces in both Bath and Helleen that had strengthened them both.

A terrible karma created from building ships armed with nuclear warheads had arrived in Bath?

But that was not all of it. The evil felt not only collective and karmic, but individual and personal and unlike the ghost that had followed me home from the haunted house in Bowdoinham when I was a reporter for the *Kennebec Journal*.

163

Maybe, I thought, grimacing, and then looking up (gratefully) at the clean starry sky of Harpswell, the horrible energy in Bath was related to ceremonies held in the woods behind the Dike Newell elementary school on High Street. That is what my friend Brenda, the psychic, said to me a few years ago. I was a poor recipient of the information. I disbelieved in evil.

I wanted to forget what she had said, but it was still clear in my mind.

"There's a group of people in Bath. People with social standing. Like judges and town politicians who are into some very bad stuff," she reported, somberly, holding an abalone shell with dried sage burning – the smoke blurring her face.

My stomach convulsed.

We had just finished a pipe ceremony with a couple of healers from the Bath area, including a pipe carrier who also performed sweat lodges in Woolwich. Myself and these two other women were sitting cross-legged on her plush red wall-to-wall carpet in her small living room. Like a robust Italian queen Brenda sat upright in her white leather chair with soft fat armrests.

"Who? What are you talking about?" I asked, with trepidation – still innocent.

"They're up to no good," she responded, ominously.

"Part of the reason we did this ceremony today was to bring healing energy to Bath. I go up to where they do their nasty business in the back of the school. We energetically cleanse the area. But I can't keep up with it by myself," she added.

How did she dare try? Was it even possible for one person to hold back a tide of evil?

I realized now, that deep down, I had been counting on it.

Bluish white smoke from a birch-wood fire still smoldering on the floor of the teepee spirals out of the hole at the top, where twenty stripped and polished thin pine trees, which are the skeleton of the teepee, interlace, like so many long fingers.

I turn away from the ocean and walk back towards the teepee. My body relaxes and thoughts of Bath drift away into the clear starry sky with the birch smoke.

On the heels of relief is an uncomfortable jumble of thoughts of a dozen other problems unresolved. As if I could really relax. I was still in the middle of a war to save my daughters from a truly evil stepmother.

Raven, shirtless and wearing faded jeans torn at both knees and battered-up sneakers, sits on a rock and pounds on his African drum, a gift from his old girlfriend, Kim, with the pointed chin. "A Virgo," he said to explain the chin) who he lived with in a cabin on a mountain in Washington where bears and cougars prowled their yard at night and hawks dropped salmon from the sky. "For us to eat," he explained.

Sweat beads on his oily, well-muscled chest, even though it is night and cold air is rising up from the earth. His skin is soft and hot. The water beads on his body. Staring at him from my perch above him on the mound, I am both repulsed and attracted.

It was Raven who convinced me to leave Bath and Academy Green. He said he would build us a house near the ocean; a log cabin; and he would make money selling his jewelry and building other people their own houses. I could, he had suggested, grow herbs and make herbal medicines and finish my screenplay. I would be safe, he had said. The girls would be safe.

I am both orphan and outcast. Cut from the pack by a black wolf called Destiny. A long time ago, I imagine. When I was seven years old and my mother left me. There is something about a young girl without a mother. Something desolate, like an island in the middle of a cold sea, never to find a mainland.

No one ever took her place. No loving Aunt, or grandmother or sister ever had a kind word or loving touch for me. I was raped, drugged, ignored, hated resented sexualized betrayed, and abandoned by the males in my so-called family. I was more like an animal in a cage that had been prodded with an electric rod to test my endurance.

Maybe if my mother had been less beautiful, less passionate, less spiritual I would have been set free.

The wind soars through the hemlock branches above my head. I stare out at the ocean.

I scoff out loud.

To think I had found love and acceptance in John's large family. Yes, we had all laughed until our sides hurt, the night in the old house in Popham, where I lived alone with Arianna after she was born and when John was out to sea. But they had all disappeared. They had all abandoned me. They must be blind to the abuse John and Helleen are inflicting on the girls. How could they? I was enraged at their silence.

I look up at the night sky and clouds racing across it. The wind in the treetops whistles low, like a spirit come to speak…

I bite my lip to keep back the tears. As if this pain could be contained! Arianna. My baby girl. Gone. I could not see her dance in shiny black patent leather shoes on the pumpkin pine floors. Did she dance anymore?

165

Did she paint anymore? Did she play with her Velveteen Bunny? Did anyone read to her? Did she still have a favorite food? It once was brown bread and baked beans.

I wrap my arms around my body to keep myself from tearing apart, and the pieces drifting away with the ocean spray. Like I had always done, with no loving arms to comfort me my whole life.

Dear God, just don't take Gwen, too. I hope I have made the right choice to be here in Harpswell. Raven promised he would protect us. I suddenly feel confused. I feel like Cathy alone with Healthcliff. A wretched loneliness and a kind of mutual strange joy were odd bedfellows. Why is it that the closer I get to Raven – the worse thing always gets for me?

The magic of the night is gone. This is the way it is. A few minutes. Then the agony is back. I cry, my moans muffled by the wind. I press away the tears with my hand.

I look back at Raven, who balances the drum between his knees. It seems he is all I have in the world. I suddenly have to see Gwen.

I run quickly down the hill, past Raven, and the teepee, to the back door of the house, and the glassed-in porch. We have rented half a house from a family – a place for Gwen to sleep and we share the kitchen and bathrooms. I have to see if she is safe. Why wouldn't she be? My heart thumps hard in my chest. I am often afraid now. Raven looks up briefly but is accustomed to my sudden movement. He exhales smoke from his hand-rolled Bugler cigarettes.

"I'll be right back," I offer.

"She's fine," he says, almost indifferently.

I walk up the new steps and inside the house. I see her body sweetly curved under the white down comforter my mother bought at Laura Ashley in Freeport. My heart beat slows. She is okay. She is here. For a few days.

I see her blonde hair tucked behind her ear. Her legs are close up to her body and her arm lies loosely over a purple Dinosaur. A half dozen other stuffed animals are strategically placed – sitting upright in a row facing forward – as if they had been abruptly left at a conference by a speaker who had gone out the front door. Or fallen asleep.

I place my hand on her back and feel the reassuring rise and fall of her body. It is a miracle to me. She has this moment of peace and I can share it with her, even if she is asleep. She must feel my love.

Tomorrow will be different. She will have to go back to Helleen. I contract my entire body, like someone expecting poison forced down their throat while salt was poured on a thousand bleeding wounds on their body. I step back with the wave of terror.

She is everything. I love her more than all the stars in the heaven, yet I have to her release her to torture every few days. If it would save her, I would gladly throw myself into the ocean. If the Gods would be appeased. My death would be my freedom.

Unfortunately, it is not that easy, I think with despair, as if I had been given a life sentence with no chance of parole. If I died there would be no hope for her, or Arianna. I am the only one who believes her. I hold the truth in my heart. The truth will die, if I die.

I hold the truth deep in my heart of hearts like a treasure I must protect. It will save them someday. That's why I can't die or drink alcohol, or smoke pot, or take prescription drugs; because I have to remember everything. So, they will know, when they are older, the Truth.

And love. Love is the only thing I understand. Love is everything.

The moon on her face illuminates her strikingly beautiful pale beauty. "Guinevere," I utter in a whisper, not knowing why exactly, except I am struck by the purity of her soul as well as her long golden blond hair and delicate blue eyes.

I suddenly feel ugly, inadequate, unwholesome, even stupid. Me, who has known only the love of trees and a horse, an old sheepdog. Me, who has been loved by many, but hated by many more. How could I even compare to her, or try to protect her? Why God, did you give me this impossible job? And what a pathetic job I have done.

Maybe if Arianna had a different mother; a mother who could have worked at BIW; who didn't fight the system; who went with the flow of the black beauty poison that drifted through the air in Bath. Instead, she got me. Somehow, I was the mortal enemy of her stepmother.

Arianna had been stolen by Helleen, only to make me suffer and Helleen did not care for my children in the least. Her only purpose with Arianna was to cause me agony. She used her like a pawn in a game invented in hell. And only she knew the rules. Just like the devil would play a game, I thought, horrified, as I always was, when I allowed myself to consider the situation.

I kiss Gwen quickly on her smooth, pale cheek, and run from the moonlit room that still smelled of fresh cut pine.

"Why is my life like this? Who am I? What am I?" I ask, more to the fire, than to Raven. I am numb like a stone. I had entered the teepee and sat on a log stump next to the fire Raven had made while I was looking after Gwen.

Silence. The fire crackles. The wind picks up outside.

"You are the Goddess. Don't you know that Jane?" Raven says, matter-of-factly as he pulls a green Bic lighter from the front pocket of his jeans. A hand-rolled cigarette hangs from his perfectly formed, full lips. He stands beside me.

"Yeah. Some Goddess I am,"

He lights his cigarette, puffs till the tip turns red, and then shoves the Bic back into his jeans. He crouches down beside the fire. The sudden movement disturbs me and I lean away – ever so slightly.

"Your father did this to you," he says and exhales a long stream of cigarette smoke.

"He destroyed you,"he continues, now rocking back and forth on his heels, his black cowboy boots leaving imprints in the dirt.

"I'm not destroyed yet, for God's sake." I retort, feeling suddenly angry, defensive and something else. Trapped?

"Well, no. I didn't mean it that way," he says, not wanting to offend me. Not this late at night.

I feel guilty and confused. In some ways he is just a tool. A means to have escaped Bath. Someone to bring us safety and security. A house. In other ways, he is everything. I love him. I Love what he represents. Another era in time. Buffalo roaming free in herds of millions. A pure earth. A blue sky. Proud warriors. The time of the Lakota Sioux, before their dissolution as the fiercest tribe in America. Why didn't they listen to White Buffalo Calf Woman who told them to live in peace! Even they seem screwed up, all of a sudden. Now, I feel completely alone.

Do I really love him? Somehow, it only seems like a fairy tale gone terribly bad. Had he put a spell on me as the other apprentices believed he did. Why was I in agony every time I tried to leave him? How did I get to this God forsaken Teepee at the edge of the earth off the coast of Maine?

I look up and watch the smoke exit the teepee hole, where twenty, twenty-foot-high pine poles, stripped of bark, interlace, like so many fingers. I had watched Raven from the stand of pines where I clipped sprays of pine needles for smudge bundles. With inhuman energy he had cut and stripped by hand with his knife, twenty trees within two hours. For the teepee.

I look back at his face. Dark like an Indian – his grandmother on his mother's side was part Sioux. Broad across his brow. Must be from his Danish ancestors. High cheekbones. Strong jaw. Like Heathcliff. The villain from my favorite book, Wuthering Heights, by Emily Bronte. Or maybe, I think, mournfully, it is just dirt on his face. Maybe he is just dirty.

"Nothing. I just hope I have not made a mistake coming to Harpswell. I couldn't stay in Bath," I say, pacing now.

"It'll be okay. We'll make it okay," he says confidently.

"Can I really run from evil? Can I run from Helleen?" I begin again, feeling even more anxious and uncertain of everything. The more he tries to make everything okay, the more uncertain I am. I search for a diversion from these disturbing topics. I spot his box of beads.

"What are you working on? I say calmly, even though my stomach is clenched and my heart is beating hard.

"Earrings. For you," he says and puffs on his cigarette. I'm irritated.

"Why?" I ask, something both bold and antagonistic rising up in me. I'm getting tired of his gifts. It kind of reminds me of my mother taking all those gifts from Hell/Hal, a zirconia diamond, amethysts, pearls; not to mention the little yellow sports car and the wigs and other trinkets and toys. Maybe I was doing the same thing – accepting bribes from an abusive man. No, it's not possible. Raven and I are spiritual. He gives me spiritual presents. And he's only raised his voice a couple of times. But there was the time he took my keys...

He crouches down again, wrapping his arms around his knees and resting his chin on his forearm. I am repulsed and fight back a wave of rage and nausea. Suddenly, I know why.

My stepfather, Hal, sat like that on the rug in the living room in Watertown, except he held a Bud tall and a cigarette. He would rock back and forth, heel to toe, just like. Just like that. Hal used to hold his knees and crouch on the floor holding a Bud tall. Just like that.

CHAPTER 31

RUNNING FROM RAVEN

I had finally gotten away from Raven. Again. I was living with my friend, Michelle.

My first thought in the morning is Gwen. How has Helleen punished her for her visit with me? I can only imagine. I choke in fear. Tears stream down my cheeks.

I stare at the white ceiling. The mattress is deflated. I'm sleeping on the floor. No wonder my back hurts. I roll on my side and then stand, my dress unraveling from a tight wave around my legs. Tears flow like I am a river that has no beginning or end. I just am. My whole life, unfelt, is draining. I don't stop anymore for tears just as the river would not stop because of water.

I wipe my eyes. Coffee brewing downstairs in Michelle's white plastic coffee maker reminds me of Raven. It burns, like a monster living in my blood starving and demanding food. I try to erase him from my mind.

Nightmares about my stepfather molesting me had followed the worse one of Gwen falling through glass. Nights when I could not sleep worrying about Arianna and Gwen, I had asked the devil, if there was one, and if indeed he was in charge these days, (which it felt like he was) to take me in exchange for them. Take me and do what you want, but set them free. Set us all free.

So unlike me, with my Pollyanna perspective of the world, to think maybe the devil had power. The lessons of Christian Science taught me evil did not exist. Was this one of the reasons I'd ignored my gut reaction to Helleen when I first met her? I'd felt repelled, as if she were a loathsome poisonous snake beneath her veneer of human perfection. If I'd acted swiftly in response to my intuition, I would have saved the girls. In my mind, bargaining with the devil is the equivalent of going into the Bath Court system in a custody battle. And I wouldn't have to hire a lawyer.

I had also dreamed of my father. It was a sunny day and I was a little girl picking blueberries with him at Fort Popham. In the dream, he left me alone on the hill. "Daddy," I called out. I just stood next to the blueberry bush. He never returned.

I've eaten mostly junk food in the past few days. Candy bars and potato chips. Milk and cookies. Maybe I'm still trying to fill myself up from the hunger I experienced in Needham – where I mostly ate Planters Peanuts.

My real food is still in my car. I feel weak. I'm wearing my clothes from last night. Day and night are no different. They are both nightmares. Why unpack and change costumes over and over again for the same scene?

Michelle suggested I apply for food stamps and welfare. I'm having other health problems. Chemical sensitivity and candida. Anxiety attacks. They are all stress related. I'm becoming allergic to the world. My immune system is breaking down. Michelle refers to the car ride from Bath to Rockland and The Department of Human Services (where you get food stamps and Welfare) as the "trail of tears."

It's a horrifying thought. I wrote about low-income women for the *Kennebec Journal*! I wasn't one of them. Was I? Didn't I have checks coming from somewhere?

I brush my hair apathetically. My dress is torn. It caught on a dead tree branch while I was running last night. It is also stained with blood from a scratch on my leg.

I continue with my hair. I suddenly remember one sunny spring day when I was twenty-two and walking along Fifth Avenue in New York City. I was dressed in a tweed Calvin Klein blazer and skirt, cream-colored silk blouse, and designer boots. Men whistled and stopped to stare. I had smiled and twirled my hair and stared down at the sidewalk – pretending not to notice. The New York Herald had just hired me as their journalist intern for the summer. I was almost out of college with a degree in journalism. I just needed this internship to graduate. A new life was on the horizon.

Dismayed, I dropped my hand with the brush onto my lap. If I had taken the internship in New York where would I be now? What in God's name made me say no? I'd gone back to Needham to be an intern at the Needham Times and rejected the Herald internship. All I'd known in Needham was abandonment and rejection from my father, and terrifying abuse from stepmother. Yet, I was drawn back.

I guess I'd wanted my father. I wanted to have a home before leaving home. I wanted love. I don't know!

He didn't even let me live at the house at Dunster Rd. in Needham while I did my internship at the *Needham Times*. He paid a divorced woman on Great Plain Avenue in Needham to give me a room while I did the internship. I was shocked to my soul at the unfathomable level of abandonment and rejection. How could he? What was so horribly wrong with me I could not even live in the same house with my father?

Dan Eramian, the editor at the *Needham Times*, sensed I was deeply depressed. He let me wander around the countryside of Needham and Dover, looking for stories or taking photographs. I remember lying on the large above-ground roots of a huge oak tree and looking up at the sun through the leaves and branches. I lied there shooting this scene over and over again with my 35 mm Nikon. These photos, like other series I shot, were featured on the front page of the newspaper. At the end of the internship in August, he gave me an "A" for my work as a reporter. I never received one word of recognition from my father. Why had I chosen hell in Needham, now hell in Bath?

If I'd chosen the *Herald* for my internship I might be another Barbara Walters by now. Instead, I am a poor, homeless, tortured woman, fighting to save the souls of her children.

The phone rings in the kitchen. Michelle's voice is muted, then she walks towards the stairs that wind up to the second-floor bedroom.

"Jane. Are you awake? she calls up.

"Yes."

Raven's on the phone. Do you want to talk to him? I told him you were sleeping," she says politely from the bottom step of the stairwell.

I'll talk to him," I respond.

"Are you OK?"

"Yeah. I'm okay"

It is impossible to describe everything that is wrong. Even to Michelle. Besides, no one can take it. It's too much. I've tried to explain. People get distracted, their eyes gloss over, they laugh nervously, they change the subject, they struggle with the right words to say, they think of something happy to tell me, they run away.

Meeting Helleen made me believe in evil. Compared to Helleen, Hal and Marion, my stepfather and stepmother, who I once perceived as evil, now just seem like bad people, training wheels in my spiritual lessons on levels of badness. They are ignorant, violent, hedonistic, self-indulgent, selfish, and greedy, but now I know evil.

I walk down the stairs and into the kitchen.

"Thanks," I say, smiling at Michelle.

I pick up the phone. My heart races.

Shoulder-length brown hair hides Michelle's face and her shoulders droop as she butters an English muffin… Eeyore. She often reminds me of Eeyore. Guilty as charged should be Michelle's motto. And mine. It is no wonder. When I still lived on South Street, I channeled information from spirit guides, who told us we were witches in another lifetime. Both of us had been hung on charges of heresy.

The psychic in Lexington I visited with Scott had offered even more detailed information.

"In another lifetime you were a witch. In England. You wrote something. A book, maybe. A document. I'm not exactly sure what it was. It revealed child abuse by Catholic priests. You were trying to expose them. You had a following of people who believed in you. But you were hunted down by the church authorities and tried on charges of witchcraft and heresy. Your punishment was to hang."

Scott and I had looked at each other, but did not speak, as if we both understood how all of this was possible, even probable. Maybe he had taken my hand.

"Raven?" I say into the phone.

"Jane. Hi. How are you?" Relief that I have picked up the phone is evident. Usually, I will not take his calls. Today, I feel there are *much worse evils than Raven.*

"I'm fair to bad," I answer.

"What's wrong?"

"Everything."

"Like…?" he asks.

"The energy here, Raven. I don't know what it is. It's much more than the toxic fumes from Bath Iron Works. It's horrible. There is something here that hates me – I mean beyond Helleen– that wants to do me in. An invisible force. I don't know. Maybe it has been with me all of my life, but it is much worse in Bath," I respond, quietly.

"It's possible," he says and means it.

Pause.

"How are the girls?" he asks.

"Not good."

"Jane, they would love it here. Where I am. In Woolwich. I think Arianna would come here. I really do. Montsweag Road is gorgeous. And there's a big swing in the living room."

"Really?" I ask, a dim ray of hope, in a world of gray.

Maybe Arianna would come home if I lived in a nice house. In a prior conversation Raven indicated he was employed as a caretaker for an eccentric elderly woman. She was wealthy and provided him with a good weekly paycheck and housing in a beautiful, renovated barn on the river in Woolwich. About ten miles from Bath. He chauffeured Chouteau to her various engagements in the Midcoast area and did repairs and upgrades on her buildings on her property. He had moved away from Harpswell soon after I had left him.

Maybe Arianna would come back, those are the words he uses that he knows I cannot resist. Does he mean it or does he just use those words?

"Why don't you just visit tonight? I have the night off. See if you like it?"

Pause.

"Were you in Bath last night? Around midnight. I thought I saw your car, the Pinto?" I ask, skirting an answer.

"Oh, the Pinto. I don't drive the Pinto anymore."

CHAPTER 32

MONTSWEAG ROAD

The next night at Raven's new place, I stare out the large picture window Raven has installed on the second floor of Choteau's old barn in Woolwich. The moon is a radiant luminescent egg set into a blue-black sky. In Maine, nights are so dark they are almost blue. Like an Indian's hair. The long black hair on Peter Lafford; the Mic Mac Indian from the reservation in Canada. I'd written a song "Mic Mac Madness" about Peter.

Fox tail-shaped clouds race horizontally across the face of the moon as if they are in route to an important gathering of the nature spirits. The narrow, winding Montsweag river, in the near distance, at the bottom of a series of softly cascading hills (which begin at the barn) is a shimmering silver ribbon.

I feel privy to the eternal emotions of nature spirits. At least I am not completely alone. Smiling, I turn to the interior of the huge renovated barn where Raven lives.

English and French antiques, polished brass fixtures, a gleaming wood floor, accented with real oriental rugs, greet my sweeping gaze. A wool L.L. Bean blanket is draped over the back of a blue Swiss dot couch. A thick white sheepskin rug on the floor in front of a massive stone fireplace softens the hard-elegant lines of the room. A shiny brass tea kettle rests on the gas stove and Arrowsic Potters clay coffee mugs hang from a black wrought iron rack near the stove in the "galley" kitchen.

It all reminds me of something. Maybe my grandparents' three-story brick house on Washington Street in Bath, which was demolished by Bath Iron Works in the 1960's. Maybe England. In a vision I'd seen a house, a mansion it could have been called, in England, in a city, probably London, possibly in the seventeenth century where Raven and I had lived together as sister and brother. We had wealthy, but mostly absent parents. It was a rich lifetime creatively. He was a musician and I was a writer.

Two hours earlier, when I first arrived, we had walked at night, on the quiet road in front of the barn that winds gently and continuously, as if a lazy meandering milk cow had set the path centuries ago. Ancient oak trees with long thick roots lined the road. Fields undulated softly in the night wind. Neat white farmhouses with black or red shutters, set deep, and close to the river, in ten and twenty acre lots, were the only signs of human life. And even they were dark.

The evil presence I feel in Bath is absent in Woolwich. Almost immediately, upon my arrival here, relief had flooded my body and soul, although it was strange. *It almost felt like enchantment.* How could I feel such magic, such relief, from my agony, by his presence, by the presence of simple trees and a simple wind. Or was it a simple wind?

To Raven's delight I even skipped, touching the buds on the tree branches. It was out of sync with what was happening in my life.

I had knelt down to caress moss and the tulips and crocuses and lilacs. *The rebirth of life.* The movement of sap in the trees in the spring is my own blood!

As we walked Raven had been quiet, smiling, nodding and occasionally, smoking with one hand, the other stuck into his jeans pocket. Watching, always watching me, as if he was mesmerized by my every movement. He had always told me I was, not just a goddess, but The Goddess. Why did he say that I wonder? Was it what he knew I wanted to hear, like "Maybe Arianna will come back"?

"The rivers of my life," I say to Raven, suddenly.

I walk to the massive fireplace and heat ignites warmth across my face and the front of my body.

"What do you mean?" Raven asks, unwinding his body to a full stance and looking at me squarely. He'd been pushing coals inside the fire with an iron claw. Choteau must pay him well. He's wearing a new green flannel shirt, probably from L.L. Bean. New jeans. Clean-shaven. Handsome – *almost a shapeshifter, I thought, fleetingly.*

I imagine him covered in bear grease and wearing only deerskins (made from the deer he killed and stitched with his own hands) inside a cave, in January, in the Yukon mountains in Canada. I laugh softly.

"What?" he says, and smiles, a little.

"Oh, nothing," I answer, but the glint in my eye must have revealed my lie.

"No, what is it?" he persists, and he is smiling more broadly now. He takes a step towards me. He reaches out like he is about to touch my hair, but then he stops.

I'm not sure. Like a cougar getting close to you; a familiar one, if that's possible. Mesmerized, but a little afraid. It's like a power animal, or someone pretending to be your power animal or ally. *But Raven must be my ally. He must. We are in this together. Right? I am asking myself these questions, in a split second and from a faraway place, from almost a different person, not myself.*

"Just thinking about the year you spent on the mountain. The Yukon. In a cave, covered in bear grease," I say and wonder if it is even true.

He laughs. "Oh Yeah."

He sets down his drink. It seems he might make a step towards me, so I walk away from him back towards the huge plate glass window he has just installed for the owner of the huge renovated barn. I stare out the window at the river that glistens under the stars.

"Everywhere I go. There's a river. Maybe there's a message," I continue, erasing images of deerskin and caves and of Raven's almost naked body in deer skin.

I walk back into the living area of the room. I run two fingers around the base of a shiny brass lamp set on an antique mahogany end-table. I am reminded of home. Somewhere. Certainly, not Needham.

Hanover? Maybe. It was hard to remember all the details of Hanover. Just a feeling.Love.

"The river I loved the most was the Indian Head River in Hanover. I rode a horse in that river. A stallion. An Appaloosa. His name was Misty." I say, remembering, suddenly.

I close my eyes and recall riding Misty through Bunny Woods. The exhilaration is the same.

I open my eyes.

"I had a horse. A black stallion. He was huge. Probably 18 hands. No one else could ride him. He was wild," Raven adds, moving towards the fire.

I know the story. A blond girl named Sue with a badly scarred back. She'd been burned in a fire. She owned a ranch in Montana and was in love with Raven. They both had horses. His was called the Black. Raven found Sue in bed with another man. That was the end of Sue and the Black and the ranch. Raven left her without looking back. That's the way he was. *Except with me. Why does he pursue me so relentlessly?*

"I remember you telling me about Sue and the Black."

"Oh yeah. I guess I did," he responds, slightly embarrassed. Men are embarrassed if they repeat things. Women see repetition as the normal flow of life. The tide comes and goes. The sun sets, the moon rises. Spring returns and so does winter.

"Everything about your life is like a fairy tale," I say, beginning to wonder why Sue had an affair with another man if she was so in love with Raven. Why had she been burned in a fire? Why did tragedy stalk Raven's women?

Silence.

"I mean, who rides a wild black stallion, except for Zorro, or Jafar in Arabian Nights? It just sounds like a movie," I continue.

He shrugs.

"I was young. I was strong. You should have seen me."

"You're still strong. You're still young." I respond, thinking how true this is. Thirty-seven is not exactly old. A sound like tapping cat feet with claws distracts me. I turn to see wet snowflakes on the plate glass window.

"A spring storm," I say, immediately excited.

Fire, water, snow, rain, spring, winter, the earth and moon. The Goddesses Becoming One. One Force. Why all these elements in one night? Is it the Goddess or some kind of other magic?

My body energy is spinning like the snowflakes in the sky under the moon and the rising wind. I am rising up to meet Her, although I already am Her. I am merely borrowing this body for an undetermined period. To contain Her – To express her joy, her compassion, her love, for all beings.

"Jane. Jane." Raven is saying.

I sink back into my body. It is heavy and awkward and very painful. Raven. Helleen. Arianna. Gwen. God, when will this hell on earth end?

I wish Raven and I were free. Free from the horrors of our childhoods, from the agony of my children, from his rage at his many torturers that can turn him into a beast, and me; free from the betrayal of my father that turns me into some kind of black widow… wanting to revenge on all men for my father's betrayal and abandonment, the sexual abuse of the men in my family, I carry within me… If it wasn't for Arianna and Gwen I would run away to the ends of the earth with Raven. I'm just like my mother. She ran away with Hal.

"Jane," he says more adamantly.

I turn to him with tears in my eyes.

"What's wrong?" he asks and concern re-forms his facial features. He sets down the iron claw and walks in my direction.

"I don't know… I'm so tired. Tired of living. I want to give up. I can't stand the pain anymore. I want to go back home. Back to the Goddess," I lament mournfully.

Fresh tears stream down my eyes.

He takes hold of my upper arms with strong hands. Arms that could fell a two-hundred-foot Montana Red Cedar; arms of the Vikings; arms of the Sioux. I understood how a Rasmussen had been the first human to reach the North Pole. Pure will and strength. These truths race through the blood in his arms that hold me now. Hold me up? I don't know. Had he changed? Had he really gone back to his roots and understood the source of his rage; seen his past mistakes, his character flaws?

He is close and I smell wood smoke, tobacco, leather and fire. Like me, he is the Earth. Because there is nowhere else for me to go, I lean into him and grab at his back, muscled and lean under the new green flannel L.L. Bean shirt. Then, I cry. I always cry. He is home. The only home I have ever known, other than Hanover.

We just hold each other for a few moments, and then I lean away and wipe away the tears on my cheeks. It is hard not to be with him, when he is all I have.

"I am such a fuck-up. I can't even save my own daughters," I say.

"You're not a fuck-up Jane. You're just different," he responds, emphatically.

I scoff. "Being different shouldn't mean not being with your children," and the pain sears my stomach. I am nothing but agony and grief. I only stay alive for my daughters.

He pulls away and looks into my eyes. He holds my wrist lightly.

"Don't you know who you are?" he says, earnestly.

"No. I guess I don't have any fucking idea who I am."

"You're the Goddess"

Is he just buttering me up? Suddenly, I'm suspicious. What does he want? It feels artificial. I'm angry and suspicious and I turn away. He turns me back towards him. I stare into his green eyes. Maybe he is sincere. The wind blows the snow, with more pressure and ferocity, into the window. The left side of me, near the window, is cold. The right is hot from the fire.

Everything about him pulls me in. His smell. Smoke. Fire. Leather. Sweat. The strength in his hands, even though they now rest lightly on my wrists.

"I love you, Jane. You know I love you. I'll never stop loving you. From the moment I saw you at Gail's house. I knew. I knew you were the Goddess. That's why I ran through the woods that night."

The wind howls in the stone hearth, whipping the flames higher. The night in the Victorian mansion by the lake in Minneapolis. The snow against the window. The fire in the hearth. The faces. The square Danish jaw and the wide forehead. Scott, oh God. I miss him. It is all the same.

I touch the cleft in Raven's chin. It is the same as Scott's. How could this be?

Raven is motionless, waiting to see how I am going to react to his words. Then he pulls me closer, his hands at my elbows, looking into my eyes as much as I will allow it. My head is tipped forward onto his chest.

He may love me. Maybe the same as Heathcliff loved Cathy. The Beast loved Bella. This wild, monstrous love. But is it love? How would I know? I've never been loved. I don't even think John really loved me. Raven, who does not die from rattlesnake and scorpion bites. What is he?

And I, raised by Trees in Hanover – no mother or father, to speak of – and beaten with the serpent tongue of my stepmother and the sly whiskey-breath of my stepfather – raped, abandoned, ridiculed, who walks now in rags, homeless, begging for knowledge of my daughters, and cursing and pledging, deep down, I would someday, somehow, find my revenge on those who had my stolen daughters.

I am a cursed lonely wolf.

Raven and I were carved from the same Wolf.

I place my hand flat on the center of his chest like I had the Mayan calendar my mother hung on my bedroom wall in Watertown. I try to feel the truth. A thousand unanswered questions race through my mind. How did he manifest this residence so quickly?

Where was his son, Jason? Why did I see his car, the one that I thought I saw in Bath last night, parked in a field near the barn? What did he do to Myrna to cause her to alarm me? Why are people saying that the elderly, white-haired lady, who walks with a cane, with a brass handle, is in love with Raven?

"Red Cloud," I murmur, remembering the dream I'd had when I called him by the same strange name.

He pulls me tight against his chest. Red Cloud was a warrior Sioux Indian Chief; a great warrior. I had seen Raven as Red Cloud, in a vision. Was it possible? Or was I under some strange spell as many of my friends believed. Since I had never had anyone I could trust in the world, how did I know who or what to trust? What did it feel like to have someone I could trust?

The sheepskin rug is soft and thick under my slim, muscular, naked body. I am glad to have thrown off the ragged dress. I wish I could have thrown it into the fire, to burn a part of me to death. A part of me would be free. The fire burns brilliantly in the hearth beside us; sparks sound like gunfire. The spring snow is heavy and wet against the window. The wind howls in the chimney.

Was the Goddess speaking or the devil I did not know. I only knew this terrifying heartless world was fading under the weight of his long lean body and the pressure of his soft, perfect lips on mine. Is it my heart that thunders or the hooves of a thousand buffalo against the hard dirt of the Great Plain? Do I hold a warrior Chief in my arms or is it Raven – or Scott?

Or, no, not that, no, it couldn't be. They all blend into one Man desiring, above all else, the Goddess. Whatever way they can have her. But for what purpose? Thunder and lightning and then soon the world is still and quiet and all is dark like the womb of the Great Mother. The last flame dies and I stay wrapped in his arms all night and there is no pain.

There is the nothingness that I crave more than anything.

CHAPTER 33

CREAM-COLORED SWEATER

I open my eyes.

Beams of sunlight speckled with ashes, stream in over my head, settling on the stone hearth. Flecks of mica embedded in the river stones sparkle in the stone. The fire is out, but in its stead, shiny black charcoal.

I close my eyes. I want to hold on to this tenuous gateway between night and day, before the reality of my life descends.

I am on the couch and naked under the wool Pendleton blanket. I reach for him, but he is not there. I pull the blanket close under my chin, feeling its roughness. Roughness of wool. It reminds me of something; of Arianna.

A child's cream-colored wool sweater – Irish – with tortoiseshell buttons I bought at a yard sale for Arianna. My slender fingers, with the diamond ring from John, buttoning it up to Arianna's chin; her cheeks are pink from the fresh air and playing outside. I smile as she runs in circles playing with a doll.

She stops and hugs me. Her long ash blonde hair has flattened under the sweater, so I gently pull it out and let it fall and then brush away brown leaves stuck to her sweater.

I kiss and hug her and she runs to her friends. She leaves me with the scent of earth and leaves, Fall and chocolate milk. Muddy tracks from her black patent leather shoes had filled my heart with joy. The wind, the air, fire, chocolate, wool, breathing, your own heart beating reminds you of your child. There is no escape.

I force the pain back down into a holding tank in my soul and I choke and bite my lip.

A coffee maker sputters to a halt. Hazelnut coffee. It's his signature.

I close my eyes and try to just smell. Raven's spoon clinks as he stirs the honey in his mug. Focus. Focus. Focus. I freeze thoughts of Arianna and think of something beautiful. The river was silver in the moonlight last night. The river. The river. The river. Remember the flow of the river. Stay alive.

Folding the blanket around my body, I turn and sit up and then stand.

Raven looks at me shyly.

"Well, hello there, bright eyes," he says.

I can't help but smile. I think about the passion of last night and my cheeks flush red and I hike up the Pendleton so it covers my breasts.

"Don't do that, "he says, mischievously.

"Don' t do what?" I ask, but know exactly what he is talking about.

"Cover yourself up," He says, taunting me.

"It's cold," I say and my cheeks burn.

We both smile.

He sits up straighter in the hardback cane chair at the far end of a long handmade pine table. He sips coffee from a huge mug. I sit at the opposite end of the long table. We are King Raven and Gwenifer, or brother and sister or Medicine Woman and Indian Chief, or *something else*. It is something else. Capturer and captured; love and lover? Sorcerer and his victim. He wears an expensive black flannel shirt and new blue jeans.

A strange night. Some of the details elude me. I remember the fire, the whip of the wind, the snow pattering against the glass. I felt more Goddess than human. Almost like I was gone and the Goddess held my place.

I had completely forgotten about any kind of birth control. It was the furthest thing from my mind. Why had I forgotten?

And what of him? Who held his place or was he fully present?

"Coffee?" he asks, holding up a coffee-filled whale tail mug that has thick streams of golden honey running down the sides.

"Sure. I'll get it," I respond, holding the blanket tight against my chest and getting up and moving toward the shiny, blue-tiled kitchen counter. I stare thoughtfully at the wrought iron wrack hung with a variety of made-in-Maine coffee mugs.

From my peripheral vision I see that Raven is scanning the curves and lines of my body. But then he drags his stare to the interior of his cup.

I chuckle lightly. Enough is enough. Maybe.

What was it we did that night in the secret, dark-of-the-moon ceremony in West Athens, Maine; Raven, along with another thirty or so people? We had dedicated our lives to serving the Goddess. What was that all about? Why has that night entered my mind this morning?

I touch a rough, sand and mud-colored mug. I see wild people, like the Saxons – drinking ale from this kind of short sturdy mug. I pass on it. More red, blue and moss green whale tale mugs, like the one Raven is drinking out of – an Edgecomb Pottery design.

I wrote about the people who made these for the Kennebec Journal. The rims are too wide for me. And holding a whale's tail while drinking from the "body" feels awkward; like I'm drinking out of a disemboweled fish.

I pick a tall mug, with a black and white polka-dot handle and delicate purple hand-painted Irises on the cup; it's from Damariscotta Pottery. The delicate blue rim is perfect.

I sigh. The days I happily traveled throughout the community, from artist, to potter, to writer, well-respected and admired for my writing skills, were gone. I was thrown from my village in the twentieth-century Puritan New England, as surely as was Hester and her baby in Hawthorne's great novel of the seventeenth century. *The Scarlet Letter* by Nathanial Hawthorne.

Not much had changed. Except witch-hanging was illegal. But if the same evil existed now, as it did then, would they still try to kill me, just find another way. Talakeal had told me they would not kill me. How did he know?

I was purposefully faithful to everyone, including my one husband, John. I wanted to be good. My virtue had done nothing to save me.

Apparently, virtue doesn't matter. It's something else. It is something deeper about me.

I pour coffee into the Damariscotta pottery mug and return to a seat at the long pine table, still holding the blanket around my naked body. I pick up a pitcher of cream and pour generously until my coffee is a light mocha. I sip and the coffee immediately provides a degree of fortitude. I never drank coffee until I met Raven.

"Do you like it here?" Raven asks, having been patient while I settled and took my first few sips.

"Yes. Very much. It's peaceful and beautiful." I answer, both hopeful and wary.

"You could live here if you like. Maybe Arianna would come back. You know Gwen would love it here," he says, and then licks honey from his thumb.

Yes. Maybe. She didn't like Academy Green because it was for low-income people. Well, that's what Helleen had told John and John had told me. Who knows? All communication is like poisoned water when dealing with a psychopath. But you drink it anyway because you're thirsty, even though you know it might kill you. I would die just to find out something – anything –about my daughters.

Images of Arianna and Gwen taking turns on the swing enter my mind. I imagine their laughter, their smiles. I imagine going to sleep at night knowing they were safe in the same house with me.

But what about Raven? Has Raven really changed? Like he said last night. "I'm a new man. Jane. Going back to Montana and seeing my mistakes in the eyes of my son changed me. I'll never go back to my old ways," he had said.

"You wouldn't have to worry about money. I make enough to take care of all of us," he adds.

Money. It seems impossible for me to create money. Bath Iron Works was out of the question. I would be selling my soul to the devil. I'd tried clerical and secretarial. I reversed numbers on receipts and blanked out in the middle of cash transactions. My PTSD and ADHD, made me unable to file two sheets of paper with one labeled "A" and the other "B." I'd been fired from a secretarial job already in Bath. Of course, I couldn't seem to sell my screenplay or any of the short stories or articles I'd sent to various women's magazines. I had been blacklisted it seems from all Maine newspapers.

My family would not help me in any way. Oh, yes, I had to remind myself. I have no family. Since John left me and Helleen stole my daughters, no one has spoken with me, except my mother, who seems increasingly sick and disabled.

Did I really have a choice?

CHAPTER 34

WINTER WIND

Spring in Maine bursts from the earth, lush, wet, fecund. Purple violets, lilacs, Iris, Lupine and lavender sprout, crawl, creep, spread and blossom. Mustard yellow daffodils – one of my mother's favorite spring flowers – rise up miraculously in the stead of ice and snow. Fields and woods layered in rich, dark, moist soil, green into a hundred shades of moss, fern, grass, and ivy.

The powers of resurrection are strong in the earth, even after a long cold harsh winter I think, staring out a small rectangular window at a row of bright yellow daffodils planted beside the ground level window in the barn. I lie in a double bed close beside Raven in a room adjacent to the living room which contains the large black woodstove and the swing attached to the roof fifty feet above.

Edgecomb pottery vases filled with fresh lilacs and pink apple blossom branches – *my favorites* – sit on the nightstand and on the old mahogany dresser and bureau in our bedroom. I'd spent many happy hours in the fields yesterday and picked flowers on my way home.

I'd been here at "the barn" for two months.

I breathe deeply. The mingled scents of lavender and apple remind me of Hanover

I clasp the edge of the mattress and squeeze. I frown. It feels like horse hair. I chuckled softly, not wanting to awaken Raven who had been out late last night with his boss, the old lady. . Is it possible? Horse hair?

I clasp my hands together on top of my stomach. A thick white down pad beneath us (on top of the horse hair mattress) and an equally heavy down L.L. Bean comforter covering us makes me feel Raven and I are sleeping in a thick heavy cloud. I close my eyes and imagine we are in a cloud bank above the mountains in Washington. Far away, floating, smiling…holding hands and talking and talking. Like we always do…imagining how life used to be in America…in the yellow plains of the Dakota.

Is my imagination harmful or helpful? The time I spend imagining happiness and peace must be better than taking prescription drugs. Prozac is the favorite these days according to Time magazine. My mother takes at least seven prescription drugs for a variety of ailments including anxiety, pain, depression. How could she feel her feelings with all those drugs? If someone cannot feel, where is his or her life? Who is living their life? Surely life does not exist in the brain, but in the heart and soul.

I would never take drugs. Never. The drug companies, the doctors, the mental institutions – they would never get me.

I'd die first. But is my imagination a drug?

I brush the back of my curved fingers lightly along Raven's long back bone, from the nape of his neck to his tailbone. Goosebumps erupt under my touch but his breathing remains steady and uninterrupted.

I am tempted to awaken him to alleviate my aloneness, but decide against it and drop my hand onto the bed. It is still early and after chopping firewood, he did not arrive home – smelling like sawdust and tobacco and sweat – until around 11 PM last night.

Why did he stay so late with her? He often arrives home at odd hours. What does he do so late at her white Cape Cod house on the river at the end of the driveway? And when he is home, he often spends hours on the phone in conversations with her, his muffled tone and strained expression indicate there are secrets and arguments.

I'd seen her only three or four times and she frightens me. Her brass-handled cane held firmly in her aged hand, she had stood squared, erect, at the doorway, her thick white hair, a crown on top of her tall, thin, big-boned body. Neither time had she stepped into the barn or looked directly at me, even though I was close to her, standing at the bedroom door, and Raven had directed several comments to me in her presence.

She refused to look at me.

She comes to collect Raven. I was simply a situation she must tolerate. I could not understand her antagonism. She called me a "divorcee." If she did not want me here, couldn't she have said as much to Raven?

I feel like a chess piece in a strange game between this strange woman who said she was roommates with Katherine Hepburn at college and Raven.

I felt both indignant and hurt. I wished for a friend so badly. A mentor. Someone who cared about me.

Hopefully, I would not have to see her today, I thought, swinging my feet out from under the warm quilt and onto the cold wooden floor. My long white cotton gown – a new gift from Raven – was laced at the bottom and around my small wrists.

After he was awake, I'd push Raven out the door with his coffee, so he would get to her house before she grew impatient and began her long awkward walk up the driveway and into the barn, I thought as I exited our bedroom. Raven's duties today included chauffeuring her to a Green Party meeting in Bath in the morning and then to a Feldenkrais appointment in Brunswick near Bowdoin College. They'd probably "lunch" on the coast somewhere with one of her many friends who lived along the coastline in Bath or Woolwich or Arrowsic.

She paid Raven regularly and well. If she only knew he promptly handed his check over to me, she would succumb in full to whatever malaise affected her when she was in my presence.

I suddenly feel dizzy and a wave of nausea rushes over me. Vomit splashes up against the back of the interior of my throat. I reach out with my left hand, now decorated with two new turquoise and silver rings from the Native Arts, in Woolwich, and grab the small nightstand.

The nausea passes.

I am so sick of the meat burritos drenched in Crisco oil and fried in the big black iron pan. My stomach is too sensitive these days. The thought of bloody red hamburger meat turns my stomach. I have to talk to Raven about not eating so much meat. I hate it.

I open the bathroom door. I step inside the bathroom and open wide the hot water faucet and steam soon fills up the small bathroom; water rises up the tub to almost spilling. I discard my clothing and slippers and sink into the hot tub. It is just dawn. I want to be clean and fresh for this new day. Arianna and Gwen are both here and asleep in the upstairs bedrooms. I want everything to be perfect! I have not dared to think about them until now.

An hour later, I am dressed and pulling a pan of homemade corn bread out of the oven; and after Raven has already departed, Gwen, in her pajamas, and holding her pink My Little Pony, descends the stairs from her second-floor bedroom.

"Hi, Gwen!" I say and walk to meet her halfway. I give her a quick hug.

"How are you this morning?" I ask. It is such a simple exchange, but it feels like a miracle. A miracle to see her beautiful, sleepy face in the morning sun. I try not to cry.

"I'm okay," she responds, twirling the blue horse mane.

"I made some cornbread."

Thank you," she says and crawls onto the cane chair at the end of the pine table.

"I had a bad nightmare." She says, tucking her blond hair behind her ears and reaching for the butter.

"I know," I said, trying not to reveal my sense of dread and doom surrounding this subject. I grabbed a sponge to wipe up my own breakfast crumbs.

So many things were beyond my control. It made me feel helpless. At 2 am last night Gwen had woken up screaming. I do not sleep well anymore, as I am always prepared for a trauma to occur with my daughters, either real, or in my nightmares, so I heard her immediately and left my bed and ran up the stairs. "What's wrong Gwen," I had asked, deeply alarmed and standing in the moonlight fearing the worst. My heart was racing in my chest, my hands were sweating.

"It was Helleen," she sputtered, tears streaming down her cheeks. It was the words I feared most.

I sat down on the twin spindle-back bed, wrapped the patchwork quilt more closely around her shoulders, and held her tightly in the little room of French antiques and hand-woven throw rugs and moonlight. There I stayed until she had told me the entire nightmare, and then in my arms, slept again, fitfully, but yet, I prayed her pain was less while she slept.

Mournfully, having received all of her pain into my heart, I had returned to my own bed heavy with Gwen' s fear and pain and my own dread and grief. Raven, so accustomed to my sleeplessness and nightly wanderings, and my eternal grief, had simply, naturally, held me tightly in his arms while I cried, my whole body shaking. I had buried my face into his chest deeply so the children would not hear my anguish.

"Be like the mountains, Jane. Be strong," he had whispered and repeatedly kissed the top of my head. "Be the Mountain."

In Raven's heart is where it all ends, I think, as I pour another cup of Hazelnut coffee. The abuse from Helleen goes to my daughters and then into my own heart, where it spills over, in rivers of tears, into his heart. I was so confused.

I hold a cup of hot coffee in a mug and smile watching Gwen eat breakfast. She takes a bite of corn bread dripping with butter and then sets it back down on her blue clam shell plate. I smile at the line of crumbs on her upper lip. She sips hot chocolate from my favorite Damariscotta Pottery mug. The one with the Iris's. To me, she is a Queen. I would not give her the Saxon mug. Ever. It would be unthinkable. Something about Gwen reminds me of a Queen and another time and place, where life was more beautiful in some way I feel in my heart, but cannot quite express.

"I'm scared of Helleen though, Mom. Please don't tell her. You can't," she says, truly terrified.

Gwen did not need to remind me of the consequences we all faced if I were to bring forth any negative information about Helleen. It lived in my heart like a knife.It could be turned at any second, creating excruciating pain and fresh blood-flow from the wound. Sometimes, just breathing could cause the wound to open.

The letter John and Helleen forced Gwen to write telling me she (Gwen) had lied to me about Helleen being sexually and emotionally abusive towards the girls had just been the beginning of a seemingly endless storage house of methods of punishment and retaliation Helleen could manifest if she felt threatened.

A month ago, Helleen had forced Gwen to go outside naked, for which she paid her $50. Horrified, I'd told John; and Gwen had been grounded for two weeks for lying. When I went to pick Gwen up Helleen came outside and told me Gwen didn't want to see me anymore and that Helleen

"Couldn't get her to come out of the house"

While Helleen lied to my face, in my peripheral vision I could see Gwen's tear-streaked face peeking through the living room curtain window. Terrified of causing Gwen more pain, I'd departed, mortified, helpless, with not one soul who would help.

I'd learned through experience that if I took Gwen to her own doctor she had grown up with, Dr, Kitfield, in Wiscasset, Gwen would be punished when she got back to John and Helleen's (if Helleen found out). Once, when Gwen was so sick she could barely talk on the phone, I said I was coming to get her to take her to the doctor. John got on the phone and threatened to call the police and have me arrested. If Gwen talked to me on the phone, she might be put to bed early. The list of horrors was endless and daily. I could not sleep or eat or think straight.

"Well, the other night when I was sleeping in my bed," Gwen began, and I steeled myself.

"It was really late and the whole house was dark. The lights were out. I heard Helleen on the stairs. She was slowly walking up the stairs. I called out her name, but she didn't answer. She just stopped walking," Gwen says, her blue eyes staring out the window.

I am astounded at her courage and her trust in me. This was dangerous information if it got back to Helleen. Gwen knew I would want to try to change things for her and I might be tempted, vainly, to tell her father. Danger was always stalking us.

"Mom. I was so scared. I don't know why. I honestly thought she might kill me or something," she said, her eyes far away now, filled with fear.

"Then she finally went back down the stairs, but I think she was outside my door."

I never wanted to kill anyone in my life. Until now. I imagine slicing Helleen into pieces with a long sharp sword. What victory and joy and relief and happiness would flood my heart and soul, to see her head roll.

I stand up and walk over to Gwen and wrap my arms around her, as if somehow, I am helping her, as if somehow, I can protect her. As if somehow this one brief moment in time, of love, would protect her from the future and the past. As if she might understand love and that would make a difference in her life. It has to. It's all I seem to have. Didn't Mary Baker Eddy say the only thing that is real and eternal is Love..

"It's okay honey. It's okay." I say, knowing nothing is okay. Knowing in my heart, that Helleen would kill Gwen if she could do it without being caught. If she could do it and still look perfect. Helleen's number one goal was to look perfect and innocent. Anything which stood before Helleen and her goal, would be destroyed, in any manner possible.

I pour as much love as I can into Gwen's heart, just standing there staring, stroking her long blonde hair, and staring at Iris's mug, now lined with chocolate on the rim. Is there anything else I can do? I don't know.

"Are you okay now?" I ask. She is not okay. We are in a war to save our souls.

"Yes," she answers, and picks up her mug.

My eyes drift down to her neck.

Red blotches scream at me.

"What is in your neck?" I ask, alarmed. I push her pajama top back a few inches, which reveals more blotches. She itches them.

"I don't know. I started itching last night," she says. The blotches seem to defy me to do something about them. I stare, numbness spreading over my body. I felt like a Wolf, my leg in an agonizing trap. If I brought her to the doctor, Gwen would suffer because Helleen would feel out of control. If I treated her with one of my many natural herbal remedies, I had made from wildcrafting, St. John's wort, feverfew, plantain, and dandelions. Helleen would make fun of me in front of both Arianna and Gwen. She would call me a "Witch" or "neglectful."

Helleen understood I was the only Love in Gwen's life and to shoot poison arrows at me was an effective weapon to demoralize Gwen. If I did nothing, Helleen would report to John I was not giving the girls proper medical care because of my insistence on only natural remedies. The trap was already tightening.

I wanted to refuse to let Gwen go – tell Gwen she could never go back to that horrifying, dangerous house where she was stalked and abused by an insane and evil stepmother and she and Arianna were housed in a tiny, unheated third floor room, if you could call it that; it was really just a widow's peak that was cold in the winter and hot and unventilated in the summer. The girls' one small window was stuck open about six inches and there wasn't a screen. They were at least two hundred feet up, with only one narrow winding staircase reaching their room in the interior, and on the exterior, no fire escape.

Against all odds of any kind of normal fatherly concern greeting my motherly concern and fear (as John was nothing now except Helleen's trained monkey) I had called John.

"John, what if there is a fire? How would the girls get out," I had asked, barely able to form the words with my lips, my terror so great. Every cell of my body was burning with triple alert. It was agonizing.

"Jane, you really need to get over this thing you have with Helleen. You'll do anything to upset her won't you," was his reply that I had expected, but had prayed, against all hope, it would not be. I had slowly hung up the phone.

Later that day, I called the Bath Fire Department. The dry, cynical, almost humorous tone in the man that answered the phone and had listened to my concerns, revealed to me what I feared. Helleen, anticipating my next move, had called the fire department. I already knew what she had said. I also could anticipate her moves.

She had told them I was the jealous ex-wife of her husband and that I was paranoid and an abusive mother trying to get back at her. She would have told them in such a way as to appear childlike and innocent and only trying to help me and the girls and her new husband and, of course, them, the fire department. She would say something to the effect she did not want them to have to waste their time coming to the house. She would tell them she would try to work with me to figure out a solution. Because she had a degree in social work, she knew the correct phraseology in every situation. She knew the textbook version of a healthy, sane mind and she copied it to perfection. Her imitation to the outside world as a perfect human being was almost seamless.

The same tone and subsequent inaction on behalf of my children and disdain towards me had been mimicked in at least a dozen individuals

to whom I have had to interact on behalf of my children. These included doctors, dentists, teachers, and friends. They all were so out of touch
with their gut instincts and so oriented around the perfect image (if you
want to call her that – she was emaciated but draped in expensive designer
clothes and jewelry) and the perfect phrases she emoted, they were both
blind and deaf to the truth. John was so hypnotized that even when she
was arrested for shoplifting at L. L. Bean and the newspaper printed details of the arrest (including her name), he denied it because she told him
it wasn't true.

I was her mortal enemy. Simply because I knew the truth about her
and I held on to it. She could not destroy or suppress me and I believed
every word that Gwen spoke and disbelieved anything that came out of
Helleen's mouth. The ferocity grew within her (she would never show it
on the outside – I simply felt it) with each instance I held firm with Gwen.

But Helleen had discovered a way to control Gwen that was way beyond my control and made it almost impossible for me to demand that
Gwen never return to that house.

Helleen was desperate for children and had taken enough fertility pills
(trying to restore to her system and her menstruation, which she had
depleted throwing up all her food for a decade, and then from living on
steamed broccoli and diet Coke, and running in marathons) to allow her
sickly womb to hold three successive pregnancies long enough to give
birth to three live. but premature male babies (one girl had died). With
each baby Gwen and Arianna were allocated more responsibility for taking care of them. Gwen, especially, was often stuck with babies much too
young for her to care for (since Gwen was disobedient in Helleen's sick
mind and her punishment was often hours of child care).

Gwen, whose heart was so loving and kind, and having essentially been
deprived of both her mother and father, and the normal love a young child
experiences from her parents, had grown deeply attached to her brothers.
Helleen, observing this connection between Gwen and her half-brothers,
used it to her advantage.

Now, in addition to robbing her of her mother and father, she would
threaten Gwen of not being able to see the boys if she stepped out of line.
If Gwen refused to go back to Helleen's she knew she might never again
see the boys and they were, in a sense, the only love she could count on,
and for which she was not punished.

It was disconcerting to Gwen for me to even suggest this course of action. I felt herthread-bare stability would be threatened by this suggestion.

I held her again, tears streaming down my own cheeks, that I quickly swept away with the back of my hand. Dear God, if there is a God, please protect where I cannot. My love for Gwen is Helleen's weapon to try to destroy me.

I do not know why this person has such hatred for me but I feel guilt and shame, as it brings pain to the ones I love most. How long could we survive? Would we survive?

And then I thought of the daffodils and the layers and layers of ice and snow in the long, long dark winter…

PART II

CHAPTER 35

LAYERS OF DEATH

*B*ut things did not get better. Things got worse. Much worse. The daffodils did not return to earth for decades. My inner world, which was all that I had left, slowly, slowly, iced over. I stopped feeling the earth, the trees any longer. I withdrew from all of life, even the flowers, the lilacs, the roses. There was nothing but darkness and not a good darkness, like a womb, or the peace of night, but of a cruel, terrifying, painful, darkness of brutality.

I tell you now as an older woman, looking back twenty years, I wonder how I am still alive. But every moment is true. I know it is true because I lived it.

If only they had let me stay with Gwen. I would not have died internally. Enough light, enough hope, enough dreams, a belief that there was some beauty, some integrity, some compassion remained in the world, for me to stay alive. But the harder I fought to protect her, the harder they retaliated. The more dangerous Gwen's world became, the harder I fought for her, in the customary channels of life. But to no avail.

I simply cannot go back there to tell you everything that happened. I cannot go over every detail, the tastes, the smells, the sights, the sheer terror, from first person I simply cannot. Instead, I will tell you bits and pieces, so as not to immerse myself completely in the twenty years of darkness, again.

I will also say, that if Gwen and I had been able to be together, it would have been enough. There would have been enough light, enough air, enough hope, enough humanness, to have given us a relatively normal life, even without Arianna. Arianna never came home. Arianna never came home. It defines me more than anything. I lost half of my heart. But I still would have had the other half.

I could have still smelled the earth, the flowers, baked cookies, tucked Gwen into bed at night, baked her favorite cookies, planted flowers, washed and folded her clothes, read her books, and watched her get on the school bus, smiling with infinite joy, with my half heart.

I would have been content to remain a mortal. But a mortal life was not for *me, no matter how much I wanted it. I wanted it with all my heart and soul. I wanted to be normal, but could not be normal and stay alive.*

This book would not have been written – and the only thing that is getting me through this part of the book is that I keep picking up the phone and calling Gwen. Just to hear her voice. "Hi, Mamma," she says, holding her cell phone against her, waiting to go into an important meeting, but she always takes the time. "I love you, Mamma," she says, because she can now. No one will punish her. We are just getting used to it. She is thirty-two, almost the same age I was at Montsweag, and she is a reporter.

"I love you, too," I say. It's a dream come true, to be able to say this to her without fear she will be punished.

"Do you have to write the book? I just don't want you in pain," she asks, and I can hear her shifting the phone. I imagine her curling a strand of her long blond hair, behind her ear. Her blue eyes wide and innocent and caring.

"I don't know. I think I do. To save other women and children. To save the world, in some strange way," I say, quietly.

I'm weak and overwhelmed by the memories. I don't know if I can go on with the writing. I'm halfway through the book.

"Well, I love you. I gotta go." She says, again.

"Come to Maine," she says.

"Ok. I love you, too" I say, hanging up the phone.

Tears are streaming down my face.

I sit on my patio chairs in the mostly-dry backyard of my house in Santa Fe, NM. Why can't anything grow here? My youngest daughter, Rose, joins me.

"I just don't know if I can write this book anymore. It feels like I'm going through it all again," I say to her after we talked about her book; about a young woman, who disguises herself as a man on a pirate ship slave ship which is captained by a lower-caste Elf.

"I guess you have to decide if the pain of writing the book is worth the rewards of finishing it," she says, very maturely for a 21-year-old woman.

I would not have become a Goddess, or a shaman, or one who knows how to rise from the dead, if Gwen had been allowed to stay with me. Names would not have been named. Every person in my life would have remained anonymous.

I would not have taken a shovel and dug down to the deepest roots of my life, my family, to try to find both the lock and the key. The key to the abomination which occurred, to myself and me and to my daughters and my mother. What kind of special hell had been reserved for us? What was down, I mean down, really down, at the bottom of the rabbit hole?

But as I said, a normal life was not to be, and maybe, just to tell my mother's story and my daughters' story, would be enough. But no, it ended up, all of humanity had to hear this story, to understand how to save themselves, from the lowest, most evil creatures on the planet, that I would have never known about, never seen, never heard of,

if Gwen had sat at my kitchen table with a coloring book and crayons... this book would not have been written...

I would not have gone back... back to my mother's birth, to her mother, even to Avalon and the ancient Goddess, and then The Hammer of Witches, to the underworld of demons, to Upper World and Hecate and Isis, and then future out, into the galaxies, to Pleiades...to Rose, the Princess of Wales...

But I would have given it all up for Gwen... but that was not to be. It was not to be.

So here is the end, I tell in a detached way, floating above my body, dreaming of fall leaves in red and yellow, and touching the face of daffodils... with my fingertips...

CHAPTER 36

JUDGE JOSEPH FIELD
AND VICTORIA MUELLER

G wen had written a letter describing how Helleen had sexually abused her and her sister. Worse, maybe, was that Helleen told John that the letter was a lie. She said Gwen was lying.

Arianna barely spoke to me. I was able, somehow, (I practically had to kidnap her) to bring her to a trusted psychotherapist, Dr. Nancy Coleman. Arianna was almost mute.

My heart raced the entire hour. I was waiting for Helleen or John to call the police. It was hell. Dr. Coleman told me afterwards she believed Arianna was in a state of disassociation.

My daughters were required to babysit continually for Helleen's three children (one was a baby). Desperate for children, and unable to become pregnant because she was deathly underweight, and could not eat anything but broccoli and diet coke, she had taken some kind of pharmaceuticals to increase her chances of pregnancy. Soon after she began the drug, she spat out, in rapid succession, four premature babies, one of whom died. A girl. Three boys lived.

Arianna and Gwen became their babysitters, to the point of servitude. The babysitting came before their own schooling, medical care, and way before any chance they ever got to see their mother. If Helleen needed Gwen (even if it was just so she could job to Brunswick and back) who was only ten, to babysit, she would manipulate the circumstances wherein I would be scheduled to pick Gwen up. Sometimes I would have to drive four or five times to the horrifying house they lived in. The front, glassed-in porch had three extra-large trash cans filled with plastic diet coke bottles – and that was it).

Gwen had also told me Helleen would often walk up the two flights of stairs to the unheated, fire trap of a bedroom the girls shared at the top of this house of hell. She would stand outside in the dark, without speaking.

I was terrified beyond what I could bear. John was going out to sea. They would be alone, with a woman, who I now truly believe was a psychopath, and potentially a murderer (f my intuition was correct).

I just knew. I absolutely knew she was capable of murder. It was already clear that she was a master liar and manipulator (almost everything I said or did was manipulated and fed back to the girls and John in a way that shocked me to my soul).

It is robotic evil. Calculated down to every word. At this point I knew she could also be charged with child sexual abuse, child neglect, leaving children in a situation which will endanger their lives (the third-floor room that did not have a fire escape, for starters.)

John had become a lost soul, as far as I could gather. I had to believe our mutual friend Brenda (who had been a guest at their wedding) that he had become a sex slave. It was the only explanation, as to why he did not save his daughters.

He was under mind control. It seemed Gwen and I were the only ones left who were still fighting this monstrous situation. Gwen did not know she was fighting anything. She was only living her life and observing and speaking the truth of what she saw. She was too young to understand the depth of evil into which she was immersed. Her love for me and mine for her was unshakeable. And this drove Helleen crazy – and this is why I feared for Gwen's life.

Helleen had shocked Arianna to the point she never came home. She visited me occasionally, but there was something very wrong. She was not the child I knew. She was contained, reserved, shocked, complacent. Like her father, Arianna seemed to be under some kind of mind control. What kind of perversion could turn a normal child so quickly against her loving mother and happy life? John absorbed lies like a sponge. He ignored Gwen's begging for mercy, to be allowed to be with me, and away from her stepmother. He discounted anything I said, any of my concern, and allegorically categorized me as "jealous" of Helleen.

Gwen seemed to have a shield, a natural defense against lies and manipulation. She did not outwardly reject Helleen's lies. This was not Gwen's way. She was gentle and quiet, but they just did not become part of her mind. She automatically and systematically rejected lies about me. Gwen was incorruptible.

Because of this trait, Gwen was in grave danger. I knew this. Psychopaths will do anything for power, to get to the top, to have complete control. The only thing that stood in the way of Helleen having complete control of my destruction was Gwen.

I was terrified of what might be next. PTSD occurred a hundred times a day – each time the phone rang, someone knocked on the door, I heard Arianna's voice, I saw Gwen, I had to talk to John. I was in a war zone.

Tobey Hollander filed a case in the West Bath District to, essentially, gain primary custody of both of my daughters when their father was out to sea as a merchant marine. It was a no-brainer in a normal world, for a normal person, like me. At least, I thought I was normal.

We did not need, as they say, a rocket scientist to figure this out. The best solution was for me to have primary custody all the time, since their father was absent half of the year. They could be with him weekends and summers, when he was not at sea, but I was being generous, I thought, by asking for full custody when he was gone.

But no, something much larger was in play. Something so big, and so evil, and so broad, and so diabolical, I could not possibly have understood it at that time. I would have called Helleen deranged, cruel, but it was not until later that I understood she was psychopathic.

I was a mother, in agony, terrified for my children. I had little or no resources. No money. No family. I could no longer work. I was also in grave danger myself but could not see the forest through the trees.

Raven was not who he said he was. And I was pregnant.

CHAPTER 37

THE GUARDIAN REPORT

A fraction of Jews are Zionists, and this is who Helleen, also a Jew (and I now believe a Zionist Jew) hired immediately. Next came the guardian ad litem, Victoria Muller. A tall, white-haired, women, who, as it turned out (from photos she showed to Gwen) was a lesbian, who lived in Brunswick.

The end report, which included the fact that Helleen had offered Gwen fifty dollars to go outside naked, and that Arianna had been strangely unwilling to go home to me (with no cause that anyone could find, even the guardian), was the most confusing and disturbing series of words. She said I had dreams about tidal waves and that I believed there was a "negative energy triangle connecting Bath Iron Works, Brunswick Naval air station and Maine Nuclear plant."

At this time, my mother, in an attempt to help the girls, had moved to Maine and I had left Montsweag Road. On North Street in Bath we had rented a beautiful, huge, four bedroom home, with an enormous living room with a large fireplace.

Both my mother and I had furnished the house, but all the guardian said about it was that it was my mother's furniture. Nothing about the two gorgeous rooms we had furnished for the girls – with antique vanities, and new rugs. In the end, she recommended the situation continue as it was, even when John was out to sea, as he could run the household "from a fax machine on the ship."

If the whole concept were not insane enough, there was no fax machine on the ship in Alaska. She dismissed the sexual abuse issues against the stepmother. She ignored Gwen's pleas that she wanted to be with me when her father was gone. She called Gwen ``co-dependent." She manipulated Arianna's words to fit her own agenda. It was a god forsaken report.

Shockingly, and maybe the most horrifying thing she did, (maybe, it is hard to measure the acts of a devil in terms of better or worse) was to bring Gwen alone, to her private home in Brunswick, and show her photographs of herself (Victoria) and her girlfriend. "It was weird. She kept showing me photos of her girlfriend and asking me what I thought," Gwen had said to me. Gwen's fear and grief, her nightmares, shingles, were increasing every day with the addition of the guardian ad litem.

As everything that was bad, was getting worse, tangibly worse, like a nightmare, that no longer ends at daybreak, but continues on through the daylight hours. There was *no peace* anymore.

Every cell in my body, in my heart, my intuition, my soul, my mind, were on red alert, twenty-four-seven. I knew their lives were in danger. Their PHYSICAL lives. Most of the time, I could not sleep. But I could not tell the Guardian this. I kept it a secret close to my heart. I had learned, after observing the Guardian's routine, that she was gaslighting me.

It was a form of mental and emotional torture. I began to realize that anything I said that was negative about the stepmother even if it was true, no, especially if it was true, became a weapon the Guardian used against me, in a two-fold manner. First, she would twist my words and turn them against me, while simultaneously making the stepmother look good because *she had not said the same thing about me.*

So, I was not so much questioned, as I was interrogated, and my words used against me in a script that had already been completed and signed and sealed. I was humiliated and made to feel I was crazy. I was quickly losing my sense of self, questioning my perceptions, feeling hopeless, confused.

It was like if you went to turn on a light, like you had done ten thousand times before, and instead of the light going on, the room fell into darkness and the light did not go on. Everything that was sane, became insane. Up was down. Down was up. Love was hate. Hate was love.

It was the old medieval method for deciding if a witch was a witch. If you throw her in the lake and she sinks, she wasn't a witch and she was forgiven, if she floats, she is a witch and she was hung. If I reported abuse by the stepmother, I would be drowned and my daughters along with me. The guardian called Gwen "co-dependent" because she had told the guardian she loved me and wanted to be with me, her mother.

I knew NOT to tell her I thought Helleen was capable of killing my daughters. That was exactly what she wanted. Something she could really sink her teeth into and report to a psychiatrist and they could call me paranoid and put me away and then have my daughters fully and completely under their control.

As John and Arianna were already completely under total mind-control and did everything they were told to do, Gwen and I were the only ones remaining who were "a problem." No matter how hard she tried, Muller could not trick, train, coerce, threaten Gwen into saying anything bad about me. I was terrified for Gwen.

Gwen was not trying to do anything one way or another. She was merely telling the truth and something in her heart and soul could not be bought or sold or tricked.

As the questioning had progressed, I learned that every time I made a negative comment or accusation against Helleen, it was used against me and the statement about Helleen was usually excluded from the report. I had learned that with each "accusation" I or Gwen made to the Guardian about Helleen, Gwen would be punished.

For the first time in my life, I begged. I'd never begged for anything. I was too proud.

All traces of pride, intelligence, strategic thought and action, were gone. With a sense of utter confoundedness, despair, in comprehensibility, I pointed out the obvious importance (I thought) of two little girls having their mother. To no avail. I was an empty space in the world. An empty, screaming space, they had to shut down. Or worse, but without anyone uttering a word against me. It was a slow, silent kill. And it did not just involve the guardian, Victoria Mueller.

The guardian engaged a therapist, Kathleen Sullivan from Freeport, then Nancy Whiteside, a therapist from Brunswick, Maine, a psychiatrist (I can't remember his name) and they walked Gwen and me through each one of them, but in the end each therapist mimicked the guardian, who had mimicked the stepmother (who was also a therapist).

In Kathleen's report, which she wrote during a time she had been informed of the sexual abuse, the excessive cruelty, the unusual punishments, and other trauma my daughters were experiencing with Heleena, she simply stated that I was "paranoid." She went on to say I was a "little off", that I thought my daughter "Ariana (real name is in the report) was crazy" and I "believed in the end of the world." Clearly, she could find nothing substantially wrong with my parenting.

To discredit me she had to regurgitate unsubstantiated gossip Heleena had relayed to her during their sessions together. I knew this with certainty. Many of the exact words and phrases Kathleen used, the girls and I and John, had all heard Heleena use. Where, if not from the stepmother, did she get the idea that I thought Arianna was crazy? And certainly, with all the important discussions to be had with Kathleen – who was supposed to help my daughters – would I spend precious moments with her talking about "the end of the world.". She got that from Heleena as well. It was the most unethical report I'd ever seen in my life and the most destructive, and it, along with the Guardian's "report", sentenced my daughters to ten years of agony.

It was an agonizing ordeal to drag my daughters through, and the result was as if one person had written all three reports. It was a charade, street theatre. Did they know it would be traumatic for two little girls to suddenly not have any parents (as my ex-husband was out to sea most of the time as a merchant marine)? What were they thinking? *Was the sole purpose to traumatize my daughters?*

In 1988, in July, Sarah Cherry, a twelve-year-old girl, who was alone at her first babysitting job in Bowdoin (near Bath), Maine, when she was found raped and murdered. Dennis Dechaine, an organic farmer, who happened to be walking in the nearby Bowdoin woods that day was arrested, tried and convicted. He was given two life sentences – without hope of parole. When he tried to kill himself in jail, with opioids, that added another six months to his jail sentence (for drug possession).

James Moore, a former FBI agent, who set out to help try and convict Dechaine, instead found him innocent and wrote a book, *Human Sacrifice.*

In Dechaine's case, Moore says there was a "ruthless cover-up of evidence" by "prosecutors who railroaded him" (Dennis) and are still hiding the truth via official cover ups. But what Moore said he found the most appalling was that the local police reports indicated the "cops could have saved the girls life, but they didn't."

The state of Maine's own scientific evidence proved Dechaine did not commit the murder, and to this day the Maine judicial system has refused to do DNA testing on the blood found under Cherry's fingernails.

Additionally, a convicted child rapist, who lived close to the location of Cherry's murder, was not even questioned by police. As far as anyone knows, he is still roaming around the woods of Maine. This rapist is an untouchable, as far as I can determine.

When my case finally went to court, and Judge Field had examined the "evidence" presented to him by Victoria Muller (and mostly ignoring my attorney, Tobey Hollander, and my witness Dr. Nancy Coleman – who had written an extensive report warning the judge against placing my daughters with the stepmother any time at all because of my ex-husband's long absences from the home and the abuse issues the stepmother had and recommending full custody for me), Field suddenly indicated the hearing was over. He said he could not hear any of my witnesses who were waiting outside in the lobby to testify on my behalf.

"I have a murder case to attend to," he said, suddenly, from his podium. There was only one murder case at the West Bath District Court at this time. Sarah Cherry.

Even though Field said it was over, they did have time for one more comment.

"A negative energy triangle. Interesting. Well, that might be true," Field said, smirking and looking up at Mueller.

Field and Muller and John and Helleen, and their attorney finished out the hearing with a jolly round of chuckling about the statement Mueller had coerced from Arianna (and included in her "report") which indicated I believed there was a negative energy triangle between Brunswick naval air station, Bath Iron Works, and Maine Yankee.

My terror and confusion and shame was heightened when John and Helleen looked over at me – triumphantly – from across the aisle. With their help, Victoria had crushed me and also managed to make me the laughingstock of the courtroom. John? Did he even have a heart any-more? Did he ever have one?

Looking over at John across the courtroom, it seemed there were still hands around his throat, but he didn't seem to be fighting back. At least there had been some fight in him way back then…when it was just his mother trying to control him; when it was just his mother trying to erad-icate me from his life; now he seemed to have jumped into being a con-trolled man, with both feet. It was like he was a different person, or maybe he was just showing his true colors, or maybe something else. It was tor-turous to see him act as if I was a criminal. What had I done to him?

I realized it was myself, my attorney and Dr. Coleman, (and all my friends who were waiting outside in the hallway who would never be heard) who were fighting to save the girls. But we were ants to be crushed. It seemed the court system, at least this court system, had been systemat-ically set up to traumatize. Maybe they were outright trying to harm the girls. What was going on in this town? Why did the police refuse to save Sarah Cherry's life? Why did police refuse to interrogate a known child molester who lived only a short distance from the site of Sarah's murder?

Why did Field focus on my comment on the negative energy in Bath? It had nothing to do with my daughters. Nothing to do with anything at all. Or did it?

Who were the high-ranking officials in Bath who were taking part in Satanic ritual behind Dike Newhall school? Maybe this comment was the most terrifying piece of information to them. That's why Mueller high-lighted and emphasized this comment – to point out to Field, I was on to them? I was some sort of threat to Satanists? That's why they wanted to crush me and they really didn't care about the girls? Or was there some-thing more to all of this? Something even bigger?

I don't know. Why do guardian ad litem's in Maine have absolute pro-tection no matter how dangerous their choice for a child.

Is Maine really the way life should be (as it says on the license plates)? As a child, picking blueberries at Fort Popham with my father, searching for sweet grass in the woods and shells on the beach, and then later, a young teenager, running along the Popham Beach coastline, in my white bikini and peace sign earrings, listening to the cry of the sea gull, smelling the wild roses and salt air, and feeling enchanted by the mica glittering like fallen stars in a dark blue ocean, I had once thought it was the most beautiful place on earth.

CHAPTER 38

NORTH STAR

Thank god I had my mother again, I had thought, opening the back door to the beautiful, huge house we had rented together on North Street in Bath. I can't remember how I got home from the courthouse. I can't remember how I had gotten to the courthouse.

Two months ago my mother had decided to help create a firm foundation and a beautiful home for the girls. We had painted walls and hallways and bought beautiful antique furniture, and put down new gorgeous braided and oriental rugs.

She bought potted floor plants – I tore out the rug on the massive staircase, and painted the steps a bright forest green – kind of like our beautiful home on South Street. We painted or wallpapered all four bedrooms on the second floor.

Arianna's room was a pretty shade of green, and for Gwen we had painted her furniture blue and white. I had gathered all their old stuffed animals and placed them on their beds and bookshelves, and the bigger ones on the floor.

I still had the mahogany twin sleigh bed that was Arianna's and each of them had a rocking chair hand painted by my mother. I got a new bookshelf for Arianna and put her old books neatly lined up on the three rows.

She had funny stories. She had brought a rocking chair for the long and elegant living room, and the few times the girls had been there, she would rock them to sleep, reading "Grandfather Twilight" and the "Velveteen Rabbit." The floor to ceiling windows had maroon velvet curtains tied back. I felt a strange stillness.

For some reason, I opened the refrigerator. It seemed unusually empty. My mother had stocked the fridge with two gallons of Sunkist orange juice and plastic gallon of milk and baby Swiss Kraft cheese, and fruit. She loved apples and oranges, and she ate oranges whole, the skin and all.

Most of her food was gone; a half-eaten can of Spam, an apple, a half-gallon of milk remained.

Where was all the food?

I opened the white wooden kitchen cupboard door. Before the Guardian's report, I'd stuffed the cabinets with the girls' favorite foods, macaroni and cheese, baked beans – everything for corn chowder and corn bread. Chocolate chips, brown sugar, vanilla. Treats again for the girls – cookies and brownies and apple pies. Maybe like the kind I watched my mother and grandmother make in Hanover. Making pies together would be a dream, better than going to Hawaii. Better than good health. Better than anything in the world. I'd hoped, prayed, dreamed, fought with everything I had.

I stared into the cabinet at short, stout, round cans of evaporated milk and creamed corn. Abandoned children all in a row in the dark. When or if I shut the door, they would be all alone again. I shut it, then opened it, staring at the cans. Tears stream down my face.

I left the door open so the little cans could see me, so they could see the sunlight from the window and I turned away, leaned against the refrigerator and then slipped to the floor, my hands wrapped around my knee, my face buried. I imagined the guardian coming into the house and taking the cans of creamed corn and I could hear their screams as they were carried away.

I was sobbing.

But, it dawned on me, as I stared out the window, at the sunset, and the encroaching darkness (that I shared only with the cans of creamed corn, who seemed to be, somehow, on my side, or at least I imagined they were) that they were not evil.

Not even my stepfather, Hal, a drunk, who had chased my mother around the house with a butcher knife, I realized now, was not evil. I'd sensed a small shred of humanness in Hal; that if he had an exorcism, or several, we might have found a human heart. What I was facing now was something different. It was a level of horror I'd never known. And I had known very little other than horror. But this was different.

CHAPTER 39

SUNSET ON NORTH STREET

The sun had set and darkness descended over the small kitchen with the open cupboards. My body, heart, soul, ached for my children. It was constant, never ending, like a child ripped from a womb, the physical agony, but a child ripped from a mother too soon, before they were meant to be, could bleed to death, too.

I wanted to call them but knew Gwen would be punished if she agreed to come to the phone. The torture it would cause for her, desperate to talk to me, but not knowing what horror might descend on her. It was late, Helleen might deprive her of a favorite television show or a favorite food. Or make her work harder on the bathroom or the kitchen. No, I'd try to call in the morning. I'd figure out a way to communicate with her. Somehow. We were walking on landmines. One wrong move on my part and Gwen could be devastated.

My heart reaching out with love, could become a can of snakes designed to attack. Anything that went through Helleen, like a phone call or a message, no matter how beautiful it began, turned into an energy of death.

I stood up and walked out of the kitchen and into the living room. Moonlight streamed into the room, through the heavy maroon velvet curtains which had been drawn back to let the light and warmth of the sun into the room that day.

The moonlight gleamed through the old, floor to ceiling windows, onto the pumpkin pine floors. Some of the glass in the windows was so old, they were beveled and leaded, and around the perimeters, and during the day, if it was sunny, near the end of the day, rainbows filtered through the glass onto the gleaming floors.

At first, I couldn't define it, a sensation, but it made me stop short. I felt apprehensive, even fearful, or something else, scared. I was somehow reminded of my sister, Sally.

Unfortunately, as it turned out, she had followed me to Maine. She was living in Brunswick with an artist and alcoholic, Mark Tibby. I felt my sister or Mark or both had been in the room. They had left an energetic imprint.

I looked over at the fireplace, and there was only a shadow where my mother's rocking chair had been beside the fireplace. The one she rocked the girls to sleep in, after she'd read *Grandfather Twilight* or the *Velveteen Rabbit*.

A coldness crept up my back into my skull. I ran to the spot and looked around frantically. Did I imagine all of this? It was gone. The chair. The chair. My mother's rocking chair was gone. Or it was moved.

I turned around frantically. I couldn't see it in the darkening room. I flicked the switch on a brass lamp on the stand beside the couch. The light shone in a circle ten feet wide onto the floor around the lampshade.

The couch was gone. I gasped and covered my mouth. My heart racing, I ran out of the room and into the front hall and up the newly painted green staircase, holding tight to the handrail. At the top, I walked quickly to the right and to her door. I knocked softly.

"Mom, Mom…Mom…" I said, my voice quavering. It was dark in the hallway.

Her car was gone, but maybe she leant it to Sally and Mark, I thought, my heart racing. It was too early for her to be asleep. Was she sick? Was she dead?

"Mom, Mom…Are you here? Are you OK?" I asked, tears brimming in my eyes.

"Mom?" I said gently.

I slowly opened the door. I gasped and raised my hand to cover my mouth. The large square room had three windows, from which the light of the moon spilled onto an empty floor. The newly painted floor and newly wallpapered walls were just about completely empty. Artwork had been removed from the walls and all the furniture, of course, even the rugs, were gone. Not even a lightbulb remained.

A broom leaned against a corner of the wall. Dirt and debris had been hastily swept into a dustbin that sat, unemptied, aside the broom.

Shocked and numb, I left the room, closed the door, and began to walk down the stairs. I realized all the knickknacks were gone. My mother had taken all of her knickknacks, including three green frogs. The wooden clock John McGuire had given John and I for a wedding present sat in the center of the mantle. They had actually left it, I thought, without humor.

A quiet click of the secondhand reminded me time was passing. It was two AM.

I sat in the only chair that remained in the living room. In the darkness I looked over at the girls' two little hand painted rocking chairs. They sat empty in the darkness. They were small, not as small as the cans of condensed milk, but they were for children. Children's little chairs.

My chair was a rust brown upholstered wingback I had bought at The Country furniture store in downtown Bath when we were married. I stared at that charcoal in the fireplace and listened to the click of the clock.

The clock reminded me of John, who had been killed late one night several years ago when his Saab hit a patch of "black ice" and he smashed head on into a tree on his way home to the isolated patch of woods called Woolwich.

It seemed so strange. He was kind. He was gentle, considerate.

Once, John even helped me wallpaper. He was so funny. Then he was gone. Why?

Click. Click. Click.

I focused on the click of the clock. Click. Click. Click. I'd frozen, from head to toe; a numbness had come over me. Then the numbness had spread, until I felt the whole world was a sheet of ice, no, a shattered pane of glass that somehow was still held together, by lack of movement.

One move, and I knew I would shatter. Breathing was the rise and fall of shattered glass in my lungs. Careful, too deep a breath and the inside of my lungs will begin to bleed. I had to breathe.

I couldn't just stop breathing. I tried not to think of Arianna and Gwen, what horrors were being imposed on Gwen for all the positive things she tried to say about me in the report…

One wrong move, the world would shatter. One wrong move. I started to count the seconds, and just stare at the charcoal; silver, gray, blue shards of charcoal attached to what was left of the unburned logs.

1, 2, 3, 4, 5, 6, 7, 8, 9, 10. I counted to three hundred and ninety, but something wasn't right – it wasn't staving off the agony. It didn't seem to be holding me together.

Four AM. Words, isolated, some in strings together, two words at a time. Mark and Sally. They had moved my mother out of the house. Where did they go? How long had they been planning this? And they did it on the worst day of my life. They planned it for this day? Is that possible? Is that human? Had they aligned with the guardian ad litem or Helleen. Had they been paid off? I couldn't imagine, but I could. They were both drug addicts. Sally and Mark would do anything for money. But, my mother?

Gwen? What might be happening to her? What if there is a fire? Was she eating OK? Would tonight be the night the stepmother poisoned her? Because of the report? It's possible.

I have no car to get her in an emergency. I'd left my car on Montsweag road, with Raven, for a new life in a beautiful home in Bath. My mother said we could share her car. We would share the rent. The girls would be so happy and safe, finally. We would be together again. We would have the most beautiful life.

Now she was gone. I was penniless, and Raven was after me, and so were John and Helleen and the guardian, and now it seemed, the judge. How would I pay the rent? How would I even get groceries?

But it wasn't me I was worried about; it was the girls. If I killed myself (which my mother tried to do) they would not live very much longer after I did. I just had this feeling I was the only person on the planet protecting them.

I kept thinking of Sarah Cherry, twelve years old, raped and murdered and thrown in the woods in Bowdoinham. Around the same age as my daughters now.

Why did she keep coming into my mind? Dechaine was not her murderer. Everybody knew that. The real murderer was still out there lurking in the woods in Bowdoinham, only a few miles from Bath. But who was protecting him? was the most terrifying question.

I had to live. Somehow, I had to stay alive.

What had happened to my mother; what had happened to her when she lost her children? You go insane inside. Not on the outside, because you wouldn't dare. You must keep being perfect, to hold the rest of the world together. It's all inside.

The secondhand ticks in the darkness on the mantel, noting every agonizing second of my life. I'm grateful to John. For the clock.

I close my eyes, and just when I'm about to fall into a stupor, I'm rushing through clouds. I'm sweeping over masses of land...and the ocean. And then I feel I'm going back in time.

And then I'm lying in a sumptuous bed, with feather quilts, enormous pillows. The room has gleaming wide wooden floors, white-washed walls, and maroon velvet curtains have been swept back and tied.

I open my eyes, stretch, stare out the window, smiling, at the sunshine, the smell of roses from the bouquet on my nightstand. I hear the clip-clop of a

214

horse's hooves, which indicates we have a visitor. I jump out of bed, my white cotton gown whirling around my ankles as I quickly cross the floor in barefoot.

On my bureau, a teapot has been left for me only moments earlier, by our maid. I turn to the nightstand and happily tip the pot and steaming amber liquid streams into the rose-decorated China cup. I add a dollop of cream to my tea and sip it and smile with deep appreciation.

I'm a happy, young, privileged English girl living in the lush green countryside in a gorgeous stone manor. I look outside my window at the long, winding driveway, lined with wild roses and sacred oak trees.

I know they are sacred, and I know the little people live within the oak groves. It is just common knowledge. The rider is greeted by our stable boy, a footman and a butler. A handsome man dismounts from his elegant and beautiful black horse, and my heartbeat accelerates. Who is this man? I will find out soon enough, I think.

I set down my tea and open the window wide, stare out at the endless blue sky, the green fields, the mature oaks, and I am filled with an incredible joy and excitement. I feel that all this beauty is within me as well as without. This is the Goddess. I am she and she is me, and we are a living, breathing, stream of pure love and joy.

A police siren. I rush back into my body. Oh god, I'm back in here, in Bath, Maine. It is like death. I'm kneeling before the dark fireplace. I have a log in my hand. I had pulled newspapers from the trash. I put the log in the fireplace. I stand up and get a long match and kneel again.

I remember the beauty and freedom of the vision, most likely a past life. It is holding me together for the moment. I light the match and ignite the newspapers...

Gwen...Gwen...Gwen...is she alive? I stare into the flames...

I close my eyes again. The small fire warms my knees and hands, as I'm on the floor, holding my knees, my head on my hands...I pray to God. I pray for help...I close my eyes.

Suddenly, I'm in Hanover...The earth shakes under the steady cadence; the hoofbeats of my wild appaloosa stallion, Misty. I'm hanging on to her mane and the bridle, clasped beneath my hand.

My legs cling to her silken silver sides and I lean forward. It is a thunderous ride through the rust-covered old logging trails, thickly lined on both sides, with young pine trees, The smell, the sound, the strength, the power, the Goddess...

I fall sideways onto the floor, next to the woodstove, screaming down to the root of my soul, down deeper and deeper. How could they do this?

215

To the Goddess...killing her... killing her... and her bloodline... I am almost done.

I scream, until there is no breath and my lungs are raw...then I cry... until all the water has been dried up...inside of me.

Misty, the stallion, is within me...her strength... I Lie on a small rug – the only one that has not been taken – in front of the tiny fire... and I fall away into blackness.

It is almost dawn. It seems impossible, but the birds are beginning to sing. The dawn light, a gentle foggy silver seeps through the curtains. To me, dawn signals another nightmare day.

When every day of your life you are trying to save your daughters from a psychopath, every day is a bad day. And there are no rewards. No one has your back. No one is saying you are good. In fact, everyone, it seems, is trying to destroy you.

Stars shine in the blue-black Maine sky. Venus is on the horizon. The cold of the night has seeped into my bones. I'd never turned up the heat and the fire was so small it was not enough. I was shivering. I pulled down a V-neck lime-colored angora sweater from the back of the chair and draped it over my shoulder – too tired to actually put it on.

Five or six fluffy angora sweaters rest, unaffected, in my wardrobe upstairs in my room. My mind is a haze, trying to think back at my old life, when things were good, when the girls were safe. Before Helleen there were colors. Lime, orange, pink. Lemon, Baby blue. The brightly colored perfect sweaters had been stuffed into a big plastic bag by the old man at Walfield-Thistle, a dimly-lit antique store on the Old Bath Road, in Brunswick.

As a young mother, it was one of my favorite getaway for an hour – to lose myself in the narrow passageways of dusty dark Victorian furniture, China, agate blue Carnivalware, gold coins, old wooden toys, diamond rings, vinyl records and thousands of books at Walfield Thistle. I even had a favorite rocking chair where he'd let me sit and read old books for an hour, before I slipped them back into their slot, and headed back to my children.

It was Ginny, my good friend, Ginny Wright, from Minnesota, who loved flying, and was related to the Wright Brothers, who had accompanied me the day I bought some of the sweaters. We had gone to Truffles Tea and Bakery shop, afterwards, for scones and tea and glowing with excitement at the great deal we'd negotiated with Thistle.

A bag of angora sweaters. We went back to my house on South Street and tried on the sweaters and brought scones for the girls. The girls walked around with a blue and green one on, the arms so long, they swept the floor. We had all laughed uproariously (Ginny with her high squeaky laugh) and had a tea party, with chamomile and Earl Grey Tea and home-made blueberry muffins and the scones. Blueberry crumbs and colors dropped like lemon drops.

The colors, the sweaters draped all over the kitchen, the blue enamel wood stove, bright with a wood fire, the antique pink dining room, with the crystal chandelier… so the green foyers, the yellow living room. And the girls' eyes were full of light and love and excitement.

I shut down the thoughts. The memory threatened to melt the ice that was preserving me; or I felt like a convicted criminal, deluded that the sun would not rise on their execution day. There was no hope.

I simply stared at the ashes. Then my vision moves away… scans the mostly empty floor… searching for something… maybe a note my mother left me… explaining everything. Or something; A scrap of paper with a note on it. But there was nothing. Mark, lit cigarette butt between his lips, loot overflowing from his arms, but still able somehow, to open the fridge door, had probably grabbed even the Sunkist Orange juice, the mixer on his way out to the getaway car.

I had asked them to not smoke pot or drink in this house (because of the constant surveillance I was under by Helleen, John, the therapists, John's mother and the Guardian). I should have known I would pay a price for that request. I'm sure they were all partying it up at their new rental house – free of my interference.

For some reason, I looked up again… across the floor… to my book-shelf, a book had fallen out… With a small amount of strength I got up and walked over and picked up the book.

It was a paperback by Sandra Ingerman, a shaman who lives in Santa Fe, New Mexico. Ginny gave me the book as a birthday present. It's like she is a friend from another lifetime. It's *Soul Retrieval; Healing the Frag-mented Soul.* I open the book and begin to read.

An hour later, I boil water in the kettle, take out a Red Rose tea bag, put in a cup and make tea. I put the sweater on, sit at the kitchen table and take a sip of tea; and continue to read.

CHAPTER 40

DEATH AND THEN LIFE

My mother did not call me the next day, or the day after. It is a blur now when she ever did call again.

The excruciating agony of attempting to orchestrate a phone call to Arianna or Gwen, to try to see Gwen (as Arianna was now completely mind controlled and I would not see her again for years, except in strange, awkward moments, when she would appear, quickly, looking not like herself at all) Once, on her birthday, I gave her an amethyst ring my mother gave me, but I think it is now lost.

An invisible umbilical cord tied to mother and child, keeps them both alive and thriving for many years after they're born. Minute details of each other's lives stream like an information channel between mother and child. All of her was being transmitted to me, all her pain, her joy, her suffering, and for the purpose of her safety and well-being, because as her mother, I could react accordingly. Arianna. Arianna. Arianna.

Hungry, boredom, fun or reading, pain, comfort, anxiety, problem solving, like an entire globe of information, which I could no longer respond to and keep myself alive. At some point, I had to stop trying. I had to cut the umbilical cord, which was like stabbing myself in the heart to save my heart for my other daughter; to keep myself alive, I had to detach, to compartmentalize all that was Arianna, all that was my beautiful firstborn. Every pulse of her life, her thoughts, her emotions, I had to stop. I had to cut it or else I would have died.

To talk to Gwen, I had to withstand a barrage of insults, accusations, lies, manipulations. Just to call Gwen I put her in danger of retaliation from Helleen. Two days of this after the court hearing and I was double exhausted. Not only that, I was completely alone.

I had broken off with Raven again – so sure now he was violent, and could not be obscured. I thought maybe even worse. I didn't know what it was. He talked in strange languages, sometimes. In his eyes, there was nothing, like nothing human, a soul... he called my daily, or tried to... I heard him knocking on the door, which sent waves of terror through me... but he went away.

I was surrounded by enemies. If I called one of the therapists on the case, I would be either ignored, no phone call returned, or I'd hear a very tense, curt, shallow voice using words like "co-dependency" or "triangulation" or "paranoid" – all the same words Helleen used to describe my relationship to the girls... the therapists simply were repeating what they had been told to repeat.

The Guardian took every word she could get from me, and put it through some kind of special trauma meat grinder, a reverse of lead to gold. She could take gold and turn it into lead and death.

John was arrogant, self-serving, merciless, condemning towards me and he, also, repeated everything Helleen had him say.

To reach out to Gwen, was like reaching through hell and I could bring hell down upon her, from Helleen and John, if they felt threatened by something I said to her, or suggestions I made or if I asked her how she was.

I simply wandered around the house for a day or so, reading Sandra Ingerman's book. Something... very big, very complicated... shocking... was taking hold in my mind and would not let go...

I walked up the emerald green-painted stairs... and walked into my mother's empty room... the broom still leaning up against the wall, trash half scooped onto a pan... the empty light socket overhead swaying in a slight breeze, to my room... beautiful in pinks and lavender.

I walked across the hall... I just lay in Gwen's blue room, the hand painted furniture, the white vanity. All of her stuffed animals, I had arranged and rearranged. Making them look as happy as possible. For Gwen...

I lay down amongst the animals. What would I do?

I was pregnant with Raven's child. I had told one friend, Brenda. Brenda had quickly recommended an abortion. Brenda said she had been Marie Antoinette in another lifetime and had written a screenplay about the life and death of Marie. Brenda believed Marie had been framed, and was innocent of all charges, even of her famous statement, "Let them eat cake."

My own experience with the justice system (which for Marie, was the French Revolutionary court) clarified for me this was an entirely accurate assumption. Words could and would be twisted. Words were weapons.

I lay in Gwen's empty bed, in the silent house. My head fell off the pillow and in between a dinosaur and a tiger. With my fingertips I played with one of the balls on the white antique popcorn bedspread I'd bought at Walfield-Thistle.

The popcorn bedspread reminded me of my bed in my pink room in Hanover. Maybe my mother had bought me a popcorn bedspread. I remember pink wallpaper with the cream cameos; my window that looked out into my father's garden of corn and tomatoes.

I could see all the neighbors – the Gerberville's, the Spinzola's and the old lady; the witch, who my mother gave tuna casseroles and butterscotch brownies.

My sister's room, painted emerald green, with a green quilt on her bed, and, I think, shockingly, a white painted vanity, just like the one I had painted for Gwen. Colors had followed me; and vanities; And popcorn quilt; and pink and green and lavender; even though my mother and I had spent most of our lives apart.

The agony, rage, despair, anger I had expelled two nights earlier, while the moon was full and I was alone, without my mother, I realized, all of that I had expelled and more, was still inside my mother. The emotions held prisoner by Prozac and Percodan and God only knows what other drugs. I hold my throat, and stare wide-eyed at the ceiling, thinking, our lives, my mother and my life, had been mapped out identically.

Everything I had done to not live my mother's life had been all for naught. My main goal had been to be a devoted wife; that way I would be safe; they would never take my children away. I wouldn't have an affair. I never did. I wasn't like my mother, I thought. It was the furthest thing from my mind. My good behavior was all for naught.

Somehow, fidelity did not matter in this strange dark game, in which I had found myself at the center. Like I was called paranoid for dreaming about tidal waves.

My mother had been called paranoid and mentally ill for taking naps in the woods. My sister had been forced to commit virtual matricide by testifying against my mother in court. Maybe that is what had destroyed her deep down.

Myself, as a seven-year-old child, was set to walk the plank and to testify against her. My mother, hearing I was to be forced to go into court and testify, withdrew from the custody battle and fled to California.

My mother had saved me from a lifetime of guilt and shame. Somewhere in my soul, it rang high and true that matricide was a crime that could lead to genocide of a family. John and Helleen and the Guardian ad litem, collectively had conspired to use Arianna in the same way my father had almost used me.

They were twisting her words, pulling words that did not exist in her brain, smothering her with dictations; they had finally managed to eke out a sentence of two from her that incriminated me, mildly, but maybe enough.

But it is there. In cold black letters. In a report. Arianna's fate had been sealed. Matricide. The killing off of the mother. She had been used, as badly as any sex slave. Human trafficked into the home of a psychopath and sexually abused stepmother. Used to destroy me, and ultimately herself, as the ties between mother and child, as young as Arianna, were as vital to life, as was the umbilical cord to a baby. They were life itself.

She still clings to The Velveteen Bunny my mother had given to her. The few times I saw her, she held it tight, even though it was in tatters. I knew what it meant. A piece of her soul clung to the love from my mother, to the beautiful. Loving, creative, world, colorful world in which she had once danced in a white lace gown I'd bought from Walfield-Thistle.

Black Mary Janes, and a velveteen bunny and Arianna dancing in circles on the purple and blue round braided rug in our foyer on South Street, which I had wallpaper in emerald green with flowers, huge, and cream. A part of her soul was still at home, dancing…

I had empathy for my mother. I knew she was also a lost soul, lost and wandering, not so much like Persephone, but Demeter, traversing the earth, in rags, turning the world to ice, in her despair, lost without her children.

I would forgive her even for this crime of abandoning me again. I knew I was stronger. I would survive, and I would not fail. Somehow, I drew strength from the past, a past life, where I was so close to something, some bountiful, colorful, extraordinary energy, I could only call the Goddess. I also knew, deep in my heart, I had been a shaman.

I had met my Lakota Sioux ancestors in visions shortly after John and I had broken up. Desperate, I had called out to the universe for help, and they had appeared.I told them I wanted to go home, they said, not yet, not yet, but we will be there in the end to take you home. I had that to give me strength. In the end I would not be alone.

Native Americans, on their painted ponies, (Just like Misty in Hanover) would be there, holding their feathered wands…to bring me home…I had my ancestors and I had my past lives, and now I knew , I just knew, I could become spiritually powerful again. I knew it from reading Sandra's book.

I put my hand on my stomach.

But what kind of world would I bring this child into? The circumstances could hardly be worse.

No help, of course, would be forthcoming from my father. I learned that on Dunster Road when I was twelve years old and he kept his face stuck in the Christian Science Monitor when we sat in the austere "funeral parlor" living room with the avocado rug in Needham, and I had cried and begged him to stop the abuse from my stepmother. His words, from behind the Monitor, still ring in my ears. "She's a great housekeeper and a bookkeeper. She keeps the business going."

Now he had prostate cancer. Joel Goldsmith, the spiritual leader who my father sought out in mountain retreats, and carried his tapes and books wherever he went (like the preachers of the past) that taught him that forgiveness healed cancer. So my father had sent me, before I was at South Street, a platter, with the words love written over and over on the, and card came, "I Love you."

Marion, his wife, had shrunk to the size of a monkey. Or at least that's how my brother, Jeffrey, had described her to me during a phone call after his visit with our father, to the "home" where she had been institutionalized for severe Alzheimer's. "Dad plays catch with her with a beach ball," he said, with a scoff, and a justifiably mirthful tone.

Tortured, minimalized, condemned, blamed, ostracized, picked on, isolated, accused; if she could have gotten away with it in an upscale, proper, blueblood town like Needham she would have beat him to death with an iron maul. Marion and my father emotionally tortured Jeffrey to the point his life was one long anxiety attack. He could not travel, he could barely move; he was terrified of everything and everyone.

A child tied me to Raven forever. A pregnancy would be just one more reason for all the systems to take me apart. Would they even let me keep the child? Would they do the same thing to this baby? Could they rip her from my arms? Could they rip her from my stomach? No, for nine months at least I could have her.

I closed my eyes and listened to the wind in the chimney…I thought of the lake near the Victorian house in Minnesota. I was with Scott. My heart hurt…I stopped the thoughts.

I still had his letter. I read it almost every day. "Please come to India"… But no…I couldn't leave Gwen…no…not like my mother had done…

I cleared my head…silence…. the soul of the child near me. A bond was already forming with the soul of this child. I could feel her. Sometimes I could see her. She wanted to be here on earth. Now. She must know my life. She must have been watching me – if she was choosing me. Why Me? Why?

She had some powers, I felt were surrounding me, maybe protecting me … I don't know. But she would be here … she would come through me to this world.

My mother had always called me an angel. I rode a white horse, my sister rode a dark horse, she said. And I had seen the true face of Raven in a vision. He was a demon, not even human. But a demon, to me, right now, far surpassed the humanity I knew. This child would be the product of the love between an angel and a demon. But…

All was lost here. John and Helleen were on fire with a kind of demonic victory. I was surrounded by enemies. There was no hope…

I stared at the little blue-painted chair, Gwen's chair, my mother had painted for her, blue, with little flowers, where her beautiful head of blond curls rested, at the top. It rocked slightly in the wind, empty, forgotten. Even the chair grieved.

I would keep this child, and try to start a life with Raven, I chose a demon and a child of a demon, to this hell on earth in Bath. Reform him, heal him. I would build my strength. I would leave Bath again, and start rebuilding my soul, putting myself back together, and then, I would be back. I would be back. Somehow, I would be back, for Gwen.

Chapter 41

Morning Glories

I kneel and pull weeds from around the roots of the blue Morning Glory flowers I'd planted at the foot of the faded trellis at our back porch on Church Street in Damariscotta. I look up and stare at the flowers. They are vibrant, almost an electric blue. It seems strange, how vibrant. It was like walking into a castle and finding out it was really a haunted house. All gleam; magic; excitement at first, and then it hits you hard. Maybe it is like a drug.

Sometimes, they were vibrant, and sometimes normal. Things seemed electric around Raven. Sometimes. Other times, they were the exact opposite. Deadly. I shudder.

I look across the street at my neighbor's hydrangea bushes. My morning glories are not as big as the dusty blue hydrangeas in the well-manicured gardens at the elegant Colonial home across the street from our apartment, but it seems they are brighter. My father's favorite flower is the blue hydrangea, I think without a whisper of emotion. It is like he is dead or never existed.

I hear the rush of the river, stand up straight and wipe the sweat from my brow. I'm holding a silver kitchen spoon. I'm always robbing kitchen silverware drawers for gardening tools. I imagine I've left a dozen silver spoons in gardens all around Maine. Amongst the many flowers I've nurtured in Maine, I've planted silver. I wonder what might grow from silver.

I look past our house, and past the lush green grass lawn, and the gently sloping hill, and beyond my garden of purple Echinacea, the tall Pink mallow and the Calendula flowers, (elegant, in the fifteen-foot-square of garden, which Raven had dug for me in an hour despite the deeply rooted thick grass) to see a glimpse of the sparkling Damariscotta river that flows in a narrow tributary behind our house.

I want to go to the river to sit on the small sand beach, and maybe rinse my face with the cold river water that co-mingles with the Atlantic Ocean, but it would be beyond earshot of , Rose's room where she sleeps in a brand-new crib under a mobile of furry Easter-egg-yellow baby chickens. She is nine months old and already running up and down the pine hallway floors.

She has powerful, strong legs and arms. Maybe she will have super-powers like her father. I shake my head. With her collection of strange creatures, all she needed was a bow and arrow slung over her shoulder. She would be emulating (at least one) of her namesakes – the Roman Goddess, Rose, Huntress and Protector of Wild Things.

I'd also named her after Princess Rose of Wales, who I believed was the embodiment of the female heart of the world; The Rose of England; the Queen of Hearts. So far, at least in her babyhood, my Diana emulated the more mythical creature of the woods.

I stay close to Diana. I am always watching her; watching the rise and fall of her chest, as she sleeps; the steady cadence of her breathing. I am sometimes waiting for her to open her eyes and then to see her smile.

I am amazed I can pick her up when she wakes and hold her tightly. It is a miracle. A miracle that held a shadow for the two girls I loved, but I could not hold. The little ones I could not hear or see. I wonder if Rose can feel this is in me, the joy and the restraint.

I guarded Rose. Raven was an enemy in a way. I knew that now for sure. I just could not figure out, yet, how to get away from him and still protect Rose. If I left him, he would demand visitation rights and that terrified me.

My mother and sister were back in my life, and they also made me very nervous, and I was guarded when they were around Rose.

I could not forget, so quickly, their brutal and callous abandonment, when I most needed them, and I was again shy and withdrawn and un-trusting, no matter how hard my mother tried to retrieve my affections. I was polite and hospitable, and even laughed a bit when we sat at my round table drinking tea and eating my homemade cake.

It still seemed I was surrounded by enemies or those who were so weak in character, that they might, at any minute, endanger Rose or myself, or even Arianna and Gwen. How could I be the only person in the world who had the strength to save my children? Why was I still so alone?

Sally showed up occasionally, at the back door, beside the blue morn-ing glories, with her new boyfriend, the town cripple, who was nicknamed "Wolfie."

Wolfie had been a victim of polio in the 1950's, (before the vaccine) and he hobbled around town with a wooden cane in one hand and a lit corn cob pipe stuck in his mouth. A respectable wool coat housed his massive hunchbacked body. From the velvet-collared neck of the coat, sprouted his very large face; perpetually tanned and weathered; and one crooked eye and one normal eye. He was, I thought, the epitome of The Beast. In my mind, at this time, Sally and Wolfie were the Beast and the Beast.

My mother called him a "dear old thing."

It was also true that Sally, my mother, and I had been so brutalized through domestic violence, sexual assaults, and for my mother and I, on-going trauma through the court systems, we all were drawn to men with self-esteems that reflected our own.

Together, we were a motley crew of pirates; mostly old blood blues; maimed and rejected. In desperation I hung out with the dejected and drugged (my sister and my mother were still sharing prescription drugs). I still would not drink or take drugs, prescription or otherwise, as I knew I held this truth I must preserve. I was, in essence, among derelicts, waiting for the pain to end.

I also felt like the ancient Goddess Demeter, who it was said, clothed herself in rags and wandered the earth, in desperate search for her lost daughter, Persephone

Rose, my strong-legged little elfin child, who snuggled lizard and snakes, was the heart of our life, and a distraction, for all of us, from all our own individual and collective pain; from what seemed like a lifetime of mistakes, abandonments, and ritual abuse from the courts, for my mother and I. But I was never so alone, as I had found my mother, but lost her. I would love her , but I would never trust her again.

Nothing was too good for Rose, and my mother came with cakes and pies, McDonalds food, and bags of new snakes and rattles and balls from Reny's store for Rose.

At the round table in the kitchen I could see both my blue hydrangea and the river. We sipped tea, and ate blueberry muffins or cake or whatev-er kind of pie I had baked or sugar-laden pink or yellow cake my mother had brought from Stop and Shop grocery store.

As we listened to the wind and the birds outside, Rose ran around and around the table, and up and down the hall. The insanity of it all was help-ful, to a degree.

Only partly, though, as each time I laughed or smiled at Rose, as we all did; because she was funny, and bright, and different; and because we were all desperate for life; for a being that felt life fresh and knew; I felt a knife being stabbed into my stomach. I had to push back tears, each of the thousands of moments, each day, each hour, each minute, each second, when I could not see or hear my other two daughters

The pain was on my face, but no one spoke of it, maybe because it was unspeakable. It was just so awful, so we all pretended it did not exist. When we did talk about Arianna and Gwen, a silence descended on all of us, even Wolfie, who could only sense what was happening. My mother and sister would look at me with veiled eyes, waiting, maybe, for me to die in front of them; hoping I would survive the question they had asked. All hope had been lost.

I could only imagine what my mother was going through, having lost me, and then her beloved granddaughters.

Raven was a steeplejack and climbed church steeples to repair and paint them. He was paid well, and he gave most of the money to me. What was left, it seemed he spent on Rose on toys, and games, and now a video recorder.

He tried to treat Arianna and Gwen as well, with presents or money or classes, but it was almost impossible. The gifts would be impounded, the classes ignored, or the girls punished for having an interaction with myself or Raven. It could be as simple as accepting a gift.

If I bought them clothes and they brought them back to John's, Helleen would punish them (usually Gwen) with either grounding her or depriving her of a phone call to me or John or by having her babysit her three very young brothers, for days and days unending; and then, additionally, destroy or "lose" the clothes. If it was something really special my mother had bought for Arianna or Gwen, Helleen would make sure she got a message to me that either Arianna or Gwen had not really cared for the item and it had been maliciously destroyed or carelessly set aside or lost. The household was poisonous and any contact was like touching toxic waste.

Gwen loved to dance and we signed her up for classes and when it was John and Helleen's turn to take her, they would call the teacher and say Gwen was "sick" or otherwise unable to attend. Eventually, she would have to drop out of anything I signed her up for because they would essentially sabotage her practices and her classes, and she would fall too far behind. In essence, they destroyed all her hope and joy related to the activity. Her dreams to be a dancer died early.

Stripped of all rights as a mother to Arianna and Gwen, Raven honored my role as mother to Rose. I was grateful. A monster who "respected," or at least acknowledged, the mother, in his own strange monster way, was light years ahead of the "perfect" psychopath and her deranged pet monkey who ceaselessly and purposefully tried to destroy myself and Arianna and Gwen, with what I was slowly beginning to realize, was some kind of trauma-based mind control.

It was if she was working from a template that the Nazi's might have used in Germany in their mental "health" torture facilities. At times, I wondered if there really was a method, a template, a formula, that was being used because it struck the heart, mind, and soul, with such agonizing accuracy, it was hard to believe it was not part of a system that had been used successfully in other places, at other times. It was the perfect way to destroy lives, family, and even an entire culture and no one would ever know, because the perpetrator of the death cult was a "perfect" citizen or institution.

It was unspeakably confusing. While John tried to destroy all traces of me, Raven unequivocally allocated all mothering to me. He was in awe of my education, my journalism skills, my vocabulary, my books by Charles Dickens and Emily Bronte. Two people could not be so opposite, I often thought. How did it happen that we were together?

Almost daily, weather permitting, during the week, when the motley gang was not around, I'd dress up Rose, put her in the carriage along with her strange toys such as a jointed wooden snake from Reny's Department store; and we would walk the three blocks to the Skidompha Library in downtown Damariscotta to get books and videos.

Flowers and apple trees were in bloom in May and green sprouted from every nook and cranny in the ancient gray rock wall that lined the sidewalk, and from the openings in the sidewalk, on Church Street.

Lawns were emerald green from endless rain. Rose would squeal excitedly and raise up her hands and legs, when we splashed through puddles. I would smile, delighted when she reached out her chunky hand to collect dew from wet leaves as we passed; again, always, with the accompanying pain, of my other daughters who I wished could see the flowers and the trees and the grass and laugh at the puddles.

Rose loved water, and in Maine the air was misty and smelled of salty ocean. I handed her little bouquets of flowers I picked along the way and she would bury her face in them, not so much with joy, like I did, but with a contemplative glazed look in her eyes, seriously aware of some kind of magic or mystical property unseen, but felt in the flower. Or maybe she was analyzing just one more piece of the puzzle of life on Earth.

Once inside Skidompha, Rose often sat on cushions in the children's book area and created a pile of mostly picture books and began to "read," which meant roughly and rapidly, flipping through the hard books and briefly scanning the colorful images. She seemed on a mission for certain information, whereas I had been contemplative and pondered and deeply digested words and thoughts and phrases.

I never understood Scorpios, which she was, having been born on November 1st, otherwise known as All Saint's Day or Day of the Dead.

Once I got my books (usually written by shamans or mystics, or by Dickens), I'd stuff them in the carriage, behind Rose's back and at her side, and I'd also have them in a plastic bag hanging from both my arms.

At home we spread the books out on the purple and blue antique braided rug (the same one Arianna used to dance on , in circles, in her white lace dress, and her image lived on and on in my mind, swirling in circles like a ghost, lost to me forever). With Mac and cheese in bowls and fruit juice boxes beside us, we'd each dive into our private world, Rose still on a mission, and me, trying to stay alive, trying to pretend, for Rose, that everything was OK.

I'd sip Red Rose tea, read about Kathy wandering the ancient moors of England. I could feel the wind in my hair, and smell the moors, and then Rose, holding a thick cardboard book, would plunk herself heavily into my lap, and say, "Read." She sometimes spilled my tea or knocked my book out of my hand. She definitely broke the spell; my rare moment of escape to another world.

As much as I liked to think of myself as different from Sally and my mother, and I was on so many levels, all of us floated, it seemed, from island to island, or home to home, in dangerous waters, seeking some kind of meaning to this life, through abusive men, although it was never an intention.

Did we call them or had they been *assigned* to us somehow? A curious word, assigned, but how did three very innocent and well-meaning women; end up in tragedies parallel to *Wuthering Heights* and worse (in some cases like the shower scene in *Psycho*).

Heathcliff glorified nature, in a sense, but nature out of control, beyond reason; a tornado, with bones, and shredded barn doors, and screaming children, and ruined crops in the whirlwind. Was it some kind of disconnection from primal nature that caused us to create a maleficent storm in our own kitchens?

Sally and my mother were the harbingers of dark information; secret money exchanges; secret exchanges of prescription drugs; secret bottles of wine and brandy; news of rape; news of illicit love affairs.

They were, to me, at times, the dark side of the Goddess – Crazy Women. They scared me and I felt both inferior and better than them, but somehow, against my will, deeply intertwined in their souls' dangerous, dark journeys.

Often arriving home early from work, Raven, after leaving spilled coffee, an open Hazelnut creamer, discarded coffee filters, and a coffee machine, still on hot, would wander into the living room and sit on the couch with a Viking-size mug of cream-colored coffee in hand.

He would take a sip, balance it on the couch arm and stare at Rose and I sitting on the rug. Still in steeplejack work clothes, (t-shirt and jeans and a leather belt with an oval sterling silver belt buckle); and smelling of ocean air, tobacco, and coffee, he would begin a commentary about Rose.

"Remember, before Rose was born, when she was still a spirit, you said you saw her riding in circles above our heads. Above the hot tub...on a painted pony. She seemed excited" he said.

"Yes, the vision was amazing. I'll never forget it," I said, sharing a warm memory with him. Almost delirious, one hour before giving birth to Rose, Raven sat with me in a whirling tub of water inside Miles Memorial Hospital.

"She's really smart for her age, isn't she?" he'd say and take another sip of coffee, often spilling on his shirt or onto the couch.

"Do you think she should go to Montessori or some kind of school like that?" he asked me. I was the authority. At least within my prison, I was.

"Yes, I really like Montessori, "I responded, quietly.

In actuality, I'd already driven by Montessori on Main Street in Damariscotta several times in my mother's yellow Prelude sports car, with Rose secure in her car seat in the back (still in diapers and drinking from a bottle) but I was already thinking ahead. I had completely distanced myself from my Bowdoin-educated father, but clearly, judging from my grandmother, who had gone to New England Institute of Music in Boston, in the late 1800's, the benefits of education ran in my blood.

That night after Raven had talked about Rose for almost an hour, (with me agreeing with all his compliments and praise of her, of course) and after a quiet dinner, and while Rose slept in a crib, in the small room right beside our room; so close, I could hear her breathing – Raven and I had lain awake.

I was on my side, facing away from Raven, my hands folded under my head, in a prayer position, staring through the three floor-to-ceiling glass windows, at the sky and the stars.

The stars and the endless black sky entered thoughts of eternity into my mind; and maybe a better life after this one – all of which gave me hope and strength and some peace of mind.

Raven, bare-chested, a cup of creamy coffee (even at ten PM) resting on his muscular, hairy chest and still wearing jeans, stared at his cup. I was fully covered in a white cotton sleeping gown from Reny's.

I told him what I always told him, and he listened with interest and respect. I told him that I believed I was from a star system called Pleiades and that the humans who had once lived in Atlantis and on The land of Mu (Hawaii being the only visible remnants of Mu) were the descendants of Pleiadeans.

I played with the purple beaded Indian earrings Raven had made for me, which were on the nightstand.

"After the cataclysm which covered Mu in tidal waves, the humans who escaped went west in their ships. They landed in Arizona, California, Mexico, and South America. They are the Hopi, the Navajo, the Aztecs and the Mayans." I said, softly.

He loved these conversations as much as I did, as they brought my mind away from Arianna and Gwen, and into another world, and into eternity, and the endless past, and the galaxies unknown and maybe undiscovered.

"I love that Hopi book," Raven said.

I knew what book he meant. *The Book of the Hopi* by Frank Waters and *Black Elk Speaks* by John G. Neihardt, were the only two books I'd ever seen him pick up and actually read.

Written from the worldview of thirty Hopi elders, *The Book of Hopi* tells the story of the migration of the Hopi from the western coast of California, east, and inland and as far north as Canada and the Arctic Pole long before the supposed migrations of Europeans to the Americas.

The Hopi book also talked about the four worlds of human life – *First World*, The Era of Earth (domination by women) *Second World*, The Era of Man (domination by men) and what we are in now, and *Third World*, The Era of Women (a time of peace, prosperity and equality between men and women and children). This third world, wherein we will see equality between men, women and children, is what the Spanish philosopher called The Tri-une culture.

The Hopis believe that what we are experiencing now on Earth, and in the next few decades would be the Great Cleansings, which would purify the earth, preparing the earth for the four thousand years of peace, i.e., the Era of Women.

Each successive world, according to the Hopi (and, according to the elders, the Hopi people went underground for at least one of the earth cleansings) had been destroyed by cataclysmic earth changes, including the Great Flood.

My mother believed she had lived on Atlantis when the third world had been destroyed. She recalled "waves so huge they covered all of the cities and all I could see was darkness" right before the end, I had told Raven.

"The Hopi probably came from Mu, too, and landed on the California coast. And then went inland, off the coast" I added.

"But there were other survivors of Mu who traveled further east and landed in Atlantis. When Atlantis was destroyed the survivors went west again to the coast of Africa. Those Lemurians are the original Egyptians," I added.

"Oh, is that from that book you're always reading ... *The Civilization of Mu* ... or something like that man, by Colonel somebody?" he asked

"Yes. Colonel James Woodward. It's a great book."

"I love to listen to you talk. I could listen to you all night," he said, sitting up, reaching for his coffee and taking a sip.

"It feels so natural, you and I, like we have known each other forever, like we have been talking like this forever," He said.

This was always hard. On a deep level I felt the same closeness; the same familiarity; the comfort of having someone who felt like a "tribe." I'd never really known a family life. Maybe for a year or two with John's family but I'd learned in the past year, that was all an illusion. Behind my back, within that family, was gossip and treachery aimed in my direction.

Continually guilt-tripping him that we were "living in sin" before we were married, John's mother, Pat, was responsible for the trauma before our marriage; then during the marriage by reporting to him while he was out to sea – mostly gossip and judgment about the dining room set I'd bought at Walfield-Thistle and the nanny I'd hired to help me with house cleaning, since I'd never been taught how to clean or cook. Marion didn't allow me in the kitchen.

And even now, after the divorce, it seemed Pat reported to John anything she heard she thought was detrimental about me. She was apparently ignorant (or did not care) that any information she funneled to Helleen and John, was slowly destroying Arianna and Gwen. You cannot destroy the mother, without also destroying the children.

"Well, we were brother and sister, in another lifetime, in Victorian England. You know that, right. And we were both Sioux. I was a medicine woman and you were a chief, a warrior. I honestly think I saw you as a chief."

"Yeah, I think you're right. That seems right," he said thoughtfully.

I was quiet. I only had so many moments when I would think of Arianna and Gwen, without starting to cry or sob or break down somehow.

"Don't stop talking. I love listening to you," he says, leaning toward me and kissing my shoulder and neck, and wiping the hair from my face and eyes.

In the moonlight, he would always see the tears on my face. Sometimes he would lay back down and stare at the ceiling. It seemed endless. My agony. Sometimes it was just the tears, other times spasms of agony wracked my body.

Then I'd feel his arms and shoulder muscles tighten around me, he was straining them ever slightly, to try to hold me together. My whole body would shake. When the shaking had subsided, and the tears dried, we would simply lie there, staring out the window at the moon or the stars. There were no words anymore.

All the words were gone.

But there was something to be grateful for, I had slowly realized. Demons and negative entities, I believe had been created in rituals by the Bath Satanists, were unable to pass over or through, or even under, the three rivers that flowed east to west in long jagged fingers to the ocean, from the mountains or lakes inland in Maine.

Additionally, on the coast, where I lived, the salty ocean water co-mingled with these rivers as they encroached upon the sea, creating rivers of a high, pure energy vibration. The spirits of ancient Mic Mac, who lived, mostly in peace, along the riverbanks, I believe, protected me. Demons, even if they could pass the three rivers between Bath and Damariscotta, would be interrupted at the river by the good spirits of the Indian Ancestor.

So, I was able to grieve without fear a demon could enter into my energy field, in my times of vulnerability. And it was often with these thoughts of Native Indians, protecting my heart and my soul, as they had done, a long time ago along Indian River in Hanover, when I was a child, when I believed I was The Queen of the River.

Malevolent entities on the unseen levels in Bath, surely created by the Satanists who worshiped behind Dike Newall school, were unable to follow me across the three rivers between Bath and Damariscotta. I had slowly figured out, after observing, after dozens and dozens of trips back and forth between Bath and Damariscotta, trying to pick up Gwen (sometimes two or three times a day, as Helleen strategically planned to make sure Gwen was either not at home or she would tell me Gwen had to babysit the three boys).

John would either be thousands of miles away on a ship and Helleen would be off jogging, exercising her already emaciated body. I could not force Gwen to get in the car and come home with me, and leave the infant and toddler children alone (even though Gwen was just a child, she was often left alone with the boys).

Helleen utilized all relationships to control or threaten Gwen. Helleen would refuse to let Gwen talk to her father on the phone. She would tell her little brothers (who were becoming Gwen's only companions) that Gwen was bad and irresponsible for not taking care of them when she had ordered it for the day. She would tell John Gwen had disobeyed her some-how, either by not doing a chore she was assigned, or neglecting the boys, or not cleaning the tub, and she would get John to agree over the phone, on what her punishment would be (and often it would be that Gwen was not allowed to talk to him).

If Gwen was ever able to get ahold of her father (which was almost im-possible as he was on a ship thousands of miles away) and she would try to tell him what was happening to her, she would have more punishment inflicted on her by both John and Helleen.

It was an infinite circle of mind-control trauma, from which there seemed no escape, and the very worst was always ahead, it would always increase. Sometimes I drove one hundred and fifty miles a day, just to try to find a moment when Helleen would let Gwen out of the house.

But Gwen never gave up. Despite the avalanche of mind-control, the punishments from John and Helleen, the threats, the cohesion, the ma-nipulation of therapists who called her "co-dependent" because she want-ed to be with me, she never gave up. Never once did she believe any of the lies, never once did it ever occur to her she would not try with all her heart to see me. She was only ten years old, and kind and sweet, and smart and loving, yet she had half an army of adults who were intent on her destruction.

All my children were alive. But I knew in every bone of my body that Helleen would and could kill them if she found an opportunity to do so without being caught; in fact, if she could kill them while appearing as if she had been trying to help them, all the better.

The death of thirteen-year-old Sarah Cherry was never far from my mind. As long as Arianna and Gwen were in Bath, and essentially without the protection of either parent, or either family, i.e., they were orphaned and living with a psychopath who was not accountable, in her actions, to anyone, they were in great danger.

Rose had me at least. I knew our bond would give her strength. I also knew Raven could and would harm her if he needed to do this to manipulate a situation.

And now a year later, I was still breathing. I was being slowly reassembled by the healers in Damariscotta and Bristol and Newcastle.

Trauma after trauma had been released as the many key points on my spine and in my acupuncture meridian points were gently urged to open and clear with super fine needles or simple gentle pressure of the fingertips. To relive the worst experience, these practitioners spoke in gentle tones, and I was coaxed to trust, in offices painted in soothing pastel colors, which were surrounded by woods or ocean or the lake or the river.

But I healed while still in a steel trap, the jagged jaws of the monster; set to clamp onto my neck or the necks of my daughters if I took one wrong move, said one wrong thing.

If I was to get out alive and to get my children out, at least physically alive, from this war, I had to figure into whose jail I had been imprisoned. Into what war had I been immersed. No one was going to stop this war. No one was going to tell me it was over. It was going to go on forever and each one of us would die, in one way or another, if I could not figure this out.

A small, infinitesimal light; no, not even a light but a memory of a light; maybe not inside of me; but as part of a greater knowledge known to me once; or maybe known in the greater overreaching intelligence of all of humanity; did exist and had not been tortured out of me.

Deep down in my soul a seed of Love had been planted; and this idea lived on in the marrow of my bones; deeper than even the physicality of them.

With her magic wand in hand (i.e. Mary Baker Eddy's big blue book, *Science and Health; With Key to the Scriptures*) Mrs. Horniman, the old Christian Science practitioner from Hanover, had said, at my birth, and even before my birth, while I was being born, "Love is the real and eternal. God is Love. We are love."

Maybe this belief lived on even without my consent. Maybe even if they had burned me at the stake, eventually they would find this Light; this truth; this belief. Rather than marrow, at the end, there would be light; or the interior; of the bone.

My life was not just a stumbled upon hell. Maybe I was living a microcosm reality of a larger macrocosm of an agenda. Or, if I was living out a legend, like Persephone and Demeter, or an archetype. There would be a key in the archetype; a message; and maybe, if I could find it, a passageway out of the archetype, and into life and freedom for my daughters and I.

An ancient evil for sure. But where did it begin, who was it, and how do we destroy it?

I'd known since I was a child the healing powers of the Earth, but questions of this magnitude needed to come from a universal source; something galactic or heavenly.

Indian Head River, the old apple tree, the lilac bushes, Misty, the half wild appaloosa stallion, even the old corn stalks and withering tomato plants, had filled me with love, a mystery, the moon, the stars…the dew on the long blades of grass. What was this love? Where did it come from? Gaia, the earth herself, but earth was only a small diamond in an infinite reality of billions of stars and planets. How did it all relate to my circumstances? I realized that enough of my brain had been healed from trauma, that I could think clearly enough to begin to ask questions.

I began a search for the source of evil; maybe an ancient evil.

CHAPTER 42

MARIJA GIIMBUTAS

The next day, instead of her riding in a carriage to the library, Rose and I walked hand in hand. Wearing jean overalls from Reny's and a red and blue flannel shirt, her light brown hair pulled back in ponytail with a red ribbon, and, in her little backpack filled with her favorite toys and strapped on her back, Rose walked along the top of the old stone wall, while I held her hand.

At the library she sat on the soft cushion on the floor, and investigated, one by one, with furrowed brow, a pile of Calvin and Hobbes books (her new favorite).

Intently, in the quiet recess of the library, I gathered books on ancient history, mythology – Joseph Campbell anthropology, ancient religion – the Gnostic Gospels, books about the legend of Persephone and Demeter, books on Atlantis, the Hopi Indians, Joan of Arc, and of course, shamanism – Lynn Andrews and Sandra Inger man.

I loved all of Lynn's books, but mostly, *Medicine Woman* and The *Women of Wyyrd*. The latter told the story of a young girl, in seventeenth century England, who lived in a beautiful manor in the English countryside, whose parents were of nobility, but who rode her horse, almost daily, deep into the woods, to meet in secret in a little cottage, with an older wise woman, she called Grandmother. Grandmother was a shapeshifter and a secret follower of the Goddess and the *Way of Wyrd*.

I gathered up my collection of books and Rose and her books, and we checked out and walked the one block back to our house. We ate quietly at the round table in the kitchen; tuna fish sandwiches, potato chips and juice and tea, and apple crisp for dessert.

Rose had a row of ceramic Red Rose animals she played with while she ate. I tried hard to focus on Rose, but my stomach was tight, and I was emotional. I remembered how Gwen had lined up her stuffed animals and put daisies in front of all of them. I had to exert such self control during these moments.

Later, when both Rose and I had settled down – she on the thick, soft braided rug – and I curled up on the couch, we began to independently plow through our books.

Sandra's book "Soul Loss" described the effects of repeated trauma on the soul – how the soul would essentially leave the body, piece by piece, until, potentially, in case of severe ongoing trauma (like being a soldier in war or in the family court systems) only half of that person's soul would remain.

The person with severe soul loss, would feel almost nothing; absent; half dead; and more trauma would follow without the soul intact. As I read on and on, I knew without a doubt, even with all the healers who had put me back together again – at least emotionally – I was now only half alive, only half present on the planet.

I put down Sandra's book, yawned and stretched and then began again with the book by anthropologist Marija Gimbutus, *The Language of the Goddess.*

I had learned there had once been peace on Earth. No wars. It had not always "just been like this" as I'd heard repeated over and over. An ancient, peaceful, highly artistic, highly spiritual civilization had once lived in Europe five thousand years before Christ. She called the artifacts she found, the language of the Goddess. It was not a world or a hierarchy of women over men, but of peace and equality. No instruments of war or torture or imprisonment were found at the excavation sites.

There it was. A time before time, a language that spoke of a Divine Feminine and respect for all of life.

In that moment, still wearing a green cashmere scarf around my neck, and a calf-length pure wool purple coat with a hood, and L.L. Bean boots – the melting snow from them creating puddles where I sat – I felt I had found the outer parameters of evil. And a time frame. Five thousand years ago.

The strength or ferocity and longevity of this evil, seemed to be based, in part, on the fact that most of us do not know there had been time *without it*. The time before time, the time before war, the time of peace, had to be kept secret, just like…The Holy Grail.

Gimbutas was marginalized and degraded by her male peers because she had provided us with a key. A key to another world, or was it the world, and what we were all living within now was an experiment; an aberration; an anomaly; a mistake?

I had found a map and a key. It showed boundaries, the onset of evil and the end of peace.

If evil had a beginning, *it could have an end*. Hope stirred faintly, like a wispy pink cloud on a light blue horizon somewhere in ancient history. Before the ancient pre-history European Goddess civilization, what existed? How far back in time did peace originate?

What about Atlantis? The sunken continent? Had Atlanteans also been peaceful? Had they done "something terrible" as my mother suggested? She said waves towered over the city and then all went black. But what before Atlantis. And why did Atlantis fall? Was it arbitrary? Was it the great flood suggested in the Bible? Had evil propagated Atlantis and then the culture had been punished? Or were the Atlanteans innocent and they were destroyed by evil? Where were the Atlanteans now? My mother, I knew, was in Damariscotta, Maine, only a mile or less from me. Would they be punished again? Or had they learned their lesson? Was I from Atlantis?

And from where had the Atlanteans originated? Humans evolving from apes, seemed like a big in-a-hurry-to-think-of-something-to-control-them lie. And, my research for my master's thesis on shamanism, had indicated that shamanism had reinvented itself repeatedly at most all points on the earth, independent of any preceding or evolutionary context. The Bearing Straits, in my opinion, had very little to do with migration from east to west or vice versa.

Rose had abandoned her pile of books and was playing with her toys and a deck of playing cards...

I stared out the window...

Almost everything else taught in school seemed like a lie now. In school, my self-esteem plummeted in the oppressive cloud of disinformation and manipulation. Peeling out of the Needham High School parking lot, mid-day, in Billy's white 1966 Corvette, with a cigarette between my lips, and Purple Haze blaring from the speakers, was maybe more than adolescent rebellion. Maybe I knew, way back then, when I was told to memorize wars and other atrocities, about the BIG LIE.

According to researcher John Churchward, The Naacal tablets, books, and inscriptions found in India, China, Burma, Tibet, and Cambodia; ancient Maya books, inscriptions; symbols and legend from Yucatan and Central America; stone tablets in Mexico, and inscriptions, symbols and legends in the Pacific Island, indicate humanity originated on Lemuria, or the Land of Mu.

Lemuria was a continent approximately 6000 miles east to west and 3000 miles north to south and situated in the Pacific Ocean between

North America and Asia. Churchward said Mu had existed for 500,000 years as a highly advanced civilization before it was submerged in an underwater gas explosion, 12,000 years ago.

The Land of Mu, or Lemuria, according to Churchward, was the origin of all human civilization on earth and the same place described in the Bible as The Garden of Eden.

Churchward contended that the people of Mu, who survived, departed (some before the cataclysm) in sailing vessels, heading east. His records indicate these people landed on various locations inland, hundreds of miles up and down the western coast of California, and Alaska, and then again inland, in Mexico, the Yucatan, and South and Central Americas. Other survivors went even further east and settled on Atlantis. A few threads of surviving Lemurians from Mu even made it as far as inland Africa and Northern Europe.

When Atlantis fell into the swirling dark seas, survivors again went eastward, again on sailing vessels, this time colonizing southern and eastern Europe. These Lemurians were the original Celts, Egyptians, The Greeks, Romans, and, I am guessing, the peaceful, nonaggressive, highly evolved spiritual and creative Civilization of the Goddess, Marija Gimbutas had recognized as having existed in European prehistory, approximately five thousand year ago in Paleolithic Old Europe.

Combined, the books and the information therein, by the English Colonel James Churchward and those by Lithuanian archeologist Dr. Marija Gimbutas, wove a fabric of both intuitive and academic information that became an ethereal map, a beacon in a dark stormy sea, a compass; something I could hold on to; information I turned until my big red compass arrow pointed at "good" (and opposite of "evil") and began to walk.

I was headed straight on into a time before time in search of freedom. I had enough information now to give me hope; something I had never had my entire life based on the information fed to me up until this point. Everything good, it appeared, had been hidden from humanity.

Was it because I had the potential to unlock this information that I was being hunted?

CHAPTER 43

SOUL RETRIEVAL

In Damariscotta, during the day hours, when my mother could babysit for Rose, I had many helpers and healers, trying to put me together again, as I have said.

Sylvia Tavares, a Reiki master, and friend, who lived in a huge white house near the Damariscotta River, just across the bridge in Newcastle, gifted me with healings and certified me as a Reiki one healer. She also said she intuitively felt it would benefit me to visit the local psychic, who lived in Damariscotta, within walking distance of my house.

So, after making an appointment, a week later, on a sunny day in February, which was cold, of course, I bundled Rose in her winter snowsuit and a wool scarf and mittens (which she hated and pulled off and threw on the ground) and Rose stuffed her Winnie the Pooh toys into the back of the carriage and, I, dressed, similarly, for winter, except in L.L. Bean coat and boots, set out to see the psychic.

I pushed the carriage down the quiet Church Street over thick frozen sheets of ice, and then, periodically, dry tarred road. It made a bumpy ride for Rose.

Pink cheeked and leaning forward with arms raised holding a jointed wooden snake in one hand, she was unconcerned about the cold; she was a happy ship figurehead cutting straight through icy seas. She seemed a confluence of the Goddess Isis with raised serpent staff, Neptune's angel, and of course (minus the snake) us together, a Rockwell postcard impression of mother and daughter, out for a walk on a Maine winter day.

Quiet, but brilliant sparkling snow lay on lawns behind white picket fences, and on the evergreen fir and pine branches. The child within somehow partially still alive, in me, pauses and ponders, at the exquisite snowflakes that fall like fairy champagne, from the fir branches, when I tap them with my gloved hand.

I stop for a moment and stare at the stark white steeple of the local church.

I wondered if Raven was hanging from a church steeple at this moment, or in his truck, cigarette butt between his lips, meandering quickly through the winding, tree-lined back road of Newcastle on his way to find me.

He grew more and more suspicious, I might try to leave –

At any rate, I pushed Rose on past the Lincoln Theatre and then left on Main Street towards Water Street, over swollen ice. At the corner by Waltz's Pharmacy, Rose and I stopped and ate banana splits, French Fries and grilled cheese at their old-fashioned soda fountain counter.

We bundled up again and departed but then saw Wolfie, who, motionless on the sidewalk, stood staring into space; somewhere only he knew.

The blue smoke from his pipe became almost invisible in the thin blue white air of Maine in February; a corncob pipe clenched in his teeth and held by one large brown hand.

"Hi Wolfie," I said, keeping my pace, as I did not have time to talk.

"Oh...Jane...Hi...I need to talk," he said, taking the pipe out of his mouth and stepping forward off the curb.

I bit my lip, not wanting to hurt him.

"Oh, really, what is it Bob, what is up?"

"Hi Rose," he says, taking the pipe out of his month, and smiling at her.

"Hi Wolfie," Rose says, distracted. She makes a wolf image with her two fingers and thumb. Then he looks at me and lowers his pipe even further.

"You know Sally and I are thinking about getting hitched"

"Yeah, I know Bob," I sigh, and pick up one boot and squeeze my toes. I think my toes are somewhat frozen.

And then he rolls his eyes.

"My mother is not gonna like it. She is not gonna like it one little bit," he says, very seriously, exactly as if he was a six-year-old boy.

"It'll be okay, Bob," I say, and stare into his eyes to determine his reaction.

I don't think it will be okay, but in the grander scheme of things, it seemed irrelevant either way. And being married to my sister, who was full of jokes, and a comedic way of looking at life, and a lot of artistic energy, he would certainly at least have fun and not be lonely for awhile anyway.

Bob had whittled a little wooden bird for Rose. She loves the awkward wooden bird and somehow the bird reminded me of Rose. He had truly captured her spirit in the bird.

And around my kitchen table, while we sat on hard back wooden chairs, before our cups of hot Red Rose tea, the winter sun low and penetrating through my kitchen window; the brown rugged hunchback beast of Bob, his expensive gray wool coat covered in wood shavings, and smelling of spruce, I could imagine Sally and Bob together.

He puts his pipe back in his mouth, puffs; a look of consternation on his face, as he digests my words. I stood, feeling emptiness, which was a relief.

Maybe he reminded me of my grandfather, the only kind man in my family. He also had a corn cob pipe. Bob did not know what was happening to me and my daughters. It was just the wind and this faint sun, and the smell of hotdogs and popcorn from Waltz's soda stand. The gentle lap of the river against the landing behind downtown; and pipe smoke dissolving into thin air.

All was well with this relative stranger who had done me no harm, who judged me not. It could have been just another Maine Norman Rockwell moment, except, if you knew what I knew, about Maine.

Satanists had infiltrated Bath and had probably killed twelve-year-old Sara Cherry and blamed it on Dennis Dechaine. Guardian ad litem and two Maine therapists had trafficked my two daughters, into the home of a psychopathic, sexually abusive, non-relative, who essentially was holding them prisoners and using them as babysitters and live pawns in a game of hell on earth.

This was the real Maine, at least for me, and probably for a lot of other poor Maine women.

"Bye Bob, I'll see you later," I said over my shoulder as I pushed Rose uphill on Main towards Water Street.

"Everything will be okay," I say, truly concerned for his feelings.

"Yeah. Well, I love Sally and Sally loves me. That's for sure," he says, and stares down at the ice. I'm reminded of the Sally, Jane and Dick books from grade school.

"That's true," I respond, pulling my scarf tighter with one hand.

"Bye Rose," he says in a cutesy tone, and smiling

"Bye Wolfe" Rose says and holds up the snake again, as we head uphill and into the wind.

Inside the huge rambling white Greek revival era house on Water Street, Rose plays quietly on a thick oriental rug beside a window framed with antique lace curtains, and the psychic and I sit in chairs, almost facing each other.

"You are a very old soul, as is your daughter, Rose," She went on. "You are both healers. In Bath, you were dealing with a great deal of evil as well as your ex-husband, who is a young soul. He is very naïve and unsure of himself and easily swept up by those he perceives as powerful. He was used as a pawn," she says.

I sip herbal tea from an old chipped China cup, my mood very somber. The almost-Norman Rockwell Maine I'd had moments earlier on Main Street, beside Walt's pharmacy, had shattered into a thousand pieces. Bob's corn cob pipe, Rose's snake, my own boots, in small fragments all over the icy ground. We are back to the endless war.

"You have an important mission to fulfill. Many have come forward to help you, and will continue to come forward, but it is up to you to bring it to a conclusion," she said.

The healing part is true. Doctors, acupuncturists, Reiki healers, psychics, chiropractors, herbalists, a new therapist, had been working hard to try to put me back together again.

"Many more will follow to help, but you have to follow the steps yourself."

She hands me a small business card. I tentatively reach out for it. Friend or foe, I never know. Business cards are potential land mines. I could lose a child, if I take the wrong card. My heart was racing. Therapists and guardian ad litems and lawyers had business cards. I trusted no one.

"Susan Bakaley Marshall," I read out loud, my palms sweating.

"She's a shaman," the psychic responds. "She lives in Freedom, at the top of a mountain. It's called Thirteenth Moon Center."

"I think you'll like her," she says.

"Get to her as soon as you can," she added.

"Be careful," she added. It was a little late for that, I thought internally.

"Squaaaaaaak," the parrot reiterated.

"Thank you," I responded, wondering exactly what she meant.

After tea and pleasantries, I gathered up Rose and her toys, and opened the front door, which was one in a series of old, white creaky doors that led down a narrow dim hall to the actual front door. The huge, rambling old house was divided up like a maze.

I helped Rose back into the stroller and as we walked away, I turned into the sunlight to see on top of the house, a widow's walk; a small square fenced in porch built on top of the roof. A captain's wife must once have prowled in circles inside this structure, periodically raising her hand to her brow, to block the sun or the wind from her eyes, so she received a clear view of ships incoming up the river from the sea.

What freedoms she had, I thought, to dream of him, at the wheel of the ship, hair blowing free in a night breeze, under a starry blue-black sky with the moon pale upon a quiet sea. To love someone without fear they would be tortured if they reached out to you or you reached out to them.

Rose, preoccupied with her toys, did not see the tears stream down my cheeks as we walked. Gwen and Arianna. Everything reminded me of them, because they were part of every cell of my body, as I had carried them each for nine months. It was like they had been dragged from my womb and I was bleeding to death, while still standing.

CHAPTER 44

THE FIRST SHAMAN

A week later, driving my mother's yellow Honda convertible sports model Prelude, I easily maneuver the narrow, winding roads inland from coastal Damariscotta to Freedom. The roads are icy, so I slow on the curves. Black ice.

Memories of Jim flood my mind. He helped me wallpaper the front foyer with the green paper with cream hydrangea. Maybe it was not the help, but his manifest kindness.

He died so suddenly and instantly. On ice. On black ice. The girls and I would have been better; safer, happier; if I'd even had the support of one member of John's family; even my marriage to John might have survived.

A few more curves and hills. Fear enters my heart. What insanity to try to go see a therapist, a licensed therapist in Maine? A card-carrying therapist. I keep telling myself she is also a shaman, but my palms sweat.

What if Susan calls Kathleen Sullivan and tells her I was there at her office. What if Susan thinks I'm paranoid, too? What if they all talk on the phone tonight after I depart. Rose could be taken away from me. I imagined a social worker coming to the door and taking Rose. The Guardian ad litem and Kathleen Sullivan would be standing at the door, too.

What was I doing? Terror stripped me of the small joy I was experiencing on the road through the backwoods of Maine. I slowed down and stopped the car. I could save myself, if I just turned around. It would be better. I shouldn't trust anyone. I wiped the sweat from my brow and just sat at the side of the road with the car running. Would Susan find a way to take Rose away from me?

I start deep breathing. I organize my thoughts. I remember goodness. I remember truth. I remember healing. I try to remember trust. Who suggested I see Susan? It was the psychic.

It felt nice at her home. Sylvia had told me to see Susan; and Sylvia was okay. I'd felt joy with the Reiki. I am healing. Maybe there was one road that was safe. Maybe. Most roads led to death in the patriarchy, but one or two might lead to life.

In my bones, I knew shamanism was healing, at least healing shamanism. I just knew. I knew it from Hanover; from being in the woods; feeling the trees; the river; the thunder of Misty's hooves in my ears. The earth was safe and shamanism was safe, at least now.

Nancy Coleman had been safe.

With thoughts of Nancy and Hanover, I put the car in drive and pressed on the accelerator.

Near Susan's house, The narrow mountain road, lined with leafless trees on both side, steep, but straight and paved, eventually led, at the top, to Susan's simple white Maine farmhouse, aside of which, thigh high in field grass, was an abandoned 1960's VW Van (in which I later learned they had arrived a couple of decades ago) and then, in the back of their property, a round unpainted natural wooden yurt.

Rectangular windows had been inserted around the yurt shoulder high and tendrils of sleepy black smoke curled skyward from its chimney. The wood-burning fire that waited for me ahead, warmed my belly and eased some of the terror which had consumed me on the journey.

Susan, a petite woman, with bifocals, and a mass of black curly hair, had, like me, bundled up for the cold weather. She met me at my car in the small driveway near the yurt. She was Jewish. Years ago, it would have meant nothing – neither good or bad. I was indifferent. But things had changed. Helleen was the evilest person I'd ever met; the most devious; diabolical; inhumane human I'd ever known and I'd known some very bad people.

I had to take a chance. I parked the car and got out. She smiled and shook my hand. I relaxed. We walked without talking toward the front steps of the yurt. I glanced back. The yellow Prelude stood out, like a fallen yellow jelly bean, from a huge Easter basket in the sky, in endless shades of gray that define a Maine spring.

So much like my mother, an Easter Goddess, so thoroughly crucified by the patriarchy. She would somehow die off, disappear, and then come back to life. She was, sometimes, the only light in my life, even though there was a barrier. I could not trust her because of her pain, but yet I understood it.

She bought us food and clothing; and she babysat for Rose; and gave me her car so I could follow this path; to find this key; to freedom. She made birthdays and holidays special and she bore witness to the agony of my life.

I close my eyes, briefly thinking of what it must be like for her to have to bear witness to my agony, the same agony she had gone through in losing me. She had tried to kill herself. Suicide was not an option for me – all three of my daughters would be left with monsters.

A wooden floor, windows, a wood fire, drums, rattles, furs laid on the floor, an opening in the center of the yurt all came into view quickly. It all felt familiar.

I was suddenly reminded of the Lakota Sioux men on horseback in a field in the southwest, another century ago, or more; I had seen in a vision. They said they would be there when I passed over; they were my ancestors; but I could not leave the earth until my destiny had been fulfilled.

Somehow, I felt them here with me now, and it gave me strength and courage. Strength and power whirled around … I held my hands over the fire that blazed inside a wood stove. My body shook suddenly; a tremor, as if I'd already cast off evil that had been attached to me from Bath: as if it could not sustain itself in this beauty and it had to flee.

We stepped inside an inner circle, inside the yurt, the floor was covered in thick animal skins; beautiful rattles and painted drums, and soft pillows, deepened my trust and aligned me with my ancestors, and also, somehow, with Susan.

Sage burned in an abalone shell, and she held it up for me to sage myself and I did, with more dark energies falling away from me; Susan smudged herself with the same smoke. I sat down on one of the pillows and Susan sat across from me and picked up a drum.

A light snow tapped on the yurt and I looked up. The snow on the river in Hanover, the trees in Bunny Forest, the pounding of Misty's hooves on the logging trail, the lilac bushes at the corner of Center and Broadway… I was reminded of all of those things …

"What would you like help with today?" Susan asked.

How could I answer? Where does one begin? Do I dare say what is happening? I looked down and then back up, my eyes lined with tears, which seemed impossible; to feel anything.

I dared to speak, even though almost every word I'd spoken to the judge, the therapists, including Kathleen Sullivan and Nancy, and the guardian, had been used against me; and ultimately, the girls.

I lay still in the yurt, breathing slowly, my heart beat a normal rhythm. Snowflakes pattered on the round skylight. I felt like I was in a tepee, in another century. Maybe that was what was helping me. I felt like I was in another lifetime – far, far away from his one. Another lifetime where I had been respected and loved by an indigenous people. I had been a powerful medicine man. The Lakota Sioux. I touched my hair to see if it was braided.

"I'm going to do a soul retrieval for you. To find the lost pieces of your soul."

I heard the gentle beat of her drum, and the snow patter, and the crackle of the fire and I relaxed and drifted. Bright lights, streaming like stars, passed through my inner vision. The colors of purple, blue, red, and green passed through my vision. I saw a mountain lion, then a lynx, a bear and maybe an angel or a Goddess in the streaming colors. I wasn't dreaming. I was looking into another world.

"I brought back three of your soul pieces," Susan said, about an hour later, as we both sat upright in the yurt. The spring snow still fell. I looked up. The light seemed brighter and I squinted.

"I believe one was at about seven years old. Then another at 39. And then again, more recently," she said.

The snow was falling harder, her voice seemed gentle, but loud. I rubbed my ear. I looked down at my feet and studied them like I'd never seen them before. I wondered if I could stand up. I was looking around like an alien who had just landed on the planet and had to figure out how to take my first step.

CHAPTER 45

THE CONSEQUENCE OF POWER

Aweek later, at a local breakfast diner in Damariscotta, I sip mocha-colored coffee from a thick-rimmed white diner-style porcelain cup. Rose is in a highchair and pulled up close to our small square table that is draped in a red and white checkered tablecloth. My mother is seated across from me and I'm trying not to stare, but it feels like I'm seeing her for the first time.

Instead, I look at the yellow and white chrysanthemum flower arrangement in a small deep blue glass vase. Even the flowers look different, somehow. I touch a flower. It's real and it feels the same. They just look more vibrant, full of themselves.

The Breakfast Place is jammed, as usual.

"So how was your meeting with Susan?" my mother asks, truly excited.

She takes a sip of her coffee. Rose is eating round oyster crackers while we wait for our meals.

My mother reminds me of Glinda, with her wand and sparkling gown. Here today and gone tomorrow. I never know when she will disappear or reappear. She has been ill. She has a pain in her back that keeps her in bed – sometimes for the whole day.

"Interesting," I respond slowly.

"She brought back three soul parts," I say.

I didn't tell her that one was the first, when I lost my mother, her, so long ago when my father and Dave Hatch and the court systems willingly implicated her for sleeping out in the forest with a pillow. I did not want to hurt her any more than she was already.

"How fascinating," she exclaims and claps her hands and then holds them in prayer position in front of her heart; her large, Zirconium diamond flashing in the stream of light, flowing in from the small window. Through the window of Damariscotta bay, blue and sparkling shone in the near distance behind the restaurant.

I smile. Her perpetual delight in new, iconoclastic, spiritual information is charming. For a moment, I imagine her at the UFO meeting in Hanover, in the early 1960's, all bright eyed and beautiful, in her white angora sweater.

As a mother of four children, a play school director, a Sunday school teacher, a wife (to a Maine man who considered her beneath him in social status) and a daughter to two elderly parents, it must have been hard, when you had dreamed of being an archaeologist.

She was also on oxygen because of her failed lungs – from smoking too late into her life. I remember her smoking in Watertown when she was in her fifties. But somehow, the breath of life, her ability to ever draw a safe breath of life, may lie at the core of her inability to take a deep breath.

At a bookstore recently I thumbed through the book *Demeter and Persephone, Lessons from a Myth*, by Tamara Agha Jaffar.

"Persephone and Demeter," I had read out loud the introduction …

"This book is about a very old story of a forced separation between a mother and her daughter… and an ancient ritual that re-enacts and commemorates their story. For over one thousand years the story quenched the spiritual thirst of our ancestors and claimed to bestow blessings and happiness on any who were initiated into its mysteries."

I had closed the book, bought it, and quickly exited the store, oblivious to the wind and the snow whirling around my head and whipping hair into my eyes, I was so deep in thought.

In the Greek Myth, young Persephone, daughter of Demeter, Goddess of the Grains, was playing outside with her friends in a field of flowers, when a chasm in the earth suddenly opened up and her Uncle, Hades, King of the Underworld, appeared on his horse-drawn chariot, and grabbed Persephone and brought her to the Underworld where he then raped and married Persephone. Persephone's screams for help were ignored by her father, Zeus.

Demeter, who had heard her screams and searched frantically to find her – to no avail – was deeply distraught and for nine days she searched the surface of the earth for Persephone and was eventually joined by Hecate, Goddess of the Crossroads.

The two Goddesses sought out Helios, the Sun God, who informed the Goddesses that Persephone had been stolen by Hades and now resided in the Underworld. Demeter was to learn that the abduction and rape had transpired with the blessings of Persephone's father, Zeus, Lord of all Gods.

Infuriated, Demeter disguises herself as an old woman, a mortal, and wanders the earth in grief – desperate to find and to rescue her daughter from her rapist. At first, being unsuccessful, Demeter becomes revengeful, and retracts all of earth's bounty and covers the earth in ice. With human starvation a real threat, and offerings to the Gods on a rapid decline, Zeus eventually bends to the pressure, and negotiates with Hades and Demeter for Persephone to be returned to the Earth's surface.

Persephone had eaten a pomegranate while in the underworld, which dictated she must return to Hades three months of the year, but nine months a year Persephone prospers. Demeter rejoices and returns the wheat and grain and flowers and trees to the earth and humanity is saved. Mother and daughter reunited; the earth is again at peace.

I had been in a state of shock, as to how this myth had played out repeatedly in my life, and my mother's and now my daughters. Truly, Arianna had been stolen into the Underworld, by a serpent-like Creature, and her father had watched it happen and done nothing to stop it. I had also been stolen from my mother and repeatedly raped and abused while my father did nothing…

What was happening on earth?

A smiling waitress, wearing a bright white ruffled apron, sets down in front of me a plate with white toast with butter, two extremely big and bright over-medium eggs and bacon. Then a large glass of orange juice. My mother is given the same breakfast. Rose receives a stack of blueberry pancakes.

"Oh my," I say, moderately alarmed, looking at the high stack.

"I don't think Rose can eat all those," I say.

"Oh, she'll have a ball" says my mother, the perpetually optimistic Persephone.

Rose reaches with her large chunky hand, sticky with crackers and juice. She wants the glass bottle of one hundred percent real Maple Syrup from Vermont. I stare at the bottle. The syrup is an amber golden brown like Indian Head River in Hanover. Suddenly, I'm on a raft, floating towards the bridge that crosses over to Hansen. The sunlight filters through the leaves onto the river…

"You want the syrup, Punky?" my mother asks, smiling and unfolding her napkin onto her lap.

Rose nods.

Rose pours the golden amber onto her stack of pancakes. Rose studies the world and how things interact. She sets down the syrup and simply watches the syrup spill down the sides and pool at the bottom of the stack.

Me, dressed like a fall fairy, in brown and moss and gold; next to my mother, in her perpetual Easter colors of bright yellow, pink, and blue, I feel drab. She is truly the Persephone, The Goddess of Spring.

Arianna, my daughter, a fairy princess, delicate, sensitive, loved flowers, trees and books; she too was abducted into hell, where she was abused, with the approval of her father, who fulfilled the role for Zeus as an accomplice to the abduction of his daughter.

"Do you want mommy to cut your pancakes for you?" I ask, hopefully.

"No," Rose responds, trying to lick the syrup from the plate.

"No, thank you" my mother says, correcting Rose.

"No, thank you," Rose mimics my mother, in compliance, but not wholeheartedly. I laugh.

The totality and the potential magnitude of the meaning of the trilogy of daughter after daughter, being abducted and raped, and separated from the Mother, was boggling my mind.

If it was an unimportant myth, then how had it been kept alive for thousands of years, since the Greek Era. Why was this scenario so important to humanity, that the Greeks re-enact the legend every year for a thousand years in the secret ceremonies of the Eurasia Mysteries?

I was myself, but more of myself, more keenly aware of everything, since the soul retrievals. I was more present in my body; I was more me.

Since the soul retrievals, I'd seen Raven clearly as the abusive man he was. Before the soul retrievals, I had been floating above my body, above the earth maybe, not here as the guardian of my own life.

I had been easily manipulated by anyone who appeared to have power or even just plain force or *animation*. Sandra Ingerman, in her book, *Soul Retrieval* had explained that from a shaman's perspective, any kind of trauma, can cause soul loss. Soul loss, which psychologists might refer to as disassociation, was the result of trauma. Violence, rape, divorce, war, surgery, or even a teacher screaming at you as a child could cause soul loss. When you have had repeated traumas, such as I had, beginning with the loss of my mother when I was seven, you have repeated soul loss, which means you are operating mostly without being present on the planet. Multiple soul losses mean you are very vulnerable to outside forces and almost incapable of directing your life.

Would I have even been in Maine at all, if I had been directing my own life; if I had not had multiple traumas and soul loss? I probably wouldn't have even known John if I was not so insecure and lost as a young woman.

I certainly would have never been with Raven. I would have gravitated towards men who were not alcoholics and drug addicts and who loved me. Where would I be right now if I had been *soul full?*

I'd been so absent from reality with Raven, I'd been able to gloss over, and further detach from reality. I thought of the thousands, no, millions of women on the planet who were probably living with abusive men. Most likely, they all had soul loss and were not actually living their reality as it truly existed.

Now, it was clear to me that I was.

Raven had detected a change in me, a new strength and this presented a more complicated problem. I was leaving his vibrational frequency.

"You think you're pretty powerful now," he said, recently, when I was sitting on our bed and drumming lightly, yesterday, and he stopped getting dressed for work, and he looked at me, menacingly.

"What do you mean?" I'd said, trying to sound casual.

Eventually I was able to calm him, but I knew he was on to me and that my power was increasing. It would be a threat; he would stop pretending to be my ally and he would become my enemy – for all the world to see.

This was a new frontier. A new battle. As soon as my other enemies in Bath found out I had left him – if I did – they would see me as even more defenseless; alone; and with new problems (financial and housing) which they could capitalize upon. Everything I did, almost every minute of the day and night, affected the very life or potential death of all three of my daughters.

I knew Raven would use the guardian's report against me. I knew that. I scoffed. As further proof that her whole report was a fabrication and just the collaborative rantings of the stepmother and Victoria Mueller, was that there was no mention of the fact I was in an abusive relationship.

It was the only truth she could have said about me which would have been damaging. But since the truth did not matter, and none of them really cared about Arianna and Gwen; and they preferred to make up all the facts. There had been no real investigation into the truth, even those they could have used against me.

Truth was irrelevant in the world of psychopaths.

A delicate bell tinkles and cold air sweeps across my feet and a door shuts. I look up through the blue glass from which I'm drinking orange juice.

Raven, his black and red checkered jacket speckled in snow, stands at the front door, inside the restaurant. I glance at the restaurant clock. It's only 10 AM. He should be at work. Splatters of white paint on his jeans indicate he has been, at least for a while this morning, painting a church steeple.

"Daddy" Rose yells out, and raises her arms and smiles, and then goes back to her pancakes, and doesn't really carry through on her interest in her arrival.

She knows. She knows who he truly is, I think. It feels like a premonition or an insight into her past lives. He steps forward. I set down my glass and stare at him, unsmiling.

I feel like I've never seen him before in my life. How did I end up with him? I didn't really make this decision. I was not even in my body. Maybe it was everywoman's answer to why they have been in abusive relationships.

I'd been lost, never knowing where to go except when someone pointed me in a certain direction. Someone, like Raven.

Maybe it wasn't just about soul loss. Somehow, maybe I'd been directed to this person. Something or someone knew he would destroy my life. The Dream. I remember the dream where I was told there was a special place for me at the herbal apprenticeship in Athens, Maine with Gail. Had the dream directed me into a curse or was it a curse? How could it be, if it felt so beautiful?

Suddenly, through my third eye, I see my power animal, a bobcat; the same one I'd seen in Freedom during the shamanic journey, and then again on the front page of a local free newspaper I'd picked up when I stopped for a cup of tea, at one of the corner stores in Freedom, on my way home.

"Hello Raven," my mother says, pleasantly. She is always pleasant to him. She is pleasant to all men, like most women of her age who have been conditioned to make everything OK. My mother probably had a hundred soul losses.

"Have a seat. Join the party." she says, and I sense her detachment from her words. But this is normal.

My mother, like myself, doesn't know how you are supposed to react to a threat. We had not the protection skills given to wolf pups by a mother wolf, according to Clarisse Estes, the author of *Women Who Run With the Wolves*. We are supposed to claw their eyes out and throw them onto the ground and handcuff them, not invite them for breakfast.

My power animal jumps forward out of my body and stands erect between myself and Raven. Raven reacts. Fear crosses his face. He stops. He notices something. He's not sure what it is, but his senses are aroused. He feels threatened.

It's a new game. I'm not sure I'm ready, but I've already made the decision to invite power into my life.

I set down my glass and stare at my power animal who then dissolves into the spirit world. Rose cuts into her pancakes with the side of her spoon. My mother digs inside of her huge white plastic purse. She pulls out a plastic dwarf in purple pants with a long white beard.

"Thanks, Polly, I think I will," he says. Raven pulls out a seat, not near me, but between Rose and my mother.

"Hi Rose, how are you?" Raven asks in a sing-song voice. My stomach clenches and the hair on my arms raise in alarm.

"I'm good. I have pancakes!" she exclaims.

"I can see that," he answers, looking at the pancakes and then at me.

"Here you go, Punky. I've been saving this for you," my mother says, thrilled.

She hands the little dwarf to Rose. At home we have leprechauns and elves, and fairy princesses, guardian angels, and dwarves with magical powers, from inside the McDonald's Happy Meals and Red Rose Tea boxes.

"Thank you," Rose responds, and, with sticky fingers, she takes the dwarf and puts him on the table and presses down on the dwarf's arms and the mouth opens. She smiles and my mother laughs. Rose stares at it. She repeats the motion.

"I just love those McDonald toys," my mother says with a truly deep sense of satisfaction. I smile, despite myself.

My mother sips coffee. She loves little toys. Shelves and tabletops and window sills at her old apartment at 174 South Street in Watertown were filled with wind-up toys and other trinkets.

So strange, how I also have little dwarfs and wizards and elephants and a dangerous, alcoholic man in my house, too.

How strange the destiny of mothers and daughters, especially when we try our hardest to not repeat them. Somehow, I felt the myth of Persephone and Demeter held the key to unraveling this mystery.

Rose repeatedly presses on the dwarf's arm lever, and the loud, rat tat tat of the dwarf's plastic arms hitting the table is the only sound. It's like Rose is making violence, visible.

We all simply stare, lost in our own private fears.

Chapter 46

Gwen, The Lion and The Golden Horse

My power animals and spirit guides had been waiting for me to actively call upon them since I'd been born in Middleboro, MA. We are not sent here alone.

My spirit guides in Upper World – Hecate, St. Paul. St. Michael, Grey Wolf, Isis – and my many guides in Lower World (which is not actually lower, but is the dream world earth), Bear, Eagle, Hawk, Jaguar, Panther, Eagle – entered my life in a more directed fashion (by me calling them in every day as I sat with my drum) and they soon became the center of my spiritual life.

I quickly advanced into shamanic journeying into the many worlds – Lower World and Upper World and Middle World – of the shaman. The alternative worlds were second nature to me I realized, or I re-remembered.

As a child, I knew the trees could speak. I knew the earth expressed love. I knew flowers could heal. I could see the spirits of Indians. My Lakota Sioux ancestors had appeared to me in a vision, while the girls and I still lived on South Street in Bath.

Thankfully, I could see into my past lives and derive hope and joy from them. My mother had always impressed upon me the idea that there were many worlds in the galaxies as well as in the past ancient history of our planet. She also made it quite easy to believe in the fairies, leprechauns, dwarves, mermaids, dragons, and flower devas that live in the unseen dream world of Mother Earth (which is called Middle World by many shamans).

A theta brain vibration, which allows you to access the unseen worlds, like Middle world, is more natural than the normal state of beta (for me). I had a higher comfort zone in a theta; the vibration of the visionary, the artist, the writer, and the shaman.

Shamanism has been on this planet for at least 100,000 years. It is not New Age. It may be the oldest form of spirituality on the planet. Jesus said, "As I do, so can you." Is that what he meant? We were all shamans and healers?

Dr. Michael Harner, a PhD from Berkeley, who had studied shamans worldwide, had retrieved the core elements of shamanism from antiquity (for the western world) and brought it back to the West in a form he called Core Shamanism.

He had, at first, taught small circles of people, including Sandra Ingerman, (who wrote Soul Retrieval) but interest in shamanism in the 1660's had quickly broadened to eventually include thousands of students (including mental health therapists and other healing practitioners) in the United States and in Europe, who were students of core shamanism. It is interesting that all of my shamanism teachers are white women from America.

If Harner had not resurrected shamanism for the Western World from the depths of its hiddenness to which it had been sequestered by political and religious powers for millennia, I truly believe my story would have ended much differently.

Shamanism was a universe of new power. My spirit guides and power animals became the center of my spiritual life. I could practice this unnoticed. It was, like silent prayer, undetected. Arianna and Gwen, I began to realize, would not be punished for my help and interaction with them, because I would be with them in spirit only.

As my shamanic powers increased, so did my urgency to use it to help the girls. I felt like I had pulled the sword, Excalibur, from the mysterious lake on the Isle of Avalon, the home of the ancient Goddess, and her priestesses, including Morgaine, the high priestess and witch, who could walk between worlds, prophesize, and who fought to preserve her pagan religion in the onslaught of Christianity during the third century.

According to British author Sir Malory, when Excalibur was first drawn by King Raven, the bright flash of its blade blinded his enemies.

"Thenne he drewe his swerd Excalibur, but it was so breyght in his enemyes eyen that it gaf light lyke thirty torchys."

I knew Gwen's spirit was in great danger. So one day, while Rose was sleeping, and Raven at work, I closed my eyes, leaned back against a couple of pillows on my blue couch, and began to pound slowly on my drum. As I had been taught by Susan, I journeyed with my spirit through Middle World from Damariscotta to Bath and into Gwen's energy field.

With my own power animal, a Black Jaguar, standing and protecting me, I looked down upon Gwen's spirit. She was losing her soul and her strength.

The longer she lived primarily with a psychopath, with no hope or help in sight, the weaker she became. Soon, I realized, with a mounting sense of terror, she would be too weak to resist, and they would take over her spirit forever.

I could see the house she was living in was filled with evil and it was only because of the protection of my Power Animals that I did not feel its influence directly. But I knew Gwen was in the middle of an evil black soup.

I reluctantly left Gwen and journeyed down to Lower World. I had completely given up on all forms of social justice, therapist, and court systems. Now my power would come from a truly powerful and sacred world.

I journeyed to Lower world, to ask for more help from my guides. It was a beautiful pine forest. I felt like I was back in Bunny Woods in Hanover. The air was scented with pine, and a stream ran fresh and clear and clean. Everything felt familiar and joyful and safe.

This was my world, I realized: my place of power. I guess it had always been this way, I had just forgotten.

One of my primary power animals, Bear, walked towards me from near the river in the forest. I smiled and my heart filled with joy. His presence was calming.

"Gwen needs help. I feel that whatever is left of her soul in her body, will leave her soon. She is a little girl fighting enormous evil and she cannot stay ahead of the traumas," I said, in silence. It was a telepathic transmission between us.

He nodded his head in agreement.

Suddenly, Bear and I were running along a small path beside a Mountain. I couldn't see on either side of me. I could only see my feet running and Bear ahead of me and then we stopped and there was an opening and light shining on Bear and I and my power animal, Black Jaguar. From the source of Light, came a beautiful Golden Horse, who immediately reminded me of Gwen. The horse had the beauty, joy and love and integrity of Gwen's soul.

As if we are all of one mind, or that thoughts were translated as fast as lightning, we all turned and ran again along the mountain side, the Golden Horse, Bear, Jaguar and myself.

We left Lower World and journeyed back into Middle World, then into Gwen's energy field. I could see part of her hair and her face. I could see the top of Gwen's head. I would know that blond hair anywhere.

The top of her head had been crusted over with something negative. She was purposefully being cut off from a connection to her higher self.

Myself and Golden Horse, and Jaguar entered her head, through her crown chakra. It was dark and at first, indiscernible. It felt like we were riding through canals or tubes – maybe nerves…

Then I saw Gwen's power animal, a lion, looking extremely sick. Jaguar lay down into the body of the Lion. Nothing happened at first. I got nervous. Jaguar stayed on as if he was giving his life force to Gwen's power animal.

I was urged to go with the Golden Horse. We ran down more tunnels. I felt something ominous. I turned and saw a fanged serpent. My heartbeat increased, and my throat went dry.

This was a serious intrusion in Gwen's brain. if I left it, it could turn into a mental illness or disease, like cancer or schizophrenia or maybe it was the spiritual equivalent to some kind of mind control. The demon energy would also lower her vibration to the point, she could be completely taken over by Helleen.

I was given a black leather bag. I was to try and capture this serpent. I lunged forward with my power animal. I felt, at this point, I had already done all of this in another lifetime, and in this lifetime, I was just brushing up old skills and I threw myself into the battle.

I called in the Goddess Demeter. She swept in like a hurricane, and she dragged the serpent into the bag. Golden Horse and I ran to the cauldron, in which a huge fire was burning. I threw the serpent into the cauldron and the lid slammed shut. The lid had a symbol on it I couldn't read.

The Golden Horse turned on his heels and we galloped off down the same mountain path. Jaguar joined us and the three of us ran, until I saw the opening into my own energy field and the three of us leaped.

I opened my eyes and looked at the green metal clock. It had been a half-hour journey. I got up and felt slightly sick and drank water. I heard Rose happily playing in her crib and I went in and picked her and her toys out of the crib and laid us all down on the rug in the living room, close to my heart; my arms in a half circle around her and the toys.

Maybe for the first time in a decade, I rested in peace, on the purple braided rug from the front foyer on South Street. The same rug on which Arianna had danced in black patent leather shoes and a white lace dress.

It was profound. I knew I had been with Gwen. I had stepped into her energy field with great allies and power. We had healed her of some form of illness in her brain. Or maybe it was the mind control. The spirit of the mind control had been trapped and then destroyed.

And no one would be punished. I had a world unexplored by enemies, at least those who were incarnate.

CHAPTER 47

THE TRUE FACE OF RAVEN

In the full moon that night, in the dark behind the house, while Raven was gone on an errand, I asked my guides to show me his true face; his true nature. Raven

Curled around Rose in my sleep, with the branches tapping the window, and Rose next to my heart, I dream of a demon.

I wake up with a start, sweat dripping down my neck ...Rose remains asleep holding a stuffed purple dragon – not Barney.

The messages were clear. Raven was either a demon or a devil, maybe born as such. I had to get away. I would be all alone. I'd had a restraining order on him once, for stealing my car keys and forcefully backing me into a hall and then screaming at me for three full hours, until I was incoherent and trembling. At the root, it was because I wanted to save Rose from being alone with him. No court in Maine would keep him from her.

I knew what I was up against in this new battle.

"I'll use the guardian's report in court, and you'll lose her. The judge will give me custody of Rose. You know what Maine judges are like," he had said, the first time I tried to leave him, after the messages from guides had become so clear.

I did it from my mother's house, while Rose was safe inside. We were on the lawn. He knew everything. He knew every inch of my case. He knew everything in the guardian's report.

My blood had turned cold, my heart sank into my feet, and tears rimmed my eyes. Even the one person I thought was on my side, was not. He had always been an enemy, just disguising himself as my ally. The wolf in sheep's clothing.

My complaints to Susan was that being around Raven made me feel drained – I had begun to see he was empty except for rage. He had been feeding off of my light – *my humanness*. He shapeshifted to become whatever I needed, whenever I needed it, in his effort to stay alive; to stay full of something human.

He was an enemy who knew all my secrets. He would know exactly who to contact.

Once, I dreamed he had set fire to a house in which Rose and I were sleeping. I'd also journeyed with my power animal, Lynx, while I was at Susan's yurt. My question had been "Why do I feel like I am drowning when I'm with Raven."

In the shamanic journey I had been taken to a lake. I saw a crocodile. I was feeling the water, the essence of life, but then there was the crocodile right below the surface. Then I was on a porch.

Then, in the journey, I'm falling off of a porch and through the air and into trees, and then deeper through different layers of the earth. Every time I try to stop myself from falling there is burning in my stomach. I pass a white-haired woman who seems angry. Or drunk. I pass a beautiful white teepee. Inside are white pillows, a white comforter. I want to go in, but I can't.

I stay with my mother but I'm strangled with grief and uncertainty. I call on my guides. I ask the question

"What happened to me, why can't I set boundaries from abuse. Why am I in this situation?" I close my eyes.

I was met by Lion, and we journeyed into the exquisite dimensions of lower world; pine scented trees, glimmering rivers, and iridescent butter-flies.

"Where are we going?" I ask, like Dorothy to the Cowardly Lion.

"Into your heart," he answers quite seriously.

Inside my heart, I see a baby, unprotected; screaming, and then we leave my heart and ascend into the galaxies. I see stars. I feel free, happy, so far away from Raven and John and Helleen. And all of the people in Maine…I see the constellation of Leo…

We descend back into my body and I stop short. I see a man; a tall, gan-gling puppet-like man with a large nose – he reminds me of my stepfather, Hal. He stepped out of a valve in my heart.

I was sitting on Lion's back – watching. We followed him as he walked through a tunnel, then unexpectedly into a beautiful room…

An exquisite warrior woman on a white horse stood in the room. She was surrounded by protective mist, and light and a circle of shields. She had a long dagger and with it, she speared the gangling man like he was a hot dog and then she held him up to the sky.

An angelic Being came and took him away to another world…

My body was shaking, my heart racing, and I was crying. But I was still in a trance. An Eagle, with golden eyes flew very close to me. His eyes were magnificent.

"Fly with me, fly with me," he said, and then tore out two black cords from my body and then he flew into the east…

I open my eyes…

I blink from the bright sunlight.

The world is somehow brighter, more exquisite, but certainly denser and slower, after a shamanic journey. Like being born, everything looks news. The shamanic journey makes me crave to be a free spirit again flying through the universe, unshackled by the demands of the body and the dense evil of the planet; but also grateful, I have not died.

I have come back to this body, to be Jane again, for a flash more of time. In the universe of the shaman I've learned there is no time, and that my life is merely a flash of light, but within that moment I am meant to make some adjustment to the world.

I inhale deeply, smelling a spicy mixture of pine tree and salt air outside where I'm sitting. The flowering daffodils, narcissus radiant with color and fragrance. I am in my skin again and relish the soft breeze on my face.

I look to my right. I see Rose play happily. I turn to pick up my cup of Red Rose Tea. It is still warm, which means my journey was less than ten minutes.

My eyes are still rimmed with tears, but my heart is lighter. Eagle had removed a blockage in my heart; A terror of my stepfather, an energetic tie to abuse. Was this the answer? Was it my ties to my abusive stepfather that had kept me tied into abuse with Raven?

And I had been given a lesson on boundaries from a Goddess. *Do not be nice to abusive people, Spear them through the heart immediately.*

I had been taught the opposite. Be nice, cook meals, mend socks, smile, have sex, clean their clothes. Somehow you can keep your universe together and your children protected if you just play nice That was not true.

I've spent my life being nice to abusive people including Helleen when I first met her. She was so emaciated and sick-looking, my former feminist self had tried to rationalize her as being a "victim" of the patriarch. Thankfully, I've now revised my feminist outlook. I realize it is not men, in particularly, that are the source of evil on the planet, but a certain type of human – whether it be male or female or black or red or white – but who have the uniting quality of having an undeveloped brain, i.e. a reptilian brain which is the leading cause I believe of what psychiatrists refer to as psychopaths or narcissists.

Then, of course, there are the slaves, and the bottom-feeders and the addicts, and sometimes just the naïve, or weak-willed who do the dirty work of the narcissists – or as someone on Facebook called them "Flying monkeys" but that is another story to tell.

If I'd been in touch with my Goddess self, i.e., my intuition, i.e., my wolf sense; I would have activated a "kill" defense. I knew in my gut the moment she walked through my front door – no, actually, it was before that, it was when I first heard her name at Helen and Matthew's bakery shop – that she was extremely dangerous. She was just presenting in a new format I had never experienced in my life. It was psychopathy.

I would have immediately begun to fight back. The same with Raven, I knew, deep down in my gut, the very first days I laid eyes on him, that something was very wrong, but I ignored my feelings and intuition.

It didn't work. It just doesn't work. All this niceness.

I'd been nice to Raven a thousand times trying to protect Rose and myself from more violence, and here I was more deeply entrenched then I'd ever imagined and he, now, is holding dangerous cards which could destroy both Rose and me. Because I'd kept him in my life so long, being nice, he knew my secrets. Giving undeserved niceness was the equivalent of slow self-destruction.

After lunch I bundled Rose in her snowsuit and hat and mittens, and, dressed similarly warm, I put her into the stroller and we walked down the quiet tree-lined road.

I am lost in thought and recent experiences of the journey. Rose plays with toys and talks happily. I want to get lost in the fresh air, and brilliant flowers. I pick a yellow wildflower for Rose and place it in her hand. She smiled with delight.

"Oh, and look, violets."

"Oh my God, they are so beautiful. They look like they are hearts,"

I give her more flowers.

"They're shaped like hearts, so that means they are good for your heart." I explain.

"Oh," she says and drops them beside her stroller, hoping I don't see her. She just isn't that into flowers, I guess.

I simply smile. Gwen is better. I saw her and I could see the light in her eyes – they had healed her – the Horse and the Lion.

My mother is dying. She spends most of her time in bed. She has given me her car. She said she could longer drive. I also had "the sight" and saw the grim reaper. He had appeared behind her, like a shadow. I knew she would soon pass.

I would be alone again so soon after she had come back into my life. I knew she was doing everything she could to help me survive, but now I would face the consequence of staying so long with Raven.

I would have to leave him and he would be mightily armed with documents. My blood turned to ice, believing he might be able to take Rose. It was a kind of inner death, to understand I could no longer be "nice" on any level. I would have to "kill" him – which meant – to take my light from him … as he had grown strong, draining my soul energy.

I had applied for a master's degree at Lesley College. The student loan would give me a reserve of money to leave him and maybe survive for a while. I'd given up trying to work. It was somehow all sabotage as if an evil fairy followed me in my path and turned all my sources of income into a dark hole of nothingness.

I walked for miles that day. I talked to her about the trees; how they all had spirits and they could provide healing and they would communicate. Like my mother had told me, I told Rose about the power of flowers and the magic in sunrise and sunset, and spirits, and God … because it felt like I might die, or she might be taken from me, and I wanted her to have all this. Information, to make her strong someday. She would have to be strong.

CHAPTER 48

LESLEY UNIVERSITY

A month later, I packed the yellow Prelude with a few items for Rose and put Rose and her handful of toys into her car seat in the back.

I'd been accepted to Lesley and already begun working on a master's thesis. The five thousand dollars from the student loan meant freedom. Rose and I moved into a new house.

The house was a beautiful, furnished single story ranch on top of a hill overlooking the Damariscotta River. I'd found a job teaching special education students at Lincoln High School and between the job and the student loan my bills were paid.

One time, when Raven and I stood in my driveway a month later and he was begging me to go back to him, a huge Snowy white Owl landed on a tree behind him right above his head.

Owl was trying to warn me, as were all of my guides, repeatedly, that if I even pondered his re-entrance into my life, it would be a disaster. The only relief of his constant attempt to engage me was that as long as he thought there was hope that I would be with him, he would leave Rose alone.

He wouldn't attempt to put forth any custody arrangements or visitations because his goal was still to be in the same house with us.

Gwen had been visiting more regularly and she seemed more herself. I saw some light had returned to her eyes and that calmed my nerves, a bit.

I had a new ghost in this house; a short, old, fat Italian woman, who cooked garlic every night on the stove in the kitchen. This only slightly unnerved me, because the smell was so strong it woke me up. I was getting used to dealing with ghosts.

Rose had a best friend she had met at the babysitter and her mother and I became good friends. For a few months, as I emotionally and spiritually was able to help Arianna and Gwen, I was able to enjoy my time with Rose and another mother and her daughter. It was almost fun – watching our girls play in little swimming pools, and dress up for Halloween, and shop for clothes together. I had a few moments of peace and happiness because I had found a way to be with my two other daughters.

My research for my thesis mainly involved shamanism, although the Divine Feminine and the ancient Goddess energies were becoming more and more central in my life. My thesis was an independent study on shamanism and, partly to fulfill the requirements of a master's degree, I'd had to find three shamans who were also master's levels or higher in academics. It seemed a hard bill to fill; shamans who were academics. It was almost an oxymoron. Shamans believe knowledge is empirical – your experience; your gnosis; is the only truth. The thoughts and beliefs of others are secondary. A master's thesis is a collection of the thoughts, beliefs, writings, and research of other people.

Shockingly, I found them: Ann Drake, Psyd, of Gloucester, Allie Knowlton, MSW, LCPC, and, of course, Susan Bakaley Marshall, who I'd been working with for several months already. They were all shamans with advanced academic degrees.

Dr. Nancy Waring, who had a PHD from Cornell and an BA from Tufts, had signed on to be my Lesley team leader and coordinator of this independent study. Patience may have been a degree she did not have externally, but earned from me, as being a student meant narrowing my broad visions as a shaman, into details that could be contained and verified and authenticated.

It was kind of like bottling a whirlwind. All forms of containment triggered me. I'd never known healthy boundaries, so all containment felt like control or abuse. It must have been a tough job reining me in from the spirit world, but Dr. Waring did it with patience and love.

"I don't know how to do this. How do I take shamanism out of the cosmos and into one sentence for my thesis title," I lamented.

Finally, after dozens of phone calls and emails, we came up with "The Potential Healing Effects of Core Shamanism for Women who Have Experienced Trauma." My thesis would also include a world view of shamanism, literary references and interviews with women who had suffered trauma, and with the shamans, Sandra Ingerman, Allie Knowlton and Ann Drake.

Like a wounded wild animal, I often battled with my superiors, but their intellect and heart-centered commentaries finally calmed my spirit.

Trauma and PTSD, and probably alcoholism, had thrown me into an undergraduate college that was so easy I don't even remember taking classes but somehow, lamely, graduated.

"I just want you to know, for you not to express your intellect would be a waste," she said.

I remember the statement because no one had ever said that to me. Everything was always about my looks, when I was a teenager

My spirituality, on the other hand, was cultivated, at first by my father, through the religion of Christian Science, and then by my mother, in the form of the Goddess energy and Mother Earth. My mother continually asked me questions about the spirit world, and power animals, and enjoyed and reveled in those conversations, although our talks were fewer and fewer as she became more bed-ridden and isolated.

My mother had a strange new friend: a woman, who, lacking the time to investigate, I'd just written off as someone temporary (so overwhelmed was I with fighting off Raven, trying to heal Arianna and Gwen, protecting Rose, and trying to survive financially *and* work on a thesis). I tried to ignore that this person was pulling my mother further and further away from me. Her expression, which had once been one of joy and anticipation, when Rose and I entered her house, was now either blank or even slightly malevolent.

The latter expression most often accompanied the presence of this strange woman who sat on the couch beside my mother in her bright white armchair. It all started to remind me of Bath and how she had disappeared and left me completely alone and I was deeply apprehensive.

Meanwhile, it became the part of the Lesley team, inadvertently, to convince me of my own capabilities. My brain slowly accepted that Susan, Nancy, Allie, and Ann were using their minds to heal and to inspire, to enlighten, educate and to liberate.

Like a kindergartener struggling with a new concept; my brain slowly re-wired this information. Compulsive fearful thoughts I mentally constrained with pure will power.

Everything went back to my daughters. If I did not survive, they would not survive. I tried to curtail my fight-or-flight reaction. Not all boundaries were cages. Not all intellectuals were out to hurt my daughters. Slowly, my PTSD, in relationship to women in authority, quieted.

The first seven years of my life with my mother, a loving, warm, creative, spiritual, and compassionate person (before she had been traumatized by the loss of her children in a custody battle, and then thirty or so years of domestic violence) provided a base from which I may have been subconsciously drawing data while evaluating this new social situation at Lesley.

Something inside of me, on a very deep level, was conditioned to expect the best in people; to believe people were primarily loving and kind; *because of my mother.*

The multiple and seemingly endless traumas which had transpired since my mother's departure when I was only seven years old; from all of my abusers including Dick, Hal Carver, Dave Hatch, my father, John and Helleen, the guardian, the therapist, Raven, and even from my own traumatized mother, may have all been secondary information to the psyche of my inner child, who understood unconditional love at my deepest core.

My survival might have been impossible without *the mother of my childhood.* This knowledge gave me hope, that my own daughters, Arianna and Gwen, that the unconditional love from me for the first seven years of their lives (almost exactly the same amount of time I had with my mother; and, again, this made me wonder, if there is systematic depopulation agenda in play) would give them the strength to survive.

My self-esteem increased *very slowly.*

I slowly realized that some people, including Dr. Nancy Coleman,(the psychotherapist, who had written a lengthy report, warning Judge Field that Arianna and Gwen should not be alone with the stepmother) and Dr. Waring, my team leader, and psychologist Dr. Ann Drake, Susan Bakaley Marshall, MSW, Allie Knowlton, MSW, and many other intelligent women, listened and respected my opinions.

This new information was dizzying considering the hellish potpourri of female misfits, saboteurs, abusers and faux intellectuals like Helleen who had been involved in the kidnapping of my children.

My submersion into the toxicity of family court had also made me realize, that my sets of beliefs about feminism (that was, basically, in a nutshell that men were the problem and women were the solution) was incorrect and immature.

Women were as infected as men with some kind of evil I had yet to completely understand. The problems in the world were not related to gender or nationality or sexual orientation; there was another layer that seemed to be controlling life on the earth.

My values were shifting and another set of questions, or one major question had risen to the surface, as a result of this quagmire. If white men were not the source of evil on the planet, who was? Or, maybe WHAT was? Was this energy even human?

I was being rebuilt just like the bionic woman. I'd had multiple soul retrievals, my mind was being energized and my heart and body were being healed with many forms of alternative healing, including a laundry list of herbs. Motherwort and dandelion were clearing my heart and my liver of stored trauma.

I began a literary review of academic research in shamanism and healing. The research included the writings of Celtic shaman, Dr. Tomas Cohen, anthropologist Michael Harner, Ph.D. (a professor at Berkeley, Columbia and Yale, who had, almost single-handedly, through field research with shamans in the Conibo, and South and North America, retrieved shamanism, or at least in a form he called Core Shamanism, for the Western world); Sandra Ingerman, MA, Dr. Joan Halifax, Ann Drake, Psyd, religious scholar Mircea Eliade, and many more.

But the books and the author which most influenced me was *The Language of the Goddess* and *The Civilization of the Goddess; The World of Old Europe*, by Lithuanian anthropologist/archeologist Dr. Marija Gimbutas. The late Gimbutas, an archeologist who was once a professor emeritus of European archeology at UCLA, is the author of over twenty books including the two I've mentioned. She used an "interdisciplinary research system – including archeological data, linguistics, mythology, and early history data – to analyze her data. Joseph Campbell wrote the following description of Gimbutas' contribution to our knowledge of prehistory.

"Gimbutas's message is of an actual age of harmony and peace in accord with the creative energies of nature which for a spell of some 4000 prehistoric years anteceded the 5000 years of what James Joyce has termed the "nightmare" of (contending tribal and national interests) from which it is now certainly time for the planet to wake," said Joseph Campbell.

In *The Language of the Goddess*, "Gimbutas dramatically brought to public attention the existence of an agrarian, earth goddess-worshiping civilization in Old Europe that was destroyed by horse-riding, patriarchal, sky-God Worshiping warriors from the east."

In `` The *Civilization of the Goddess*, "Contrary to popular belief, she shows civilization did not start at Sumer with its patriarchal hierarchy and beliefs. Instead, the goddess culture of Old Europe represents a very different but just as authentic form of civilization, one with a highly developed social structure based on a harmonious, non-warfare-oriented agricultural economy. Presenting a wealth of findings concerning religion, customs, rituals and art, Gimbutas establishes beyond doubt that this was a matrifocal goddess-centered civilization that in its peaceful and earth-respecting values has much to teach us today."

Gimbutas, in her evaluation of ancient artifacts in Old Europe, had determined that a Goddess culture had existed and had lived in peace and harmony. No objects of war had been found during her excavations, for a period of almost five thousand years prior to the onslaught by a tribe Gimbutas called the Kurgans – a mounted, violent, warrior tribe that rode down from the mountains to the north, to rape and kill and conquer the peaceful Goddess tribes.

I had found a key.

There had been a beginning to evil. At least it seemed that maybe approximately nine thousand years ago, according to Gimbutas, there had been peace. No instruments of war. And that women did not rule over men, but we lived in equality in a mother-honoring culture. Is that possible? And what about other cultures in that same time frame?

From where had this ancient culture derived? The women and men who lived without swords and armor within a culture of peace and equality/? Gimbutas referred to this Goddess Era as a matriarchy, but specifically said this did NOT mean women ruled over men, but that they lived in equality. Surely mother and daughters were honored, maybe above all else?

Was it possible, even, that the Persephone and Demeter legend, the Eleusinian Mysteries, had originated in this ancient Goddess culture and that a greater mystery; a mystery of peace and prosperity was contained in those mysteries and was that peace somehow tied to mothers and daughters?

My mind was racing. Was it possible that war and torture and slavery and all things evil had more chance of surviving if the sacred bonds, especially between mothers and daughters, were broken. The Eleusinian mysteries indicated this bond was sacred. It was presented in three phases: "The descent," "the search" and "the ascent" in ancient Greece beginning around 1200 BC.

Would there be an ascent for myself and my daughters as there had been for Persephone? And what would be the price we paid (above and beyond what had already been sacrificed, which, I knew, essentially would be our lives, because none of us would truly ever be innocent again and the traumas would take a lifetime to heal).

An owl hooted. Was it the same white owl that had landed in the tree above Raven's head when he was begging me to go back with him? I shuddered.

Was it possible, maybe even unbeknownst to the scavengers who did the low, dirty work, like the guardian and Helleen and Kathleen, that there were "higher," potentially even more evil, more widespread; more epidemic and incipient entities, that had, from the beginning of my life, wanted to destroy my connection to my mother; and then, my connection to my daughters?

Was all of this information somehow tied together? Was it happening to other mothers and daughters? Again, as I said earlier, I believed that if I could find the origin of evil, a map, if you will, of the beginning, I could find the end, I could find the door, into which I could put a key and open it and find the light. I needed to see the beginning of evil, to be able to find the end and the "Ascent." I believed I had found it in the world of Marija Gimbutas.

I went into the small white kitchen where all the back windows of the house looked out over the river. I turned on the tea kettle and stared out at the glistening river.

Where had it all begun? I did not believe in the theory of evolution. It seemed like a quick fix someone had thrown into the history books and they had never explained the missing link. Chimpanzees were a completely different species, I believed, than humans

And if we evolved from them, why are they still here? Did only some chimpanzees evolve into humans and some just said, "No thanks. I think I'll just stay here with the monkeys." Also How did humanity evolve to what I perceived to be such a low vibration; into a hell, or at least that's how I'd experienced Life. We have devolved, if anything.

I made lemon balm tea, grown from my own lemon balm, and went back to the living room and sank into one end of a soft upholstered couch. The room was infused with Love. Since leaving Raven, my connection to my guides and God and the Goddess grew stronger. Drumming and a shamanic journey hardly even seemed necessary. My spirit guides seemed to be in the room with me, easily accessible and immediate. I was surrounded by Spirit.

I sat down my tea, crossed my legs under me on the couch, and covered myself with a wool blanket I pulled off the back of the couch. I took one last look at the moonbeams on the river and I closed my eyes and called upon the Goddess.

Was she also God, the same God I'd prayed to in Sunday School at the Christian Science Church in Needham, or that the Christian Science practitioner, Mr. Horniman, had espoused, even at my birth? Who was the Goddess in relationship to God: to Jesus? I had these questions and many more in my mind as I closed my eyes.

At first, as I beat lightly on my drum, and all I saw was darkness, then the darkness shifted, to the sky, the black sky with stars and I could feel my soul traveling ... back in time ... and here is what was revealed.

At first in my journey I saw myself as a child, alone, on the wet grass at night in Hanover, crying for my mother. I heard a voice, that night, a woman's voice saying she was with me, would always be with me, forever.

The Goddess Isis appears and this is her channeled message on the Goddess and the history of humans on earth. She says:

"She was everything and everywhere. It was Her; She had given birth to God, but she was not God, she was the womb, the origin of all life, she was ecstasy of creation, unconditional love, the magic of twilight, the purity of dawn, the innocence of a flower; the meaning of all life. The purpose of all life was to embrace her and live life to the fullest.

She had both given birth to God and had been a thought of God. God had a thought aside from himself and it was She and she became the rivers and the lakes and the mountain streams, and in every single song of nature and even in the rainbow in a raindrop. She was not so much life, as the energy that infused Life. He was the chalice; she was the water. She was life, he was form.

Then She narrowed herself, to be seen in the physical and she became Gods and Goddess and many planets and many galaxies and she continued to express herself as joy and love and peace and she narrowed herself into form and became lady Guadalupe and Mary Magdalene, Mary, and Rose and Astarte, and Pele and White Buffalo Calf Woman.

At the next level of incarnation, she was resisted. Religions were formed expressly to repress and control her and or eliminate her, as she was the liberator, she was freedom for humankind. I am told in my journey that the story of the Goddess here on Earth began a long, long time ago, before organized religion.

I see an ancient land called Lemuria.

It was star-seeded with souls from many different advanced planets and galaxies, including from the Seven Sisters of Pleiades. It looked like Lemuria was a continent about the size of Africa and located in the Pacific Ocean east of California.

Their bodies were formed from the earth's soil which had been formed from the ashes of exploded stars. Lemuria was the same as The Garden of Eden described in The Bible. The Pleiadian souls held a strong connection to The Goddess and utopian life of abundance and peace and joy which they duplicated on Lemuria – which was also known as Mu, the Motherland.

This advanced population of Beings grew and grew, never departing from a connection to creation, to a feminine, loving aspect of God; and understanding of the life-giving powers of the universe came from the sun, until a succession of tsunamis, a natural event, which transpired over hundreds of years, eroded the massive land structure to what is now the islands of Hawaii.

Lemurians journeyed east from Lemuria on sailing vessels, landing on various points from along the coast of California and Mexico and South America. Some even went further east through a channel of water and into the Atlantic Ocean to a continent called Atlantis. At first the ancient teachings of Lemuria continued on Atlantis, a continent about half the size of Lemuria or "Mu" and was generally located in the center of the ocean between what is now North America and Europe.

In 400 BC Plato stated that Greek philosopher Solon had shared with him that "Atlantis was the center of civilization and conquered the whole world" but Atlanteans eventually lost their connection to Mu, and diverted from the original teaching of the Motherland, and digressed into Satanism and blood sacrifice.

They forgot about the Mother Goddess and began to worship kings, including King Poseidon and the many successive kingdoms of Poseidon. Drenched in their own forgetfulness and the blood of sacrifice and the misuse of technology (crystals), Atlantis was destroyed by water.

("The waves were so high. I've never seen anything like them. We Atlanteans must have done something terrible," my mother told me once when I was a very young child, I recall in the middle of this shamanic journey)

Many died that night, they drowned in the turbulent seas. Kane and his followers survived to repopulate areas along the west banks of Africa, others who had gone out earlier, who had been warned – those who still held the mysteries and secrets of Mu, populated the coastal area of Europe – they became the early Goddess cultures (In my mind, I thought this might be the beginning of the early European culture Gimbutas had studied) Kane's descendants went up into northern areas that are now Finland and Denmark – they became the steppe people or the Kurgs.

Those along the coastline prospered and many maintained the ancient ways. For thousands of years after Atlantis, there was peace and prosperity, a high degree of creativity and spirituality. There were no wars...for over five thousand years...

In Egypt food was in abundance; there were fields of golden wheat, fruit-laden trees, clean, fresh, water, rivers, beautiful skies, temperate weather, and no disease. All disease comes from discord in the energy field around humans. Human auras were strong and almost impenetrable.

I see boys learning bow and arrow early, playing warriors, running free, riding horses, girls naturally formed into groups, to share knowledge of the land, but they also could be warriors if they chose.

She shows me the heart line of the earth, Gaia. The heart ley line ran under England, and even Hanover, where I grew up and lived for the first ten years of my life. A deep mystery school arose naturally from the earth, the very heart of the Goddess, on the heart ley lines. Ancient magic and a connection to all levels of life – the fairy realm, the intergalactic, was normal and accepted – was rich and a natural part of the life of humans.

The Arthurian legends – Camelot, Avalon, Lady of the Lake, The Knights of the Round Table, Guinevere – thousands of years later, all arose from the heart ley line of the earth in England. Like Princess Diana, I had grown up on a heart ley line, and one of the few energy spots on the planet which still held the vibrations of the Goddess.

At one point, it seems, portals were opened in the Middle East, in northern Europe, in South America, and another species entered our atmosphere, one of Annika origins.

It was the reptilians, who had been thrown from another planet in a war lost.

I see that they are the scourge of the entire universe and they feed on our light. They had pierced the energy field of the earth, seeking a new home; they did come as actual physical entities on aircraft. They also began to sit right outside our earth aura in energetic forms. They were so dense, at first, they couldn't even exist in our environment.

The first had to first downgrade the earth to a vibration where they could co-exist with us. They are horrifying creatures and rape was one of their primary means of introducing their species to our planet. The peaceful Goddess tribes were infiltrated with these reptilian rapists and murderers.

The offspring became the gangs of murderers that swept down from the steppes of Russia into the more southern regions of Europe and invaded the peaceful tribes Gimbutas described in her book *Language of the Goddess*. They raped the women and destroyed temples. They were being empowered by off-world reptiles as well as the bloodline that was now being created.

Egypt was taken over by the reptilians and the pure human female bloodline of leaders faded and was taken over by the male reptilian Pharaohs; and the sacred ceremonies were usurped and co-opted and used for evil, slavery, Luciferian and Satanic worship. They stole energy from children through rape and blood sacrifice; this gave them power as it empowered Lucifer, their God, who rewarded them richly.

With the exception of small pockets of healers and shamans and priestesses that remained hidden, the ancient ways of much of Europe and Africa were taken over by the Luciferian agenda. Religion was formed to oppress the people, creating hierarchies of men who secretly worshiped Lucifer and despised women who held in their hearts a memory of the Goddess.

People began to worship these reptilian religious leaders as if they were the real leaders. These ancient civilizations of peace were omitted from history books until only the history of the reptilians existed. America, for a while, had a purity; and escaped from the torture, war, and death which had taken over Europe, but now it has become now completely taken over by the reptilians.

You humans are waking up for the first time since Atlantis, continued Isis, but it will take a large number of people to wake up to the reptilian invasions, which was for humans to wake up to their own power, to create a force of God, to become gods and goddesses again, to acknowledge the existence of this other species, and to eradicate them from the planet and to seal the planet against them ever returning, so that we can once again have a Paradise Earth.

They have used my name Isis, in vain, again, trying to use real power for evil. They have nothing of their own, it is only what they can take from our creativity and God self. They have made you believe you are weak; but they are weak, they have no power except for what you give to them. Call in God and your ancestors and remember they are nothing without us. But to avoid another Atlantis, you must take your power..." she says, with strength and then she was gone.

"What is my power?" I ask, through thought vibration communication.

"Your Power is the Goddess. You remember peace. You remember love. You remember a time on Earth before the invasion. You remember the interconnectedness of all life. You come from a Goddess lineage. Your mother remembers the Goddess; and your daughters, if the reptilians do not take over their minds, will also remember the Goddess. You are a Goddess. You are the most dangerous of all beings to this evil. That is why they are trying to destroy you," she said, from beyond my vision.

I opened my eyes. I stood up slowly and walked over to the glass picture window, which gave me a panoramic view of miles of the wide, deep, tree-lined river, still illuminated by the moon. I could feel the moon as if she were inside of me, I felt the river as if her waterways were my water. The rich, dark fertile soil beneath the tall, dark, ancient pines felt like my body...

My hometown, Hanover, MA was on a heart ley line – maybe the same ley line that ran through Northamptonshire, England – where Princess Diana has also been born and raised and who became The Queen of Hearts. I had been born on the heart ley line of the earth, so that maybe I would remember the power of the Love; the energy of the Goddess; of a lost Paradise Earth.

It is no wonder Gimbutas's findings were highly ridiculed by her predominately male academic contemporaries. It is no wonder her work is sidelined as "myth" and conjecture. It is no wonder her discovery of an ancient peaceful culture is not taught at schools, because if everyone knew that most of the 400,000 years on earth had been one of peace, we would all realize we are living in an anomaly.

And the duration and predominance of all the wars – all the male heroes, all the battles and revolutions; the immortalization of endless male warriors and conquerors; all of the pharaohs, kings and queens, prime ministers, the religious "leaders: the Catholic priests, the Popes, the Protestant witch hunters during the Inquisitions; the "royals" (of every country to England to China to Japan to Russia to America) the generals and commanders; the invasions and battles; the endless torture of humans such as the native Americans, and Aborigines, the witches – was just a small, almost insignificant blip, in human history.

The past five thousand years or so had been a bad blip – it had been just that – a blip where we had been temporarily ruled by an invading race and their descendants; evil usurpers. It had been a mistake. The entire recorded history, force fed to every child on the planet in school, would be reduced to a mistake.

It is no wonder that anyone who remembers the era of prehistory, would be a threat to those who wanted to perpetrate the concepts that the recorded history was the ONLY reality in human history. It is no wonder that anyone who remembers there are intergalactic species; and that we in fact had come from other star systems; would be a threat.

If humans understood that this planet; and our "leaders," were not the only game in the galaxy; the authority and power of the ruling elite on the planet; would certainly be diminished. We would perceive our own leaders, were somewhat trivial, in the broader expanse of reality.

Suppression, suppression, suppression. Suppress all truth and live off our soul energy and keep us as slaves in not-stop wars for profit and greed and acquisition of goods for the ruling elite. That was the plan.

NO WONDER "they" potentially wanted to eliminate me; either through my own suicide from despair, or accident, or maybe someday, a direct hit. I remember the Paradise Earth. I remember the Goddess, not in a forced kind of way; or even a cerebral context; or academic; or even philosophical; or religious. I purely was the Goddess – as sheer stream of pure loving life energy

The Druids believed all of life came from a spiritual womb,the darkness. The Goddess was manifested in a blue light of creation. For the Dark womb precedes life, the goddess precedes life, manifestation from dark to light, as I had been taught by Dr. a Geo Cameron Treatheran – a direct descendent of the High Kings of Tara, including Conair Mor – who I had met at in Massachusetts.

The Women of Wyrrd, an ancient, secret society of men and women in England, who knew the mysteries of the universe and lived in great harmony with the earth(who Lynn Andrews had written about in The Woman of Wyrrd; The Arousal of the Inner Fire

Whoever I was, in ancient England, I had seen her in a vision one night in Bath – one of the worst nights of my life; the night I read the guardian's report – and the vision helped me survive.

The young girl, in the beautiful bedroom that looked out into the wildflower gardens, and forests, and rolling hills, in a past life in England, she was connected, I suddenly realized, to the Goddess.

If I did hold this knowledge, which I knew I did, how did they know where I was? Did this pursuit of me begin at birth? Did this explain the ongoing trauma, pain, betrayal and abuse? How deep and how broad was this assault? Was it limited to Maine?

I didn't think so – this was a much bigger plan than I ever imagined. I also understand that some of the players in this game were simply either demon-possessed through greed and the want of power – like potentially the guardian. Maybe most of the guardians in Maine were trafficking children into abusive situations. I didn't know. I just suddenly knew it was a much bigger game, and maybe more dangerous then II realized.

At the same time, as I was acknowledging this huge plan by an evil force, I felt stronger; part of a broader knowledge; a wisdom that was deep and also powerful and strong.

I was not an arbitrary nobody being thrown around by rabid dogs like a piece of discarded meat – there was a larger methodology to my destruction and coming from a higher place than maybe most of the people in the game realized. I was much more important than I'd ever realized in my life of being completely marginalized by my father and most of the men in my life.

Had the Inquisition and other mass extermination of sensitives, and shamans and witches, which I had found out about in my research for my masters' thesis, been part of a larger plan, not just to exterminate the sensitives, but to set an example to the rest of the society, NOT TO BE intuitive.

In Siberia, for example, officials had thrown shamans out of helicopters, and we all know how thousands, if not millions, of women in Europe had been hung, burned to the stake, crushed under rocks, and drowned on accusations of witchcraft during the European Inquisition.

A powerful Impetus behind the "witch" killing craze in Europe was the book, Malleus Maleficarum, otherwise known as "The Hammer of Witches." Written in 1487 by Heinrich Kramer (in Germany). "The Hammer" describes in details how to identify, torture and execute "witches."

Wikileaks describes Kramer as a man who was so obsessed with the sex life of an accused woman, Helena Scheuber (who was in love with a Templar knight Jorg Spiess) and for another unspecified illegal activities, that he was discredited and banned from the town of Innsbruck by the local Bishop.

Malleus Maleficarum, a book that was reportedly more widely read than the Bible for a period of two hundred years, was written by Kramer, after he was expelled from Innsbruck. His perverse opinion on the Innsbruck witch trials (in which all seven women were eventually released) were ignored and even criticized by his fellow ministers.

It is believed that Kramer wrote Malleus in retaliation for his expulsion from Innsbruck. So, think about it. An angry, resentful, sexual deviant, who was disrespected by his peers and banished from his town; writes a book and it becomes the most popular book on the planet for two hundred years. For TWO HUNDRED YEARS, people's heads were stuck in a sewer alongside Kramer's.

The Hammer was directly responsible for the torture and death of thousands or even millions of women in the Middle Ages – most of whom were just normal woman who stood slightly askew – they were either too old, too beautiful, too ugly, too smart, owned too much land, to thin, to fat, to talkative, to happy, to sad, to social, too much of a recluse. Ultimately The Hammer gave license to kill women for almost any reason imaginable.

I believe I know why, the real reason women are tortured and killed.

Women, regardless of their religion, race, country, have been the most feared humans by this invading race because we are most strongly connected to the life force of planet earth, of each other, and of the Goddess. Our intuition is generally strong; our belief in myth and legend and folklore is stronger than men because we are often more connected to our higher selves, and the collective consciousness of humanity. Within the collective consciousness is all information, past, present and future is contained. We remember a Paradise Earth

Dr. Gimbutas's contemporaries criticized the conclusions from her field work in Europe, primarily because she interwove myth, legend, and folklore into standard linear cerebral academic anthropological study. She dared to try to expand our basic concept of what comprises intelligence. She bravely went where no one had gone before –into the wisdom of universal consciousness.

My opinion is, that if you don't include intuition, in your assessment of anything (whether it be an archeological find, a partner, a friend, a doctor, or whether or not your child is doing drugs or, a potential business partner, and on and on into infinity) then you will often be misled. Intuition is wisdom connected to universal intelligence; intellect is a closed-circuit re-circulating inside your brain. In other words, Marija Gimbutas was the first anthropologist to include wisdom into her assessments. All prior examinations of the same material by other professionals were limited by the limited by mind.

Intuition is the highest form of intelligence we have accessible to us. And if you can tap into the collective consciousness, which is also your intuition, you remember the Paradise Earth: The Goddess; and i.e. the beginning of invasion.

When they needed more extermination of sensitives, the Illuminati families worldwide created the German Holocaust.

This was just one more of thousand attempts eliminate the free thinking and deeply sensitive, shamanic, feeling humans – the intelligentsia has always been a target of the Nazi's – because the most intelligent, intuitive, perceptive, amongst us are naturally often more equipped to figure out systems (system analysts) potentially unveiling, the systems and codes of the reptilian race.

And much information indicates the Nazi's did not lose the war, the simply went underground in some cases. The brightest amongst them; the scientists; were brought to America, and thus began the MK-Ultra non-consensual human experimentation on American citizens.

In any kind of normal scenario, if evil intentions were not behind society pulling the strings of human minds; how could this happen? I would guess now, knowing what I do, that Mr. Kramer, was most likely, barely human. How many humans do you know that write books about torture? Did you count? How many? Zero. Normal human beings do not two hundred pages of ways to torture women. You have been programmed to believe this is just business as usual on planet earth. I'm beginning to believe this is not business as usual, but massive manipulation and brainwashing on humanity.

The highly insightful, shamanic Aborigines and Native Americans were hunted, diseased to near extinction (or spiritually crushed by the Jesuits priests and/or relocation to reservations). The Huna shamans from Hawaii were all but decimated. The monks of Tibet, the African shamans, certainly the magical Celts of Ireland, England, Scotland had all been marginalized and almost eliminated.

Gimbutas's Lithuanian heritage links her to the ancient Goddess Brigette. All the Nordic Goddesses were put into deep freeze, while the war mongering infiltrators took over religion, politics, education, the money system, medicine and brainwashed us into believing torture, untimely death, disease and war was just business as usual.

The truth was the invaders brought hell with them and enslaved humanity and brainwashed us into forgetting our power and the glory of living on earth.

But maybe the most profound revelation in my literary review for my thesis was information contained in the revolutionary (other would say "heretical") book *The Gnostic Gospels* by religious historian and Harvard educated, Dr. Elaine Pagels. The Modern Library named The Gnostic Gospels one of the hundred best books of the twentieth century.

The main focus of the book *The Gnostic Gospels* is the revolutionary information contained in the ancient papyrus scripture found in the desert in Nag Hamm Egypt in 1945. The scripture was discovered, in an earthen jar buried in the sand in the desert by accident by an Arabian peasant, on a blood revenge quest.

While most of the texts were burned, by the peasant's mother, twelve were ultimately saved and were bought by antique dealers. Eventually they made into mainstreaming academia where Pagels was able to examine them.

Carbon dating placed the papyrus writings to around 200 AD. Examinations by a host of professionals deemed that scripts to be the original teachings given by Christ to his twelve disciples.

Mary Magdalene, according to these scriptures, was not only a disciple, but Jesus's most valued disciple and his wife. She was deemed by Jesus to be spiritually and emotionally superior to the other disciples. Mary had been chosen by Jesus's choice to lead the Christian faith after his death.

In addition, The Gospel of Thomas, The Gospel of Mary, reveal this early Christian religion as one that valued gnostic knowledge – a belief in our own divinity and ability to connect with God on our own (without the need of a translator such as a priest) terms and based by our own inner knowing. True knowledge of God was Gnostic (inner).

"There is a light within each person and that light shines on the whole universe. If it does not shine, there is darkness" The Gospel of Thomas.

In the texts, God is portrayed as both mother and father, and therefore women were leaders in Gnosticism and considered equal to men. Additionally, Jesus was portrayed as a real man, with a real wife (Mary Magdalene); a spiritual master and an inspiring leader.

Pagels believed it was to the advantage of the early political and religious leader to re-write these gospels (and to destroy most of them) so that the population believed the only avenue to God was through the hierarchical Pope system (or in Christians, through the church).

It was heretical to believe, as did the Gnostics, that the path to enlighten was gnostic. This latter is the information that allowed the churches to maintain control of humanity for the past two thousand years. It seemed there was a global network that wants us to not embody; to not feel; to not find our shaman center: to maybe not remember that time of peace on earth – information that could only be gained through intuition and gut instinct, i.e. the shaman center.

CHAPTER 49

ISIS

It is no wonder Gimbutas's findings were highly ridiculed by her predominately male academic contemporaries. It is no wonder her work is sidelined as "myth" and conjecture. It is no wonder her discovery of an ancient peaceful culture is not taught at schools, because if everyone knew that most of the 400,000 years on earth had been one of peace, we would all realize we are living in an anomaly.

And the duration and predominance of all the wars – all the male heroes, all the battles and revolutions; the immortalization of endless male warriors and conquerors; all of the pharaohs, kings and queens, prime ministers, the religious "leaders: the Catholic priests, the Popes, the Protestant witch hunters during the Inquisitions; the "royals" (of every country to England to China to Japan to Russia to America) the generals and commanders; the invasions and battles; the endless torture of humans such as the native Americans, and Aborigines, the witches – was just a small, almost insignificant blip, in human history.

The past five thousand years or so had been a bad blip – it had been just that – a blip where we had been temporarily ruled by an invading race and their descendants; evil usurpers. It had been a mistake. The entire recorded history, force fed to every child on the planet in school, would be reduced to a mistake.

It is no wonder that anyone who remembers the era of pre-history, would be a threat to those who wanted to perpetrate the concepts that the recorded history was the ONLY reality in human history. It is no wonder that anyone who remembers there is intergalactic species; and that we in fact had come from other star systems; would be a threat.

If humans understood that this planet; and our "leaders"; were not the only game in the galaxy; the authority and power of the ruling elite on the planet; would certainly be diminished. We would perceive our own leaders, were somewhat trivial, in the broader expanse of reality.

Suppression, suppression, suppression. Suppress all truth and live off our soul energy and keep us as slaves in not-stop wars for profit and greed and acquisition of goods for the ruling elite. That was the plan.

NO WONDER "they" potentially wanted to eliminate me; either through my own suicide from despair, or accident, or maybe someday, a direct hit. I remember the Paradise Earth. I remember the Goddess, not in a forced kind of way; or even a cerebral context; or academic; or even philosophical; or religious. I purely was the Goddess – as sheer stream of pure loving life energy

The Druids believed all of life came from a spiritual womb,the darkness. The Goddess was manifested in a blue light of creation. For the Dark womb precedes life, the goddess precedes life, manifestation from dark to light, as I had been taught by Dr. a Geo Cameron Treatheran – a direct descendent of the High Kings of Tara, including Conair Mor – who I had met at in Massachusetts.

The Women of Wyrrd, an ancient, secret society of men and women in England, who knew the mysteries of the universe and lived in great harmony with the earth(who Lynn Andrews had written about in The Woman of Wyrrd; The Arousal of the Inner Fire

Whoever I was, in ancient England, I had seen her in a vision one night in Bath – one of the worst nights of my life; the night I read the guardian's report – and the vision helped me survive.

The young girl, in the beautiful bedroom that looked out into the wildflower gardens, and forests, and rolling hills, in a past life and a memory of the Goddess. Somewhere inside of me was this Goddess, I had known it then..

If I did hold this knowledge, which I knew I did, how did they know where I was? Did this pursuit of me begin at birth? Did this explain the ongoing trauma, pain, betrayal and abuse? How deep and how broad was this assault? Was it limited to Maine?

I didn't think so – this was much bigger plan then I ever imagined. I also understand that some of the players in this game were simply either demon-possessed through greed and the want of power – like potentially the guardian. Maybe most of the guardians in Maine were trafficking children into abusive situation. I didn't know. I just suddenly knew it was much bigger game, and maybe more dangerous then I REALIZED.

At the same time, as I was acknowledging this huge plan by an evil force, I felt stronger; part of a broader knowledge; a wisdom that was deep and also powerful and strong.

I was not an arbitrary nobody being thrown around by rabid dogs like a piece of discarded meat – there was a larger methodology to my destruction and coming from a higher place than maybe most of the people in in the game realized. I was much more important then I'd ever realized in my life of being completely marginalized by my father and most of the men in my life.

The Inquisition

Had the Inquisition and other mass extermination of sensitives, and shamans and witches, which I had found out about in my research for my masters' thesis, been part of a larger plan, not just to exterminate the sensitives, but to set an example to the rest of the society, NOT TO BE intuitive.

In Siberia, for example, officials had thrown shamans out of helicopters, and we all know how thousands, if not millions, of women in Europe had been hung, burned to the stake, crushed under rocks, and drowned on accusations of witchcraft during the European Inquisition.

A powerful Impetus behind the "witch" killing craze in Europe was the book, Mallus Maleficarum, otherwise known as "The Hammer of Witches." Written in 1487 by Heinrich Kramer(in Germany) "The Hammer" describes in details how to identify, torture and execute "witches."

Wikileaks describes Kramer as a man who was so obsessed with the sex life of an accused woman, Helena Scheuber (who was in love with a Templar knight Jorg Spiess) and for another unspecified illegal activities, that he was discredited and banned from the town of Innsbruck by the local Bishop.

Malleus Melficarum, a book that was reportedly more widely read then the Bible for a period of two hundred years, was written by Kramer, after he was expelled from Innsbruck. His perverse opinion on the Innsbruck witch trials (in which all seven women were eventually released) were ignored and even criticized by his fellow ministers.

It is believed that Kramer wrote Malleus in retaliation for his expulsion from Innsbruck. So, think about it. An angry, resentful, sexual deviant, who was disrespected by his peers and banished from his town; writes a book and it becomes the most popular book on the planet for two hundred years. For TWO HUNDRED YEARS, people's heads were stuck in a sewer alongside Kramer's.

The Hammer was directly responsible for the torture and death of thousands or even millions of women in the Middle Ages – most of whom were just normal woman who stood slightly askew – they were either too old, too beautiful, too ugly, too smart, owned too much land, to thin, to fat, to talkative, to happy, to sad, to social, too much of a recluse.

Ultimately The Hammer gave license to kill women for almost any reason imagineable.

I believe I know why, the real reason women are tortured and killed.

Women, regardless of their religion, race, country, have been the most feared humans by this invading race because we are most strongly connected to the life force of planet earth, of each other, and of the Goddess. Our intuition is generally strong; our belief in myth and legend and folklore, is stronger than men because we are often more connected to our higher selves, and the collective consciousness of humanity. Within the collective consciousness is all information, past, present and future is contained. We remember a Paradise Earth

Dr. Gimbutas's contemporaries criticized the conclusions from her field work in Europe, primarily because she interwove myth, legend, and folklore into standard linear cerebral academic anthropological study. She dared to try to expand our basic concept of what comprises intelligence. She bravely went where no one had gone before –into the wisdom of universal consciousness.

My opinion is, that if you don't include intuition, in your assessment of anything (whether it be an archeological find, a partner, a friend, a doctor, or whether or not your child is doing drugs or, a potential business partner, and on and on into infinity) then you will often be misled. Intuition is wisdom connected to universal intelligence; intellect is a closed-circuit re-circulating inside your brain. In other words, Marija Gimbutas was the first anthropologist to include wisdom into her assessments. All prior examination of the same material by other professionals were limited by the limited by mind.

Intuition is the highest form of intelligence we have accessible to us. And If you can tap into the collective consciousness, which is also your intuition, you remember the Paradise Earth: The Goddess; and i.e. the beginning of invasion

Also from Germany, was not only the Malleus Malificurium, but the Nazis and the holocaust of "sensitives" – beginning with gypsies, and a certain strain Jews, and women. When The Inquisition failed, or whenever another holocaust was needed, the Illuminati families worldwide created the German Holocaust.

This was just one more of thousand attempts eliminate the free thinking and deeply sensitive, shamanic, feeling humans – the intelligentsia has always been a target of the Nazi's and other "royals": because the most intelligent, intuitive, perceptive, amongst us are naturally often more equipped to figure out systems (system analysts) potentially unveiling, them systems and codes of the reptilian race.

And much information indicates the Nazi's did not lose the war, the simply went underground in some cases. The brightest amongst them; the scientists; were brought to America, and thus began the MK-Ultra non-consensual human experimentation on American citizens.

IN any kind of normal scenario, if evil intentions were not behind society pulling the strings of human minds; how could this happen? I would guess now, knowing what I do, hat Mr. Kramer, was most likely, barely human. How many humans do you know that write books about torture? Did you count? How many? Zero. Normal human beings do not two hundred pages of ways to torture women. You have been programmed to believe this is just business as usual on planet earth. I'm beginning to believe this is not business as usual, but big time manipulation and brainwashing.

The highly insightful, shamanic Aborigines and Native Americans were hunted, diseased to near extinction (or spiritually crushed by the Jesuits priests and/or relocation to reservations). The Huna shamans from Hawaii were all but decimated. The monks of Tibet, the African shamans, certainly the magical Celts of Ireland, England, Scotland had all been marginalized and almost eliminated.

Gimbutas's Lithuanian heritage links her to the ancient Goddess Brigette. All the Nordic Goddesses were put into deep freeze, while the war mongering infiltrators took over religion, politics, education, the money system, medicine and brainwashed us into believing torture, untimely death, disease and war was just business as usual.

The truth was they had brought hell with them and enslaved humanity and brainwashed us into forgetting our power and the glory of living on earth.

But maybe the most profound revelation in my literary review for my thesis was information contained in the revolutionary (other would say "heretical") book The Gnostic Gospels by religious historian and Harvard educated, Dr. Elaine Pagels. Modern Library named The Gnostic Gospels one of the hundred best books of the twentieth century.

The main focus of the book The Gnostic Gospels, Pagels is the revolutionary information contained in the ancient papyrus scripture found in the desert in Nag Hamm Egypt in 1945. The scripture were discovered, in an earthen jar buried in the sand in the desert by accident by an Arabian peasant, on a blood revenge quest.

While most of the texts were burned, by his mother, twelve were ultimately saved and were bought by. Eventually they made into mainstreaming academia where Pagels was able to examine them.

Carbon dating placed the papyrus writings to around 200 AD. Examinations by a host of professionals deemed that scripts to be the original teachings given by Christ to his twelve disciples.

Mary Magdalene, according to these scriptures, was not only a disciple, but Jesus's most valued disciple and his wife. She was deemed by Jesus to be spiritually and emotionally superior to the other disciples. Mary had been chosen by Jesus's choice to lead the Christian faith after his death.

In addition, The Gospel of Thomas, The Gospel's of Mary, reveal this early Christian religion as one that valued gnostic knowledge – a belief in our own divinity and ability to connect with God on our own (without the need of a translator such as a priest) terms and based by our own inner knowing. True knowledge of God was Gnostic (inner).

"There is a light within each person and that light shines on the whole universe. If it does not shine, there is darkness" The Gospel of Thomas.

In the texts God is portrayed as both mother and father, and therefore women were leaders in Gnosticism and considered equal to men. Additionally, Jesus was portrayed as a real man, with a real wife (Mary Magdalene); a spiritual master and an inspiring leader.

Pagels believed it was to the advantage of the early political and religious leader to re-write these gospels (and to destroy most of them) so that the population believed the only avenue to God was through the hierarchal Pope system (or in Christians, through the church).

It was heretical to believe, as did the Gnostics, that the path to enlighten was gnostic. This latter is the information that allowed the churches to maintain control of humanity for the past two thousand years.

It seemed there was a global network that wanted us to not to embody; to not feel; to not find our shaman center: to maybe not remember that time of peace on earth (information that could only be gained through intuition and gut instinct).

CHAPTER 50

SPELLS UNWINDING

I went through a period where I frequently wasted my time and my spirit guides' time and my power animals' time journeying into the spirit world to ask about Raven. A part of me was still a lost little girl (although I did not realize it at the time) desperate for love. I wanted one guide to tell me Raven was redeemable; we could make it; hang in there; don't give up.

I asked for a vision of Raven, as he truly is; his soul. Before sleeping, I put a mugwort leaf under my pillow.

In my dreams, I saw a fanged serpent, and Raven nailing boards all over our house, covering windows, and then he slunk back into an interior that was dark and murky and foreboding I saw an angry warrior with white pain, then a fierce demon; crocodiles just below the surface of a dark water. Then I found myself in Middle World, in an ancient time in the Himalayan mountains range where a solemn monk shook his head,

"No" and then went back to feeding sticks to a smoking campfire.

"How do I know how to trust my instincts? "I asked . .

"Trust feels like these mountains," he said, waving expansively towards the mountain range behind him.

"Do you trust these mountains?" he asked.

"Yes," I answered, "I can trust the mountain. I know what the mountains feel like."

"That is what your intuition feels like," he said.

I'm unresponsive, uncaring, and distracted.

I wake up and stare out at the stars. The visions and dreams and guidance was dramatic and clear. Raven, I realize, is like heroin to me. I'm wallowing in self-pity and addiction. I don't want to listen to my spiritual guidance. I always wondered why my mother went back to Hal over and over and other women went back to their personal monsters so frequently. It disgusted me.

I thought I was above stooping so low, but here I was feeling like an addict, even sweating and shaking with withdrawal symptoms: feeling like I want to kill Suzanne; mad with jealousy. What was wrong with me? I wanted to get into the car and speed away into the night, to Walpole, to fall into his arms, surrounded by stars and ghosts, and Easter-colored rooms.

Just one touch; just once more let him hold me and make me feel I am not alone. Let me hear the thunder of the hooves of our wild horses, as we ride once more through the plains of the ancient Lakota Sioux. Is that what heroin feels like? Let us sweep, like soaring Ravens, over all the rivers of my life; all the waters of the Goddess. Together.

I fall back asleep and dream my teeth fall out; Raven burns down our house and I am dismembered. I fly away with Rose. I dream Raven is running, running, fast, away – fast away from something, something that is going to catch him, I know IT is going to get Rose and I too, if I don't get away. Sure enough, whatever is chasing him enters my body. I wake up shaking and feel spiritually sick. It took me days to cleanse myself of this horrible energy.

I am going through withdrawals from Raven. Even the wind in the trees was like fingernails across a chalkboard; missing the Beast so much I wanted to scream; without the Beast I couldn't even be Beauty. I was just nothing.

So, I journey again to Upper World. I'm greeted by a council of serious-looking Native American elders, including Beautiful Painted Feather (who, in a real-life ceremony in Maine, had recently given Rose the Native name "Moonflower" and Gwen, "Starflower") The Peacemaker, Grey Wolf, and someone, set apart, I thought maybe he was the Sioux Warrior Chief, Red Cloud.

"Do not even look into his eyes. Never trust him," telepathically, they told me.

My stomach sank. I was furious, like an addict. It was a consensus amongst them that there was "no hope" for Raven; he had gone over to the other side; to evil. The Native elders were somber, serious and unwaveringly strong in their opinion.

In response, they said,

"This is your power. This power will be available to you, if you let him go."

A fox appeared and together we traveled to a grassy plain in the Southwest of America where I saw a woman who I thought was White Buffalo Calf Woman. She indicated she wanted me to work with her energy.

I sense danger and have a choking sensation in my neck. I feel Raven's presence – his rage.

I understand now that he is a sorcerer and has powers, maybe like me, but he is misusing them. He is using the dead and demons to do his dirty work; to align women to him; to spin webs around them; to curse them; to make them like Dracula's brides.

What else is he doing with his sorcery? What has he done in the past? Even to me, I think, shockingly. I am under the spell. Was the dream, which was sent to me the night after I withdrew from the Herb Class, part of his spell? Or was it someone else who wanted me to walk into the nightmare? I remember the dream of the room, with sparkling soup, and the beautiful faces of the apprentices; the dream that prompted me, anxiously and with dead seriousness, to sign back up for the class first thing the next morning.

I see the white owl in a tree – a sign of betrayal – and then Raven's face looking like a demon; deranged, and contorted with rage and evil; and understand, more fully even, that he has gone over to the dark side. I'm shown Suzanne and Raven in a stage coach – it's loaded with whiskey barrels and ammunition. With Suzanne holding the reins, they burst out from a circle of wagons, trying to make a break for it.

The next day, after this journey, Sally and Wolfe (in real life) got married. They arrived at the church in a horse-drawn carriage. Sally wore a silk orange dress my mother made (and she looked like a pumpkin). She had a ring of fall flowers around her hair and she reminded me of some kind, fall fairy godmother, who had walked out of a Maple tree flush with red and orange leaves sprouting from her head.

Wolfie actually looked debonair in a black tuxedo. I was the maid of honor, and Rose was the flower girl. I wore a black velvet dress with gold lace trim and a gold headband around my forehead, to which Sally's son, Richie, reacted, saying, "Hey, Pocahontas," as he passed me going into the wedding.

I bowed my head in embarrassment. I felt like a whore.

The truth is the *exact* opposite.

Mary Magdalene, the "whore" and the Divine Feminine are the true Christians, according to the Gnostic Gospels. So, I was a kind of Magdalene; hated even more than the average woman, because I represented the original truth; the original threat to Satanism. Not a whore, as they would like me to believe, but a spiritual healer. The Christ threatens to dissolve with love the foundation of Satanism.

These were my thoughts as I went into the Church…

CHAPTER 51

A MAGDALENE IN A TENT

My father had dementia. In reaction, Dave Hatch had moved into the house at Dunster Road, hoping, I was quite sure, to capitalize on my father's vulnerability.

A shark cannot resist the smell of blood.

Her body, shrunk to the size of a monkey and her brain to something much smaller, Marion, my stepmother; most likely from ingesting pounds of toxic Teflon and her own rage; had been institutionalized a few years ago as an Alzheimer patient. She had died (I believed) and so our father was alone.

The small white Cape Cod house at Dunster Road was perched on the highest point in Needham, near the green water tower (as I have said in one of the first chapters). The house with the avocado carpet; the black and white photo of Bobby Orr; the bathroom with the blue plastic cup which had been there since I was thirteen-years-old; the old Teflon pans, scratched to their deaths (and everyone's else's) with metal forks and knives and spatulas; the dank cellar of spider webs, and mold, and cracked cement floors; and now Dave Hatch.

It seemed nothing had changed, really. It was an almost predictable series of events.

Never caring, really, if Marion was dead or alive, I only ever thought of her with pain, and barely controlled rage. I was aware that most of my childhood anxiety and low self-esteem, and indeed, PTSD, was due, in great measure, to my short, but torturous stay with my father and stemother, when I was a young child and teenager.

I identified deeply with Charlotte Bronte's *Jane Eyre*; who was also emotionally tortured and half-starved by her stepmother; and throughout the years I had read the book repeatedly trying to find some sort of poetic justice in tying my life to Jane Eyre.

My brother, Jeffrey, who also hated Marion (with good reason) but who had a macabre interest in viewing her ill health (which I did not), had visited her hospital with our father, during the last days of her wretched life.

Alzheimer's disease had shrunk her body to the size of "a monkey" and she looked like "the crypt keeper" while she lay prone on a hospital bed holding a colorful beach ball, Jeffrey had observed. My father, who sat in a chair next to her bed, had proceeded to try to play catch with her, but she had reportedly failed at even this simple exercise.

It is ironic, considering she had held so tightly to a can of Comet scrub cleaner for most of her life that she was to end up clinging to a symbol of fun and frolicking. Her horrid final days and death did nothing to heal me, of course, but it absolutely did solidify in my mind the concept of karma. You are born with the face God gave you and you die with the one you create.

For my father, the seething hatred, and uncontrolled bitterness from Marion, had been swirled into the toxic gasses released from Teflon pans, and served up to him three times a day for thirty years. The brew had proven to be a bad combination for the brain cells in both Marion's and my father's brain function.

I imagined, for a moment, Marion, beaded sweat on her drooped eyelids, her forever furrowed brow, mumbling viciously, and standing before her suburban stove in Needham; and digging the steel or aluminum spoon deeper and deeper into the Teflon pan; successfully digging off most of the protective covering of the pan; and poisoning and killing both of them with the noxious gasses released into her stewed meats and grasshopper pies.

I was grateful now, for having mostly eaten the greasy Planters Peanuts I stole from the cabinet, in the dark, while they were both sleeping. My intuition had been correct all along. Marion had swirled hate and death into her Hamburger Helper.

Ironically, the hundreds of Meals on Wheels my father delivered to old people, the hours of volunteering at the YMCA, all the church attendance; trips to the mountain retreats with the spiritual leader, Joel Goldsmith and all the boat trips he gave to his grandchildren and nephews and nieces, had not saved my father; had not released him from karma; from the very real responsibility of caring and loving his own children.

In the very end, he had drowned, along with the rest of us, in Marion's poison. So much for being a good bookkeeper.

In the Tarot systems of analysis, Hierophant represents a religious, legal, or political male leader, i.e. a "good" member of the patriarchy. Re-

versed, you are the swill of the patriarch, the bottom feeder, not completely evil, but a low IQ envoy of a system. The bottom feeder is willing to do
the dirty work of a corrupt system without even much pay or recognition,
but purely for the illusion of power or dominance that comes with subju-
gating innocent people, through malicious intent.

The many reversed hierophants of the world, are responsible, I have
come to believe, for the slow, but constant degradation, and oppression
of the many Magdalenes of the world. The reversed Hierophants are the
nearly-rabid dogs nipping at our heels; weakening us; depleting us and
setting us up for the final blow that comes from people like Dave and Victoria Mueller. Helleen is in a category all by herself.

The Inquisition never ended, it merely changed in appearance.

But I digress; about a month ago, my father began to call me, which is
mainly how I found out about his condition and about the arrival of Dave
Hatch at his doorstep.

"What do you think Dave would think if I moved up there with you,"
he had said, recently, after somehow finding my number and calling me
up. I had stood in my kitchen stunned, almost unable to talk. We had lost
each other a long time ago. I was a teenager at Popham, when I had turned
away from my father's neglect and never looked back. I barely knew this
person on the other end of the line.

We both chuckle, but inside I grimace. His intellectual capabilities had
clearly been compromised, but he also sounds like a child who is trapped.
I feel sorry for him. I actually feel for him.

"I don't know what Dave is doing, but he's around here all of the time.
I think he's even got a room here," he continues, his voice lowered, like a
child hiding in a closet.

We both chuckle again, but a dread creeps into my consciousness. He has
been imprisoned in his own house. Dave has taken over where Marion left off.

"Yeah, I think Dave does live at your house, Dad. Dave Pacosha, you
know, your other roommate; he's been visiting me. He said Dave lives
there. In the front bedroom," I say, as gently as possible, in a polite nod to
his confusion and complete loss of control over his entire life, including
his own home.

"Oh, yeah. That other guy. He seems like a nice guy. Works for the
post office, I guess," my father says, more curious than anything. He is
detached, but he seems kinder and gentler.

"Wow, wouldn't that be something, if I just sold this house and went
up to live there with you," he says, his spirit rising.

He chuckles, gleeful, again like a naughty child.

"Yeah, that would be great dad. Maybe we could live at Popham," I answer, detached, wary. I can feel my heart.

This would never happen. Dave had his claws sunk deep into this situation and he would not retract them and I simply did not have the energy for one more battle.

But it was a happy thought to go for walks on the beach, to make Welsh Rarebit or brown bread, together again, maybe picking blueberries. I imagined Arianna, Gwen, Rose and I and my father in a beautiful house on the ocean. Maybe he would read *Winnie the Pooh* to them, and we would all be free and safe and happy together.

But I knew it would never happen.

He laughs hard, like the geeky kid who just heard a crazy fun idea from his cooler friends but knows he would never be part of the eventual plan.

"Popham. I used to deliver baked goods there in the Pepperidge Farm truck. That sure was a long time ago, "he says, quieter now.

"I remember you told me you used to deliver to the Donnells," I answer, feeling both increasingly sad for, but increasingly closer to him, as if while his mind had clouded, his heart was suddenly opening.

"Oh, yeah, Jane. She was great. I'd go into the kitchen and they'd have something hot for me to drink and maybe a piece of homemade pie. Blueberry, I think." he continues.

"I think you are right. Blueberry," I answered.

He pauses.

"You know I named you after her," he said, thoughtfully.

I laughed.

"I know. I don't think Mom was too happy about that."

"No, she probably wasn't," he says, even quieter. I imagine he is looking down at the floor.

And from the lowered tone of his voice, I could tell he was actually feeling the weight of that decision, *maybe for the first time in his life*. It almost sounded like he *cared*.

Everything, of course, was still *all about him*. He knew nothing about my life. He didn't ask. And I wasn't about to begin to tell him. He never asked about Arianna or Gwen or Rose. He never really asked me about my life.

But there was actually a gentleness about him I'd only seen on occasion, maybe like the day he thought I might have drowned in the storm at Popham; and when my body was streaked with blood, from the tiny rocks and shells that had scraped my bare stomach on the shore as I dove forward; in a wave of broken sticks and tangled seaweed,

He laughs, more nervously this time.

"Oh, Dave wouldn't like that, if I went up there," he says.

I knew he was in a trap.

"So, don't tell Dave. That wouldn't go over very well," he says, more serious.

"No, I won't, don't worry," I say, my heart sinking, just a little, because I had one moment of a dream, one happy vision of laughter and fun and love and safety and acceptance, with my father, then it was gone.

"Well, you have a great evening. And never forget, you are a magnificent person."

"Gee, thanks Dad," I say, genuinely surprised.

"You're welcome," he says, with a little bit of his old vigor.

I did make one attempt to see my father at this time, as I felt he might not remember me at all if I waited too much longer. I went with Rose to Dunster Road.

It was good. At least parts of it.

In the living room we talked excitedly about Elaine Pagel's publication of the book *The Gnostic Gospels.* And then we moved from the living room to the kitchen. While my father sat at the humble, ugly small kitchen table reading to me from Joel Goldsmith's book, I made grilled tomato and cheese on white Pepperidge Farm Bread.

I flipped the sandwich and stared at the golden crust and the bubbling butter on the black iron pan and silently rejoiced that Marion was dead.

Ding-dong, the wicked witch really is *dead.* Really dead. Gone. Forever.

In this state of wonder, I ate my sandwich, and then, after lunch, we moved back into the living room and I sat on Marion's flowered upholstered chair and sipped Lipton tea.

The room was much less terrifying. Cold ashes lingered in the fireplace from an old fire (wow, I hadn't seen ashes in a fireplace since Hanover); newspapers were spread about casually on the floor: even a dirty drinking glass, probably from a five o'clock whiskey and water the night prior (with a square soiled cocktail napkin underneath), sat on a pine side table beside the large brown lazy boy recliner, where my father sat.

It was *relaxed.*

The antique clock tick-tocked.

As the sun set, he told me how important the teachings of Joel Goldsmith were; and we compared them to Mary Baker Eddy and Christian Science.

Like the snake he was, Dave came and went, ever watchful; forever hovering over my father and making sure we were not discussing money or anything which might affect Dave's financial interests. My father, to my astonishment, knew exactly what was going on. He looked at me right in my eyes, nodded his head towards Dave, and rolled his eyes.

I was so shocked I couldn't even respond. Throughout my entire life he had aligned with Dave, against me, my brother Jeffrey, partly my sister Sally. I believed at this moment, it had not been his true self. It was the little boy with the bi-focal glass who never got picked for the basketball team and suddenly, Dave, who had been a macho football player and generally all around con man, was on his team. He felt like he finally had a team. It was the wrong team, but it was a team.

On the scale of creepiness, Dave was one step up from Marion. He was cunning, but semi-jovial. He was like having a used car salesman in the house, rather than a malevolent dangerous mental patient.

He would not interfere in our spiritual conversation as he had nothing to add. It most likely disgusted him. In some sense, we had freedom to be ourselves and to talk quietly, and to laugh and we talked about Popham. We were being ourselves; two intensely spiritual people, which was also shocking to me. Sadly, I slowly comprehended that at his core my father was a gentle soul. He was also an intellect. He was deeply spiritual. He was a gentleman. But maybe his parents had not recognized any of these qualities in him and maybe that's why he had anxiety attacks all his life and maybe that's why he could not face his own inadequacies that his own children tried to present to him. Instead of self-reflection, he deflected his pain and lack of self love, onto us, his children.

He had surrounded himself with sycophants (Dave) and other relatives and friends who did not know him intimately like we did, but worshiped and adored his public persona. But in the end, I realized, it is how we treat those closest to us; those to whom we owe the greatest responsibility; that we will be judged by God.

Not many brownie points are given, I realized, for delivering a meals of wheel, when your own daughter is home being tortured and you are doing nothing to protect her.

Dave wouldn't let me sleep in Dave Pachoca's room, nor would he go and spend the night at one of his other rent-free spaces with his ex-wife or children.

Instead, after my father had gone to bed, he handed me a tent and a sleeping bag and blanket. Rose and I wandered out into the backyard in the dark and I slowly set up the tent. I could have argued with Dave, but it would have confused my father and I didn't want him upset. I just couldn't deal with Dave. I was battle weary and they say you have to choose your battles. I brought a flashlight and once we were snuggled in, I made the best of it, and began to read to Rose her favorite book, Calvin and Hobbes.

We must have laughed too loud, or talked too loud, because soon after Rose went to sleep, I saw my father standing on the slate tiled back porch in his old thin white pajamas, in bare feet, looking for all the world like the ghost of Christmas past.

"Are you out there, Janie?" he asked, speaking into the darkness. He sounded like he cared.

"Yes, Dad" I answered, finally, quietly, trying not to sound sad. Tears started to stream down my cheeks, for everything. For my mother, my brother Jeffrey, myself, Rose, for Arianna and Gwen and even for my father. For all of us.

"Well, what the hell are you doing out there in a tent?" he asked and kind of did his funny, Hatch scoff and laugh. He wasn't mad, he was worried. I couldn't believe it.

"We're just camping," I said, trying not to reveal the shaking in my voice. I didn't want him to feel bad. I didn't want him to know how hurt I felt being out here in on the lawn.

I peak out the tent flap. He's confused. He puts his hands on his hips and stares down at the porch. In the moonlight, I can see him clearly. Sadly, he reminds me of Winnie the Pooh, when Pooh was afraid of the Heffalump, but he couldn't seem to find him anywhere. Pooh just knew the Heffalump was out there somewhere. I remember how, when I was little, we both used to laugh about the Heffalump.

"Well, are you ok?" he says.

"Yes, we're fine," I lie.

"It's fun," I lie again.

"Well… okay. Seems kinda strange" he says, confused, then angrily.

"I bet Dave is behind this. Did he take over that upstairs room? Did he make you stay out here? I bet he did," he says.

And, then, without waiting for an answer, and barefoot, he pads slowly towards the old pine table, weathered and broken from forty years of sitting on the porch in rain and snow. He had built the table by hand for his family – my mother and the four of us children – and he had set it beneath a chandelier and beside the brick fire hearth in the kitchen in Hanover.

He just stands, with one hand on the table, looking into the darkness.

I can't answer because I am crying too hard and trying not to make any noise. I don't want to scare him or Rose, because I know if I really opened up, the tears would never ever end.

"It's OK Dad," I manage to say, in jagged breaths, but he does not notice.

I lie back down and stare at the moon, and the gentle shadows, dappling onto the top of the tent, and pray to the Goddess just as I had done in my father's cornfield in Hanover…

Finally, he pads across the slate porch and up the three brick steps opens the screen door and goes into the breezeway, and he is gone again.

CHAPTER 52

I DREAM OF A FIRE IN BATH

"Stop, Raven, please turn the car around," I scream, in a voice filled with fear and panic, the kind unique to mothers when they are afraid for their children.

Raven, Rose, and I are in the car on our way back from Bath around 5 PM. We had tried to pick up Gwen, but no one would answer the door. I had seen curtains on the third floor of the girl's room, but Gwen, or maybe it was Arianna, did not dare answer the door. It was terrifying.

After we had gone back over the Bath Bridge, headed back to Damariscotta, I had turned and seen black smoke spiraling up from a house in Bath, near South Bath. Near where the girls were housed by Helleen and John.

"There's a fire. There's black smoke. The house is on fire. I knew she would set them on fire. I knew it. I even called the fire department to report the girls were living on a third floor without insulation and no fire escape. And Gwen said the windows wouldn't open.

Oh my god. Oh God," I say, gasping for breath.

"Please Raven!" I scream. "I have to go back. Please, I'm begging you."

He keeps driving north, towards' Damariscotta, and away from Bath.

"I have to get Arianna and Gwen, Please." I said, beyond terrified.

"She made her bed, let her lie in it," he said, nonchalantly lighting up a hand rolled American Spirit cigarette.

"No ... no ... no!" I scream,

"She's just a child. She's just a little girl. She didn't know what she was doing. She would never. Ever. Ever. Helleen did something to her. I know it. She loved me so much. They killed her spirit!" I shout at him.

I'm mortified, he is talking about Arianna. He thinks Arianna has caused all this pain. Little Arianna, with her Velveteen Bunny and lace dress, and all her books, baby Arianna, with her first little footsteps across the pumpkin pine floor on South Street, from my arms to her grandmother's. The grandmother who, I once thought, loved us, John's mother.

I opened my eyes. It was just a nightmare. I had been sleeping on our couch in Damariscotta. Exhausted from my trip to Needham, I had fallen asleep after bringing Rose to Montessori.

It was just another nightmare. Or was it?

My heart was racing. I was terrified. I sat up quickly and looked around. I was alone. Arianna and Gwen? Were they OK? Was the guardian here? Or gone? Or the Police? Or the fire department. My body was shaking violently now. My throat went dry.

Then I remember the dream. The nightmare. Almost every night I have a nightmare about the girls.

This one was especially bad. I dreamt the girls were locked in the house on North Street and it was on fire. Oh God. I can't call them. If Gwen gets a chance to say hello to me, she will be punished. I'm afraid to hear Arianna's voice, the distance, the trauma; the complete loss of soul. I had to calm down.

I reached for a purple amethyst crystal. I had just cleared it in the sunlight and snow. I held it close to my stomach. I started to deep breath. I imagined the Reiki symbol on my stomach to release my terror. I had to calm down.

I was alone. No one to call. Any call I made to anyone, including John, a therapist, a doctor, a guardian, or the girls, or especially Helleen, the girls would be punished and we would all slip further into the abysses. Evil could transmute my love into hate; like reverse alchemy they turned gold to lead, lead which they would use to slowly suffocate us all.

Last night I had driven home from Needham and gone to bed and fallen asleep. I had dreamed of the fire. It was a very real possibility that the girls could be killed in a fire, and the Bath Police Department had done nothing.

I know for sure they were just waiting to officially drive me insane or to kill myself, so they could officially call me unfit as a mother (so far they had not been able to find anything wrong with me other than I had dreams about tidal waves) or dead.

Gwen was already having dreams that Helleen was trying to poison her and she was afraid to sleep at night. I knew the dreams could be real, very real.

I decided I could call the fire department, anonymously.

I got up and dialed the phone. The sound of the fireman's voice accelerated my heart. I thought I would have a heart attack, but with all my strength, as my blood was quickly draining to my feet in sheer terror, I spoke. Everyone, just about in Bath, had been infected with poisonour lies from Helleen.

"Was there, is there a fire, anywhere reported in Bath today," I ask, trying to sound normal.

"No, nothing this morning," he says, uncaring,

I looked at my watch. It was only 10:11.

"Nothing" I said.

"No nothing," he responds

"Thank you" I said and hung up.

I was weak. No fire. Then the dreams were a warning, I realized. I had to do something.

I already knew my daughters were in constant danger from living most of their time with no parents and a woman who had proven to be a psychopath, a sexual deviant.

It is illegal in Maine to take a child from fit parents, but the guardian had worked with the stepmother, to create such a state of terror in both me and the girls; and such a deep state of mind control trauma on Arianna, and control over their father, that I couldn't make a move to save them.

Absolutely, a deal had been made behind closed doors, involving the judge, the guardian, maybe even my own attorney, maybe even Helleen's parents, who were millionaires, maybe even the State of Maine; somebody wanted them, these two absolutely beautiful, intelligent, elegant little girls.

But the dream signified another danger, something I wasn't totally aware of, yet.

The spirit world. It was my only hope.

I shut off the phone, locked the door, pulled down the shades. I bundled up in my wool journeying blanket, surrounded myself in a circle of stones and crystals, I held a Raven feather over my heart.

I held my drum and began to beat it in a slow rhythmic cadence. I called in my helping spirits from all directions: from the north the wise ones, wolf, snowy owl; the east, eagles; the south was coyote. And my inner child; the power of the sun, high noon, from the west; dolphin, whale.

I called in the Goddess of all four directions, and the spirits of air, water, fire, and earth. I closed my eyes. I was calm. I was surrounded by love. I felt roses fall on my face. I felt a gentle wind spirit. I felt the middle world fairies, maybe even Gwen's leprechaun.

"What do I need to do right now to help Arianna?" I asked.

Somehow, I knew it was about Arianna.

A striped tiger met me in Middle World on a green hill.

"Come with me," he said.

I followed him with Snowy White Owl flying above my head and Black Panther running alongside me.

We went, suddenly, into the earth, and through many underground tunnels it seemed and under three waterways (three rivers) until we rose up to a field.

Ahead I saw a cave. We walked forward and, I with great trepidation, walked into the mouth of the cave. A young, thin, naked, girl about eight years old stood alone in the cave in front of a very small fire. I shuddered but could only feel the love and support of my power animals.

I walked closer – my owl perched on a ridge of the cave. Panther lay down in front of the fire, which meant it was safe for me to be at this location. This was not a decoy or a trap for my soul. I gently reached out with my hand and gently brushed back the hair that fell across the little girl's face. It was Arianna.

I wavered slightly, but still the love from my allies was strong, I was held in deep sacred love. Arianna looked up at me imploringly, but her eyes were blank and empty. If this had occurred in real life, I would have collapsed at seeing the enormity of her despair. I decided to speak.

"It's Mommy, Arianna. It's mommy" I said and smiled.

I stroked her hair. I tucked it into her ear, like I used to do when she was little. I could not believe I could touch her hair. It had been so long. I loved her hair. I had loved making ponytails and braids, and brushing them, at night before she went to sleep, while she played with her stuffed animals on her bed. The house was silent back then, with John out to sea. But we would smile and laugh and listen to the snowflakes on the windows and the fire crackled in the woodstove, in the living room.

But I did not say anything more. I did not want to frighten her. She looked like a holocaust victim.

She didn't say anything but just stared into the fire.

She is not really here, I thought. She has had so much soul-loss, her soul is scattered.

She looked at me solemnly, and then back at the fire. I had the feeling she felt the world was too scary even for her to speak. She was alive, but not quite. She had so many soul losses and so much trauma, she was hanging onto life by a thread.

I wanted to begin to go in all directions, to retrieve her soul from the many places it must have gone to hide; to find comfort, maybe back in her old room on South Street, but there was a silence, a pink love, a stillness of the Goddess, which said to me,

"Be calm. Be calm. Go slowly. Bring in her power animals. This will keep her alive, for now. Be careful. Be gentle. Be quiet."

I had a steely manner now. This was life or death, but my eyes were rimmed with tears. I demanded for clothes for her and a beautiful little coat of red appeared. I gently place it over her shoulders. She did not move. I closed my eyes. I prayed for her. I called in all of her protection. She must have been a Goddess in another life, or priestess, because many ancestors and spirit guides and angels appeared. I also saw mermaids, a unicorn, a mountain lion, and Middle World Fairies. Who had she been in another lifetime, to come with so many guides? It made me wonder about all three of us – Arianna, Gwen, Rose and I. Who had we been?

"Are you all from Love?" I demanded. This is the standard question all shamans must ask spirits.

"Yes," they each said to me, and I allowed them to pass. The lion and the mermaids. I could see they were filling Arianna with strength and hope and love, through a kind of osmosis.

It was time to go. I could do no more at this time, I was told.

"I have to go, Arianna. But I will be back. You will not be here forever. Mommy will save you. I love you. " I said. My voice was quavering.

I could feel tears on my real face streaming down onto my lips and my chin and into my drum. But in the journey, I did not quaver or cry, because I was immersed, like Arianna, in spiritual love.

She turned and looked at me with empty eyes, but she did not smile or show hope. I dared to touch her hand and raise it to my lips and I kissed it. Maybe I saw a flicker of light, a flicker of memory of love. I wasn't sure but I felt better. I felt something had been returned to her that would survive.

Panther rose, which meant it was time to go.

"I will be back for you. I will save you. I love you," I said.

She smiled, ever so slightly, but then turned back to the fire and her hair slid in front of her face.

I journeyed back with Owl and Tiger and Lion through many fields and underwater, and through tunnels, until we were back and I was back into my body. I sat my drum on the floor, and simply stared out at the river.

I cried for many hours, the enormous grief of having lost my first baby, my precious girl, and that she was being tortured and I was unable to drive the fourteen minutes to get her.

I cried until the snow did not reflect into my eyes any longer.

CHAPTER 53

HEALING

Jill was the new guardian ad litem for Suzanne and Raven. The three of them were frothing at the bit to get their hands on the Witches Hammer, i.e., Victoria Mueller's report where she enticed Arianna to commit matricide. The guardian had forced Arianna to tell lies about me. I simply knew it. I remember suddenly, with gratitude and love, that my mother, when I was little, had dropped the custody case, when she found out my father was going to parade me in front of a judge to testify against her. She had sacrificed herself for me.

Helleen and the guardian had included the fact that Helleen had told Gwen she would pay her $50 if she (Gwen) would go outside naked, as if it was nothing – almost as if the judge would approve – as if the judge would even see Helleen in a more favorable light for being a proponent of child sex abuse.

It was if there was a calculated plan to destroy Arianna by Helleen and the guardian; it was formula; or a pre-designed, oft used plan, to strip a child of their spirit; their soul.

And Raven, having lived through every single step of witnessing the unfolding of the guardian's report; who had seen my anguish, my dismay, my shock; who had firsthand knowledge that it was all untrue; who knew the destruction and torture it held therein for all the children; had agreed to have Suzaane use the report against me.

"How do I protect myself from the guardian?" I asked my spirit guides after that first dreadful meeting with the three of them and the guardian's report.

At first, I saw monkeys...then I entered a tunnel. At the end of a small meadow was Jill. As if she had been waiting for me.

She took me to another place...far, far, away... It seemed we were traveling through clouds in space. It was a home, a simple home; I saw Jill as a little girl, being screamed at by her mother. Jill, a tiny girl, frozen, terrified. She went up through a tunnel to grandfather Twilight.

" I am the grandfather of both of you. I want you to heal your relationship" he said.

I looked at Jill. Her eyes were blank. it wasn't working. We leave and go back to the room where she was screamed at. I asked her mother to stop, and to see her daughter as just a helpless child. The mother suddenly stopped as if she had been awakened from a dream. She stared at Jill with compassion.

Then my lion power animal took me into a cave, a very decorative, beautiful cave where-in a banquet was being held.

I was told it was a banquet, at which sat the archetypes of my own personality. At the head of the table was a fairy of English heritage – privileged, sensitive, delicate – she loved everything fantastical and mystical.

Then there is an English Lord; an academic, like my father. He is busy with records and lists and figures and equations. He wants everyone to have proper schooling and licensing.

Then an Indian comes and roughly sits and slams his fist on the table. He wants revenge. He wants justice.

Then there is the Goddess/White Dove/Crystal woman. She is quiet and serene and respected by all the other characters. She is dressed in white. She is the divine aspect of myself.

Then into the room, file the seven dwarfs. I'm surprised. They sit and fill the rest of the seats at the massive oak table. I'm reminded of the Knights of the Round Table.

The dwarves start to criticize all the other archetypes. They are blatantly and pointlessly blaming and judgmental.

I observe that none of the other components of myself can operate under this kind of constant criticism. White Dove looks at me, and indicates she cannot intervene, unless I request her to do so.

Lion looks at me.

"Bring the self-criticism and judgment under control in your own mind and heart and you will have less critics," he said with love and respect.

I journey back to my couch. I look at the clock. I still have almost an hour before I have to pick up Rose at Montessori. I think about my father and the thirty (ish) years I lived under his crippling judgment. Nothing was ever good enough. The kids at the Y were better than me. The people on meals on wheels were better than me. I was nothing. I was worse than nothing, really. I barely existed except to be criticized.

Tears ran down my cheeks. I realized that self-criticism was the most prominent operating system in my psyche, despite all the strength and power I possessed; all the powerful archtypes within me.

And this truth was being reflected in the outside world.

I closed my eyes, just to rest them, *I thought*. I guess I nodded off. Lynn Andrews, the shaman from Santa Fe, New Mexico and the author of two of my favorite books, *Woman of Wyyrd* and *Medicine Woman*, is knocking at my front door. In the dream, I get up and answer the door.

"I've come to pick up something," she says. She has long blond hair and is wearing turquoise jewelry and a long white skirt. I can feel her love and power.

"Lynn," I stutter.

Her blond hair is pulled back in a barrette. She has with her a dog and two children. A boy who looks like an Indian and a little white girl with pigtails.

"You have some jewels." she says. It wasn't a question. Her eyes are wise, loving, and kind.

"I do?" I ask.

"Yes. you have some jewels for me," she states again. Her eyes are glowing with deep secrets and old wisdom.

"Oh," I stammer. I have no idea what to say. It is like a god walking in. She enters the house and walks into a bedroom and then onto a porch I'd never seen. We turn to face each other, and we shake hands and the sky lights up and deafening loud lightning cracks.

I wake up from the dream, as if lightning were striking the house. It's the phone rings.

The phone rang. Adrenaline spreads through my body. I hated the phone these days. It mostly held news that felt like it had come straight from hell. I slowly picked it up.

"Hello," I said with trepidation.

"Hello, Mommy," It was Gwen. My heart froze. I was immediately terrified.

"Mommy," she said.

"Yes honey," I answered, my blood freezing and my throat constricting as I tried to sound normal.

"I'm scared. I'm scared of Helleena."

The most terrifying words in the world to me. I close my eyes, press the receiver too tightly to my head. I pray. Silently.

"It will be okay honey. I know you are. It's okay..."

My body is flooded with grief, panic. Fear, shame – but I try to stay strong.

"We'll figure it out," I say.

"Don't tell her."

"I won't. I promise."

And I mean it. I know the consequence for Gwen if Helleen finds out about the content of this call. She will have no one. No one she can trust. She is completely alone.

"And don't tell dad, either," she says. "Because he won't believe me. Just like he didn't believe anything else. Like when I told him what Helleen did to us in the hot tub. And then he will tell Helleen."

She starts to cry.

"It's okay honey. I promise I won't tell," I say as tears stream down my cheeks.

I silently pray to God that she trusts me enough to tell the truth. I realize she is risking her life telling me these things.

"Gwen, remember when you were little and we used to gather flowers and make flower rings for our hair and we would sing and dance...and then we'd have a tea party."

"Yes," she sniffles. It was kind of like a prayer.

"I'm going to pray for us and help you. No one will know."

"Are you sure?"

"Yes honey, I'm sure. Prayers are invisible. I know you will feel better. And someday everything is going to be okay."

"Okay...I gotta go mommy. Helleen's home."

"I love you Gwen."

"I love you Mommy."

She hangs up quickly.

Every cell in my being is grief-stricken, like an acid poison has spread, like cancer. I'm also terrified. I hold my head in my hands and drop the phone. I'm aware of the ticking of the clock. The pile of unpaid bills fluttering as a breeze rolls in from the window. I'm aware of the passage of time, the almost empty gas tank in the Prelude. I'm aware I must stay alive. I remember the dream of Lynn, and somehow, it's enough. It's enough. I can go on. I've been give some special power from Lynn. I just know it.

I hang up the phone. I stand and get my keys. I rinse my face; I pet the cat. I open and shut the door. I have to meet with the guardian ad Litem before I pick up Rose.

I was in a war, maybe like Vietnam, only worse, because they have shoved, not just you, but your children, into the center of the thick, hot jungle filled with snakes, snipers, and landmines.

Twenty minutes later, I pick up Rose at Montessori and she runs into my arms. I was being allowed that moment; They could take her if I did one wrong thing. If I did one wrong thing...

We drove home and she chats happily, playing with her snake and her paper cups. She takes cheese and crackers and a juice box into her adorable room. She sits down and open a book. I hear her singing.

I grab my blanket, my drum. Please dear God. Sometimes that's all I can say. Please dear God. Has God given me all these allies for this purpose? I don't know. I knew everything came from God/Goddess, even my panther, Lion, and Owl...

Please. I could barely form the request. What should I say? Maybe they will just know. I wrap myself in the blanket.

"Please hear me, my loving and compassionate guides," I ask.

I see owl and eagle and fox, clearing me of dark substances, angry words, fearful thoughts, and intrusions in my stomach, until I'm clear. I light sage and let it burn; the smoke circling my body.

I close my eyes. I fall into a vision.

Panther and I run through a dark jungle. I'm aware of dangerous animals. I see a fanged serpent and an alligator. Not sure what it means, but I stay close to Panther. We race out of the jungle and we are running down a pathway and into Middle World. We are passing clouds. We pass over three rivers, and my stomach turns and tightens.

I know where we are heading – to Bath.

Then I see Gwen. Panther shows me her mind has separated from her body, from trauma. She has shut off her feelings. It felt very dangerous.

I was surrounded by evil, again the fanged serpents. But we stayed. Panther was fighting off the attack on me; more power animals arrived. It was Eagle and then Hawk, they were picking up the creature and carrying them...away...I saw a creature who seemed to have Gwen's soul...Panther and I stared at this creature...Panther slowly walked forward. It moved back. I offered the creature a jewel I manifested in my hands; a ruby, a crystal ruby – and his beady eyes brightened."

"Do you have any more of these," he snarled. I will trade her soul for the ruby crystal."

With that he released Gwen's soul part.

Panther went forward to protect Gwen. I pulled out another crystal. I threw the ruby at the creature and he slinked off somewhere...

I saw Gwen and blew the soul into her heart and then rotated four times around her...Then I knew we had to work fast to put her body and mind back. I knew the dangers: the mental illness of split mind. Panther and I had to travel back to when she was eight years old.

Gwen and I were laughing and playing in the foyer of South St. I saw Gwen dance in front of rows of her animals.

"Gwen, please accept this power. Your lion." I said to her younger, trusting self.

"Of course. I love lions," she said.

Lion jumped into her body. I sent Reiki to Gwen's young self, before we left South Street where we still had joy, and trust.

"Hold on, Gwen," I say.

I call upon the youngest Gwen to bring her lighter thirteen-year-old who was spiritual, emotionally, and psychically traumatized.

We brought the thirteen-year-old back to South Street. First Eagle had to clear layers of demonic energy from her skull, put there by Helleen, my guides said, to try to destroy her connection to her higher self. It was a method used by the Nazi's I am told in the journey.

Panther, the integrated Gwen, and myself, were surprised by the appearance of a green leprechaun.

"Gwen, this is the same leprechaun you saw behind the chair in the green foyer on South Street when you were little. Do you remember?" I said excitedly.

"Yes," she said in awe, and a slow brimming excitement.

"He wants us to follow him," I said.

We did...at a fast pace (it seemed everything had to be done quickly) we ran...we entered a beautiful field of green grass and there were apple trees in full bloom. Apple blossoms flew in the wind and we all laughed, and Gwen held up her hands as if she was in awe of the apple blossoms.

The elf leprechaun kept moving quickly and saying, "Follow me. Follow me"

I felt we were in England or Ireland; a place of power for Gwen in one of her past lifetimes. He was trying to have her remember her power; her strength; her magic. We came upon a clearing in the orchard. In the middle stood a beautiful gold palomino horse – his pure white mane was blowing in the breeze. He neighed and shook his head, as if to greet us.

Gwen ran forward and climbed the tree, and from an apple tree limb, she mounted her horse. In all her glory, with her long hair blowing...and apple blossoms blowing around her hair, she stood in her power.

"There you are, Gwen. This is your power. This is you. Never forget. I promised you it would be a secret. No one knows. You are safe," I said.

She smiled...and her leprechaun and her palomino and Gwen galloped off down an old truck path kind of like the one I remember riding Misty on in Hanover...and I watched.

I feel in my heart. When an apple blossom had stuck to my cheek when I was a child in Hanover. I touched my cheek. I realized I was crying. Panther curled up at my feet. I petted Panther, not moving...and the tears flowed.

CHAPTER 54

VERY LITTLE STRENGTH LEFT

I felt I was failing. On every front. I had very little strength. The destruction of my children on every front, my father lost now forever, to Dave and dementia; my mother dying. She had now moved into a nursing home.

My mother seemed happy and at peace now, maybe for the first time in her life, since she lost her children in Hanover. Maybe she is like every other woman who loses her children. You simply wait for death on some level. I knew her ancestors were moving in closer, because the vibration in her nursing home room was high.

Everyone loved her of course, she had such a bright spirit. Even towards the end she kept everyone else entertained; she complimented nurses and helpers and gave them small gifts and tokens.

"I see the fairies on the river outside my window," she said, smiling excitedly, like she did when I was a child and we were in Hanover and we went to Bunny Woods with the playgroup. I had stopped to see her one morning after at the nursing home.

I'd dropped Rose off at playschool.

There was some peace for her, maybe as there would be for me at the end of it all, waiting for my Lakota Sioux ancestors.

They would be there for me with my pony, maybe even the Appaloosa stallion, Misty.

I never had forgotten the day in the Bunny Woods, where I had rested my head on her warm shoulder, and the wind had swept through the trees, and the children laughed.

Then she looked at me and smiled.

"How are the girls?" she asked, but she already knew, and she had tried so hard for this not to happen to me and my daughter. But now, it was over for her and she was happy. She would find peace. The strange woman who had been hanging around her apartment had taken her to her house and then someone abused her and myself and Dave had rescued her and brought her to this nursing home.

She was near the end. It was one of the few times Dave and I had ever worked together in peace. He was quiet. Maybe he actually cared for the woman he had helped to destroy.

I always told her something positive about the girls, even if I had to make it up. I knew she wanted to leave. I could not believe she had lived this long, even now that I knew what her life had been like, having lived it myself.

I knew that before they were divorced, she had begged my father to let her come home. She dreamed almost every night, she once told me, of knocking on our front door at Hanover.

"Bob, please let me come home."

In the dream, the answer had always been the same as in real life.

No answer. Just an unopened door. I wanted her to be free, to go home, to be with the ancestors. I did not want her to see what was happening to me and the girls anymore... I could not stand her pain, on top of mine.

Our talks were light and happy, but we both knew. Everything...without saying much of anything. It was such a short distance from the nursing home to my house on the hill above the river.

I drove slowly home in her yellow Prelude; she had given me everything she could think of – to save me.

It was freezing cold in Maine, gray and many shades of darkness, and the wind-whipped tree branches...I did not know how to go on... so desperately alone...and with so many enemies...

I stepped out of the car and onto the driveway and went into my little house.

I was terrified of a new situation looming, Rose was scheduled to spend the weekend with Raven and his new girlfriend, Suzanne. For some reason, I was scared of the situation. It would be deep in the woods, much further north, and it would be just Suzanne, Raven and Rose. Something was wrong. I felt Rose was in danger.

I hardly ate anymore...

I walked past my computer and the books and papers. Past the coffee table with my drum sitting in the middle of it. I sank to the floor...held my head. I closed my eyes.

I was drifting through Middle World with Panther.

I was a little girl back in Hanover sitting under the apple tree. Pink blossoms floated through the air and I was at peace. I felt a warm presence.

I saw an angel. Suddenly we were not under the apple tree anymore, but on a beautiful beach. The sun was brilliant and warm. I smiled and took a deep breath, loving the air and the wind and the sun and the sparkling beach sand.

"Look in the sand. You lost something here. It is time for you to find it." The angel said, holding my hand.

We walked along the shoreline...the waves were washing the rocks and crystals, clear and sparkling. I gasped. Up ahead I noticed the most extraordinary necklace, slightly submerged, sparkling in the sand.

I ran towards it. I picked it up, because I felt it had been mine once upon a time...

The angel took it gently from my hand and placed it around my neck... She tied it in the back. I touched it, awash with wonder and love and a sense of power.

"Do you remember this necklace?" she asked.

"You lost it over time...because of the difficulties you have encountered in your life. You stopped believing in magic. The necklace is magic."

I smiled. I could feel the diamond necklace becoming me...I felt a piece of my heart had returned.

I sat on the beach aware of this new vitality I felt. We both watched dolphins jumping into the air from the ocean.

"You need to leave where you are when this is all over. Find the sun."

I feel angel wings flapping in the air.

CHAPTER 55

SPIRIT MOTHER AND SPIRIT FATHER

I awoke from this vision and the sun was setting. I glanced at the clock, I had only forty minutes before picking up Rose. I still felt weak.

My heart froze when I remembered Rose would spend the weekend with Suzanne and Raven.

They were going up north, to Suzanne's cabin, deep in the woods, beside a tumultuous, dark, Maine ocean. Suzanne had a canoe. A winter snowstorm was reported to be hitting the Maine coast this weekend.

"It won't stop him." I said out loud. "It won't stop him," I said again out loud.

I knew he would want to show off for Rose and Suzanne, and he would take Rose out in the ocean on a canoe, in the storm. Death stalked him...

"Am I getting paranoid?" I thought. No, just gaining a deeper understanding of Raven; and now Suzanne.

She was like most of us, I thought. A long string of Dracula's wives – deaf, dumb, and blind to his evil. She had said recently, she thought he was Christ.

I closed my eyes.

"I need help to protect Rose"

I started to drum.

I was suddenly in a hot air balloon with Tiger. We went higher and higher and higher...through clouds of white and pink and floating gently through the air...

We passed through Middle World and into Upper world. When the balloon stopped, Tiger and I stepped out onto a cloud...and before us stepped the most exquisite white horse, with flowing white mane. His body did not seem solid, but was like an opal, translucent. He had a muscular back, thighs, and neck, and it was rippled with colors and he pawed at the sky, and then reared.

I was mesmerized with his beauty...He was a male guide. Male power... This horse was maybe the most magnificent being I'd ever laid eyes upon...

"Please stay with me," I asked. I braided a bouquet of flowers from a field into his mane...

I swung up on his back and we raced through the clouds...faster and faster, my hair pulled back, straight, with the wind, rainbows flashed by, and the wind, the north wind. I could see all of the clouds had spirits, and the wind and air was filled with spirit and power, and blessings...

Tears of joy streamed down my cheeks. We stopped on top of a mountain. I leaned forward and I held my head to his neck, just like I did with Misty In Hanover.

"I will come to you anytime you call," he said, the flowers still wound in braids in his mane.

"Thank you" I said, he turned and flew off into the clouds, and a blue sky far, far, far away…

I stood on the mountain not wanting to ever go back to the world I was living in. It was just too much. I was too alone. I was losing my parents again...

Then a small monkey appeared.

"Follow me," he said.

We jumped onto what looked like a Christmas tree and slid down to Middle world.

Suddenly we were sitting on a strong tree branch looking in through a window to the most idyllic scene...

There was a Santa Claus-looking man; stout with a white beard and his wife, I assumed, who looked, of course, like Mrs. Claus. They sat on comfortable upholstered chairs before a fire that burned brightly in a brick fireplace in a living room.

I could not believe the peace. I closed my eyes.

I suddenly felt a shift and opened my eyes. I was sitting on a braided rug, like the one I had on South Street, before a fireplace. And the gentle, older couple began to speak.

"You need us. You need fire. You cannot give up. Take our power." The flames shot up higher...my spirit slipped into the fire and I rose up through the chimney and into the sky with the sparks … flying higher and higher...I was suddenly a volcanic eruption...

The older man smiled and telepathically I heard him say,

"We are your spirit parents. You have a home with us. This is your spirit home."

I descended back into the room after having absorbed the power of fire.

Soft moonlight illuminated shiny wooden floors. I was suddenly filled with joy. I ran into the kitchen and looked at the perfect white cupboards, and the copper tea kettle and the brick floors.

And then I ran upstairs. I was looking for my room. I must have a room! I opened a door and gasped. A little room, with pink wallpaper and a round window. I ran to the window and looked out on fields of green grass with ponies, grazing peacefully.

A fluffy white, soft quilt like a big marshmallow lay atop the double bed. Big soft pillows propped against the headboard. An antique rocker, a vanity, and a braided rug were placed with care in the room. The floor was painted a soft peach.It was everything I would have dreamed of for a perfect little room.

I peeled off my shoes, and slipped under the quilt, dreaming of love, and more love, of pink apple blossom, and Misty, and the white horse and the fire.

"Fire is always here for you. Call upon us whenever you need us," I heard as a I fell into a deep, peaceful, warm sleep…

Chapter 56

Raven's Demons

Two days later, it was excruciating to turn over Rose to Suzanne.

After I had dropped off Rose at her house, my gut burned all the way back to my house I passed my mother's nursing home, also on the river, and I wanted to stop, but I felt a pressing need to go home, to connect with my guides, to try to understand the fear I felt about Rose's trip with Raven into the northern Maine woods.

To the rest of the world, she was just going on a trip to a cabin in the woods, but to me it was a Stephen King cabin, where unexpected horrors could manifest.

Once inside my house, I stare out the kitchen window at the river and drink herbal tea. It is red clover that I picked inland, near Jefferson, not long ago. Fields full of clover

I went to the couch and pulled my blanket over my lap and picked up my drum.

"How can I help Rose? I feel she is in danger right now," was my question and statement.

A fierce timber wolf, a power animal, showed himself almost immediately. Together, side by side we began to run down a path into Lower World...

This was not the Lower World which was familiar. Maybe it wasn't Lower World. It was a dark, rather ominous energy .

We were going lower, and lower, maybe even leaving Lower World. I noticed distinct changes in the scenery, and the encroachment, within myself, of fear and wariness. We were not in Lower World. I was sure my power animal was a creature of Love, so I proceeded. I had asked for help for Rose, now I was being shown a path that may or may not fulfill my request. I had to follow.

We started to run down a path, deeper into this other world. On his suggestions, for my own protection, I was now riding on the back of Timber Wolf. I felt evil forces were trying to pull me off his back. I clasped my hands tighter around his neck and leaned my head into the bushy gray fur on his neck, and I tightened my grip on his body with my legs and knees.

Suddenly, Wolf stopped. We had arrived near the dingy, dark, bank of an unmoving sludge-filled river. I saw dark, semi-transparent figures, like dead men; ghosts, or ghosts of their former human selves, trudging in the mud along the riverbanks. It was sickening and dangerous.

We moved closer, but stayed hidden behind a dark tree. No life exited here. I saw angry, Native American men who were stuck in this no man's land – this land of eternal anger and bitterness and death. This was, I realized, shockingly, and remembering Sandra Ingerman's description, The Land of the Dead. I shuddered, but kept breathing, and maintained a tight grip on Wolf's neck fur.

Why are we here?" I asked Wolf telepathically.

"Raven and these dead men are feeding off each other. The zombies work for him in the land of the living. They do his bidding. He has sold his soul for this power," said Timber Wolf.

It seemed the zombies (who were clearly neither alive or dead) had apparently become alerted to our presence, and they stood up and started to amble around aimlessly at first, but with menace, and with sounds, like growls. When they started in our direction, Wolf growled back ferociously and they stopped, seemingly confused.

"This is the demonic power he uses on the earth to control his victims," Wolf said.

"We need to send them onto the light. To go back to their ancestors. Otherwise, they will remain here forever, available to the living for demonic use," I whispered.

He reared up and growled and the zombies, frightened and confused, turned, and began, at first, to walk and then run, at a hobbled pace, along the filthy banks of the dark slimy river.

We chased them until we reached a tunnel of light. They ran, like the mindless zombies they were or sheep; or sheeple; over a cliff and into the spirit world. I knew they would be there for a long time, healing from their mistakes.

Our job complete, Wolf turns, and we run back alongside the river, and then follow the exact path up we had followed downwards. With each step away from the Land of the Dead, my heart feels lighter. The scenery changed, too. The grass became green, the wind became clearer, the birds sang. There are no bird songs in the Land of the Dead. Butterflies gathered to welcome us back to Lower World.

So those were demons Raven had conjured.

I slid off the back of Timber Wolf.

"Thank you," I said and hugged him. I looked into his eyes of love. I didn't want to leave Lower World. The birds; the vibrant, psychedelic color (almost like the posters from the 1960s), the sweet smells of lavender and jasmine, all the sounds of nature. It is brighter, richer, warmer, and kinder, here. Lower world is the dream world of Mother Earth.

Reluctantly, I follow the glowing light from the lanterns hung on the walls, up the stairs in the center of an old oak tree, and then step out into the woods beside my house.

For a few minutes I was at peace, staring at the Damariscotta River, and the blue sky, and the beautiful wood, remembering the Wolf and Lower World. This was my world.

CHAPTER 57

MY ANCESTORS RETURN TO SAVE US

It is late afternoon. I pace back and forth in front of the picture window. I wanted to call the girls, but I knew everything would be filtered through Helleen. If I said love, it was fed back to the girls as hate. If I said, free, they girls heard "enslaved." If I said I wanted to "help" my daughters the guardian or Helleen or Kathleen would feed it to John or the girls as "hopeless" or "helpless." If I indicated I was "terrified" for my daughters, Helleen would tell John I was "paranoid." Love was hate, hot was cold, life was death, truth was a lie, abuse was love, love was hate in the world of the psychopath.

If I acted anywhere within the system, I would be cut down and the girls would be shredded. It was just like the witch in the dunking chair.

It had taken a while to learn the machinery of the system. I'd always looked for light. I'd looked for hope. I'd looked for signs of humanness; signs of wisdom, insights; but maybe more than anything; signs of intelligence; signs of a heart or compassion; in the court system, the guardian, the therapist and in John and Helleen.

There was none, even in John, who I often daydreamed would somehow save us all. With one word, it could all be over. One Word, on a phone call from him and all the agony would end.

All he had to do was call Helleen and say, "Bring the girls to their mother."

That would have been the end to what was now a decade of agony. All the power of the courts, the guardian, the therapists, the lawyers, and Helleen would be null. That is the extreme power parents who are united are given. That is the extreme power parents, whether they are divorced or separated, have to protect their children from the courts.

It never happened. He never made the calls. I had given up hope.

And there was no light in the machinery. Everyone that is fed into a psychopathic system or person, whether it be truth or love, or goodness, or hope, or joy, or mercy, or compassion, is transformed into mental, emotional, spiritual and sometimes, physical, death.

As I did almost a dozen times a day, I ran through my head all the people who would not, could not help the girls. John's mother, my daughters' grandmother, Pat McGuire had become an accomplice to Helleen and John, calling them with any new "dirt" she could find on me, or anything she heard on her scanner or around town.

Rose was at Montessori for a few more hours. I felt like I was going crazy. Arianna's words were like an unexploded hand grenade in my heart.

I ran outside. I ran through the woods, winding quickly through the tall river-side pines. I could feel this screaming coming out of my lungs, but I was detached, as if it was happening to someone else...I stopped and sat on the earth and covered my face and screamed and screamed and screamed.

I got up and ran, falling twice. I didn't know where to go. There was no escape, as long as they held my daughters in their jaws. I kept thinking...just one word. John...just one word, maybe five words. I had begged him...please, please...let them come home, but he was always angry, cold, and predictable.

Tears were streaming down my face, not like rain, but like an ocean had flooded out from my heart. I reached the river. My father would never be here for me. What was happening to him? Why were they transferring him? Dave was transferring him somewhere.

My body is racked in agony.

That night, after Rose had come home, and happily ate her dinner, and we had played with her toys on the floor of her room and she was tucked in, safe, for now, into her warm bed, I sighed and touched her soft face. Somehow, she had escaped the system, maybe because her father was a demon, not a psychopath. I had learned that the lowest form of life was not demonic, but psychopathic.

I had not seen my mother today. I was anguished at not having enough time. I could not keep doing soul retrieval and clearing negative entities from that hell house...I did not know what to do...I had tried to call Arianna several times. Helleen kept answering and telling me, the first time, she was not home; second time, she was "doing her homework"; third time she was "watching her favorite show."

It was beyond impossible.

I stared out at the river. It was dark. It was the dark of the moon. A stillness hung in the air.

I did not know what to do. Gwen had gotten through to me. She said John and Helleen were going away, taking their children (Arianna and Gwen were really not considered part of their family) to Disney world, leaving Arianna and Gwen home alone. Of course, John and Helleen never told me anything. They especially would not want me to know of any "imperfections" in their life (apparently, they did not consider it wrong or imperfect to be holding two girls hostage).

Gwen had also told me Arianna had tried to run away and John had nailed wood panels across the front door.

It had to end. It all had to end. We would not survive much longer...

I lit a fire. I smudged the house. I drank a tall glass of water. I smudged myself. I painted my face with red and yellow. I was going to be a warrior. I had been a warrior. I could be one again.

I closed my eyes, I prayed to all the Goddesses for strength. I bathed in roses and lavender. I dressed in silk and velvet. I glittered my eyes and cheeks.

I would die or free them. I no longer cared what it took. I had to do this for my mother, too. For all mothers. For all daughters.

They were all guilty of matricide. The killing off of the mother, a crime punishable by death in the old days.

I stood before the river...my heart racing, beating, thumping. I raised my arms and called out to all of the Goddesses of all times, I called to my ancestors, the Lakota Sioux; I called out to all my Power Animals and Angels and Spirit Guides and Ancestors.

I called out for the Power of Hawk, Eagle, Bear, Wolf, Owl, and my Horse, my White Horse, my male energy.

I fell to the ground and slipped out of my body. Suddenly, I was riding my White Horse, his mane, flipping in my face. We rode high in the sky, above the clouds, in the stars. Hundreds of Goddesses and Power Animals flew together over the Damariscotta river, faster and faster. Icy tears were ripped from my cheeks with the wind like when I rode Misty in Bunny woods.

We cross the Wiscasset River: we are gathering strength. We are unstoppable. Hundreds of us are flying through the sky. I was given an obsidian spear, from which hung feathers from my people, the Sioux.

Finally,

I knew my allies. I knew my enemies. We cross the Kennebec River.

I see the house come into view. The pathetic white house, with super-size plastic garbage bins of trash outside. It was disgusting. Lifetimes of rage fill me.

We descend down from Upper World to Middle World, and I aim my spear at a window and with all my might – with all my pent up rage and my daughter's being tortured for almost ten years – hurl my spear, breaking a window in the house. It crashes and splinters to the ground. My Native Ancestors break more windows, tear apart woodwork, and enter the house, from all angles and entryways. We tear down the boards nailed to the door. My power animals attack and eliminate the negative spirits living in the house. A war is transpiring inside this house of hell.

I set down a new spear I had been given. I was looking for them. I was looking for my daughters. I was still mounted on my white stallion. I galloped my horse up the stairs to the firetrap of a room on the third floor; the small, cold, room where they kept the girls.

I see Gwen sitting on her bed and my heart opens.

"Gwen, it's Mommy. Come with me. Come with me now. We need to leave now," I say, with open heart, with love.

I see it in her eyes. I see her spirit. I see her trust and my heart leaps with hope. She could feel my love. She could feel. She could trust. They had not broken her spirit. Tears of joy streamed down my cheeks.

I hold out my hand to her and she holds out her hand. We grab hands and I swing her onto the horse. I feel her tender face upon my back. I feel her arms around my waist.

It is a moment of joy I will never forget.

We race down the steps. I see Aborgine warriors, The Native American warriors, My Power Animals, battling with the evil entities guarding and inhabiting this hell hole.

"Gwen, where is Arianna, where is Arianna?" I yell.

"In there," Gwen points.

We ride into what looks like a living room. I see Arianna. She is sad and her soul is shriveled and she is a shadow of her former spirit.

"Arianna. It's mommy...It's mommy. We can go. You can leave now. Take my hand. I will protect you. It will be okay. They can't get you anymore. They can't punish you anymore," I say, my heart racing. Will she respond? I can't take her against her will. It is a law of the universe. Does she have enough spirit? Enough will? Does she remember the love we shared, my newborn baby girl, my life.

"Mommieeee" she cries and runs to me and holds out her arms. I can't believe it. Ten years of trying to just touch her hand. Touch her face. See her smile. I was shaken with relief. We had somehow broken the mind control.

I hold out my hand. She grabs it and I pull her onto the horse behind Gwen. Together, holding each other tightly, Tehran, my white Stallion, flies out the broken window and into the starry night sky. We sail through the clouds as we fly higher and higher.

It is a wonder they knew me, underneath my warrior glitter and paint. I laugh and the wind blows our hair and we are smiling and crying and sailing aside other horses, and power animals, and Indians, and with Eagle and Hawk beside us, and the Goddess, over the three rivers.

We land in my home, the fire still glowing in the fireplace...I see Rose still sleeping.

I slip from Tehran, and he neighs and stomps his feet, and nods his head. I hold my arms up for the girls, first Gwen and then Arianna. They slide off Tehran and into my arms. We are all still smiling.

"Thank you," I say to Tehran and give him one last hug before he flies off to his home in Upper World. We climb onto a chair together beside the fire, and we sleep, our arms around each other, in peace, for the first time in a decade.

It was over ... I just knew it was over ... they were free.

Chapter 58

The End

It was the evening of the same day. I was sleeping. I heard a phone ringing. I struggled for consciousness but kept lapsing back to sleep. The ringing stopped.

I open my eyes. I'm on Rose's bed and she is sleeping soundly. I feel light, clear, almost peaceful. Then I remember the powerful journey to Bath where my spirit guides, our Native American ancestors, and the power animals had eradicated the evil, and set the girls free.

The phone rang, again.

Groggily I rose from the bed and went to the kitchen and picked it up. To this day, I cannot remember who called but I remember the conversation clearly.

"Jane, the police are at John's house in Bath. The girls are alone. John and Helleen left them alone and went to Disneyland with the three boys."

"What?"

Alone. Police. Disneyland.

"What? Why are the police there?" I stammered. "Is there a fire? Is there a fire?" I ask, my heart racing, my palms sweating. A fire was almost my worst fear. All I could think of was the two girls in that third floor; a small room, with no fire escape, the window barely able to be opened; A total fire trap. Helleen.

"No. There is no fire. I don't know what is going on, but you should get over there," the friendly voice said. This was not a prank.

OK. Ok. I will," I said, numbness overcoming me and fear; but on a deeper level, something else.

"Good-bye. Thank you," I responded. I hung up the phone.

How much gas did I have in the Prelude? What about Rose? I looked at the clock. It was late, not quite midnight. I simply could not wake Rose, drive with her into the middle of mayhem, which included the Bath police, who, in my opinion, were no friends of children.

I stood there thinking. I had to get there. I called my neighbor, a young woman I hardly knew, but she had small children, and a husband. I opened my address book and dialed, my hands trembling.

A moment of confusion; I said it was an emergency, and I had to get to Bath and then she agreed to help.

A cold dark night. A Maine night. My spirit felt clear as I crossed the three rivers, for the third time that fateful day, into Bath. The first two on the back of my spirit horse, Tehran. I arrived, my heart racing. The town seemed quiet and, somehow, it didn't seem as malevolent.

The stars shone brightly in the night sky and I felt they were guiding and protecting, rather than illuminating my presence, like a dragonfly caught in the light of danger. We were all together, the stars and the river and me.

John and Helleen were gone, I reminded myself for the hundredth time. That thought eased my thumping heart.

Sadly, horribly, in my opinion John had become an extension of Helleen, *and his ongoing betrayal of his children was even more painful to witness than her criminal psychopathy.*

At least the two people primarily responsible for the girl's imprisonment and abuse were out of the way. It was a time out of time. One opportunity. I may actually be able to give the girls support or love amidst whatever tragedy was transpiring in the house of horror (John and Helleen's house)

But the Bath police were involved, and that was bad.

It was moments like these – when the lives of children are involved in any way in the Maine legal system or with the police– that I think of 12-year-old Sarah Cherry who was strangled, raped and murdered and Bath police officer Mark Westrum altered evidence, it appeared, to push through a conviction of Denis Dechaine, a young, organic farmer with no prior record and no motive.

Not just Westrum (who, years later resigned as sheriff after being accused of sexual assault on another male officer and after two DUI arrests) covered up evidence of Cherry's murder, but so did the courts. The rape kit, clothing at the site of the murder, hair, DNA found under Sarah's fingernail and also the testimony of four doctors who stated the time of the murder was approximately 30-36 hours before her body was found – and at the time Dennis was already in custody – was also not presented in court.

Dennis was tried and convicted in a makeshift trial and ordered to serve a life term which in Maine means "until you are dead."

It seems Bath police and the entire judicial system went to great lengths to cover up the real murderer who most likely still walks the Maine woods. Most people in Maine have a good idea of who the real murderer is – he was related to Sarah and was highly motivated and he was seen in a car with a young girl who was crying – shortly before Sarah was murdered. A woman, Sarah Cook, who worked with this man, said she saw scratches on his face shortly after Sarah Cherry was murdered. She said "The sheriff" – I assume this was Westrum – basically, told her to get lost and it "was none of her business."

I understood what Dennis had gone through. In my own trial, all positive information about me or reports which were contrary to the conviction and the outcome Judge Field and Victoria Mueller, wanted were ignored or destroyed. Field would not see any of my witnesses and he ignored the report –as I have said before – from Dr. Nancy Coleman, Psyd, who stated grave warnings about leaving the girls for any time at all with the stepmother.

Years later I would learn that during almost 30 years of imprisonment Dennis Dechaine had created a "horticultural paradise" at the Thomaston State prison complete with 100 rose bushes, lilac bushes, apple trees, perennials, annuals, and trees. Dennis was overjoyed, he said, in a newspaper report, when he overheard a newly sentenced criminal – who had just arrived at the prison in chains– had looked around at the beautiful landscape and said, "I think I've died and gone to heaven")

Thinking of Sarah Cherry, the malevolent actions of the Bath Sheriff, and also that the real murderer was undoubtedly somewhere near Bath, made me drive faster. I was speeding down the narrow, dark, silent Washington Ave, with the wind whipping in my hair, and it felt good. I knew something had shifted. Something was going to happen. It already has. On the spirit level.

I arrive at the house. I gasp. Police lights are flashing. I observe teenagers, in groups and some standing alone, outside John and Helleen's house; looking at the house, mostly. My worst fear was a fire, but the person on the phone never said fire.

Police cars lined the road. Revolving red police lights blinded me every time they flashed. Arianna and Gwen, where are they? What has happened?

I park the car discreetly; any sign of me would be reason for all hell to break loose. I had begun to know how criminal minds operate; any sight of those who represent the light or truth and they begin to grow fangs and salivate.

Lights were on throughout the house. I saw a broken window. Rough and ragged wooden boards, which had been nailed up to prevent the girls from escaping, had been torn off the house and thrown on the ground haphazardly.

The girls, increasingly angry and suddenly empowered, had repeatedly tried to run away, in recent months. In response, John had begun to "ground" them. John had boarded up doors and windows, I was told.

I was never informed by John or Helleen, or anyone, that this was going on with the girls. Of course not, they would go to any lengths, no matter how much it hurt the girls, to keep me out of the picture. Helleen, absolutely would not want anyone in Bath to think the girls would want to escape. She wanted to be thought of as a perfect parent.

The exterior of the house had begun to resemble a monster house, with the boarded up windows and walls. A fence was put up that was so high around the house that even a six-foot person could not see over it into the small, mostly dirt, flowerless brown lawn. Giant green and black plastic trash cans, filled and often overflowing, with empty bonus size diet coke bottles, stood like addicted demons, vomiting over their sides, along the outside fence. Bulimia dictated that Helleen drink endless gallons of diet soda.

I walked closer to the house, the red police light intermittently illuminating the scene with a red flash. A teenage boy stood, clearly drunk, and kind of swaying right in front of the house, near the steps.

"Where are Gwen and Arianna?" I whispered, tensely.

"Gwen's in the police car," he mumbled. He was drunk.

I turned immediately and started to walk quickly towards the police cars. A cop held his arm out to stop me.

"Who are you," he demanded.

"I'm Arianna and Gwen's mother" I answered, determinedly.

He looked at me with dismay, as did so many people in Bath, who had either forgotten I existed or who had been told Helleen was my daughter's mother. It was a town of matricide.

Anyone who dared to stick up for me soon found their reputation destroyed and they slinked away damaged and with lessons learned. Helleen was an expert at spreading carefully designed lies. And she always managed to do it by making it look like she was helping the person she was intent on destroying. It was beyond the comprehension of most people.

I kept walking.

I saw Gwen's little blond head in the back seat in the dark interior of a police car. She is only thirteen for God sake. I went around to the passenger side and opened and got into the car.

"Mommy, " Gwen said...tears were streaming down her cheeks

She tried to reach out to me, but forgot she was in handcuffs. Instead, I stroked her hair and tucked a strand behind her ears. Her eyes were red and she had definitely been drinking. She leaned against me and I hugged her.

"It's gonna be okay. Everything's gonna be okay now. It's over"

"Helleen is going to kill us, Mom. She really is, this time!" she cried, terrified.

"No, not anymore. You're safe…everything is going to be OK now. I just know it." I said, soothingly.

"Where is Arianna?" I asked.

"She ran away with the rest of the kids. But she's … she's with our friends. I tried to run but they got me," she said.

"We had a party, a huge party, and the kids tore down the boards, and broke windows and some of the boys, they tipped over a police car," she said, trying to wipe the tears from her face, but she was handcuffed.

"Where is everybody…they all ran...they just caught me," Gwen said.

"I'll stay with you. Don't worry." I said and moved closer to her and held her.

The cops got into the car, asked me a stream of questions, then started the car and with lights and siren departed the house towards the Bath police station.

We were silent but I held her, as best I could...and we slipped further and further into the darkness with police lights flashing.

On that night, with stars bright overhead, and the lights of the police car, swirling red, and amongst the tears and the handcuffs, a war had been won. My ten-year battle to save the souls of my daughters had been won.

I didn't really understand it that night, it took me years, to place the moment, to this day… and I do not remember the exact date. I'm sure the Bath police have a record, if it was not destroyed, of this night.

The transition was not simple.

Seething, John and Helleen, upon their arrival home, immediately barred the girls from the house. John, shockingly (I thought I was beyond shock) filed a police report against Arianna and Gwen. He demanded the girls be put on probation, be charged with criminal theft, destruction of property, and for punishment they wanted the girls to be put in a detention center in Portland and banned from ever entering the city of Bath again

. I believe there were between ten and twenty charges against the girls – for having a party. Even for John, who I had come to see as heartless, this was beyond the pale. Gwen went home with me that night and the next morning,I stood in attorney Jonathon Hull's office in Damariscotta with the "document" – the charges against my daughters. I was numb. I kept shaking my head, but desperation and hopelessness and panic was gone… something had shifted.

"I just can't believe their own father would do this to them." It was beyond shocking.

Jonathon nudged his glasses up his nose. He looked at me. He was a hefty man, from an old Maine family – Hull. Yankee to the core. He was intimidating, but not evil. NOT evil. That's what matters these days. I even think he actually cared. I'm not sure how. I was probably one of thousands of single poor women in Maine who had fallen between the cracks; just one more woman whose children were under threat by the Maine Guardian Ad Litem System, The Maine Judicial systems, and Maine police.

I had no money. I can't even remember if I had paid him. I had so much trauma, I had disassociated from all but the very few goals which were unwavering – saving my daughters. All else had fallen to the wayside. .

"Well, that' it then, " he said.

"What's it?" I said, although deep down, I knew. I knew because I had set the course last night with Tehran, my white horse and all of my angels and power animals and spirit guides.

But still, here I was just a poor, single, Maine mother, alone. Just one in a million, whose children were most likely in jeopardy, one way or another, if they were in the system.

"We're going before a judge today. In Bath." he said, emphatically.

"Let's do this quickly, " he continued.

"Where are Arianna and Gwen?" he asked

"At my house. I am trying to enroll them at Lincoln Academy," I answered, robotically.

"Good," he answered, getting up.

I stared at him, unable to speak. Ten years ago– one year into this battle– I would have broken down in tears of joy, then laughter, gone out for champagne, and called everyone I knew with the good news. I would have raised a Chalice of Wine to the Goddesses, but too much time had passed. Now, I understand, warriors, who come home from war, are simply home. It was simply over. The scars go deep, so deep...as to have changed you on a cellular level. I could hardly speak.

"Meet me at the Bath Courthouse at 3," he said. "Bring your paper-work." He put on his coat. "I need to go home to see my daughter and have lunch."

"OK. I'll be there," was all I could say.

I slowly turned and walked into the entryway and picked up my coat. I stared at the window. He was exiting the driveway already, in his old Saab. It seemed like he did everything fast.

After ten years of battle every day of my life, could it really be over?

At three PM Jonathon Hull and I walked into the courtroom in West Bath. It was like a dream and I don't recall all the details, maybe Jonathon remembers, maybe I should call him, now, today, twenty years later. I was almost sleepwalking at this point in the war, barely present in my body. Thousands and thousands of traumas, had left me almost not here on the earth.

Jonathon presented the Judge (I don't believe it was Field. I would have remembered that hawk face – who was too busy covering up for the real murderer of Sarah Cherry to even listen to my witnesses during the custody battle ten years ago). The "argument" was simple. My former husband and his wife had thrown the girls out of the house. They had been "banned" from Bath, were on the precipice of being sent into State care (in a detention center in Portland) and were essentially homeless. I believe the entire hearing lasted twenty minutes. It was just myself and Jonathon. No witnesses. No therapists. No guardian ad litems. Nothing. You could almost hear a pin drop. The judge signed the papers, returning full custody of the girls to me.

I stared at the document in disbelief.

CHAPTER 59

SET THE GIRLS FREE

Maybe a week or so later Gwen told me that a group of teenage boys, their friends, I guess, on the night of the party had begun a chant of "set the girls free" while tipping over a police car.

I thought about this for some time; all the events of that night. The shamanic journey to Bath, to "set the girls free," the ancestors, the power animals, the angels, the Goddess, had unwoven a spell, captured and dispelled demons, broken down doors, shattered glass, while I went inside to rescue the girls' souls. Only hours later, a similar series of events followed in the wake of my actions that night.

Physical matter follows spiritual. I had learned that in Christian Science, and now, unequivocally as a shaman. This is power. This is the power the Satanists do not want you to know that you have. A power to transform the world.

Maybe this knowledge that I acquired (shamanism and journeying) – is why they tried to get me to suicide myself, was so I would not write this book – or maybe even more books – so they could permanently capture my daughters. Much later in my life, through thorough research, I have learned that many of these judges and lawyers and guardians – often with the help of corrupt police and social services – create "cash cows" out of vulnerable children from "cradle to grave." They receive kick-backs and profits from every stage – from the custody decision, to the detention centers, then to child sex trafficking and foster homes.

I knew, absolutely, that Arianna and Gwen would not have survived much longer, and that Helleen may well have been planning to poison them, or at least Gwen (who slept with a knife by her side for almost ten years). Gwen felt she was going to be killed. It was because they could not put Gwen under complete mind control. The love she had in her heart was to powerful. It would not surprise me if the stepmother "accidentally" killed her to get her "under control." Logan Marr was killed by Maine

State Courts. Only five-years-old she was taken from her loving mother and given to Maine foster care worker Sally Schofield who suffocated her to death.

My dream of the house burning down in Bath was probably metaphoric. My spirit guides were trying to tell me that the girls were in extreme danger and the end was near.

They were rescued from the entire corrupt system and their primary abuser on that night. As above, so below. The spirit guides had changed the reality on the unseen level and so this manifested in a physical reality less than eight hours later.

Every human being has the power to become a shaman. It is a gift from God to humans who have the courage to be here on the planet. You do not come here alone and you have many universes of souls and Being here to assist – should you call on them, as I did.

But, one of the hardest realities I had to accept, over time, was that I had lost my little girls. I would never see them again. They were gone. The thousands and thousands of moments we could have shared, were gone.

My daughters were my daughters, but they were on the run. They were angry, confused, traumatized, defensive and enraged. Shock and confusion, as to why they had not been able to be with their mother, was an ongoing. This shock made them wild for the first ten years after their escape.

At least, at first…

Arianna ran from Damariscotta, to Hawaii and kept going, almost never looking back. She went from Hawaii, where she slept on the beach, and listened to the waves, and roamed in bare feet on strawberry farms. Then she went to Santa Fe for four years; then to California, and then to almost every point on the planet; the Steppes region of Russian, deep into Africa, with armed guards, the jungle of Guatemala where she came down with typhoid fever and was healed. I flew down to Guatemala and sat by her bed and stroked her face, for the first time in over a decade. She recovered through a blood transfusion, but she kept running.

All the time, she would call; "I love you mom."

"I love you too," I would say.

We were speaking like two people in different worlds. Trying to hang on. Arianna, almost more than Gwen, realized what Helleen had done to her, what she had taken from her, and how her father allowed it, and was enraged. Fierce power and will somehow found her and she began to fight back, through emails and phone calls and letters to her father.

"How could you? How could you? How could you?"

CHAPTER 60

MY MOTHER AND
THE LAVENDER SACHET

The first week the girls were officially "home" (with me in Damariscotta) we all went to see my mother, at the last, and final, resting home. We brought her a lavender sachet that she loved. I knew she was going to pass. I had hardly had time to see her in the last few weeks, because of the battles I was fighting both for Arianna and Gwen and now for Rose.

I knew she understood. She knew the battle I was fighting because she had fought it too. I did not want her to go through it in the last years of her life.

I kept it all from her. She was barely coherent, but she seemed happy. She wanted to leave this planet. Her life, because of matricide, had been hell. And on her last birthday on this earth Arianna, Gwen, and Rose were all together and her and I were all together. It felt like a miracle and a gift for my mother who had been shattered by the loss of her granddaughters, Arianna and Gwen.

We baked her a cake. The nurses wouldn't let us light the candles inside so Gwen ran outside with the cake and stood outside her window and she lit the candles.

We all sang "Happy Birthday" to her. I could see Gwen mouthing the words from outside the window in the dark night with the candles lighting up her face.

I will never forget Gwen's face, lit up in the dark, by the candles. I saw her beauty, joy, innocence, and love. It was still there. Everything she had been as a little girl. She had never stopped trusting me against an avalanche of mind control propaganda. It was a miracle.

Later, Rose played in the room with her dragons. She hummed a song I did not recognize. Arianna, Gwen, my mother and I talked softly and we all ate the cake. It was a quiet, gentle night..

"I just love this lavender sachet. Thank you so much Janie" she said.

"You're welcome. I thought you would like it. You love flowers so much," I answer, biting back tears.

I remember in Hanover, how much you loved pansies and daffodils and the lilac bush."

"Oh yes," she said, "I just loved those sweet little faces," she said, and smiled brightly remembering her days as a young mother with a garden and her children. She was probably thinking about Mandy, her black cat and maybe even Rose, her pet skunk. She was smiling.

We knew the end was near...

It was the one night in thousands when all four of us had been safe and together. It was a moment in time where somehow God had given us one day of peace before it was over....

That night, after we all went home, and miraculously all my daughters were with me in the same house, while I was sleeping..my mother came to me in a dream..She was beautiful and young, and finally, free.

"I love you," she said and smiled.

In death, she was everything I remembered her as a little girl. Her loving hands, her warm and generous heart, her bright spirit. She had become mine again only as she passed away from the earth to heaven.

I woke with a start. I knew she had died and that she had come to say goodbye.

It was still dark, but I could not sleep. I went downstairs and made tea, went outside with my steaming cup and stared out at the black starry sky –just as I had as a little girl, when I was calling out for my mother, when I was alone and only seven years old.- – Tears ran down my cheeks. It was a broken crystal. Dreams half filled.

"I just got her back..God, why...I just got her back." I lamented

But I had not really ever gotten her back, not the mother of a little girl's dream, as matricide had stolen her soul and crushed her heart, by the time we were reunited when I was thirteen.

At seven AM the phone rang. It was the morning receptionist from the nursing home and she said my mother had passed over during the night. I got dressed, left a note for the girls – just saying I was going to the nursing home – and then got in my car; and praying my daughters would be safe for a few hours (which they were not as Helleen drove thirty miles from Bath to Waldobor to leave a box of dirty kitty litter in front of our door that day – just trying to terrorize us in whatever manner she could manifest in her perverted mind)

But I had to go. I had to see her one more time.

…I was alone in her room. She had the lavender sachet I had made for her still on her chest , next to her head…Tears streamed down my cheeks. I picked up her hand. It was still warm.

"Look at these old hands. They're just so ugly now. You wait until you get older. You'll understand." she had said more than once about her aging hands. Sometimes she would even sit on them, to make the point.

She had given all her rings away to me and the girls as she no longer wanted to display anything on her hands.

But as I held her hand I thought it was the most beautiful hand in the world. I just kept holding her hand. I could not let go.

I was the seven-year-old girl again thinking

"Mommie..please please..don't leave."

I knew it was the little girl in me, who had never really understood why she had gone… all of a sudden, with no trace, except, in her wake. A white kitten. A shiny red purse she sent from California and postcards of little animals, like bunnies, squirrels and baby bears. …

Through blurred vision, I stared at my hand on her hand … and thought of my own daughters: for ten years they did not have my hands, to curl their hair around their ears when it was in their eyes, to tuck the covers under their chin at night, to tie their little wool hats, to zip up their coats, to hold their heads against my chest, to make them cookies, to straighten their dresses, to button their buttons, and help them hold their pencils, to give them vitamins, fold their clothes. A thousand times a day a mother reaches out to help, and when there is no child…

The pain was almost unbearable … but I tried to control myself.

I reminded myself it was over. The worst was over and my mother was free and I had seen her face and she was finally happy. And in her freedom, as she passed from this world to another, she was just as beautiful as everyone said she had been. I could not remember her beauty, only her love.

"Oh, and Mom I'm sorry, I don't think you knew … I was so busy … but the girls are going to be ok. They are Ok. They're free too. I got them back, Mom. I did it. I think I actually saved them … and no one will ever know but you and I."

And then she was gone…

Chapter 61

Waldoboro and The Apple Orchards

Many months after my mother's death, and Arianna and Gwen were somewhat safely out of Bath (Gwen was still being traumatized at her new school by her stepmother, who had followed Gwen and got a position as a school teacher at the school). Again, one thing I had learned from this situation is that psychopaths never stop trying to destroy. They are like machines.

I also had begun to believe that our culture consisted of a certain segment of individuals with an entirely different brain structure which made them capable of massive destruction, deceit, and criminal behavior, for which they felt no remorse. I had learned a lot from dealing with this stepmother who had a (real) last name associated with one of Hitler's closest allies.

Gwen could speak to me on the phone without her stepmother monitoring. I could actually go and I could see her. It was the beginning of a long, long healing – which would ultimately take decades.

Rose and I were alone on a 100-acre farm in Waldoboro.

The old farmhouse was haunted – I was quite sure of that – but it was miles of hardwood floors, and of green grass, an orchard of apple trees, and far below us, a lake, where we could hear the cry of ospreys.

Rose had a rabbit and a cat, and she played happily for hours with her pets. She climbed trees and chased chickens, and she was enrolled in a school that she loved next to the ocean in Rockport.

I had a job –for a while – as a newspaper reporter for The Courier Gazette. It was short-lived. Only a few months after I began my boss told me he was giving me a going away party and that my job had been suspended. It was the most depressing, nonsensical, goodbye party anyone had ever attended. No one, mostly myself, understood what was going on, I knew my writing was good and my reporting was at least average . I was certainly just getting going.

I soon realized, after this happened a couple of more times at Maine newspapers, that I was on some kind of blacklist list that was circulating through Maine after I did the reports on sexual harassment at Bath Iron Works. I was slowly learning that there were much bigger actors in this attempt to take me down, than just the Bath court system. I was being targeted from every angle, including, I thought, possibly. from the federal government.

Suzanne and Raven were fighting hard for more time with Rose, and it was beginning to scare me as Suzanne was as clever as Raven was diabolical and she, like I had been, was under his spell. The difference between Helleen and Suzanne was enormous though.

Suzanne, as enslaved as she was by Raven, was a decent human being. She treated Rose with love and kindness and she never spoke badly of me in front of Rose. The difference between Ariana and Gwen coming home to me, at the beginning, from their stepmother, and Rose, arriving back from Suzanne, was night and day. Parental alienation had begun to destroy the psyches of my older daughters from the first day they had contact with their stepmother

So even when I knew Suzanne was carefully planning my loss in court, by running around collecting all the court documentation from Bath, including the guardian's reports – I still felt grateful to her for not harming Rose.

I did know, though, that Suzanne would figure out a way to never allow me to leave the state of Maine, and now that Arianna and Gwen had escaped, I felt alone and scared – and I wanted to be near them,

To me, Maine was a death sentence.

So, I did the unthinkable.

I used Ravens' love for me, or whatever it was – his addiction to me– his undying passion. It was a calculated plan, an enormously dangerous plan – considering the warning from my spirit guides – but I knew it would get me out of Maine.

I went back with Raven.

He thought nothing of stepping out of his marriage to Suzanne and back into my life.

For a few months it was a strange kind of joy

It was a family – the only thing I'd ever wanted in my whole life – was to be a mother and wife. We had family meals, and walked in the woods, and made campfires, and fell asleep beside them. We lounged on the white wicker chairs in the sun porch, when the lilacs were in bloom and the window open. He had his arm slung over my shoulder and we could talk forever. He asked me about the night my mother passed; and a dozen more questions about the vision I had of her the night she died. He seemed pacified that she was now free.

There were months of catching up about all that had happened in Bath. I told him I had journeyed with the Goddess, and my Arabian horse, Tehran, and my ancestors and power animals. He listened and he nodded and believed in me and he believed that I had freed them from evil–at least the worst evil. He was quiet as he rolled his Camel cigarettes, and smoked them, blowing the smoke away from me and out the window.

I knew I was dealing with a sorcerer, and I did not have much time to activate my plan. I had to be careful not to get too caught up in the dream, or the spell he had cast on me a long time ago. But I would be inside the spell, using it against him– for the freedom of Rose and myself.

Compared to a psychopath, a sorcerer is almost a decent kind of person. I learned that there is no greater evil on the planet than a psychopath. At least sorcerers, even those that work with underworld demons, have a heart.

He still called me "Goddess." My ties to him were extremely strong. I knew we had lived a life together as Native Americans and then in the 1800's we had been brother and sisters in a life in London, England, where we enjoyed relative opulence and our family seemed to be artistically and musically inclined. Feeling like I had a brother that cared about me, was one of the ways I had been entrapped. I wanted so badly to be looked after by someone.

But I knew in my heart he had sold his soul. The dark spirit had given him a charm that pulled in women– with the most love and light– and then he would drain them and slowly destroy their lives.

I could already feel the drain I knew would take my soul eventually, and that of Rose's.

I had once journeyed to my spirit guides and asked them where Raven's soul was in the universe. They brought me to a steamboat somewhere in the ocean in the late 1800's. He was dressed richly, in a gentlemen's suit, with fur across his lap.

I asked him,

"Why are you here?."

"Because this was a happy life; a good life,"

"But we need you." I had said, " You have a daughter. And something has taken over your body. You have sold your soul!" I exclaimed.

341

But he would not come back to his body. ....

During the brief time we were together as a family– myself, Raven and Rose – I never talked of all the betrayals, how he had used the guardian against me – Victoria Mueller's report – ``The Hammer of Witches."

It was all part of the enchantment. Did I really love him? What do I know of love? I had never been loved. I knew I loved my daughters and they loved me, and that my mother had loved me once, and that my spirit guides and power animals loved me. I'd never known a man's love that I could remember.

So maybe it was not love, but it felt like something close. There was something I could not name that I felt when he held me those moonlit nights in the apple orchard in Waldoboro.

I felt like I was home. Since I did not know home, and I did not know love, he felt like both; in reality, he was neither.

He was my Heathcliff and I was his Kathy, and we were again on the moors of England, the fresh wild wind in our hair, forever laughing and loving, and obedient to no one except our love for the earth and each other..

It was reckless.

But, with the unification of the biological mother and father, the wheel of injustice had ground to an immediate halt. All lawyers, guardians, judges, stepparents, lost their power. That is how powerful the family unit is and I marveled at how infinitely beautiful a real family was. So, all court orders dissolved when Raven and I were together, and Suzanne was out of the picture.

We watched tentatively, as our little girl, Rose, walked, in her red ruby slippers, down the long driveway to the bus stop. We could not take our eyes off her- on her first day of school.

It is a moment only biological parents understand. The tense moments when the bus stops and she steps her little foot onto the big wide bus step, and then you see her little head, for a moment, and then she sits, and then her small hand waves, and the bus lurches into second gear and up the hill and gone...

It was my a few months of indulgence. I was able to escape the court, for a few months', because I had an intact family.

But the spell began to fade, as I knew it would. The violence began.

I began to calculate my escape from Maine. It was complicated and it involved going to Cape Cod to be with my father, who was now dying, also of cancer, but he had dementia. I had begun to talk with my brother

Robbie, and he was interested in me coming down there to my father's new house on Cape Cod to help him take care of our father. Dave had talked my father into leaving Needham and buying a house on Cape Cod, so here we all were going to be.

I was also talking to Arianna and Gwen, almost every day or every other day. It was hard. It was painful and it was just the beginning. Thirty years later, we would still be trying to heal and to understand what happened.

I did not tell Raven my plans to try to help my father. I was slowly planning what to pack. What to bring...

But then I was ready, our little purple car was packed. Raven was away on a job for the weekend. The bunny, Cabby, had thankfully gone wild, so we only had the cat, and all of Rose's stuffed animals, and her books and clothes.

We would leave early in the morning before the sun was up. I had told Rose, but not Raven we would leave Maine. I could hardly believe it. I would have a steady income from my father's estate – an hourly wage for taking care of my father – and Rose and I would have an entire second floor apartment in a beautiful house on Cape Cod.

All we had to do was get there.

That night, in the middle of the night, the night before we would depart, I left my body and I was taken to our old house on South Street – where Arianna and Gwen and I had been so happy.

CHAPTER 62

MOTHER MARY AND 62 SOUTH STREET

M y power animals and spirit guides took me back to 62 South Street, in Bath. The beautiful four-bedroom Victorian where I had painted the front foyer rose, and the dining room pink, and the kitchen blue, and front foyer I had wallpapered in dark green with cream color hyacinth John McGuire, Johns older brother, had been so nice and helped put up the wallpaper.

In my ghostly form – as I had traveled through the spirit world to reach my old house – I looked down at the purple and red wool braided rug and I remembered Arianna dancing in a white lace dress and black patent leather shoes going round in round on the rug smiling and laughing full of joy. I started up the staircase … I remember Gwen had put stuffed animals on every step of the foyer steps – all thirty of them. and danced for them all, at the bottom platform. I looked into the living room where a fire had burned brightly in a wood stove and where Gewn had seen a leprechaun.

I touched the walls of the house where all my dreams had been born *and all of them had died.*

I had brought my two daughters home from Miles Memorial Hospital to this house. They had been born into the loving care of Dr. Kitfield, and Sarah Robey, in a birthing room, with homemade quilts on the beds. My babies never left my side that I can recall until we left together for home.

My guides said to walk up the stairs. In a state of awe, I walked, touching the thick, expensive, emerald green paper, remembering the joy of having my own home and family.

I was a ghost floating through the spaces of my old home, I reached the second floor and looked down at the beautiful pumpkin floors. I remembered everything. Arianna in her room reading books and hugging her Velveteen rabbit, Gwen in her yellow room with all her lions and tigers laughing. She was the sunshine. Arianna was the moon, the mystery.

I touched the tall black candelabra made of wrought iron where I burned small white candles on dark winter nights. I touched the beautiful Victorian couch. It was so beautiful. I had loved this room more than any room in the world. It wasn't much in the grander scale of things, but it was beyond what I ever dreamed I could have for myself after having grown up feeling I deserved nothing more than ragged towels and torn and thin blankets, and ugly furniture which I had no love for at Dunster Road in Needham. .

I step onto the pumpkin floors on the second floor. I loved these floors. I walked a little bit and looked to my right into Gwen's old room. I had painted the room a beautiful soft yellow. I had painted her bureau white and my mother painted the little rocking chair blue, with flowers.

I remember touching Gwen's warm pink face as she slept peacefully in the sunshine in her crib – her blond curls falling over her eyes.....I had loved washing and drying her little clothes and tucking them neatly into the drawers, and taking so much time and effort to make sure all her stuff animals were around her when she slept. I had wound up the Easter yellow fuzzy little chicken mobile, when I laid her down to sleep, so she would close her eyes to the sweet melody.

I went further straight ahead into Arianna's room. I stepped onto the plush royal blue and looked up at her old white wrought iron bookshelves that I had kept filled with books.

She could never get enough books. Most of the time, her floor was covered with books. I saw the mahogany sleigh back twin bed and her white popcorn quilt – like mine – when I was a little girl. The walls were wallpapered in a white background with tiny purple and blue flowers. I had always marveled at how beautiful every room was in this house. A minister had lived here before me and he had made it beautiful and sacred, I think.

I remembered how the wind, when I kept her window up – not too high to make her cold, but just high enough to let in a slight breeze – it would blow on the lace curtains. I could see her window from my room down the hall. I would watch the wind, to make sure it was just right.

I kept going. I was being called.

" Keep going," my guides said, "Don't stop."

I went up another flight of stairs into the dark attic. Moonlight illuminated a small corner and there I saw Arianna and Gwen and myself standing in a corner in the moonlight. I was a beautiful young mother… about thirty years-old, Arianna and Gwen were only three and five years old. We were all together, as if we had always been…

I was shaken…

"Why are you all here?" I asked

"We stayed here because it was safe," they told me.

"It's before anything happened. Before it all happened. We were safe here."

"Before I lost my little girls" she said, the woman who was my younger self.

I stood before this soul part with tears streaming down my face.

"I'm sorry," I said. "I'm sorry for everything. For everything that went wrong. I wish I could have stopped it all. I wish I could have saved you. I'm so sorry, I am sorry," I cried, and gathered them all into my arms. The girl's eyes were still full of joy and love and trust and innocence.

I saw how innocent my old self was; how loving, and kind, thinking the best of everyone; she was everything I could no longer be. I had changed.

I was being called to go upstairs. I held the white stair rail and began to ascend.

I step onto the pumpkin floors on the second floor. I loved these floors. I walked a little bit and looked to my right into Gwen's old room. I had painted the room a beautiful soft yellow. I had painted her bureau white and my mother painted the little rocking chair blue, with flowers where her head leaned.

I remember touching Gwen's warm pink face as she slept peacefully in the sunshine in her crib – her blond curls falling over her eyes. I loved washing and drying her little clothes and tucking them neatly into the drawers, and taking time to make sure all her stuffed animals were around her when she slept. I had wound up the Easter yellow fuzzy little chicken mobile, when I laid her down to sleep, so she would close her eyes to the sweet melody.

I went further straight ahead into Arianna's room. I stepped onto the plush royal blue and looked up at her old white wrought iron bookshelves that I had kept filled with books.

She could never get enough books. Most of the time, her floor was covered with books. I see the mahogany sleigh back twin bed and her white popcorn quilt – like mine – when I was a little girl. The walls were wallpapered in a white background with tiny purple and blue flowers. I had always marveled at how beautiful every room was in this house. A minister had lived here before me and he had made it beautiful and sacred, I think.

I remember how the wind, when I kept her window up – not too high to make her cold, but just high enough to let in a slight breeze – would blow on the lace curtains. I could see her window from my room down the hall. I would always watch the wind, to make sure it was just right.

I kept going. I was being called.

I went through the laundry room behind Arianna's room and stopped. Was I to go up to the attic?

I was not in emotional pain, I realized. I was enveloped in love by angels and maybe by God and maybe Mary. I knew that this was what it was like to be dead, you could go over the past without pain, but with love.

The answer came – yes, keep going. I started to walk up the steep stairs – where Martha, the long haired-beautiful girl had lived – and the Indian girl – A brilliant light was shining down the stairs at me from the attic.

How could that be – It is so dark. But I kept following this light – it was like illuminated rays of moonlight..I got to the top stair and turned left – then looked right toward the river – The Kennebec River where my grandparents had built a four story brick house for my father and his brothers...Then I saw an image of a woman – was she a ghost?

I went up another flight of stairs into the dark attic. Moonlight illuminated a small corner and there I saw Arianna and Gwen and myself standing in a corner in the moonlight. I was as I was back then – before all of the hell. I was a beautiful young mother, Arianna and Gwen were only three and five years old. We were all three together, as if we had always been together....

I was shaken...

"Why are you all here?" I asked, my voice quavering.

"We stayed here because it was safe," they told me.

"It's before anything happened. Before it all happened. We were safe here."

"Before I lost my little girls" she said – the woman who was my younger self.

I stood before this soul part with tears streaming down my face.

"I'm sorry," I said. "I'm sorry for everything. For everything that went wrong. I wish I could have stopped it all. I wish I could have saved you. I'm so sorry, I am sorry," I cried, and gathered them all into my arms. The girl's eyes were still full of joy and love and trust and innocence.

I felt and saw a beautiful light being entering the old attic. The energy was serene. It was Mother Mary. She held out her arms and she embraced Arianna and Gwen, as little girls. She was holding my daughters in her loving arms. A brilliant light enveloped them.

I kneeled and bowed my head.

She touched my head with her hands and her love flowed down through my head, and then through my body. Light and love filled the house and then the whole town. And the whole world was different, for that one moment. It was a world of love and the Goddess had returned. Tears streamed down my cheeks

"Jane, I will hold them now and into eternity. They will never be alone again. I promise you," she said.

And then they were fading…

And on my beautiful White Spirit Horse, Tehran, I took my last spirit ride from Bath and over the three rivers to safety..

CHAPTER 63

ESCAPE FROM MAINE

In the morning, Rose and I, and our cat, Felix, slipped from the dark house, and into the car. Sitting in the back seat, Rose switched on a flashlight and opened her Calvin Hobbs book and began to read, her cat soon fell asleep in her lap.

We drove through the darkness; we traveled over the three rivers, from Waldoboro to Bath, unscathed. I held my breath, in Bath, I knew the demons could be woken...but we were safe...I knew Mary was still watching over us.

I drove, holding my breath at times, wondering if I would be stopped by the police, or psychically attacked. We finally crossed the Maine New Hampshire border and I pulled over and stopped the car. I looked at Rose. She was sleeping peacefully, as was her orange cat.

I tried to remember. Arianna was free. She was sleeping on a beach in Hawaii at night...but she was free, listening to the waves and birds and picking strawberries on a farm in the daytime. It would be a lifetime of healing, but it had begun.

Gwen was almost free. Gwen would be ok. Our bond was unbreakable. She was powerful. I had seen in a vision, Gwen, in another life, Gwenivere – a magical white lady, a powerful leader – who was destined to bring love and light and purity and the Goddess to the earth once again, if she could find her strength. No wonder they had tried to destroy her.

The sun was rising...I silently thanked Mary for her protection and love, and I started the car again. I drove towards the rising sun. I saw Mother Mary in a vision ... and heard her voice. She had stayed in the house, in the attic, looking towards the river, protecting the spirits of my two daughters – and all children – for all of eternity.

I will hold your love, for your children, here forever, You and your children will never be forgotten.. " Go in peace,"

As I drove, in the silence, happily saying good-bye to the tall, dark pine trees of Maine – which had felt, for years, more like ominous "watchers," than benevolent nature spirits – I wondered if all of my searching, which had begun as a search for my mother, and then the Goddess, and then for the source evil on the planet, was somehow tied into knowing myself.

Who was I really? And why the enormous effort to keep me blind to my own power? They wanted me to think I was a poor, helpless, victim, but maybe I was more like Demeter: a powerful being living in disguise.

I looked down onto the front passenger seat.

A dozen or so crystals – clear, pink, purple, topaz, blue – lay in a jumbled pile on an old LL Bean blanket on the seat beside a plastic Tupperware container full of Rose's toy snakes and dragons, and an open package of Ritz crackers. On the floor, a round, flowered tin containing some of my mother's ashes – that I had actually stolen from Dave – sat on top of a painting by activist Ray Shadis. The painting was a rainbow-colored Pegasus horse. The horse, in flight, kind of reminded me of Tehran, the white Arabian horse, who had help rescue my daughter's souls.

Dave had taken control of every aspect of my mother's memorial. He had decided the memorial would be at Popham and he would pay a helicopter pilot to throw her ashes into the air over Popham Beach.

I never attended. I felt it was blasphemous, what he had done.

She had been rejected from Popham. After the divorce, my father and all his kin and friends at Popham had rejected her, in one way or another. It was my father's spot. It was, I have decided, the patriarch. It was war. It was Fort Popham and Fort Baldwin. It was nuclear-armed war ships which sailed down the Kennebec River, past Popham, to the Atlantic and then on to unnamed and named wars.

Yes, there was sweet grass, and blueberries, crashing waves and starlit nights, but it held a history of repression. It might have been the first English settlement in the New World, but it was not my mother's world.

Her dream had been to return to Hanover. She had dreamed of this for most of her life. I had suggested we scatter her ashes at the bridge at Indian Head River. She loved the river. She had many happy memories of her family all together in Hanover. My mother and her friend, Clara, had dreamed of opening an art store near the river. She could have come home again, one last time.

Dave had laughed "What are we gonna do, ask the new owners of the house on Broadway, if we can have a funeral on their property under the apple tree?"

It felt like a knife in my stomach, but I was so battle weary at the time of her death, I had simply given up – as had my other siblings.

We mostly always gave up with him because we did not believe in our-selves. We could not often hold a position. It is the nature of a family who loses a mother, and then the mother is vilified. We were not unified. None of us knew who to believe, who to trust. Plus, we were artists and creators and spiritual and easily wounded; sensitive. He was something outside of our understanding. He was a blank wall. I'm sure it is against that hard blank wall, in part, that shattered Greg.

I wanted something of her. Of my mother. Something I could keep next to me. Something he could not control. So, I had taken some of her ashes.

I find it strange that Dave is even mentioned once in my book. I never had a real relationship with him, and I avoided him at all costs most of the time.

It makes me wonder if I needed the dark to illuminate the light. The toxic masculine had become a general theme in this book almost on its own accord. Or, as I would describe the Light, the dark would automat-ically appear as if to reveal the truth; to reveal how Love and The Divine Feminine was being systematically destroyed. But it was not the worst en-ergy. The toxic male. Neither was sorcery. It was the psychopathy which, I had learned, was the most evil energy on earth. And it did not feel human.

And so here I was escaping Maine with what was left of my moth-er, my youngest daughter (believing the other two were safe – or at least moderately free – from the stepmother), my crystals, my drum, children's books, a spider plant, and an orange cat, named Felix. The future would soon begin to reveal how deeply my older daughters had been affected by the trauma-based MK Ultra mind control imposed on them. Had I saved them in time? Would they ever trust themselves: their own power; their own hearts?

I was broken, just like some of my crystals. But I had been reforged by shamans. Maybe I was more like a mosaic – pieces of colored glass shattered – and then recreated into something even more powerful. But would I hold together? What was the glue holding me together?

My mother had escaped this beast of hell only through death. I'll nev-er forget how happy and beautiful she looked as she passed on into the West, saying her last farewell to me. She was in The Land of our Ancestors, but sometimes I feel her spirit near me.

I felt America was broken or something had taken over this country to bring it down, maybe beginning with the mothers and children; the most vulnerable. I was deeply affected by Princess Diana' death. It felt like confirmation that the toxin that had taken hold of America, was also in England. Michael Jackson had said on the day she died, "The Heart of the World is gone" and I agreed.

Tears threatened my eyes. I looked over at the pile of crystals. They were always so haphazard. Half of them were broken. Why couldn't I be a normal shaman and have everything in order? A yurt on a mountain, with crystals safe on conch shells or in medicine mags. Instead, my crystals were like comrades running alongside me trying to hold themselves and me together.

Some had had tips broken off, when I, for instance, having forgotten I was sleeping with them on my chest or stomach, and woke up, often from a nightmare, and they would fall off onto the floor, as I jumped up to run to a phone – to try to call my daughters – or to the window looking for some kind of good omen; some hope – leaving in my wake a scattering of broken crystals.

I carried them in pockets, in my bra, in my purse – and since I was often on the run it seemed they were often damaged. I'd drop my purse on a hard floor and hear a crack and my stomach would contract in fear. I knew it was crystal. It was a broken crystal.

I'd given away dozens of crystals. Maybe those ones were safe. I'd infused them with love and set them in rivers and trees and gardens. I'd given love-filled crystals to my daughters, knowing, even if they tried to hide them, their stepmother would find them and quickly dispose of this tie to me. I had hoped they could feel my love in the crystal and, because it was not me, but a crystal, it would be safe for them to smile.

I'd returned lost souls using crystals. Crystals are often used to transport the souls from Middle World and Upper and Lower World.

Crystals healed me too. They had absorbed so much of my pain, I felt guilty.

Similar to how I could see – in one single flower – the magnificent and unconditional love of God; and the magic of the universe; so, I could see and feel the goodness of the universe – of the Goddess – in a crystal. They gave me hope and inspiration and joy on days when otherwise there was nothing but darkness.

Strangely, one crystal suddenly seemed it was staring up. It was a large single terminated purple amethyst crystal. A gift from Raven. It was unbroken.

My own spirit guides, including my Native ancestor guides, had said he had left his body and allowed it to be inhabited by a demon. They had said there is "no hope."

Other shamans had shared similar perspectives on Raven. He was a sorcerer sent into my life to try and destroy it. He was, as the devil often is, everything I valued – on the surface. That is how a curse operates. You are shown what you most desire, until the curse dissipates, and you see the truth, if you are still alive.

I had known by the time I left Maine that there would be no going back, although I feared I would have many battles ahead to truly rid him from our lives.

Still, I wondered why the amethyst crystal seemed so vital; and why was it whole? Maybe, this quest was not over. What role would I play – outside of Maine – and in the larger world of bringing light and truth to the world? In my quest to find the origin of evil, I had learned it was not men – it was not white men or red men or black men – it was something else much more malevolent and females were as much a part of IT as men. What was the unnamed beast? Did it exist beyond the Maine woods? I felt sure it did.

The last of the tall dark pine trees faded into the distance in my rear-view mirror. I had truly escaped. I could not believe it. Again, as I drove, I could feel Mother Mary, The Goddess, and I felt they would be with me as I journeyed into another dimension of my life, on another journey into the unknown. I also felt that someday soon I would truly understand the enormous power of humans who have been re-forged from broken pieces of Light.

ACKNOWLEDGMENTS

To Dr. Nancy Coleman, PHD, a clinical psychologist from Topsham, Maine, who courageously presented her recommendations, in a comprehensive report, and personally, on the stand, in front of an openly hostile judge and guardian at the West Bath court. Judge Field refused to acknowledge the contents of her report (which warned him of the danger of taking two little girls away from their loving mother, especially when their father was not present half of the time at the other household) and into the primary care of a stepmother. Field also refused to address her as "doctor." Thank you. I will never forget your intelligent, sane, and powerful presence in that courtroom.

To my master's thesis team at Lesley University including Professor Nancy Waring Ph.D, shaman Allie Knowlton, MSW, LCSW, DCSW, and shaman Ann Drake, Psy.D. (also, with Ann, for curse unravelling and energy clearings). Thank you all for believing in my vision, my intelligence, my abilities as a shaman. You restored my faith in humans and in myself.

To the four women who I interviewed for my thesis, who were victims of trauma, but who choose shamanic healing primarily over (but often in conjunction with) Western traditional cognitive healing, thank you for your trust and for sharing your very personal stories. I want to thank "Mimi" in particular (Ann Drake's patient) for sharing her life story as a victim of the Catholic Church and the Boston area priests who abused her with MK Ultra mind control and Satanic ritual. It was an invaluable insight into this type of trauma, which I have since learned is epidemic in our world. Your experience also enlightened me to the Satanic influence in the family court room.

(Also, of particular interest, was how your power animals – and the energy clearings and soul retrievals from Ann Drake – helped you to integrate the 13 different personalities within your psyche which you had created to survive. I remember you said you trusted your power animals more than any religion, because religion had become so tainted (The thesis and interview can be read in full at my website bethedastar.com or at janeceliahatch.com).

To my friends in Bath, Maine-- who stood in the hallway outside the courtroom waiting to testify on my behalf-- but who were blocked by Field, who declared, he was "too busy with a murder case" (which was the Dennis Dechaine trial) to hear your testimony. Thank you. I'll never forget your support.

To Leila Jane Percy, former Maine State Representative, and an outspoken advocate for girls and women, and my lifelong friend-- for her heroic efforts-- to rescue "Gwen." It involved weeks of planning, but Leila arranged for Gwen to escape Bath, Maine (even though the girls were back in my custody at this point, the stepmother was stalking them with the kind of irrational vengeance typical to domestic abusers who are losing control of their victim) to attend a first-class girl's private school specializing in her two favorite activities, writing and dancing. Gwen, an extremely smart and talented girl (but whose school grades, while with her stepmother and father, had plummeted to all "F's) was so excited. Unfortunately, the stepmother got wind of the plan and lashed out brutally. All our plans unraveled overnight. Nonetheless, Gwen and I will never forget the love and concern and caring behind the effort. Just the fact you believed in us, was like a miracle back then.

To all of my Power Animals and Spirit Guides – Lion, Jaguar, Wolf, Tehran, The White Horse, Owl, Eagle – And to My Spirit Guides, The Goddess, Princess Diana, Lady Guadalupe, Mother Mary, Black Elk – and To My Creator, God. Thank you.

To Sandra Ingerman, MA, shaman and trauma expert, family counsellor, award-winning author, international teacher, who took taught me about the important relationship between trauma and healing shamanism. Thank you, also, for your book, Soul Retrieval: Mending the Fragmented Self. It was a lifeline.

To Susan Bakaley Marshall, MPS, ATR, of Freedom, Maine, a shaman, who, with her Spirit Guides and Power Animals, retrieved the pieces of my split soul, which had fled from the unspeakable trauma of court and into the outward edges of the universe.

To my other shaman teachers, John Amaroso, Geo Cameron-Trevarthen, PHD, Nan Moss, David Corbin, Ann Drucker, and the late Belgian physicist, Claude Poncelet, Ph.D. Thank you.

To the late Lynn Andrews, a shaman, and the author of over ten best-selling "Medicine Woman" books on shamanism, you lent me your

ACKNOWLEDGMENTS

power when I needed it most. Thank you for your brilliant understanding of the ancient powers of woman. You provided courage, strength, direction, and – at least for a time – the power of the Lightening.

To the many healers – psychics, Reiki Masters, chiropractors, therapists, herbalists – in the small riverside village of Damariscotta, Maine, who gently put the stuffing back into the scarecrow that had arrived at your doorstep.

And, in Damariscotta, thank you to my attorney, Jonathon Hull, who seized the moment, to have my daughter's custody legally transferred into my sole custody. It was an opening in time that was brief and I was just too battle fatigued to even recognize it

(An interesting note here, is that Jonathon, a Vietnam Veteran, was recently disbarred and charged with embezzling money from his own (in part) highly successful non-profits which had served homeless and troubled youths in Maine since the early 1970's.

My educated guess – and this is strictly hypothetical – is that the real reason Jonathon Hull was charged and prosecuted by Judge Bruce Mallonee in 2020, was not because of embezzlement, but because Jonathon was NOT part of Maine judicial child trafficking. In my experience, Jonathon worked hard and long, with very little pay from me, and often under duress, as he had many health problems. I'm not saying, he did not embezzle, I'm saying he was prosecuted because he had somehow displeased important people in the system.

(To learn more about Maine judicial sex trafficking, please see the documentary by Frontline "Failure to Protect" about the murder of five-year-old Logan Marr, of Maine, who was taken from her loving mother and given to Sally Schofield, a State of Maine social worker who suffocated her to death with duct tape. No charge, of course, has ever been brought against the judge who knowingly ignored the warnings from Logan's mother, Christy, who told him Logan was being sexually and physical abused by Schofield and her husband.

Instead of helping Logan, the judge threatened Christy. He said that if she made any more complaints against Schofield – she would never see her daughter again. In this case, as in mine, any attempt to help save our children, threatened our children. Sadly, in Logan's case, they followed through on the threat. Christy never did see her daughter again until they returned her tiny body to be buried.

Also, another example, is Dr. Lori Handrahan, whose daughter, Mila, was trafficked by a Maine judge to her ex-husband, an illegal immigrant, who had raped Logan. Lori, who is from Maine, is an international expert

357

on gender equality and feminism. She also wrote the five-star book *Epidemic: Americas Trade In Child Rape* published by TrineDay)

(Additionally, and to highlight a system that seems to care very little about the children in Maine, a ten-page report I sent to the State of Maine Board of Social Work Licensure, in 1998, highlighting my deep concerns about the ethical behavior of Kathleen Sullivan, was completely dismissed. No one contacted me. No one was interviewed, nothing was done to investigate my concerns. I received, by mail, a brief, standard issue, we-are-basically-not-interested reply)

And more recently, and on a lighter note, to my technical team, thank you to M Designs for their unshakable support in all my projects and for last minute critical editing of this book.

To Ras, Raven's father – you are the man I thought Raven was. Thank you for being a kind and caring and generous grandfather to Rose. And, also, for taking Rose and I – and three of our pets – into your home when a new form of evil had threatened, and we were again in a bit of a whirlwind. Your love and non-judgment I will never forget.

And, almost thirty years after the court experience, to my therapist Joan Heiden, MA, LPCC, of Santa Fe, NM for EMDR treatments for PTSD and for your unconditional support and belief in my personal journey.

(My daughters "Gwen" and "Arianna" are in their thirties as this book goes to print. They have both, also, for almost two decades, participated in deep and profound healing work. I can't reveal all the details of their healing journey. Hopefully they will write their own books. I can say, that like myself, they have had EMDR treatment for PTSD and soul retrievals, energy clearings, and power animal retrieval, as part of their lifelong journey to heal from court trauma. They are now grounded, highly educated, intelligent, creative, powerful women and the three of us are very close)

To my friend, artist Mahara Daniel – for portraying so well that magical night where the souls of my two daughters and I rode on the white spirit horse, Tehran, to safety across the three rivers – which is the cover image of this book. Thank you. To my friend and healer, Elizabeth Rose, for reading the first draft and saying, after she finished the book, "I'm honored to know you", which changed my view of myself, probably for forever.

To one of my best friends, and my landlord, Prax, who handmade a wooden frame for an image of Lady Guadalupe, The Patron Saint of the Southwest, which he gave to me as a gift and I treasure. Prax has provided my youngest daughter, Rose, and I (and my crystals) a safe and loving home. At long last.

And believe it or not, to my x-husband, who I call "John", the father of Gwen and Arianna, who finally believed what the girls (and I) had been telling him for over a decade. He finally understood he was being manipulated and lied to by "Heleena" and they are divorced. He has spent much of the last twenty years trying to make up to the girls for what they felt was his betrayal. To me, more than once, he has said, with tears in his eyes, "I'm sorry." We are friends – to the degree that I can be -- and five years ago we all spent one amazing Christmas together that none of us will ever forget.

(This situation with the stepmother is an excellent example of how family courts only need one person in the family who is malevolent, mentally ill, to destroy an entire family. All the courts needed was the stepmother, in our case. My x-husband, I believe, was weak-minded (admittedly as I was with Raven) possibly a bit power hungry, a victim of mind control, but he was not evil.

Make no mistake about it – courts, detention centers, foster care, social services, police, (some) therapists, reform schools, politicians, Catholic Churches and even royals – (which is the topic for my next book) often want mind-controlled and traumatized children because these children can be used for sex trafficking, sex trade, sexual abuse, income, ritual abuse, sacrifice, trade, and more. It is a billion-dollar industry. Children are often "cash cows from cradle to grave" for our courts.

Kathleen Russel, Executive Director of the Center for Judicial Excellence, concurs. She said --and I found her quote on a Facebook page "Mainers Against Morowitz" (Morowitz is a judge in Maine) – "We used to be cautious about alleging corruption in the court system, but after 16 years of doing this work, I can say that it is almost like a form of judicial child trafficking by family courts")

And in memory of my late sister-in-law, Susan Hatch, who died recently, but who was, I believe, the sweetest person in our family. Since I was a little, she always had a smile and a kind word. When she passed, her spirit stopped and said good-bye. She looked beautiful and young and full of mischief and fun. She was with my mother, who she adored. Thank you. Kindness was so rare in my childhood, that I remember yours very clearly.

And of course, Trine Press, who consistently publishes groundbreaking, iconoclastic books that are changing the world.

ABOUT "ROSE"

My next book, which is about Princess Diana and the royal family, will also include the ongoing steps in Rose's life (as she was only eight years old at the end of *Broken Crystals*) and she was deeply affected by the court's decision about her sisters, and by her father's anger. Having a mother who was in grief about her other two daughters was more hurtful to Rose than I imagined. Matricide effects all members of the family, from grandparents to grandchildren, and often, for several generations. Her healing journey is one of the many subjects I cover in my new book – the working title of which is *Princess Diana: The Ties That Bind Us: The Fleur De Lei, Matricide, and The Tree Spirits of England.*

ABOUT SHAMANS

In my acknowledgements I refer to all the shamans, as shamans. They may refer to themselves as practitioners or shamanic healers, I'm not sure. I perceive them as shamans. In my master's thesis, as part of the literary review of shamanism, I discovered that shamans originated on almost every point on earth at one time or another, independent of each other, yet possessing impressive commonalities. Shamanism is reported to be, by historian Mircea Eliade, the oldest form of spirituality on the planet – potentially going back a hundred thousand years.

One of the oldest archeological remains of a shaman is the skeleton of a female Celtic shaman who is believed to be 60,000 years old. It was discovered at the Upper Paleolithic archaeological site Dolni Vestinice in the Czech Republic. She was buried with a splint, a fox, skeletal remains of a mammoth, and thousands of baked clay animal figurines.

The word, shaman, is from a Siberian word "saman" and loosely translated means "one who sees in the dark" or one able to access "techniques of ecstasy." Certainly, all the woman (and one man) who I call shamans can "see in the dark" and beyond the veil of illusion and into the unseen worlds which exist all around us. What we see with our eyes is a very small degree of the reality which surrounds us.

Humans from all over the world – including Aboriginal, Celtic, Russian, Hawaiian, South Americans, English, Irish, Chinese, Japanese, Lithuanian, African – on all continents and all countries have ancient roots in shamanism. Most all humans have the power of shamans if they choose to activate and cultivate these powers. It is a gift from God. Shamanism did not originate with Native Americans, nor is the word "shaman" associated with Native Americans.

MIND CONTROL

I feel it is important to reclaim our God self, our innate power, our complete and total freedom, before it is too late. Shamanism is an antidote for mind-control because its power is intuition and connecting with the Earth, and your heart and the Beings of great love and compassion. If there was ever a time in history, we needed to find our shaman power – our ancient roots – it is right now. I advise everyone to learn shamanism. It does not matter what religion you are. Shamanism is not a religion. It is, in part, spiritual surgery.

Please see my website www.janeceliahatch.com to see my master's thesis in full and more information about my writing, shamanism, book signings, talks, and other events.